Troubled Industries

A volume in the series

Cornell Studies in Political Economy

EDITED BY PETER J. KATZENSTEIN

A full list of titles in the series appears at the end of the book.

A Study of the East Asian Institute, Columbia University

The East Asian Institute is Columbia University's center
for research, publication, and teaching on modern East Asia.
The Studies of the East Asian Institute were inaugurated
in 1962 to bring to a wider public the results of significant
new research on modern and contemporary East Asia.

Troubled Industries

CONFRONTING ECONOMIC
CHANGE IN JAPAN

ROBERT M. URIU

CORNELL UNIVERSITY PRESS

Ithaca and London

First published 1996 by Cornell University Press.

Printed in the United States of America

♾ The paper in this book meets the minimum requirements
of the American National Standard for Information Sciences—
Permanence of Paper for Printed Library Materials, ANSI Z39.48–1984.

Library of Congress Cataloging-in-Publication Data

Uriu, Robert M. 1959–
    Troubled industries : confronting economic change in Japan / Robert M. Uriu.
        p.   cm. — (Studies of the East Asian Institute)
    Includes bibliographical references and index.
    ISBN 0–8014–3029–1 (cloth : alk. paper)
    1. Industrial policy—Japan.   2. Industries—Japan.   I. Title.   II. Series.
HD3616.J33U74   1996
338.952—dc20   96–3229

For Noriho

Contents

Tables and Charts

Preface

The idea for this book came to me a decade ago from an offhand comment that the Japanese government has had great success in forcing its declining industries to adjust to market pressures. That notion intrigued me. It certainly seemed to confirm the orthodox view of the Japanese political economy, that bureaucrats would be both smart enough to design economic policies that force its declining industries out of the market and powerful enough to avoid political pressures for protection. Yet I was skeptical. Could things be that simple?

I also found the issue area intriguing because it offered a better test of the "bureaucratic dominance" approach. It seemed that every analyst of Japan's industrial policy stressed the role of the government in fostering growing industries—in other words, bureaucrats "picked the winners" and supported them through public policy. The bureaucrats made the decisions, and the private sector followed docilely along. But were the industries merely getting from the bureaucrats everything they were asking for? It is hard to tell when interests overlap. In troubled industries, at least, bureaucrats may be forced to implement policies that take something away from industries, rather than giving them what they may have wanted. If the interests of industry actors and those of bureaucrats are potentially in conflict, we have a better chance of assessing the extent to which bureaucrats are indeed insulated from industry preferences.

Columbia University's Political Science Department, East Asian Institute, and Center on Japanese Economy and Business helped fund my early research. I carried out the bulk of the research in Japan between 1988 and 1990, when I was funded by a scholarship from the Fulbright-Hays Graduate Research Program. During that time I was affiliated with two institutions: first, Professor Inoguchi Takashi arranged an affiliation with the Institute of Oriental Culture of Tokyo University; second, I was a visiting foreign research scholar at the Ministry of International Trade and Industry's research institute, MITI/RI. The staff of MITI/RI was also very helpful in arranging interviews with bureaucrats and industry officials. (Although some of the detailed information in the case studies was gathered via interviews, I have in most cases verified it from written or published sources. I indicate in the footnotes the handful of cases in which no independent verification was possible.) Upon returning to the United States, I was supported by a grant from the Joint Committee on Japanese Studies of the Social Science Research Council, the Wellington Koo Fellowship from the East Asian Institute, and Columbia University's Council on Research in the Humanities and Social Sciences.

A first book is grueling and humbling, but also rewarding. There are so many friends and colleagues to whom I owe a debt of gratitude either for intellectual or for emotional support (and in some cases, for both). Hugh Patrick was involved in all phases of this project. His academic advice has always been thought-provoking, and his personal support always wise and uplifting. James Morley has served as a role model of a true scholar; I am nowhere close, but his example is still something I strive for. Gerald Curtis has gone out of his way to offer guidance and encouragement; his contributions have been very important to me. I also thank Dennis Encarnation for helping me clarify the conceptual framework of this project. Many others have offered valuable comments or suggestions, including T. J. Pempel, Richard Samuels, Mark Mason, Inoguchi Takashi, Frank Upham, Greg Noble, Robert Jervis, Helen Milner, Jack Snyder, David Weinstein, Taka Suzuki, Peter Drysdale, John Campbell, Frank Packer, Tom Roehl, Tony Iaquinto, Kenji Hayao, Marc Busch, Robert Pekkanen, Peter Evans, Mark Tilton, Junko Kato, and Barry Keehn. I owe special thanks to my friend and colleague Taka Suzuki, for his helpful comments and his personal encouragement. I have also benefited from close interaction with a great group of political science graduate students at Columbia University, many of whom are now colleagues. There is no harsher critic than an advanced graduate student, and some of the sharpest and most challenging criticisms have come from members of our political science "Friday group" meetings. I thank especially Jennifer Holt-Dwyer, Patti Machlachlan, Taka Suzuki, Anne Marie Murphy, Mike Chambers, Hiroshi Ohta, Aki Miyashita, Allan Song, Victor Cha, Anne Emig, Takako Kobori, Galia Press, Yoshiko Motoyama, Leslie Vinjamuri Wright, and Masayo Ohara. Finally, many have helped in the research for and editing of the book, including Aki Miyashita, Galia Press, Mary O'Donnell, Shigeo Hirano, Miles Wixon, and Masayo Ohara. I am also grateful to Roger Haydon of Cornell University Press, both for his early interest in this project and for his help in pushing things along to their conclusion, and to Kay Scheuer for her help in the final editing process.

Most important, I thank my family. My parents, my brother, and my sisters have always been supportive and encouraging. My sons, Masato and Jackson, have reminded me what is important in life and helped me keep my priorities straight. My wife, Noriho, has been always patient and understanding. She was my significant other when this project was first conceived; had become my wife by the time I began the research; and gave birth to Masato while the dissertation was being written and to Jackson while the book manuscript was being prepared. (So much for a quick and easy first book!) I dedicate this book to her.

ROBERT M. URIU

New York City

PART I

THE POLITICAL ECONOMY
OF INDUSTRIAL ADJUSTMENT

CHAPTER ONE

Introduction

The emergence of troubled industries is a fact of economic life that confronts all industrialized countries. If dynamic growth and development of an economy are dependent on the "gales of destruction" posited by Joseph Schumpeter, then some industries will inevitably become troubled: that is, they will reach economic maturity and will face significant periods of economic distress. Japan has been no exception. The phenomenal growth of the postwar Japanese economy has involved the fundamental transformation of its industrial structure. In the process, numerous primary and manufacturing industries have lost out in the competitive race and have had to adapt to the onset of industrial maturity, distress, or decline.

This book analyzes how Japan has dealt with its troubled industries. My aims are twofold. First, I use this issue area to assess business-government relations in Japan. By focusing on the role that industry actors (firms and their labor forces) play in the policy process, I call into question the orthodox image of a Japanese bureaucracy that is largely insulated from societal pressures. Second, I seek a better balance between societal- and systemic-centered approaches by focusing on how industry actors interact with the broader policy-making environment, which I define to include not only domestic actors but also the constraints and opportunities provided by the international environment.

An examination of policy for troubled industries forces into the open some of the hidden assumptions on which the "bureaucratic autonomy" thesis rests. The majority of case studies of Japanese industrial policy emphasize the role of the bureaucracy during the era of high-speed economic growth. In particular these analyses emphasize how state actors "pick" and promote likely "winner" industries, nurturing them into internationally competitive forces. This emphasis on growth industries is understandable given our preoccupation with explaining Japan's postwar "economic miracle," but it makes it difficult to weigh the relative influence that state and societal actors have on the policy process. The fundamental problem is that studies that stress bureaucratic autonomy in Japan begin with the assumption that industries are not central to the policy-making process. Chalmers Johnson, for instance, argues that industries are "responsively dependent" on the bureaucracy; this assumption allows him to dismiss, from the outset, the possibility that industry actors exert a decisive influence on policy choices.[1] Most other analysts of Japan's industrial policy similarly focus on bureaucratic goals and interests and on how these goals are achieved, paying little attention to what industry actors may have wanted or may have actually asked for.[2] Because they dismiss a major policy role for industry in their *initial assumptions*, these analysts tend to equate the extent of government intervention with government initiative and autonomy.[3]

The assumption that industry actors are "responsively dependent" on the bureaucrats often goes unnoticed and unchallenged when we look only at industrial policy for growing industries. In the case of those industries, public and private interests tend to overlap, with both state and industry actors working to promote growth, expansion, and competitiveness. State actors can pursue policies that both promote the "national interest" of an expanding and efficient economy and at the same time satisfy the more narrowly defined interests of particular industries. But precisely because interests tend to overlap, it is difficult to tell who is influencing whom and where autonomy lies. Those who see the state as autonomous assert that state actors make all the difference. But how are we to tell? As Peter Gourevitch puts it, "when [state] policy and the interests of the strongest coincide, it is not clear that the state has produced the result"; in such situations we must carefully ask, "who has co-opted whom?"[4]

[1] Johnson 1982, p. 24. Johnson's book, *MITI and the Japanese Miracle*, remains the classic statement of the "bureaucratic autonomy" approach. Others applying this approach to Japan include Anchordoguy 1989 and 1990, and Pempel 1978.

[2] Anchordoguy, for instance, in her discussion of industrial policy for the computer industry (1989, 1990), devotes almost no attention to the policy agenda the industry itself was pursuing. Even Okimoto, who stresses the political dimension of policy making, argues that MITI has a free hand in formulating industrial policy. His implicit assumption that state and societal interests are in harmony may apply more to growing high-technology industries, the main focus of Okimoto's analysis (1989, pp. 226–228).

[3] The assumptions of the bureaucratic autonomy approach have been accepted by many generalist political scientists who have turned their attention to Japan. See, for example, Katzenstein 1978 and 1988, Krasner 1987, Tyson 1992, and Huntington 1993. The notion that bureaucrats enjoy power and autonomy has also become recent orthodoxy among American government officials and trade policy makers.

[4] Gourevitch 1978, pp. 906–907.

It is easier to distinguish between the interests of state actors and those of industry when the subject is policy for troubled industries. From the point of view of state policy makers, the public interest in a more efficient and competitive economy is best served by the smooth rationalization of these industries and the transfer of resources to more optimal uses. Things appear quite different, however, to the industry in distress. With the economic pie shrinking, someone must bear the painful burdens of adjustment—the loss of profits, bankruptcies, unemployment, and the like. However, as Lester Thurow puts it, when economic losses must be allocated, "no group wants to be the group that must suffer economic losses for the general good."[5] Nations are often unwilling, or unable, to accept the political consequences of leaving troubled industries to their market-determined fates.

Troubled industry policy thus provides a better test of the argument that the Japanese bureaucracy is insulated from industry preferences. Because public and private interests are more likely to diverge, the analyst cannot simply ignore the preferences of industries or explain them away via initial assumptions.[6] The analyst's task is to come to an understanding of the preferences of important actors, both public and private, and then to analyze the extent to which these various interests are reflected in policy choices. In short, we must answer Gourevitch's question—who is co-opting whom?

Nations can take one of three general approaches to deal with their troubled industries. First, governments can forgo intervention and allow the market to force the rationalization of the industry. By resisting pressures for intervention, governments thereby leave industries to their market-determined fates. Second, governments can actively intervene in the market to promote adjustment and foster industrial restructuring. Such policies of "industrial euthanasia" have been labeled "positive adjustment policies" (PAP) by the OECD. Third, governments can intervene in an attempt to preserve the industry in question. Governments often use such policy tools as import protection, subsidization, and bailouts to protect an industry from pressures for change or to retard the pace and severity of the adjustment process. Not surprisingly, nations most often find this third approach to be attractive in political terms.

---

[5] Thurow 1980, p. 10.

[6] Several colleagues have commented that we should expect neither a full convergence of public-private interests in growing industries nor a full divergence of interests in declining industries. I agree there will be some conflict in the former and some consensus in the latter. But common sense suggests that there will be fewer conflicting interests when the economic pie is growing and that conflicts will be exacerbated when the pie is shrinking.

Japan is routinely credited with a successful record of industrial adjustment. Especially after the Oil Shocks, industries in Japan such as aluminum smelting and synthetic fibers adjusted rapidly in response to economic change. The Japanese government is often praised for following consistent and coherent policies to encourage industrial adjustment. Some analysts give policy makers credit for not bowing to industry pressures for excessive protection and coddling, in particular, for protection against imports. By forgoing intervention, policy makers have thus given industries no choice but to adapt to market forces.[7]

Others go one step further and give the economic bureaucracy credit for following more active restructuring policies that have induced successful industrial adjustment. Peter Katzenstein, for instance, argues that the Japanese bureaucracy is able to anticipate industrial decline and acts to "preempt the costs of change" through a policy of forced structural adjustment. Michael Trebilcock describes Japan's approach as both anticipatory and positive and argues that the Japanese bureaucracy effectively intervenes to rationalize its troubled industries.[8]

I describe Japan's policy choices for its troubled industries quite differently. First, Japan's policies have not been as coherent and consistent as is often argued, but rather have varied widely across industries. Its policy has been relatively unobtrusive in such cases as the synthetic fiber industry, but has been highly interventionist in industries such as cotton textiles and coal mining. In addition, the pace and degree of adjustment have varied according to the industry in question. Certain industries, notably aluminum smelting and synthetic fibers, have adjusted successfully. Others, such as cotton textiles and coal mining, have not adjusted successfully or in a timely fashion. Rather, as discussed in Chapter 4, these industries have been able to utilize government policy to delay and draw out industrial adjustment over a period of 30 years.[9]

Second, when faced with policy demands from industry actors, the bureaucrats have not been able to resist these pressures. Bureaucrats have

---

[7] Examples include Alexander 1994, McKean 1993, p. 83, Patrick 1991, Okimoto 1989, pp. 27–28, Macomber 1987, Dore 1986, OECD 1983a, Boyer 1983, and Johnson 1982, p. 28.

[8] Katzenstein 1985, pp. 23, 26; Trebilcock 1986b, pp. 223–242. These arguments are based on the conviction that the Japanese bureaucracy is effectively insulated from domestic interest groups and is thus free from politicization and political pressures. In this conception, the bureaucracy is able to favor the interests of growth industries over those of mature industries and thus pursues policies that promote national economic efficiency.

Japanese government policy pronouncements are also consistent with this appraisal—Japanese bureaucrats are quick to take credit for adhering to the OECD's norm of "positive adjustment." When it intervenes, the Japanese government stresses that its goal is the positive one of promoting adjustment and fostering industrial restructuring.

[9] It is probably no coincidence that analysts who have a more "positive" view of Japan's approach to distressed industries often ignore these less successful cases.

certainly not been able to force industries to adjust against their will: I find no evidence that the government has been able to "preempt" industrial decline by anticipating market forces ahead of the private sector. Bureaucrats have also not been able to take a hands-off approach, letting market forces determine the pace and direction of adjustment.

Rather, the policy process has been highly politicized, and policy makers have consistently had to respond to pressures from troubled industries. Most troubled industries in Japan, I will argue, have been able to utilize public policy in their attempts to shield themselves from the adjustment process. In particular, they have utilized cartels extensively in an effort to stabilize conditions and attenuate adjustment pressures. These industries have been granted a wide variety of cartels, both formal and informal, that have helped to control production levels or reduce surplus capacity. By "managing competition" in the domestic market, industries have sought to avoid more rapid change and dislocation.

Thus, Japanese policy makers, like policy makers elsewhere, have not been insulated from political pressures from the nation's troubled industries and have shown themselves quite willing to use policy tools to shield domestic industries from adjustment pressures. Policy tools have been utilized to prop up the least competitive firms, rather than support the most competitive. While eschewing overt import protection, Japanese policy has relied on other methods to accomplish the same political goal that prevails elsewhere—the goal of shielding industries from the need for difficult industrial adjustment.[10]

To explain the variations in Japan's policy choices, I use a two-step process. First, I explicate the economic and political preferences of key actors in the industry in question—the individual firms and their labor forces—and I posit that their fundamental preferences will depend on the industry's economic structure. In Chapter 2 I use two industrial organization variables, industrial concentration and the size of the labor force, to construct a skeletal typology of four industry types, and then derive hypotheses linking industry structure to the likely preferences of firms and labor.

The second step is to trace the extent to which industry actors are able to translate their preferences into policy choices. It will be rare for them to

---

[10] This assessment is consistent with the growing body of evidence that Japanese industrial policy has tended to focus more on distressed rather than growing industries, and that these policies have tended to delay rather than promote adjustment (Weinstein and Beason 1994; Tan and Shimada 1994; Sekiguchi 1991; and Komiya 1988, p. 10).

In this sense Japanese policy behavior has been similar to the small, trade-dependent states of continental Europe, as described by Katzenstein. Japan has compensated its distressed industries for the costs of adjustment, while at the same time eschewing the option of overt import protection. Like Katzenstein's small states, Japan "live[s] with change by compensating for it" (1985, p. 24).

get everything they want. Rather, in the process of policy making, their preferences are often deflected or altered to some degree. Thus, industry preferences are likely to determine the general contours of policy choices, but a fuller account of the specifics of these choices requires that we trace the process through which industry actors interact with the industrial policy-making environment. In Chapter 3 I describe this environment, which I define to include the industrial policy bureaucrats, the politicians, and the officials in charge of antitrust enforcement. Industry actors also function within an even broader context: the constraints and opportunities afforded by the international environment.

I present in Part II a series of detailed case studies of how firms and labor have responded to economic distress. Each of the four chapters corresponds to one of the industry types set out in Chapter 2.

I present my conclusions in Part III. In Chapter 8 I reassess my industrial organization hypotheses. I find that industry groups are not simply political animals following rent-seeking goals; rather, they have had incentives to pursue a combination of economic and political strategies. Their specific choice of strategy has depended, I argue, on the structural features of the industry in question. (In Chapter 8 I also apply my hypotheses to cases of industrial adjustment in Germany.)

In Chapter 9 I reassess business-government relations in Japan. I find that firms and labor have been direct participants in all phases of industrial policy making. In many cases, through their political demands they have actually driven the policy-making process and have heavily influenced policy decisions. I also find that MITI bureaucrats have not been able to make and implement policy free from specific industry or political pressures. Rather, bureaucrats have been subject to strong constraints and pressures from industry and their political allies. In this sense, the autonomy of the Japanese bureaucracy can best be described as compromised or "permeated." I also find that Japan's industrial policy environment has evolved significantly over time. In particular, both antitrust considerations and Japan's international context have shifted, leading to stronger constraints on the use of domestic cartels and import protection, all of which must be factored in to the analysis.

This book stresses the central role of industry actors in the policy process in Japan, rather than the importance of institutional actors and environmental constraints. But this is not an exclusive focus. On the one hand, an analysis of the preferences of industry actors does not alone provide an adequate explanation of Japan's policy choices for troubled industries. On the other hand, if we focus only on the policy-making environment, we can understand constraints on policy choices but not the choices that are actually made. Analyses that stress structural elements—the international system or state structures and institutions—focus far too much on the constraining effects imposed by unchanging structural determinants. These constraints may explain the broad parameters of what is possible and what is not, but as John Ikenberry has noted, "what is possible" covers a lot of ground; there is always considerable room for choice within these environmental constraints.[11] Those who favor structural approaches need to pay more attention to how industry actors interact with the policy environment.

Any analysis that focuses on only one element of policy making—one level of analysis, one set of institutions, or one type of actors—will leave us with an overly narrow and ultimately misleading view of policy choices. Rather, our explanations need to acknowledge a more complex causality. It is the process of interaction between choice and constraint that best explains Japan's policies toward its troubled industries.

[11] Ikenberry 1988, p. 242.

CHAPTER TWO

Industrial Structure and
Industry Preferences

I posit that the interests and preferences of industry actors are a central and necessary part of explaining Japan's policy choices for its troubled industries. However, instead of inferring the most influential industry actors by simply looking at policy outcomes, we must develop some a priori expectations. First, we must establish which actors are most likely to be involved in the policy process, then we must derive expectations of their likely preferences. In this chapter, I argue that the main actors within an industry—individual firms and their labor forces—will be the ones most likely to influence policy outcomes. I then posit that the interests of firms and labor will depend on the structure of the industry in question. I use two industrial structure variables—concentration and the size of the labor force—to derive expected patterns of preferences for the different industry types.

The collective action approach provides a useful first cut in establishing which societal actors are most likely to organize and influence the policy process. A fundamental tenet of this approach is that not all groups will be able to translate passive preferences into active demand for political action. Rather, those groups whose members have intense and concentrated stakes in an issue are more likely to be able to organize sufficiently to initiate policy action or to otherwise exert influence over the policy process.

The collective action approach has been criticized on a number of grounds. But as Joanne Gowa points out, this approach is likely to be best suited where it was intended—in the study of economic interest groups.[1]

---

[1] Gowa 1988, pp. 20–22.

The very nature of industrial policy means that benefits are likely to be both concentrated and excludable—that is, the regulated industry will be the main beneficiary of public policy. Although any attempt at organization will encounter problems with free riders, the ability to exclude benefits implies that the costs of organizing will tend to be low relative to expected benefits. Even in diffuse industries with dozens of firms, organizational problems such as free riding are not likely to be on the same scale as those faced by general voters or taxpayers; enforcing agreements among 50 firms may be difficult, but it will surely be easier than actions that involve millions of individuals. Not surprisingly, industry actors are often found at the center of the industrial policy-making process.

Declining industries should be considered a special subset of economic interest groups. Given that their very survival is at stake, declining industry actors are even more likely to be involved in the policy process than their counterparts in flourishing industries. Firms will face falling profits, declining market shares, and possible bankruptcy, while workers will face the loss of jobs and the difficult process of employment adjustment. As Russell Hardin argues, the prospect of *losing* something valuable provides one of the strongest incentives to organize. The intensity, salience, and concentration of costs that declining industries face implies that they will have extremely high incentives to overcome barriers to organizing.[2]

Certainly, other societal actors may have a stake in distressed industry policy, but their interests are likely to be considerably less concentrated. Banks, shareholders, and creditors may have financial ties to individual firms, but because any creditor generally has diversified investments, its stake in any particular industry is often low. Suppliers of the industry's inputs and buyers of the industry's outputs will also be affected by troubled industry policies but, again, their fates will not often hinge on how the industries are dealt with.[3] Stakes in an industry for general taxpayers and final consumers are likely to be lowest of all.

What is most important, then, is the *asymmetry* of stakes involved in troubled industry policy. Relative to those of other actors, the stakes involved for firms and labor in the troubled industry—their very survival—means that they should have the most intense and compelling incentives to become involved in the policy process. Consequently, their voices are likely to be the most persistent and, all else equal, the most influential.

---

[2] In Hardin's terms (1982, pp. 82–83), actors in troubled industries will enjoy asymmetrical incentives to organize.

[3] The stakes of buyer firms will be high when troubled industry products account for a high percentage of their inputs. Aluminum ingots, for example, are the main input for the aluminum rolling industry, while steel accounts for a good proportion of inputs for auto makers and shipbuilders. Especially when buyer firms are themselves in economic distress or are facing tough competition, their stakes in troubled industry policy may be relatively high.

TROUBLED INDUSTRY OPTIONS

Although the public choice approach can tell us *who* is likely to mobilize and exert influence over policy makers, we need to know more about *how* these groups will respond to adjustment pressures and *what* types of policies they will prefer. Unfortunately, the collective action approach tells us little more than that actors will pursue their preferences; it says nothing about what those preferences are likely to be. We must therefore go beyond this approach to specify relevant preferences. I turn to the literature on industry structure and strategy in order to generalize about the expected preferences of industry actors.[4] I posit that the economic and political preferences of the main industry actors will depend on the structure of the industry in question.

In the following analysis, I divide the economic choices available to firms in distressed industries into two categories, divestment and adjustment, and the political choices into three, compensation, stabilization, and preservation (see Table 2-1).[5] Political solutions do not differ from economic ones only in intent. By definition, they cannot be achieved by individual firms; rather, achieving political solutions requires cooperation, and in most cases some degree of direct government involvement.

I refer to the efforts made by individual firms to reduce or move resources out of the distressed industry as economic adjustment options. Kathryn Harrigan argues that firms in distress can either "flee" (through divestiture) or "fight" (by remaining in the industry but taking steps to regain profitability).[6]

A firm that is able to anticipate decline may pursue a strategy of divestment in order to minimize long-term losses. This divestiture option, however, may not be equally attractive to all firms. In particular, a firm may face exit barriers, which Michael Porter defines as "economic, strategic, and emotional factors that keep companies competing in businesses even

---

[4] I draw heavily, albeit selectively, on the analysis of industries by Michael Porter (1980), which links firm strategy to industrial structure. Kathryn Harrigan (1980, 1988) extends this approach to deal with mature and declining industries. I further extend their analyses, which focus only on economic or market strategies, by linking an industry's structure with its political preferences and strategies. Porter refers only once to government policy, which he treats as a part of the fixed environment facing an industry rather than as a variable that can be influenced (1980, p. 92).

[5] See Zysman 1983, pp. 87–89, and Gourevitch 1986, pp. 37–54, for other typologies of options open to firms facing economic change. See also Porter 1980 and Harrigan 1980 and 1988 for a full discussion of possible adjustment strategies.

[6] Harrigan 1988, pp. 13–16. In the following sections I assume that it is the firm and its management that will choose different options and strategies. The interests of labor will largely depend on how the firm chooses to respond. This assumption is consistent with the views of Porter and Harrigan, who focus only on the strategies that management should choose. They both treat labor as simply a supplier of a needed economic input—indeed, labor is hardly mentioned in their analyses.

Table 2-1. Responses to economic change

Economic adjustment options	
Divestment	Bankruptcy
	Selective divestiture
Adjustment	Rationalization of production
	Diversification
	Overseas investment
Political solutions	
Compensation	Adjustment subsidies
Stabilization	Supply-side stablization (cartels)
	Demand management
Preservation	Subsidies
	Bailouts
	Trade protection

though they may be earning low or even negative returns on investment."[7] These barriers include the "fixed costs of exit," for instance, the costs of disposing of capital facilities or those required by labor settlements. Harrigan and Porter, however, argue that such barriers are more likely to be "emotional" than economic—feelings of loyalty or attachment to the firm, to employees, to the community, or to customers, as well as more self-serving concerns, such as avoiding damage to one's reputation or prestige.[8] Finally, the ability to divest will be a function of the availability of alternatives: where capital or labor lack attractive alternative uses, the relative costs of divestment will be high.

A firm that cannot divest will have incentives to adjust to changing market conditions. Every firm can attempt to improve productivity by streamlining its operations, shedding redundant resources, or cutting costs. A firm can pursue more aggressive adjustment options by diversifying up the value-added chain or into unrelated fields, or it may be able to lower production costs through overseas investment. However, in order to pursue these adjustment options, the firm will require access to adequate resources, including financing, technology, and information about markets and future trends. Not all firms will have access to such resources.[9]

[7] Porter 1980, p. 20.
[8] Harrigan 1988, p. 56; Porter 1980, pp. 261–267.
[9] Access to resources needed to pursue adjustment is not a central concern for Porter or Harrigan. Most analysts simply assume that firms and labor will have some attractive alternative opportunities. John Zysman notes that "firms may exit from an existing activity without seeking protection if they have some alternative use for their resources" (1983, p. 87). The attractiveness of alternative opportunities is dependent upon mobility barriers, namely, the specificity of capital or labor. See Porter 1980, pp. 259–267. To the extent that facilities are specific to the current task, their resale value will be low, and firms will have difficulty finding new uses for them. The lack of alternatives depends also upon emotional barriers to exit; to the extent that alternative employment opportunities are limited, emotional exit barriers will be high.

There is a critical difference between a firm that chooses to divest as part of its business strategy and a firm that is forced to exit through bankruptcy. Economists, however, do not distinguish between the two: in both cases the firm acts according to a rational calculation of the costs and benefits of exit, and so, by definition, the exit decision is rational and thus efficient. As noted above, however, not all firms will be able to pursue economic options. Divestiture may be more costly than its benefits. The lack of alternatives, or the lack of resources to pursue those alternatives, may make adjustment unattractive. Firms that find themselves "pushed to the wall" and into bankruptcy, however, have an important alternative to the marketplace—politics. In Albert Hirschman's apt phrase, firms that cannot exit can attempt to exercise voice.[10]

Even where firms have incentives to respond flexibly to economic distress, adjustment is never without costs, and industry actors will also be tempted to seek government compensation for their adjustment efforts. Subsidies that compensate producers for the cost of scrapping capacity or retraining labor, for instance, turn private costs into social ones; as a result, the costs of adjustment are shifted to the taxpayer.

Firms can attempt to smooth out the process of adjustment by stabilizing supply-side conditions. Mechanisms such as cartels aim to control surplus production, manage excess capacity, or cooperatively determine market shares. The purpose of cartelization is to artificially control output in an effort to alleviate downward pressures on prices and thus to stabilize profits. Industry actors benefit to the extent that stabilizing industry conditions reduces the risk of damaging price wars. The costs of adjustment would be passed on to downstream buyers and final consumers in the form of higher prices.[11]

To an even greater degree than stabilization strategies, preservation strategies seek to alleviate market pressures and to protect the industry from the need to make adjustments. "Preservation" implies resorting to the political realm to, in essence, force others to make the needed adjustments. Examples of preservationist measures run a gamut of strategies, including import protection, direct subsidies, government bailouts, and

---

[10] Hirschman notes that "the role of voice would increase as the opportunities for exit decline, up the point where, with exit wholly unavailable, voice must carry the entire burden" (1970, p. 34).

[11] See Zysman 1983 and Gourevitch 1986 for a discussion of the use of recession cartels in Germany, France, and Britain. Porter (while not advocating the use of cartels) argues that one pitfall a troubled industry should avoid is destabilizing cutthroat competition. His advice pertains not only to the weak firms but strong ones as well, for even when a firm is dominant, "a war of attrition is costly to the victor and vanquished alike and is best avoided" (Porter 1980, p. 92).

An industry might also seek to stabilize itself through management of the demand side, in particular through public-works spending or targeted government procurements; however, it is unlikely that any one industry would have such political clout.

adjustment-retarding legislation. Industries that achieve political solutions pass adjustment costs on to others: to buyer firms and final consumers to the extent that prices are artificially propped up; to taxpayers to the extent that government policy entails subsidies and bailouts; and to foreign producers to the extent that domestic capacity is maintained or that imports are limited.

INDUSTRIAL STRUCTURE

Political scientists typically assume that firms will respond to economic distress by pursuing political solutions to their problems.[12] But even firms that possess great political influence may have incentives to pursue economic options as well—for instance, to minimize long-term losses, to restore profitability, or to regain their competitiveness. In practice, then, the options outlined above will not be mutually exclusive, and firms may pursue a combination of political and economic responses—divestment, adjustment, compensation, stabilization, and preservation. For example, a firm can choose to diversify so as to maintain its economic viability, while at the same time seeking public policies to stabilize the industry's conditions.

In this section I explicate the link between the structural features of an industry and the general patterns of industry preferences. Here I stress the importance of economic alternatives, arguing that industries with viable economic alternatives available to them will have fewer incentives to seek political solutions.

The key structural variable is the industry's degree of concentration.[13] *Large oligopolistic firms are more likely to have both the capabilities and the incentives to pursue the economic strategies of divestment or adjustment.* Although these firms may find it difficult to divest from the industry completely (because, for instance, the high economic costs of disposing of their large capital facilities may make complete divestiture unattractive), they are also likely to have the resources to make adjustments such as diversification up the value-

---

[12] Examples include Olson 1965, Olson 1982, Strange 1979, pp. 310–327, McKeown 1984, p. 216, and Garrett and Lange 1986, p. 526. In contrast, economists tend to ignore a firm's political options and focus by default on market strategies. One exception is Rajan and Brahm (1994, p. 421), who argue that economists should pay more attention to the political and institutional environment that influences the choices that firms make.

[13] I use the Herfindahl index (H-index) to measure industrial concentration. I prefer this measure to simple concentration ratios or average firm size because it is a composite measure that reflects the number, size, and distribution of firms in an industry. The H-index is closely related to the size of firms, since high concentration generally indicates high entry barriers due to scale economies, high levels of capital and labor resources, and so forth (Scherer 1980). Industries with Herfindahl scores over 1,000 are treated as concentrated, following Peck et al. 1987.

added chain, into other fields, or into overseas markets. Large firms tend to have an adequate technological base and adequate capital to pursue and finance adjustment. The larger the firm the more likely these resources will be available. In addition, large firms already tend to be diversified and so should find it easier to "divest selectively" by repositioning resources internally or ridding themselves of the part of the firm that is in distress.

This argument departs from the usual assumption that concentrated industries, because they face lower obstacles to political organization, tend to pursue political solutions.[14] I argue that the ability to organize is only one determinant of the behavior of firms. More critical is that firms in concentrated industries have a fuller range of options open to them. These firms may be more interested in regaining their competitiveness through the market than in rent seeking via politics.

In contrast, the numerous, small firms in fragmented industries are in a more vulnerable position. The relatively small size of the firms makes them more susceptible to bankruptcy. The usual assumption is that the small size of their capital facilities means that small firms can easily exit an industry. However, the costs of exit are not limited to the disposal of capital facilities; rather, as Harrigan and Porter argue, "emotional" and other barriers may be equally, if not more, important.[15] Thus, even if the cost of disposing of capital facilities is low, the decision to do so may be extremely difficult, thus giving small firms strong incentives to avoid exiting. Furthermore, firms in fragmented industries are less likely to enjoy attractive economic alternatives, making the exit decision even less palatable. First, as these firms are generally small, they often lack the financial and other critical resources needed to pursue economic adjustment. Second, small firms will also tend to be less diversified than large firms so cannot divest selectively or shift resources internally to alternative uses. If small firms were to follow the dictates of the market, their only economic "option" may be death through bankruptcy. These firms, however, have a different, and much more attractive, route that they can pursue in order to survive: politics. *Lacking easy access to economic adjustment options, firms in fragmented industries are more likely to pursue political strategies to stabilize or preserve their industry's status quo.*[16]

---

[14] Aggarwal et al. (1987, pp. 348–350) and Anderson and Baldwin (1981, pp. 5–9) posit that high exit barriers will be correlated with incentives to seek political solutions. However, they define exit barriers only in terms of the size of capital assets, which leads them to posit that concentrated industries are the most likely to seek political solutions.

[15] I thus agree with Harrigan (1988, p. 56) and Porter (1980, pp. 259–267) that our definition of exit barriers should be broadened to include "emotional" ones as well.

[16] This specification of the interests of fragmented industries is consistent with Frieden's discussion of industries whose assets are highly specific—that is, assets that have few alternative uses. These industries should have the strongest incentives to lobby for desirable public policies (1991, pp. 19–22).

The fundamental interest of the labor force is to preserve jobs, so we can expect labor to oppose adjustment efforts that entail layoffs, such as rationalization, diversification, or efforts by firms to invest abroad. Labor is likely to press for public policies to preserve employment; it can resort to protests or can appeal directly to policy makers to seek legislation to prevent plant closures, for instance. To the extent that unemployment or layoffs cannot be avoided, labor will seek public policy compensation for the costs of adjustment, for example, through retraining programs, unemployment insurance, and other transfer payments.

Industries with larger labor forces will find it more difficult to absorb excess workers or to compensate them easily for their adjustment efforts. As a result, adjustment of labor will be more costly and the resistance to adjustment efforts will be greater. *Large numbers of workers in an industry pose a constraint on adjustment efforts and provide a strong bias toward political solutions to stabilize or preserve the industry.*

In contrast, the adjustment of workers in industries with a small labor force will entail lower total costs, as firms may be able to absorb redundant workers or find relatively easy ways to compensate them. The difficulties associated with labor adjustment will not be as severe, so small labor forces will pose less of a political constraint.[17]

Industry Preferences: Four Industry Types

Using the two industrial organization variables, industrial concentration and size of the labor force, we can derive rudimentary expectations regarding the preferences of industry actors. Table 2-2 lists four industry types, categorized according to the size of the labor force and the concentration of the industry. Expected economic preferences and policy demands are listed for each industry type.

Conversely, my analysis contradicts the arguments of proponents of "flexible manufacturing" who say that smaller firms will be more flexible and will find it less costly to adjust to international competition. See Piore and Sabel 1984, and Sabel et al. 1987. (See also Friedman 1988 for an application of the flexible manufacturing thesis to Japan.) It is important to note that the Piore and Sabel thesis is more a prescription for how production should be organized in the future than a description of how much of today's manufacturing is organized. Most of today's "small" industries are not flexibly organized or specialized in small pockets of demand. Rather, the current batch of declining industries in Japan is precisely composed of those that are locked into the old methods of mass production that Piore and Sabel criticize. Since this is the case, my assumptions regarding the vulnerability and lack of flexibility of small firms are more likely to hold.

[17] I use 100,000 workers as an arbitrary cutoff mark between small and large labor forces. Labor's opposition to adjustment efforts will be muted to the extent that the current work force is retained, either in their present capacity or in new jobs after retraining. To the extent that the firm retains its labor force, we can expect labor's interests to coincide with those of the firm.

Table 2-2. Four industry types: Industrial structure and industry preferences

Degree of industrial concentration	Small labor force	Large labor force
Concentrated	**Type I** (Concentrated, small labor force) 1. Firms will have both the incentives and capabilities to pursue economic adjustment options. 2. Labor's resistance to adjustment is likely to be low. (Total adjustment costs are low, and the ability of firms to absorb labor is high.) *Costs of adjustment are relatively low, so neither firms nor labor will have strong incentives to resist adjustment; they are most likely to pursue economic adjustment options.*	**Type II** (Concentrated, large labor force) 1. Firms will have both the incentives and capabilities to pursue economic adjustment options. 2. Labor's resistance to adjustment is likely to be high. (Total adjustment costs are high, and the ability of firms to absorb labor is constrained.) *Firms and labor will pursue a mixture of adjustment and stabilization strategies. The high costs of adjusting labor, however, may bias incentives toward political solutions.*
Fragmented	**Type III** (Fragmented, small labor force) 1. Firms are vulnerable to exit through bankruptcy and lack resources to pursue economic adjustment options; they are more likely to seek political solutions. 2. Labor is likely to endorse the firm's efforts to seek political solutions. It will oppose efforts to rationalize labor, but the small labor force implies low total adjustment costs. *Economic adjustment options are limited, so firms are likely to pursue political solutions.*	**Type IV** (Fragmented, large labor force) 1. Firms are vulnerable to exit through bankruptcy and lack resources to pursue economic adjustment options; they are more likely to seek political solutions. 2. Labor is likely to endorse the firm's efforts to seek political solutions. It will strongly oppose efforts to rationalize labor, since adjustment costs to labor are high. *Costs of adjustment are high for both firms and labor, so both will have strong incentives to pursue political solutions.*

Type I Industries (Concentrated, Small Labor Force). Industry actors in a concentrated industry with a small labor force are the most likely to pursue the economic strategies of divestment or adjustment. The critical factor is on the side of capital: firms in a concentrated industry (one dominated by a small number of large firms) are more likely to have the opportunities and the necessary resources to adjust in order to remain competitive.[18]

As the labor force's interest is to preserve jobs, it is likely to demand public policies that slow adjustment efforts. For a Type I industry, however, two factors will mute the intensity of this opposition. First, the small size of the labor force implies that total adjustment costs will be low. Second, the "absorptive capacity" of firms in this category is likely to be the highest of that among the four industry types—that is, large firms are more likely to be able to compensate displaced workers through separation bonuses and the like, or they may be able to absorb the small number of workers by shifting them to other sections of the firm or to related firms.

It may also prove easier for firms in concentrated industries to pass the burden of adjustment on to others. To the extent that firms in concentrated industries can act strategically, they may be able to pass adjustment costs on to downstream buyers in the form of higher prices. And because of the small number of firms involved, a concentrated industry may be able to coordinate and privately enforce cartel-like behavior.

The costs of economic adjustment in a Type I industry are likely to be the lowest for both firms and labor; at the same time, industry actors have the resources and incentives to pursue economic alternatives. Consequently, they are the least likely to seek preservationist solutions to shield themselves from pressures for change. Such pressures on policy makers will tend to be limited to seeking compensation for adjustment efforts and enforcement mechanisms to help stabilize the industry. Thus, pressures on the government to become involved in a Type I industry are likely to be relatively limited, both in terms of the time frame and obtrusiveness of intervention.

Type II Industries (Concentrated, Large Labor Force). Like Type I industries, firms in a concentrated industry with a large labor force also tend to have incentives to pursue economic options. Large, oligopolistic Type II firms generally have access to necessary resources to make adjustments such as diversification or overseas investment.[19]

In contrast to the situation in a Type I industry, however, the large size of the labor force imposes a constraint on such forms of adjustment. Although some workers may be absorbed internally by each firm, the sheer number of workers will strain the firm's "absorptive capacity." Labor will strongly resist strategies that entail layoffs or employment adjustment, and this will increase the firm's incentives to seek political solutions.

---

[18] A typical example of a Type I industry is aluminum smelting. In most countries this industry consists of a small number of large, capital-intensive firms, with a labor force typically under 10,000 workers (Peck 1988).

[19] A typical Type II industry is the integrated steel industry. In the OECD countries, the average steel industry consists of very large, capital-intensive concerns, with a labor force in the 100,000 to 200,000 range.

Thus, industry actors in Type II industries are likely to pursue a mixture of both economic and political strategies. They also have an interest in passing adjustment costs on to others through collective stabilization efforts or though public policy compensation. In particular, both firms and labor are likely to favor policies that help them deal with the adjustment of the labor force.

Type III Industries (Fragmented, Small Labor Force). In contrast, fragmented industries face quite different incentives. The critical difference between a fragmented industry and those discussed above is that the smaller firms often lack the resources to pursue economic adjustment.[20] The small size of these firms increases their vulnerability to bankruptcy. As a result, these firms will have strong incentives to pursue the alternative route of politics. *Firms in Type III industries are thus likely to be in favor of political measures to stabilize the industry, and to delay or dampen adjustment pressures.*

The interests of the labor force are likely to coincide with these efforts. To the extent that stabilization or preservation prevents drastic layoffs, labor should endorse the firms' efforts. However, to the extent that firms try to rationalize the labor force, their interests will conflict. Because firms are small, they are less likely to have the capability to shift workers internally or to affiliated firms. The small size of the work force, however, means that total adjustment costs to labor will be low, thus mitigating, to some extent, labor's resistance to change.

The fragmented nature of a Type III industry will make it more difficult to pass adjustment costs on to others through cartel-like behavior. The large number of firms may make tacit market collusion difficult to enforce. In practice, private enforcement mechanisms are not likely to be strong enough to overcome incentives to cheat, and so if attempts to stabilize an industry through a cartel are to succeed, they will probably require that the state intervene to enforce collective agreements.

Type IV Industries (Fragmented, Large Labor Force). Industry actors in an industry that is fragmented and has a large labor force are the most likely to resort to the political process to resist adjustment pressures.[21] Economically, such firms will lack adjustment options and will be highly vulnerable to bankruptcy, giving them strong incentives to seek preservationist policies. As in Type III industries, the choice facing firms is a stark one: death through bankruptcy or stabilization through politics. Labor will favor political solutions and will oppose efforts to rationalize the work force. Ra-

---

[20] There are numerous examples of industries that fit the Type III profile. In the Japanese case, examples include cement, paper, pulp, sugar refining, electric furnace steel, lumber, and plywood.

[21] Examples of a Type IV industry include the natural textile industries and coal mining. These industries typically consist of over 100 relatively small firms. Because these industries are highly labor-intensive, the work force in each often surpasses the 200,000 mark.

tionalization of the labor force will be extremely costly and difficult in a Type IV industry, as the large number of workers and the relatively small size of firms means that the ability to absorb excess labor will be the lowest of the four industry categories. Strong incentives on the part of labor to resist adjustment will complement the firms' interest in achieving political solutions. *Because adjustment in a Type IV industry is the most difficult and costly, both firms and labor will have strong incentives to resist adjustment and to pursue the full range of political solutions.*

Firms and labor will thus have strong incentives to apply political pressures on policy makers. If this kind of industry pursues stabilization strategies, the outside enforcement mechanisms of the state become essential for it to overcome the problems inherent in cartel-like behavior. To the extent that adjustment occurs, demands for compensation will be quite high, particularly in order to cope with the rationalization of excess labor. To the extent that the industry tries to preserve the status quo, actors in a Type IV industry are likely to demand that the government become significantly involved in the industry, in terms of time-frame, intensity, and the scope of policy intervention.

Obviously, any two variables will not explain everything we need to know about an industry's structural characteristics and its actual behavior—there are simply too many other factors involved.[22] Industrial structure matters, but it will not yield ironclad predictions. Still, the initial expectations laid out in this chapter give us a general idea of the economic and political preferences of industry actors in each industry type. At the very least, establishing this baseline of expected behavior is a prerequisite for any approach that focuses on the role that societal actors play in the policy process.

[22] However, one further factor does deserve mention at the outset: the issue of whether firms in each industry are in fact homogeneous. In the case studies that follow, we should remain sensitive to potential differences between firms within an industry. Porter captures such variations in his concept of "strategic groups"—that is, discrete groupings of firms within an industry that share common structural positions. To give one example from a case discussed in Chapter 4, the Japanese cotton spinning industry was fragmented, but on closer examination we find that the industry was led by a handful of large firms co-existing with many tiny firms. The larger firms enjoyed some competitive advantages and were also members of the *keiretsu*, which gave them greater access to resources and an added degree of flexibility in absorbing or re-employing labor. These firms were thus more likely to prevail in a market situation and so had less of an interest in seeking political solutions. In contrast, the smaller firms enjoyed no such advantages. To the extent that such "strategic groups" exist, their behavior may differ somewhat from the majority of firms in each industry type. Indeed, the work of Porter (1980, pp. 126–155) and Harrigan (1980, pp. 33–36) is premised on the assumption that firms will have different strengths and weaknesses, and that managers must choose strategies accordingly.

CHAPTER THREE

Turning Industry Preferences into Policy Choices: The Industrial Policy-Making Environment

In the last chapter I focused on the expected preferences of firms and labor, postulating that these preferences will be linked to the industry's structure. However, these actors must *act* if they are to translate their preferences into policy. In the process of policy-making, these preferences are likely to be deflected or altered, with the specifics of final policy choices reflecting some degree of compromise. Thus, understanding the preferences of the industry is only the first step in explaining eventual policy choices. The second step is to trace the process through which firms and labor interact with the broader policy-making environment.

In this chapter I first discuss two main routes through which industry actors can try to achieve their goals: through direct interactions with bureaucrats and through mobilization of political supporters. I contend that industry actors are better able to constrain bureaucratic behavior than they are generally given credit for. MITI's autonomy, thus, can be fundamentally constrained by at least two sets of actors—the party politicians and the industries being regulated. Taking these constraints into account, I then discuss how the goals of a more "politicized" MITI might differ from the usual image of an autonomous bureaucracy.

The policy process, however, is not merely confined to the "iron triangle" linking industry actors, bureaucrats, and politicians: rather, all domestic actors are constrained and influenced by elements of an even broader policy-making environment. In the last section of this chapter I turn to a discussion of the domestic antitrust environment and Japan's position in the international economy I argue that changes in both of these conditions have led to the growing constraints on the range of policy tools available to industry groups and policy makers.

Thus, as I define it, the policy-making environment consists of the political and bureaucratic actors and institutions, both domestic and international, that are involved in, or influence, the policy process. This
environment includes all important determinants of the policy process
that are *external* to my unit of analysis—the firms and labor forces that
comprise each industry.[1] Because the effects of this environment may vary
over time, it is difficult to derive explicit hypotheses or predictions. I therefore refrain from making strong a priori hypotheses and, instead, limit my
discussion to an assessment of how the key features of the environment are
interrelated and how they have evolved over time.

THE QUESTION OF BUREAUCRATIC AUTONOMY

The fundamental issue that divides analysts of Japanese political economy is a simple one: a deep disagreement over the extent to which bureaucratic actors can define and implement policy in relative autonomy
from political or particularistic pressures. The "bureaucratic dominance"
view asserts that bureaucratic behavior is not subject to strong constraints
from either the party politicians or industry actors. This paradigm describes bureaucratic actors as impervious to political intervention and un-
responsive to particularistic pressures and, thus, able to design economic
and industrial polices that achieve broader, national-level objectives. In a
policy process in which politicians reign but bureaucrats rule, politicians
are described as powerless or deferential, allowing the bureaucracy to initiate and implement policy free from political interference.[2] And if industry actors are indeed "responsively dependent" on the bureaucrats, their
interests will be only incidental to the bureaucratic decision-making
process. To understand Japan's policy choices in this apolitical world of
unconstrained and autonomous bureaucrats, we need only focus on the
goals and objectives of the relevant ministry.

In the case of industrial policy-making the relevant ministry is MITI.
MITI bureaucrats have jurisdiction over virtually every manufacturing industry, enjoy a broad mandate to oversee the industrial policy process, and
are involved in all aspects of that process. Indeed, analysts often describe

---

[1] That is, all elements of the policy-making process, including international factors, consti-
tute what Daniel Little calls the "environment of choice" relevant to industry actors (Little
1991). If one were to focus on a different actor the environment external to that actor would
differ accordingly. For example, system-level theories take the nation-state as the central actor and then focus on how the environment external to the state—i.e., the international system—influences and constrains these states.

[2] As Chalmers Johnson puts it, for the "developmental state" to be effective, the bureaucracy has to be "protected from all but the most powerful interest groups so that it can set
and achieve long-range industrial priorities" (1982, p. 44).

industrial policy-making as dominated by MITI, or at best limited to narrowly defined "policy segments" consisting of the MITI bureaucrats and the industry being regulated, with the politicians and other actors operating only in the background.[3]

If MITI bureaucrats are impervious to political and interest group pressures, what should be MITI's policy goals for troubled industries? The bureaucratic dominance perspective offers two sets of expectations. First, if the bureaucracy is truly insulated from the particularistic interests and able to implement policies that further national-level goals, then it will prefer to take a hands-off approach, refraining from intervening in the market and letting market pressures, by default, force the industry to adjust. MITI should have an interest in leaving the industry to its market-determined fate and should be able to resist efforts by industries to prevent economic adjustment.[4] Second, if the Japanese bureaucracy follows the goals of a "capitalist developmental state," we can expect the bureaucracy to take a more active, "positive," and anticipatory approach to distressed industries. MITI's goal of promoting strategic or growth industries will be hampered to the extent that distressed industries do not adjust or continue to hold on to capital, skilled labor, or other scarce resources. If the bureaucracy is interested in fostering overall economic growth and development, it should prefer intervention fostering rapid adjustment and rationalization of inefficient or uncompetitive industries so that adequate resources are made available to the more promising growth industries. In short, the bureaucracy should intervene to wipe out pockets of lingering economic inefficiency and favor sectors that contribute more to the nation's overall economic strength.[5]

This description of MITI's policy goals, however, makes sense only if we assume that MITI is indifferent to political pressures and constraints and that it defines and implements policies based on its own conception of "the national interest." In contrast, I conceive of MITI and the rest of the Japanese bureaucracy as political organizations that are as likely to pursue organizational goals as national ones. To further these goals MITI relies

---

[3] In this chapter I focus my attention on MITI. However, the points made here are also relevant to the Ministry of Transport, which has jurisdiction over the shipbuilding industry discussed in Chapter 7.

[4] Johnson mentions that the developmental state "simply ignores the nonstrategic sectors of the society" (1982, p. 316). Unfortunately, Johnson says little else about distressed industries. This is partly because his analysis ends with the advent of the Oil Shock of 1973, when the majority of the cases of industrial adjustment appeared in Japan. But he ignores troubled industries mostly because his main concern is with Japan's growth and development.

[5] Okimoto 1989, p. 128. Johnson, for instance, mentions that the heart of MITI's industrial structure policy is the selection of industries "to be developed *or converted to other lines of work*" (1982, p. 28; my italics) Elsewhere, Johnson notes that "no doubt Japan will find it painful to adjust to declining competitiveness in the steel and automobile industries, but it already has more experience in the deliberate change of industrial structure than any other country and should therefore be able to manage this one" (1988, p. 94).

on and needs cooperation from industry actors and their political allies. This reliance makes the bureaucrats receptive, at least to some extent, to the interests and preferences voiced by these groups.

Troubled Industries and the Bureaucrats

The first avenue through which industry actors can seek to influence policy choices is through their direct interactions with the bureaucrats that oversee them. Until recently, the extent to which these industries could use their relationships with the bureaucrats to influence policy has been relatively neglected. Richard Samuels, in *The Business of the Japanese State*, remains one of the few scholars of Japanese industrial policy who pays explicit attention to the preferences of industry actors and the extent to which those preferences have been reflected in ultimate policy choices.[6]

Analysts of Japanese industrial policy agree that bureaucrats and the industries under their jurisdiction enjoy close interrelationships, but often disagree over what these links imply. Those who see autonomous bureaucrats in Japan assume that influence flows from the top down and that these linkages give the bureaucracy the ability to influence or control the behavior of societal actors.[7] Daniel Okimoto, for instance, argues that MITI's extensive policy networks and informal links with the private sector give MITI "multiple points of entry [into the market] through which to exert a direct influence on market outcomes."[8] The "old boys' networks" that link the bureaucrats with firms and industries presumably allow the bureaucrats to take advantage of similar mind-sets and a common agenda. Another personal linkage is *amakudari* ("descent from heaven"), the practice of bureaucrats retiring and taking positions in the private sector. As Johnson puts it, this "institution" is a part of MITI's overall development strategy, with retired officials sent to serve on the boards of industries that MITI deems to be economically strategic.[9] Finally, the existence of nu-

---

[6] Samuels 1986. Since the publication of that path-breaking book, a number of scholars have emphasized the policy roles played by industries or organized actors, including Rosenbluth 1989, Friedman 1988, Noble 1988, and the present study.

[7] Johnson 1982, pp. 55–67; Katzenstein 1978; Krasner 1987. In fact, both Peter Katzenstein and Stephen Krasner see these linkages as so pervasive and deep that they portray the state and society in Japan as one and the same. According to Katzenstein, in Japan "relations between business and the state are so symbiotic that it is virtually impossible to determine where one stops and the other begins" (1978, p. 315). However, as McKean points out, the inclusion of private actors in the definition of the state is "a grievous error" (1993, p. 77).

[8] Okimoto 1989, pp. 17–18. Furthermore, he continues, these points of access allow "MITI to bend and shape the market without having to go through the political channels of the LDP and the parliament" (1989, p. 18).

[9] The targeting of key industries for *amakudari* bureaucrats is thus "not an unintended consequence of the developmental state; it is in fact an objective of the developmental state. . . . [The most senior of these positions provide] bases from which to coordinate the strategic sectors" (Johnson 1982, p. 70–71).

merous industry associations is said to facilitate MITI's job of coordinating industry behavior. According to Okimoto, these associations, or *gyōkai*, play a "role in aggregating individual company interests, building intra-industry consensus, and serving as a vehicle of communication between industry and government. . . . [As a result, they] insulate industrial policy from the kind of parochialism and politicization" caused by interest groups in other countries.[10]

I argue that all of these linkages allow influence to run in both directions—that is, these points of access also enable industries to influence policy makers in ways that suit their interests. This is obviously the case for informal linkages such as the old boys' networks; if state and industrial actors share similar mind-sets and a common agenda, these similarities could merely reflect the interests of the industrial actors. The mechanism of *amakudari* can also allow industry actors to exert influence on the bureaucracy. Kent Calder argues that firms seek out retired officials to increase their access to the ministry and to change the policy environment they face. That is, *amakudari* plays an "equalizing role" in that it "broadens and strengthens access to the national economic decision-making process for groups with relatively weak connections to it."[11] Most importantly, the existence of industry associations increases the political bargaining power of each industry. These organizations provide the industry with a forum for coming to an intra-industry consensus and allow industry actors to speak in a more unified, organized voice. These organizations at times also serve as forums for collective action within the industry and occasionally act as the enforcer of industry-wide agreements. Finally, these associations play the key role of direct lobbying of the bureaucracy. Far from insulating the policy process from parochialism, the *gyōkai* serve to increase that particularism.[12]

An industry's influence over its regulators also stems from the fact that the bureaucrats depend on industry actors to provide necessary information and to cooperate in the implementation of policies. MITI bureaucrats, for example, simply do not have the information sources and market expertise that businessmen do. Trained as generalists, with only limited experience in any one industry, the bureaucrats must rely on the industry for accurate information as well as policy advice. This is especially true for high-technology industries, where the industry associations are key sources of information on rapidly changing markets and new technologi-

---

[10] Okimoto 1989, pp. 165–166. It must be remembered that Okimoto assumes that state and private sector actors agree on the goal of promoting high technology industries and that they thus have incentives to realize their "collective interests." This assumption allows Okimoto to portray the *gyōkai* as an instrument through which MITI coordinates private behavior. Again, one must stop to ask: who is influencing whom?

[11] Calder 1989, p. 383.

[12] Sone 1993; Lynn and McKeown 1988.

cal developments. In the case of troubled industries, no one knows the industry's problems better than the industry actors themselves; bureaucrats are likely to hear very clear ideas as to what policies are needed to help solve the industry's problems. In addition, the bureaucrats rely on the industry's cooperation in terms of implementing agreed upon policies. Not surprisingly, the implementation of informal policies has been smoothest when those policies promote industrial growth. In these cases, as John O. Haley argues, "it did not require coercion to elicit compliance when all agreed that the consequences would be mutually rewarding."[13]

When industries are not satisfied with policy decisions, they can act to withhold information, they can ignore or evade policy advice, or they can refuse to cooperate with policy decisions. In the past, when MITI bureaucrats have attempted to implement policies that have gone against industry interests or that were opposed by some or all industry actors, the policy process invariably became politicized and controversial. MITI bureaucrats in most cases have shown themselves to be very sensitive to industry demands and have tried to avoid political controversy.[14] If industry actors are truly dissatisfied with their treatment by the bureaucracy, they can try to raise the degree of controversy by openly protesting MITI behavior and stepping up their direct lobbying and pressure tactics. The prospect of open confrontation and controversy is one that MITI bureaucrats prefer to avoid. As one analyst puts it:

> [When] firms go bankrupt or at any rate clear losers appear ... they and third parties who suffer losses go running to the government to ask for aid and succor. It is the bureaucrats who then suffer in trying to clear up the mess. In such situations, bureaucrats may have to answer questions from the Diet or face the examining eye of the press about what is going on and how they could have permitted such a situation to arise. ... Thus officials have tried to see to it that, whenever possible, measures are instituted that assure that none of their firms get into trouble, that their firms remain profitable, and that their industry is not faced with the specter of import competition or the entry of foreign firms.[15]

---

[13] In these cases, most of which occurred during Japan's rapid growth phase, because "all concerned agree on the desirability of a particular policy, there is hardly any need for formal procedures. ... The pervasive use of administrative guidance by the economic ministries can be explained in part therefore by the promotional nature of much of Japan's postwar economic policy" (Haley 1987, p. 187).

[14] Komiya 1988. One notable example is the 1965 Sumitomo Metals incident, when MITI was pressured by the steel industry to force the noncooperating firm to comply with a production cutback agreement. MITI eventually prevailed, but in the process endured a great deal of criticism from the FTC, the media, and the opposition. Others have pointed to MITI's failed attempts to force Japanese auto firms to merge in the late 1960s (Johnson 1982, pp. 268–271).

[15] Komiya 1988, p. 12.

If industry actors remain truly dissatisfied with policy choices, they can try to increase their influence through a second route: mobilizing the party politicians to apply pressures on the bureaucrats. Whether these efforts will be effective or not depends on two conditions: first, industry actors must be able to offer politicians attractive resources, and second, the politicians must be able to effectively constrain bureaucratic behavior. Neither of these conditions is automatically fulfilled in practice, so there may be a great deal of uncertainty as to whether politicians will actually intervene. I discuss these two prerequisites in the following sections.

Troubled Industries and the Politicians

Industry actors that are highly motivated are likely to have relatively greater influence over the politicians. As discussed in Chapter 2, troubled industries should be among the most highly motivated societal actors simply because firms and labor in these industries have their very survival at stake. And because of the asymmetry of incentives involved, actors in troubled industries are likely to be considerably more motivated than other groups that may be affected by policy choices, such as final consumers and taxpayers.[16]

Industry actors will also have influence over politicians to the extent that they are able to supply the critical resources that politicians need—money and votes. The typology outlined in Chapter 2 suggests that the four industry types will vary in their ability to provide political resources. All else being equal, the larger the labor force, the greater the industry's political influence. In terms of obstacles to organization, the concentrated industries, which have fewer firms to be coordinated, should have an easier time mobilizing for effective political pressure.[17] In contrast, a frag-

[16] A partial exception to this may be buyer firms that have high stakes in troubled industry policy and face low organizational barriers. The incentives of buyer firms to become involved in the policy process will be higher to the extent that they rely on troubled industry products for a high proportion of their inputs; that they face competition at home or abroad; and that their industry is more concentrated than the troubled industry.

A further factor determining the political influence of the troubled industry is the extent to which it is regionally concentrated. This variable, however, can work two ways: on the one hand, regional concentration implies that the costs of adjustment will be higher for both firms and labor, due to the lack of exit or re-employment opportunities; regional concentration thus is likely to increase the intensity of pressures that are brought to bear on the local politicians. On the other hand, troubled industries that are spread throughout the country may have an advantage in mobilizing politicians from a greater number of electoral districts. This opens up possibilities like log-rolling and other mobilization tactics (Anderson and Baldwin 1981).

[17] In addition, high concentration implies that barriers to entry are high, which in turn implies that the benefits of collective action are likely to accrue exclusively to the firms in the industry. In contrast, for a fragmented industry, barriers to entry are low and the benefits of collective action may be captured by the entry of new or upstart firms (Anderson and Baldwin 1981; Gowa 1988; Stigler 1971).

mented industry, with a large number of firms, will have greater difficulty in overcoming inevitable problems of free riding.

These two factors suggest that a Type II industry should have the strongest political influence because it will have low barriers to organization and because its large labor force adds to its political weight. Type II industries are thus the most likely to receive the policies they demand of the politicians. (However, recall that Type II industries generally have incentives to follow a mixed strategy of economic adjustment and political stabilization.) A Type IV industry will enjoy somewhat less political power: it will hold the same degree of voting power as the Type II industry, but its fragmented nature makes it difficult for firms to organize for collective lobbying efforts. In contrast, industries with small labor forces will tend to enjoy less political power. Of the two, Type I industries will have an advantage because the firms face relatively low barriers to political organization. The Type III industry will be the weakest in terms of political power, both because of the small size of the labor force and because it will be more difficult for its numerous firms to organize for political action. As a result, these industries are the ones most likely to be politically marginalized.[18]

The ruling party politicians, however, may face mixed incentives and at times may prefer to *refrain* from supporting troubled industries, even those which have large political resources. First, in many cases members of distressed industries have not been core constituents of the ruling party. This was true of the textile industry, for instance, which has had stronger ties with the opposition Democratic Socialist Party than with the ruling Liberal Democratic Party (LDP). And organized labor in Japan generally has developed political relationships only with the opposition parties.[19] Second, in some cases intervention in support of a single industry may involve trade-offs with other party interests. For instance, a policy to subsidize the steel industry may be unpopular with the automobile and shipbuilding industries.[20]

---

[18] However, we must not dismiss the ability of these industries to achieve political solutions. Two caveats are in order. First, organizational barriers are never insurmountable; given the extremity of stakes involved, even a Type III industry may find that the benefits of organization outweigh its costs (Gowa 1988). Second, if likely opponents (in this case consumers, taxpayers, and voters) are even less organized, the industry's political preferences may be the only ones to reach the ear of the politicians.

[19] Although the opposition parties can make life for the bureaucrats uncomfortable—for instance, by grilling them during testimony before Diet subcommittees—they lack the direct political clout that has been enjoyed by the LDP.

[20] To the extent that policies impose costs on constituents, politicians have incentives to distribute these costs in an indirect manner and, further, will have incentives to "assign the administration of the policies to an 'independent' agency of government, so that the causal relationship between the costs and the party is attenuated" (Trebilcock 1986a, pp. 22–24). In other words, ruling party politicians may have incentives to remain uninvolved and to delegate to the bureaucracy the more visible role of implementing unpopular policies. In as much as policies are popular with constituents, politicians have incentives to make the benefits as visible as possible.

Similarly, for the ruling party, intervening too heavily to protect industries in distress may also contradict broader party goals such as the desire for an efficient growth-economy. Thus, an industry's exact level of political influence will depend on numerous situation-specific factors and is thus difficult to determine in an a priori fashion.

The Politicians and the Bureaucrats

Even if industry actors enjoy influence over the politicians, their influence over policy choices will be affected by the extent to which politicians are able to control bureaucratic behavior or constrain the policy parameters under which bureaucrats operate, a matter of great controversy among scholars of Japan's political economy. The bureaucratic dominance approach, on the one hand, takes the extreme position that politicians do not matter, and that these policy boundaries are so wide that they are effectively nonexistent: bureaucrats are highly autonomous, can exercise complete discretion, and can define and implement policy free from political interference. Bureaucrats enjoy this autonomy not because the politicians have delegated it to them, but because the politicians have already abdicated their power and authority. Most analysts of Japanese political economy, on the other hand, argue that these boundaries are more tightly drawn. Party politicians in Japan, as in other democracies, have created mechanisms to control the bureaucracy, including powers of oversight and the ability to reject undesirable legislation. The ruling party for most of the postwar period, the LDP, through its long-term domination of the Diet, had ultimate control over the purse strings and thus controlled the one commodity all bureaucracies must have: money. The bureaucracy's dependence on the good will of the party politicians made them susceptible to political interference. Most analysts now agree that bureaucratic autonomy was in fact heavily compromised by the LDP politicians during that party's long reign. The LDP was able to set the broad policy parameters under which bureaucrats operated and the scope of the policy space within which bureaucrats were allowed to exercise discretion. And when the bureaucrats stepped beyond these politically defined boundaries and behaved in ways that contradicted political interests, the politicians were able to intervene to shape or reshape those parameters.[21] The goals and interests of the ruling party politicians have thus been important in constraining bureaucratic autonomy; bureaucrats have never been powers unto themselves.

[21] Most scholars of Japan now take this balanced view of the role that ruling party politicians have played in the policy process (Muramatsu and Krauss 1987; Samuels 1986; Curtis 1988; Okimoto 1989; Pempel 1987; Calder 1988; Campbell 1989, Rosenbluth 1989, Suzuki 1995; Noble 1988). Even Johnson 1989 stresses the importance of the LDP politicians, albeit in particular issue areas.

The growing consensus that ruling party politicians have constrained bureaucratic autonomy is an important corrective to the simplistic view of completely autonomous bureaucrats. However, some recent scholarship, utilizing an explicit rational choice framework, takes the analysis of political constraints to the opposite, but equally extreme, position.[22] Proponents of this approach, notably Mark Ramseyer and Frances Rosenbluth, assert that the LDP did in fact possess finely-tuned and fully effective mechanisms to control the bureaucrats. These authors postulate that the policy parameters drawn by LDP politicians were so tight and so sensitive to political interests that bureaucrats have had virtually no autonomy at all. In this conception, the only roles that bureaucrats were allowed to play were those that the LDP politicians were willing to delegate to them. Bureaucrats were docile and obedient because they anticipated the reactions of their political masters.[23] While I agree that politicians can indeed constrain the bureaucrats, this insight—one already made by numerous scholars—loses its impact when the claim is made that these political constraints have been absolute. By asserting that realities in Japan in fact have corresponded to their theoretical postulates, Ramseyer and Rosenbluth have replaced the simplistic assumption of bureaucratic autonomy with the equally simplistic assumption that the bureaucracy has lacked autonomy altogether.[24]

It is a truism that party politicians will intervene to force the bureaucracy to do their bidding when they have high enough incentives to do so. But the question is, when will the political gains be worth the costs of intervention? Politicians' attempts to constrain or influence the bureaucrats involve the expenditure of time, effort, and other resources. These costs may in practice be significant, and the threshold of political intervention quite high. First, politicians' abilities to overrule the bureaucrats will depend on the extent to which policy must be formally ratified by the politicians themselves. They may be able to reject undesirable legislation in the Diet, but they will have a harder time influencing bureaucratic behavior that does not involve explicit legislative approval. Yet a great deal of industrial policy—indeed, any sort of policy—is formulated and implemented at the administrative level, outside of direct legislative oversight.

---

[22] Kernell 1991; Ramseyer and Rosenbluth 1993.

[23] This characterization is from McKean (1993, p. 80). See also Kernell who argues explicitly that the bureaucracy is fully accountable to the politicians (1991, pp. 367–369).

[24] Some Japanese specialists now describe the debate as between those who see a dominant bureaucracy and those who stress political constraints on the bureaucrats as "sterile" or unproductive. Certainly this debate is longstanding. However, it can be labeled sterile only if one is satisfied with the consensus that has emerged. It seems to me that the debate has if anything become more polarized over time, with the dividing line in the field becoming stronger rather than weaker. Until we reach some reasonable middle ground, there is still a need for this debate to continue. See McKean 1993 for the single best summary of this debate.

This may be especially true in Japan, where ministries are given broad mandates and considerable leeway in administering policies under their jurisdictions. In these cases politicians have to rely on less direct, and usually less effective, mechanisms to influence bureaucratic behavior.[25]

Second, scholars have drawn differing conclusions regarding the strength of the mechanisms through which LDP politicians historically were able to control bureaucratic behavior. For instance, Ramseyer and Rosenbluth argue that politicians are able to control bureaucratic promotions and post-retirement employment decisions, while others have refuted this claim in very strong terms.[26] Surely, at some threshold, when a bureaucrat has completely alienated powerful politicians, politicians can indeed make life miserable for the bureaucrat or even ruin his or her career. However, the point at which the politician will take such a drastic step is often quite high. And in any case, this leverage tends to be very general, allowing the politicians to set only the broadest of policy parameters; thus, leverage may not translate into fine-tuned control over bureaucratic behavior.

Third, the politicians must have adequate information and expertise to effectively intervene in the policy process. Again, scholars disagree vehemently on this point. On the one hand, some argue that the LDP, over the forty years of its reign, had the luxury of relying on the bureaucracy for much of its policy expertise and legislative drafting ability; others portray the politician's lack of independent legislative expertise as one of their biggest weaknesses. Again, reality is somewhere in between these two positions. It is possible that the LDP at some point did delegate responsibilities to the bureaucracy, but that over time its reliance became so extensive and institutionalized that its powers of oversight and control were effectively weakened. In this view, the rise of *zoku giin* ("policy tribesmen") or the

---

[25] As one example, consider the decision to form a recession cartel between the industry and MITI. The industry must gain the approval of the FTC, but at no point does it require the explicit approval of the politicians. Political influence on such decisions is at best indirect. In addition, the founding laws of most ministries are also vague, allowing bureaucrats great leeway in interpreting their roles and powers.

[26] Ramseyer and Rosenbluth's assertions stand or fall on the issue of whether the LDP's mechanisms to indirectly control bureaucratic behavior were in fact as effective as they have postulated. On this score, they greatly exaggerate the ability of LDP politicians to control bureaucratic appointments and promotions. As many have pointed out, political appointments in Japan are limited to positions at the apex of each ministry, and promotion decisions are handled within the bureaucracy itself. At the top of the career ladder political backing may become important, but in comparative terms, career advancement is relatively insulated from political control. Given this degree of insulation from political interference, political control over bureaucrats in Japan is not nearly as effective as it may appear to be in theory. Ramseyer and Rosenbluth do at least recognize the possibility that "agency slack" exists but assert that this slack is as limited in Japan as it is in the United States—or as it should be in theory. They also exaggerate the ability of LDP politicians to determine the post-retirement careers of the bureaucrats. Here, their evidence is only anecdotal and is, even then, shaky at best.

LDP's Policy Affairs Research Council (PARC) were imperfect substitutes for direct and concrete policy expertise; thus, the LDP's lack of adequate access to independent sources made it costly for the politicians to intervene effectively.

Finally, the ability of party politicians to control the bureaucrats has varied over time. In the LDP's early period, political constraints on the bureaucracy were relatively weak.[27] These constraints grew stronger during the height of LDP hegemony when bureaucratic antennae had become, out of necessity, highly sensitive to the LDP and its interests. However, with the LDP's loss of its majority in the lower house of the Diet in the summer of 1993, political constraints on the bureaucrats again weakened. Until a strong, dominant party emerges, bureaucrats will be able to operate in a relative political vacuum; in the absence of decisive political constraints bureaucratic autonomy by default will appear to be higher.[28]

If political control over the bureaucrats is not absolute and the costs of intervention are in practice high, then politicians may not be able to intervene as freely, as often, or as effectively as they would like. Politicians thus may become selective regarding the issues on which they commit their resources and intervene only when the benefits clearly outweigh the costs. In practice, then, some uncertainty will exist as to whether politicians will actually intervene in any particular case.

When industry actors are able to mobilize their political supporters, however, the role of the politicians can be decisive. In practice, MITI bureaucrats are quite sensitive to the threat of political interference. As others have pointed out, MITI's autonomy is maximized so long as the policy-making process remains confined within well-defined "policy segments," with decisions negotiated directly between industry actors and the MITI bureaucrats.[29] However, forestalling interference by "outside" political actors is possible only so long as policy choices are not controversial, and the policy process remains routine and smooth. MITI bureaucrats realize that the politicians, once mobilized, may become permanent fixtures in the policy process. In these cases, MITI bureaucrats will find themselves embroiled in messy struggles with outraged industry actors and their political allies. Since the bureaucrats need political cooperation and support in order to get their own programs implemented, they cannot afford to disregard the concerns raised by the politicians. This desire to avoid polit-

---

[27] Even in this period, however, Muramatsu and Krauss (1987) argue that the LDP was able to define the general directions of national policy—the pursuit of economic growth at home combined with the US alliance abroad—but left the details of implementing this "conservative party line" to the bureaucrats.

[28] Suzuki and Uriu 1994.

[29] See, for instance, Campbell 1989, p. 125, and Komiya 1988, p. 11. Okimoto (1989, pp. 152–161) refers to these as "policy networks."

ical controversy gives MITI strong incentives to tailor its policies in ways that industries find acceptable.

Troubled Industry Policy: The Permeated Bureaucracy

Industry actors can thus hope to influence policy choices via two routes: directly, through their interactions with bureaucrats and, indirectly, through the mobilization of their political allies. However, one must not conclude that MITI bureaucrats are somehow completely "captured." Given its broad jurisdiction, MITI is able to play a mediating role when the interests of different industries are in conflict. By playing the interests of one industry off against another, MITI is able to resist the most egregious demands. As Okimoto puts it, "no single industry or interest group, no matter how powerful, exercises dominant influence on MITI or dictates the substance of industrial policy."[30] Second, the diversity of industries under MITI's jurisdiction means that its organizational stake in preserving any particular industry will be low. If the coal mining industry were to disappear, for example, MITI bureaucrats could be easily shifted to work on other industries. The possibility of capture should be lower in bureaucracies with broad-based jurisdictions.[31] Thus, MITI bureaucrats are sensitive to industry interests, yet they are not pawns of any one set of industry actors. MITI's autonomy is permeated and constrained, not non-existent.

Given the potential constraints imposed by the industry and politicians, what should MITI's goals for distressed industry policy be? On the one hand, the desire to avoid politicization gives MITI ample reason to be sympathetic to the preferences of the industry and refrain from forcing it to undergo difficult adjustments. If MITI pursues policies that go against the interests of the industry, it faces the difficult task of forcing it to accept an unpopular policy and, furthermore, runs the risk that the policy process will become heavily politicized. On the other hand, because MITI is neither completely captured by its constituents nor completely beholden to

[30] Okimoto 1989, p. 114. See also McKean 1993. As an example, MITI has been able to resist pressures from the textile industry for outright protection against imports because it can point to the broader ramifications for the rest of Japanese industry. As discussed in Chapter 7, the Ministry of Transport also oversees industries with conflicting interests, and this has allowed it to play a mediating role between these groups. Okimoto points out that MITI's internal organization, which combines vertical bureaus responsible for particular industries with horizontal bureaus concerned with broader interests, ensures that policy makers take into account the interests of all industries under MITI's jurisdiction. This also ensures that it will be able to resist the most extreme parochial political pressures (1989, pp. 114–119). Similarly, at least after 1984, the MOT has been organized along horizontal as well as vertical lines.

[31] In contrast, single-interest bureaucracies such as the Ministry of Agriculture would be organizationally devastated if their clients, the farmers, were to be greatly rationalized or reduced in number.

34

the politicians, it can strike a balance among multiple objectives: the developmental goal of fostering economic growth and the organizational goal of avoiding politicization.

In choosing between these competing goals, MITI will, I expect, pursue development only to the extent that doing so does not run the risk of creating political controversy. If politicization is not a problem, then MITI can be expected to maximize industrial development. But if achieving this goal entails high political costs, I posit that bureaucrats will be willing to forgo development. Thus, when faced with a choice between a policy that promotes development but risks becoming politicized and a policy that retards development but avoids politicization, bureaucrats will opt for the latter.[32]

In as much as politicization, controversy, or conflict is likely, we should expect the bureaucracy to be responsive to the various demands for stabilization by the troubled industries. The bureaucracy should be sympathetic to efforts by industry to pass on the costs of adjustment to others, and should compensate it for adjustment, support its stabilization efforts, or help it to retard adjustment. Similarly, the bureaucracy should help industry prevent major bankruptcies and large-scale unemployment, actions that threaten to cause social disruption and politicize the policy process.

THE BROADER POLICY-MAKING ENVIRONMENT

The discussion thus far has been limited to the "iron triangle" linking bureaucratic, political, and industrial actors. However, the policy-making environment as I define it includes two broader elements—the legal antitrust environment and the international political environment. These elements have imposed constraints and afforded opportunities that have influenced industry actors, politicians, and bureaucrats alike.

Over the postwar period the most important policy tool for troubled industries, the use of cartels, has become more and more constrained by changes in the domestic antitrust environment. The effectiveness of cartels has declined over time due to the growing openness of the Japanese economy. To be effective, cartels require at least implicit barriers to imports; if imports are not somehow impeded, then efforts to control output are doomed to fail.[33] Cartels were thus much more effective earlier in the postwar period, when the economy was relatively closed and protected. Although Japan today is still criticized for maintaining implicit or hidden barriers to imports, it is no longer able to overtly impede imports. The

---

[32] Ikenberry 1986, pp. 60–61. As he puts it, "when push comes to shove, [the state] will choose organizational over national goals" (p. 61).

[33] Lawrence 1987.

rapid decline in the use of cartels beginning in the mid-1970s is indicative of these developments.

An increasingly assertive Japan Fair Trade Commission (FTC) has raised further obstacles to the use of cartels. The usual image of a politically weak and subordinate FTC, while accurate for much of the postwar period, began to change in the 1970s. In that decade, the FTC began a legal attack on MITI's administrative guidance prerogatives, an attack that culminated in the petroleum cartel case of 1974. As I discuss in Chapter 5, this FTC court challenge was eventually upheld and served as an important legal constraint on MITI's use of its administrative guidance powers. In addition, pressures from Japan's trading partners have served to strengthen the FTC. During the mid-1980s the U.S. trade agenda with Japan increasingly focused on allegations that domestic cartels implied de facto barriers to imports. The FTC received a huge boost in the Structural Impediments Initiative talks, in which one of the U.S. demands was that the Japanese government enhance the FTC's antitrust enforcement capabilities.[34] The likelihood that attempts to enforce cartel arrangements would run into domestic or international opposition made it more difficult for MITI to support such industry efforts. And because the bureaucracy became less likely to enforce collective action, over time industry actors found it more difficult to achieve cooperative, coordinated solutions.

At first glance, troubled industry policy may appear to be an entirely domestic issue. But the international environment has been a source of both opportunities and constraints that have influenced all actors in the domestic policy process. Thus, even for a domestically centered issue, the international context cannot be ignored.

The relatively open international economic system in the postwar era has been a two-edged sword for Japan's troubled industries. On the one hand, exposure to the international economy has meant that domestic industries have been vulnerable to exogenous shocks—sudden shifts in world demand, drastic rises in resource prices, pressures from trading partners to restrain Japanese exports, and so on. On the other hand, the relatively open international economy has also led to the temptation to shift the costs of adjustment to its trading partners.[35] Many instances of Japan's early postwar "export deluges," for example, were attempts by distressed industries to export their way out of their domestic problems of surplus capacity. And in as much as a troubled industry is implicitly or explicitly protected from imports, foreign trading partners must adjust to reduced export opportunities.

---

[34] See Schoppa 1993, pp. 362–363, and Janow 1994, pp. 66–71.
[35] Susan Strange (1979, pp. 308–310) argues this point.

Attempts to shift the burden of adjustment to trading partners, however, also run the risk of invoking retaliation. For Japan, both the likelihood of retaliation by foreign trading partners and the potential costs of that retaliation have increased during the postwar period. The combination of higher risks and higher costs of retaliation has made Japanese policy makers extremely sensitive to international concerns and constraints.

First, the *likelihood* that foreign governments will retaliate against Japan has increased. In the 1950s and 1960s, when the external impact of the Japanese economy was low, Japan was a "small economy," one that could shift the costs of adjustment to its trading partners without much fear of retaliation.[36] By the 1970s, however, Japan was certainly no longer a small economy. Persistent Japanese trade surpluses and sectoral displacements caused by growing Japanese competitiveness have led to growing frictions with the United States and the European Community. As a result of Japan's growing economic impact, international attention has become increasingly focused on Japanese policy. In an atmosphere of heightened criticism, Japan's trading partners are less likely to permit it to shift the burden of economic adjustment to them. Attempts by Japanese industry to export domestic surpluses or to try to pass the costs of economic change on to others through import protection are now more likely to lead to retaliation abroad.

Second, the potential *costs* of foreign retaliation against the Japanese economy have also grown over time. The dramatic shift in Japan's position in the international economy has changed Japanese interests at both the national and sectoral levels: Japan has developed high and tangible stakes in maintaining an open international economy. These growing stakes can be seen from structural analyses of Japan's changing position in the international economy. David Lake, for instance, argues that as Japan's relative size and productivity have increased, so too have its stakes in maintaining the international system.[37] Similarly, Richard Rosecrance

---

[36] Kindleberger 1973, p. 249–250. Kindleberger also describes Japan as a "price taker" in the international economy. Katzenstein (1985, p. 23) argues that large countries, given their political advantages, are most likely to be able to export the costs of adjustment. Paradoxically, very small countries may also be able to do this in so far as their actions are unimportant to, and therefore unnoticed by, their trading partners (Yoffie 1983).

[37] According to Lake's analysis Japan in 1950 was a "protectionist free rider," given its small share of world trade and its low relative productivity. By 1977, Lake labels Japan as a "spoiler" economy—a middle-sized economy with low relative productivity (1983, pp. 538–542, and 1984, pp. 150–152). Lake argues that Japan is likely to have become a "supporter" by the late 1980s (1983, p. 540). It is interesting that Lake now describes Japan as an "opportunist" rather than a "supporter"; I agree with him that this is a more appropriate term, since a nation in this category will favor open markets at home only so far as failing to do so runs the risk of losing access to markets abroad. Lake's framework is emulated by Inoguchi (1986).

and Jennifer Taw argue that Japan's rise to the position of "incipient hegemon" implies that its interests will be better served by cooperative rather than predatory behavior.[38] These structural analyses give a clear sense that Japan's stakes in the system have grown enormously, and that it stands to lose the most if existing economic arrangements were to fall apart. Japan's growing stakes in the international economy are also visible on the sectoral level. Of particular importance is the growing number of internationally competitive industries that have developed strong preferences in maintaining access to international markets for trade and investment and in avoiding retaliation and closure abroad. The high costs these industries would face if Japan's trading partners were to close their markets make them highly sensitive to foreign pressures and threats of retaliation.

Increasingly, then, Japanese policy makers have had to factor in the probable reactions of foreign trading partners in their deliberations over how to deal with distressed industries. What were previously considered purely domestic policy decisions now carry growing international ramifications. Japan's trading partners have grown increasingly aware of, and more critical of, Japanese policies that shift the burdens of adjustment to foreign producers. In particular, since the late 1980s Japan's trading partners have applied pressures on it to strengthen its domestic antitrust enforcement efforts and to dismantle the protectionist aspects of the government's administrative guidance, the recession cartels, and troubled industry legislation.

International factors also make the use of import barriers politically unfeasible. As the world's attention has increasingly focused on opening the Japanese market, efforts by Japan to erect new import barriers to protect its distressed industries are not likely to be politically acceptable to its trading partners.[39] Efforts by distressed industries to receive overt protection against imports tend to arouse the opposition of Japan's many export-oriented industries. Normally, these internationalized firms are disinterested in policy towards troubled industries; but when their access to foreign markets is threatened, these industries may become mobilized. Thus, troubled industries seeking import protection must overcome the opposition of Japanese export interests and convince policy makers to defy considerable international criticism and possibly retaliation. Changes in Japan's position in the international economy have thus been translated, through do-

---

[38] Rosecrance and Taw 1990, pp. 193–200.

[39] Japan is not likely to receive what John Ruggie calls the "intersubjective understanding" of its partners in terms of the "embedded liberalism" compromise—that is, the notion that states can deviate from liberal trade when domestic industries are damaged by international trade (Ruggie 1983). There is a double standard at work here: what is considered legitimate by and for some countries is not considered legitimate in the case of others.

mestic politics, into strong constraints on the overt protection of troubled industries.[40]

I have argued thus far that understanding the preferences of industry actors is the first step in explaining Japan's policy towards its troubled industries. In Chapter 2 I contended that any approach that focuses on actor preferences must first establish a priori expectations of those preferences. I therefore set forth some core hypotheses linking an industry's structure to the general economic and political preferences of firms and labor within an industry. Actor preferences are rarely translated directly into policy choices, however, as I discussed in this chapter. As industry actors work through the industrial policy-making environment, these preferences may be deflected or modified (though rarely rejected, at least in Japan). The policy environment consists of the bureaucrats, the politicians, domestic antitrust laws, and Japan's position internationally.

In the second part of the book I present the findings of my empirical research on industrial adjustment in Japan. Each of the chapters covers one of the four industry types discussed in Chapter 2. In each chapter I present a detailed case study of the adjustment experience of a representative industry and then bolster my findings by using secondary sources to discuss an additional example for each industry type. Table 3-1 lists representative cases of distressed industries in each of these four types.[41] In choosing which industries to study I was often constrained because the list of troubled industries in Japan for some industry types is still quite short. For my main cases I tried to choose industries not covered in the existing literature. For the additional cases I relied exclusively on case studies already done by others.[42] The cases are arranged in roughly chronological

[40] These external constraints, however, have not prevented Japan from attempting to erect less formal barriers to imports. For instance, some Japanese industries have sought tacit industry-to-industry "understandings" about the need to maintain "market order" with its more dependent trading partners in Asia. The cotton spinning industry was a key beneficiary of such agreements (discussed in Chapter 4). Some industries have also tried to pressure importers and buyers to refrain from dealing with foreign suppliers, at times with government support. I present anecdotal evidence on these efforts in my case studies, but I am not primarily interested in assessing the trade implications of Japan's policies for its troubled industries.

It should be noted that not all distressed industries in Japan have faced import competition, while others have remained net exporters even while undergoing distress at home. In addition, some of Japan's troubled industries have been dependent on an open international environment for exports, imports, and investment ties. As Helen Milner (1988) points out, these stakes in the international economy will dilute their interest in seeking protectionist solutions.

[41] Employment figures are for direct employment only. The statistics for concentration and the size of the labor force reflect each industry's situation at the beginning of its competitive decline. The H-index, or Herfindahl index, is a measure of industry concentration; an industry with an H-index score of over 1,000 is considered to be concentrated.

[42] Relying on existing case studies may introduce a potential selection bias, as the authors might have selected these cases precisely because they were the most politicized and controversial.

Table 3-1. Representative troubled industries in Japan

| Type I (Concentrated, small labor force) | | | | Type II (Concentrated, large labor force) | | | |
Industry	Herfindahl index	Labor force	Peak year	Industry	Herfindahl index	Labor force	Peak year
Aluminum	2,547	13,935	1970	Integrated steel	1,631	212,143	1975
Petrochemicals	1,330	8,952	1970				
Synthetic fibers	1,096	53,871	1971	Shipbuilding	1,041	314,132	1975

| Type III (Fragmented, small labor force) | | | | Type IV (Fragmented, large labor force) | | | |
Industry	Herfindahl index	Labor force	Peak year	Industry	Herfindahl index	Labor force	Peak year
Cement	835	21,799	1964	Coal mining	525	397,737	1951
Rayon	781	62,352	1956	Silk reeling	324	106,197	1951
Paper	708	81,579	1953	Cotton spinning	286	145,162	1960
Petroleum refining	585	35,423	1978	Cotton weaving	68	208,658	1960
Sugar refining	579	10,752	1966				
Paper pulp	576	9,433	1959				
Bicycles	437	37,925	1954				
Electric furnace steel	294	72,609	1964				
Plywood	124	81,013	1970				

SOURCES: *Kōgyō Tōkei* (Tsūshō Sangyōsho); Japan Fair Trade Commission 1976, 1987; *Historical Statistics of Japan*, 1986.

order, allowing me to trace relevant changes in the policy-making environment over time. I begin with the fragmented Type IV industries (cotton spinning and coal mining), the first industries to experience industrial distress. I next analyze Type III industries (electric furnace steel and paper) which differ from Type IV industries only in having a much smaller labor force. I then analyze concentrated industries: Type I industries, which have small labor forces (synthetic fibers and aluminum smelting), and Type II industries, which have large labor forces (shipbuilding and integrated steel).

In each chapter I utilize the method of process tracing, or what Margaret McKean refers to as "political archaeology," to analyze the process through which industry actors have attempted to influence policy making.[43] While the method of process tracing is labor-intensive and time consuming, it is also necessary. Too often in the field of Japanese political economy, proponents of opposing views "argue by assumption"—that is,

[43] McKean 1993, p. 75. See also Snyder 1984, pp. 92–93.

they make strong causal assumptions and then look only at policy outcomes (and, far too often, only at those outcomes that conform to their assumptions). In this way, proponents of the different approaches often point to the same evidence but interpret that evidence in diametrically opposite ways.[44] Process tracing at least forces us to more explicitly demonstrate that our assumptions and hypotheses are plausible and that our independent variables operate in practice the way they do in theory. In short, the method of process tracing forces us to show the plausibility of each link in the causal chain and thus to make clear the relationship between hypothesized causes and observed outcomes.

In each case study I focus on the following issues:

—To what extent is the industry's structure correlated with the economic responses and political preferences of industry actors? Has the behavior of industry actors been consistent with the hypothesized preferences?

—Through what mechanisms have industry actors organized themselves? In as much as there are conflicting positions within each industry, how have the opponents tried to negotiate common, industry-wide policy positions? Through what mechanisms have the various groups tried to influence the policy-making process?

—To what extent and through which mechanisms have industry actors been able to translate their preferences into final policy choices? Which groups have acted, and which have been merely "responsive"? What role have the party politicians played, directly or indirectly, in the policy process?

—What have been the interests of bureaucrats, and what policy roles have they played? In what ways have MITI bureaucrats behaved consistently with the expectations of the bureaucratic dominance approach? Conversely, has the policy process been politicized, with bureaucrats willing to forgo developmental goals in favor of the interests of industry?

—How have changes in the domestic antitrust environment constrained the use of certain policy tools? Similarly, how have changes in Japan's position in the international economy led to growing constraints on policy choices?

[44] To take one stark example, the fact that most successful Diet bills are drafted by the bureaucracy is treated by some researchers as evidence of the bureaucrat's lock on policy expertise; in contrast, others argue that because bureaucrats anticipate the reactions of the politicians, the bills that are presented are exactly what the politicians desire. At least one of these assertions has to be wrong—but without going beyond initial assumptions there is no way to determine which one.

PART II

CONFRONTING
ECONOMIC CHANGE

CHAPTER FOUR

Politicized Industries: Cotton
Spinning and Coal Mining (Type IV)

In this chapter I discuss the adjustment experience of industries that are composed of numerous small firms that have a large labor force. In terms of the initial hypotheses set out in Chapter 2, economic adjustment strategies will be relatively costly for both firms and labor. The small size of the average firm means that firms will lack the financial and technological resources needed to diversify or adjust economically in other ways. For labor, adjustment costs are likely to be the highest in this type of industry, because of the large number of workers and because small firms will be unable to shift workers internally or to related firms. As a result, firms and labor will face a stark choice: either exit, via bankruptcy or unemployment, or voice their interests through politics. With such a choice, they will tend to pursue political solutions to alleviate the costs of adjustment. To test this hypothesis, I present a detailed case study of the cotton spinning industry, covering the period from 1950 to 1975, relying mostly on secondary sources for the period after 1975. Afterward, I present a brief study of the coal mining industry, based on secondary works.

The process of adjustment in the cotton spinning industry began in the immediate postwar period. Cotton spinning in 1952 was a representative Type IV industry: it was composed of 112 firms, most of which were small, and had a labor force of over 111,000 workers. The cotton spinning process is a relatively simple one: raw cotton is treated and processed and then spun into cotton yarn. The industry's main equipment, the cotton spindle, is relatively cheap to build and operate and relies on technology that by the 1950s was already considered to be standardized. Economies of scale in this industry are thus low, and so even very small firms can operate efficiently. These characteristics mean that barriers to entry (as well as exit) are low.

The textile industry as a whole is divided into the upstream stage of yarn production, the midstream stage of weaving and knitting, and the downstream stage of apparel-making and distribution. The cotton spinners occupy one part of the upstream yarn stage, along with two other natural fiber industries (wool spinning and silk reeling) and the man-made fiber producers. Unless otherwise indicated, my analysis is limited to the cotton spinning sector.[1]

FROM RECOVERY TO STRUCTURAL RECESSION, 1945–1955

The year 1952 marked the beginning of four-decades of continuous public policy support for the cotton spinning industry. Early in that year MITI "recommended" that all firms temporarily cut production by 40 percent. This was the first time that MITI used a policy instrument that later came to be used in virtually every declining industry—recommendations to curtail operations, or *kankoku sōtan* (*kankoku sōgyō tanshuku*). This episode has been described as MITI's "first totally independent action as a new ministry"—that is, this was the first time that MITI acted independently of the Occupation authorities.[2] But although MITI may have been acting independently of Occupation officials, its decision was by no means made independently of the preferences of the industry involved. Industrial politics was a central part of the policy process from early on.

The industry's first postwar recession period, in 1952, revealed deep-rooted structural problems of excess capacity. Excess capacity had its origins in the SCAP decision to promote the recovery of a more "democratic" cotton spinning industry. SCAP was determined to bring more openness and competition to an industry that during the war had been consolidated around only ten firms (the "Big 10"), and the cotton textile industry was thus one of the first designated for industrial deconcentration. Eventually, SCAP forced nine of the ten firms to dispose of their non-textile operations, although it eventually decided to forgo further steps to break the firms up. In addition, SCAP announced in May 1946 that new cotton spinning firms would be free to enter the industry. In February MITI recognized 25 firms (all of which had existed before the war) as new entrants

[1] The cotton spinning industry is only one part of a much larger industrial sector. In the Japan Standard Industrial Classification (JSIC) system the two-digit code for the textile industry is 20; the yarn spinning stage is represented at the three-digit level by 202; and cotton spinning is a four-digit industry, 2021.

[2] Johnson 1982, p. 224.

into the industry.[3] And two days after the outbreak of the Korean War, on June 27, 1950, SCAP removed all remaining restrictions on cotton spinning facilities.

As Table 4-1 shows, the new entrants initially made little headway in breaking up the dominance of the Big 10. But the situation changed with the outbreak of the Korean War, as the U.S. Army's special procurements (*tokuju*) boosted textile demand and caused cotton yarn prices to explode. Almost overnight, over 100 small-scale spinning firms entered the industry and quickly embarked on an aggressive campaign of capacity expansion. Between 1950 and 1952, these new firms increased their capacity more than fourfold. This spate of new entry established a dual structure in the industry, with the Big 10 coexisting with numerous small firms. Because of this dramatic rise in the number of smaller firms, the market share of the Big 10 fell sharply, from 96.2 percent in 1948, to 64.4 percent in 1952, and then to 54.6 percent by 1958. Almost overnight the industry had become highly fragmented.

The Dynamics of Cartel Behavior:
The Industry Seeks Administrative Guidance

The period of expansion was short-lived. The major source of demand, U.S. Army procurements, began to dry up in 1951, with the beginning of armistice negotiations in Korea. Also, the industry could no longer rely on Japan's prewar colonies as a stable source of demand; industry officials openly bemoaned the loss of Japan's colonial markets in Manchuria, Korea, and China.[4] In spite of depressed demand, however, the output of cotton yarn continued to increase. Inventories of excess production accumulated, and prices for cotton yarn fell dramatically during 1951 and early 1952.

The large cotton spinners reacted to this economic downturn by attempting to coordinate industry-wide cutbacks in production. The goal of this implicit cartel arrangement was to balance supply and demand, stabilize prices, and thus stabilize profits. Industry leaders reasoned that because they could not raise demand in the short term, their only hope was to manage the supply side. Although the market mechanism would eventually reduce supply as less competitive firms reduced production, this process could take a considerable amount of time; meanwhile, prices and profits would remain depressed. More desirable from the industry's point

---

[3] Significantly, SCAP also forced the cotton spinners to concentrate only on natural textiles, rather than the newer and more promising chemical fibers. According to SCAP's plan, the 25 new entrants were to account for only 334,000 of the industry's initial target of 4 million spindles (Tanaka 1965, p. 99; Seiji Keizai Kenkyūjo 1958, p. 232; Fujii 1971, p. 76; Lynch 1968, pp. 54–58).

[4] See, for instance, Seki 1956.

Table 4-1. Japan's cotton spinning industry, 1945–1964

Year	Number of firms		Number of spindles (thousands)			Employment		
	Big Ten	Other firms	Total spindles	Big Ten (percent of total)	Other firms (percent of total)	Total	Male	Female
1946	10	0	2,307	2,307 (100.0)	0 (0)	NA	NA	NA
1948	10	9	3,155	3,035 (96.2)	120 (3.8)	NA	NA	NA
1950	10	41	3,942	3,363 (85.3)	579 (14.7)	NA	NA	NA
1952	10	112	6,873	4,426 (64.4)	2,447 (35.6)	111,245	17,243	94,002
1954	10	120	7,830	4,800 (61.3)	3,030 (38.7)	101,140	16,081	85,059
1956	10	119	8,551	5,002 (58.5)	3,549 (41.5)	95,473	15,085	80,388
1958	10	135	9,019	4,924 (54.6)	4,095 (45.4)	87,041	14,014	73,027
1960	10	131	7,753	4,225 (54.5)	3,528 (45.5)	91,976	12,877	79,099
1962	10	127	7,955	4,431 (55.7)	3,524 (44.3)	80,978	11,580	69,398
1964	9	124	7,764	4,216 (54.3)	3,548 (45.7)	76,610	10,649	65,961

SOURCES: Seki 1956, p. 312; Seiji Keizai Kenkyūjo 1958, p. 195; Fujii 1971, p. 89; Nihon Bōseki Kyōkai 1982, p. 51; Iwata 1984, p. 96; Iwata 1984, p. 51; Bōsei Jijō Sankōsho, 1986, pp. 33–34.

of view was an implicit cartel to reduce overall output, since sufficient cutbacks would provide the collective benefit of stabilized prices.

Internal industry discussions on the need to cut production began as early as September 1951. On January 10, 1952, the industry association, the Japan Spinners Association (JSA, the Nihon Bōseki Kyōkai), held its first formal subcommittee meeting to discuss the production curtailment issue. The association estimated that excess capacity was more than 50 percent of existing spindles, so some immediate action was essential. It was decided that the major firms would begin autonomously to curtail their production levels. The original curtailments were carried out by only 13 of the industry's total of 122 firms—the Big 10 plus three of the larger new entrants (Minseibo, Kowabo, and Teikoku Sangyo)—which accounted for 77 percent of total industry capacity.

How to enforce compliance with the agreement was a difficult problem. Without effective enforcement mechanisms, cartels face the classic problem of collective action: all firms stand to benefit from cooperation, but each benefits even more if it can exploit the cooperative behavior of others. That is, each firm has an incentive to expand production while others cut back; the maverick firm would enjoy the collective good of stabilized prices and profits and would also enjoy a larger market share. The dilemma for cartels is that all firms have similar incentives to cheat, and if enough firms pursue these incentives, the cartel will collapse. The large number of firms in the cotton spinning industry complicated the task of negotiating and enforcing a cartel. With large numbers, the transaction costs of reaching consensus are higher, and monitoring and enforcing the agreement becomes more difficult. As a result, cheating is more likely to go undetected, thus undermining the confidence of would-be cooperators that their cooperation will be reciprocated. In the absence of adequate mechanisms for communication and enforcement, collective action is likely to end in failure.[5]

In 1952 the industry faced an even more difficult enforcement problem: how to elicit cooperation from the nearly 100 firms that were not party to the agreement. Soon after beginning the cutback, the larger firms complained that the small firms were producing more than necessary, making the curtailment meaningless.[6] Something would have to be done to ensure that

[5] Scherer 1980, pp. 212–220, contains an excellent discussion of cartel behavior in cases of both cyclical downturns and long-term decline. Itoh et al. (1988, pp. 251–253) presents a formal analysis of the Prisoner's Dilemma for the scrapping of capacity. The dynamics for the limitation of production levels is similar. It should be noted that cooperation to achieve a collective good may not be a positive thing for the society as a whole—rather, in the case of cartel behavior, firms attempt to pursue anticompetitive strategies that pass costs on to others, including taxpayers, consumers, and foreign trading partners.

[6] Industry discussions are described in *Yomiuri Shimbun*, Sept. 8, 1951, *Asahi Shimbun*, Nov. 16, 1951, *Nihon Keizai Shimbun*, Jan. 12, 1952, and *Tōyō Keizai*, Feb. 9, 1952. The critical JSA meeting is referred to in *Tōyōbō Kenkyūjo Geppō*, no. 26 (Feb. 1952), p. 2. Fujii (1971, pp. 100–101) describes the industry's initial curtailment efforts.

these smaller firms did not simply increase their output to offset the cutbacks taken by the 13 larger firms. If the cartel members could not persuade the small firms to cooperate, the goal of stabilizing prices would be unattainable.

The major cotton spinners in 1952 found that they had no private mechanisms to enforce the cartel agreement. This situation was quite different from the industry's situation before the war: then, the industry had enjoyed very strong private enforcement mechanisms and was in fact famous for its long tradition of resorting to cartels to regulate production levels. The JSA, known before the war as the Nihon Bōseki Rengōkai, describes its own history as "the history of cooperative curtailments of production." The Rengōkai initiated its first production curtailment in 1891, just ten years after it was established. Thereafter, it was quick to resort to restraints on output whenever the industry encountered a downward swing in the business cycle: curtailments were in force for 20 of the 47 years between 1891 and 1938. These prewar production cutbacks were private agreements, initiated and enforced by the Rengōkai. The industry association was able to ensure compliance by all firms because it controlled overlapping cartel mechanisms: all spinning firms had to buy their raw cotton supply from the Japan Cotton Association and had to market their products through the Japan Cotton Textile Trade Association. Because the Rengōkai could deny access to these cartel arrangements, the spinning firms were under powerful constraints to adhere to industry agreements.[7]

By the time the newly reconstituted industry association, the JSA, initiated the first postwar *sōtan* (production curtailment) in 1952, however, the industry found itself facing an entirely different legal environment. Specifically, SCAP's creation of the FTC and imposition of antitrust legislation had rendered prewar practices impossible. The enactment of the Anti-Monopoly Law in April 1947 made cartels and cartel-like agreements clearly illegal restraints on trade, making the industry's prewar cartel system explicitly illegal.[8] A second difference in the postwar environment was

[7] These early curtailments were implemented without governmental authorization or enforcement. The JSA reports that each curtailment agreement required months of arguments and negotiations between firms; in a number of instances many firms did not participate. The government's role in these early curtailments was indirect. During the first cutback in 1891, the industry gave written agreements to the mayor of Osaka, who then notified other prefectural mayors. As the association wryly notes in its official history, this was "a different world compared to trying to receive the approval of the FTC today" (Nihon Bōseki Kyōkai 1982, pp. 18–19). Prewar cartel efforts are also discussed in Seki 1956, Iijima 1949, and Lynch 1968, pp. 41–54.

[8] For good descriptions of the original Anti-Monopoly Law, see Yamamura (1967, Chapter 1) and Misono (1987, pp. 58–65). The Anti-Monopoly Law was first amended in 1949. Article 3 outlawed cartels, while Article 4 made industry agreements illegal that set prices, production levels, and capacity (Misono 1987, p. 59). In addition, SCAP heavily restricted the activities of trade associations through the Trade Association Law of July 1948. Efforts by the Japanese leadership to relax antitrust restrictions and to exempt the recession cartels from antitrust considerations had been underway since June 1951, but the cotton spinners could not wait for these efforts to bear fruit. See Yamamura 1967, pp. 39–41.

that the large number of new cotton spinning firms made the enforcement of collective agreements more difficult. The industry now no longer had the ability, legal or otherwise, to compel all firms to cooperate.

However, the industry did have recourse to a different mechanism that would avoid antitrust complications but still ensure compliance: MITI's informal administrative guidance. If the industry could no longer rely on its own enforcement powers, it would instead enlist the enforcement powers of the government. In fact, industry leaders felt that given MITI's control over foreign exchange allotments, such "administrative measures" (*gyōsei sochi*) would be an even more powerful enforcement mechanism than the prewar cartel arrangements.[9]

MITI's initial reaction to the approach taken by the cotton spinning industry was divided. On the one hand, the industry still occupied an important place in the national economy. The textile industry was one of the few industries then able to compete in the export market and accounted for 36 percent of Japan's total exports in 1953. It thus was recognized as an important source of foreign exchange. In 1951 the country's two largest firms, Kanebo and Toyobo, and nine of the largest 20 firms, were cotton spinners.

On the other hand, MITI was reluctant to provide support for the industry. First, cotton spinning was not considered to be a strategic industry. Second, MITI had already begun to recognize the limited growth potential of natural textiles and instead was shifting its attention to a sector competing with the cotton spinners, chemical fibers.[10] This sector was seen as more promising in terms of profitability and export competitiveness. As MITI was already beginning to support the development of chemical fibers, it was reluctant to prop up a nonstrategic competitor such as cotton textiles. Third, MITI was concerned about the FTC's legal objections to collusive trade practices. In September 1951 the FTC had made it clear that collusion to restrict production would violate Articles 3 and 4 of the new Anti-Monopoly and Trade Association Laws.

However, the cotton spinning firms were highly organized and spoke with a loud voice. The industry association, the JSA, magnified the industry's political influence. The JSA's most important mechanism to coordinate industry pressure was its "Tuesday Club," a forum established in 1951

---

[9] Seiji Keizai Kenkyūjo 1958, p. 240. MITI's authority to engage in administrative guidance is based on the vaguely worded MITI Establishment Act, so its specific legal powers have been ambiguous (Misonō 1987, p. 60). It does not have formal authority to enforce compliance, so it must rely on voluntary cooperation. Johnson (1982) views administrative guidance as one of MITI's most powerful policy tools, while others, such as Haley (1987), stress the voluntary nature of compliance. The FTC challenged this policy tool on antitrust grounds as early as 1950 but was unable to deter its use until the 1970s (Iyori 1986, p. 69).

[10] Tsūshō Sangyōshō 1972, pp. 312–340.

to bring representatives of the Big 10 firms together for talks on how to respond to the recession.[11]

The cartel members, through the association, applied strong pressures on MITI to convince it to help enforce the cartel. Open industry pressure on MITI to take regulatory action began in November of 1951, at the time the industry began to discuss production curtailments. Industry insiders argued that if their "autonomous" efforts to control production were not effective, then they would need some administrative measures.[12] A series of bankruptcies among the medium-sized textile trading companies in January 1952 raised a sense of crisis in the industry. Industry officials warned that some drastic measure was now clearly needed. On January 18, 1952, one week after the large firms began to cut production, the leaders of the JSA and other textile organizations met directly with MITI and Liberal Party representatives to voice their concerns. The industry drew up a proposal for the necessary production cutbacks and presented it as a petition to the Textile Bureau of MITI. In this proposal the industry asked MITI to instruct all firms to honor the production cutbacks.[13]

Persistence on the part of the major firms eventually overcame MITI's reluctance to intervene. By mid-February MITI had become persuaded to use its administrative guidance powers to recommend that all firms cut output. Overcoming the objections of the FTC was not difficult. First, the FTC was in a weak political position vis-à-vis MITI, as it had lost the support of its principle backer and source of power—the SCAP authorities. Second, MITI influence over the FTC was considerable because it was staffed by ex-MITI officials, including many in top positions. In addition, MITI held a veiled political threat over the FTC's head: it argued that if the FTC were to declare *kankoku sōtan* illegal, or otherwise delay the action, then prices would collapse and the industry would be in great trouble. The FTC would then be responsible for whatever political fallout ensued.[14]

MITI announced its *kankoku sōtan* recommendation on February 25, 1952, calling on all firms in the industry to cut output by 40 percent as of March 1. This was an across-the-board cut, applying to all 122 firms in the industry, with production cutbacks calculated according to each firms' ex-

---

[11] Nihon Bōseki Kyōkai 1982, pp. 88–91. Members usually included the presidents of firms and/or their managing directors. As far as I can tell, such direct contacts were never challenged by the FTC.

[12] *Asahi Shimbun*, Nov. 22, 1951; *Nihon Keizai Shimbun*, Jan. 12, 1952.

[13] Misono 1987, p. 62.

[14] Misono 1987, pp. 62–63. Misono refers to this political threat as MITI's "trump card." Indeed, around this time the FTC did challenge the legality of similar MITI recommendations to the rubber industry and the chemical fiber sector. The main reason the FTC did not challenge the cotton spinning curtailment, according to Misono, was the "political considerations involved in the case" (1987, p. 65).

isting capacity and recent production record.[15] Although firms were not legally required to comply with these recommendations, MITI issued an explicit administrative threat: any firm not cooperating with the cutback would be considered delinquent (*furyō*) and would suffer a reduction in foreign exchange. Particularly for the smaller firms, access to raw cotton imports was a matter of life and death. Clearly, noncompliance with MITI's policy recommendation was not an option for most firms.

The industry's labor force was not involved in the *kankoku sōtan* decision and was only able to protest after the fact. Zensen Dōmei (the Japan Federation of Textile Industry Workers Unions) argued that the prewar curtailments had led to enormous sacrifices by the labor force; it was now displeased that the government was stepping in to support the *sōtan* efforts of the large firms. The union could do little more than protest, however. As a result of meetings between the JSA leadership and Zensen on February 29, labor agreed to accept the *sōtan* as necessary and inevitable. It did succeed, however, in reaching an agreement with the major firms to pledge not to fire workers as a result of the curtailments and to guarantee that wages would not fall below a certain level.

MITI's decision to use its administrative guidance powers in this earliest postwar episode of industrial regulation was clearly in response to initiatives taken by the main firms in the industry: the major spinners had been attempting on their own to stabilize the market through curtailments and applied direct pressure on MITI to intervene to help them.[16] These pressures eventually compelled MITI to overcome its initial reluctance to use its *kankoku sōtan* enforcement powers. MITI's "first independent action" as a new ministry, then, was not at all independent of industry preferences. Even in the early postwar period, with MITI's relative power at its peak, industry preferences played a key role in the policy process.

ORIGINS OF THE 1956 TEXTILE BILL

The immediate result of this informal cartel was a slight rebound in prices, but prices dropped again toward the end of the year, prompting an extension of *kankoku sōtan* recommendations. By the time administrative guidance ended in June 1953, prices were more than 50 percent higher than when regulation had begun. The industry's recovery was a short-lived

[15] Tsūshō Sangyōshō 1972, p. 784. *Zensen* later reported that the smaller firms were tacitly allowed slightly higher operating rates, as a means to insure their compliance (Zensen Dōmei 1966, p. 189).

[16] An unpublished MITI document entitled "Sen'i sangyō no sangyō chōsei seisaku" makes a similar argument (Tsūshō Sangyōshō 1988). Most foreign analysts, however, argue that MITI acted autonomously (Hadley 1970; Johnson 1982).

53

one, however, as it ran into another significant recession in 1953–1954. The cotton spinning industry by the mid-1950s had clearly become mature and increasingly troubled.

The JSA leadership was well aware of the signs of future decline. By 1954 industry leaders had come to recognize a number of trends, both domestic and international, that were moving against it. First, domestic demand for textiles was not predicted to increase significantly in the future. Second, the government's deflationary policies beginning in late 1953 led to a domestic recession that hit the textile sector particularly hard. Third, export markets were also seen as increasingly problematic, because many of Japan's former markets in Asia were developing their own indigenous industries, and because pressures to restrain textile exports were building in Europe and the United States. Fourth, the natural textile sector was now facing a major domestic challenger for the dwindling textile demand: the man-made fibers, which were then enjoying a world-wide boom and were predicted to dominate the future textile industry. In fact, a handful of the larger firms in the cotton spinning industry were already taking steps to diversify into this new field.

The 1954 recession saw a drastic fall in prices, with cotton yarn prices falling more than 30 percent in the space of nine months and reaching a trough in June 1954. More alarming, excess inventories nearly doubled between late 1953 and mid-1955. One sign of impending crisis was the high number of bankruptcies among textile trading firms: in 1954 some 645 textile trading firms went bankrupt. That year the cotton spinners recorded their lowest profits since the war.

The industry initially dealt with these downward pressures on prices with the same method used three years earlier: coordinated production curtailments. There were two differences this time around. First, the industry was no longer divided internally. Now, all firms recognized the benefits of a production cartel. Second, MITI was less worried about antitrust restrictions. Immediately after the end of the occupation, industry leaders, conservative politicians, and MITI bureaucrats had set out to loosen SCAP's Anti-Monopoly Law. These efforts succeeded with the 1953 revision of the law, which among other things specifically authorized antitrust exemptions for recession and rationalization cartels when both MITI and the FTC deemed them necessary.[17] After the industry's committee on production curtailments estimated that the industry needed to reduce overall production by 12 percent, the industry did not hesitate in appealing to

---

[17] Yamamura 1967 provides an excellent review of early antitrust policy. The 1953 revision was a major retreat from the occupation's antitrust program. In addition to the creation of the recession cartels, SCAP's Trade Association Law was abolished (Johnson 1982, p. 222). According to Misonō (1987, pp. 60, 66), MITI's use of *kankoku sōtan* for the cotton spinning industry in 1952 was the first salvo fired in the fight to revise the Anti-Monopoly Law.

MITI. According to MITI's official history, "the cotton spinning industry now called loudly on the ministry to reinstate *kankoku sōtan*."[18] MITI agreed to issue new *sōtan* recommendations at the end of April 1955.

The Dynamics of Capacity Regulation

By 1955 it was becoming clear to the JSA membership that the industry's problems were too deep to be solved by temporary production curtailments. Industry leaders recognized that the fundamental problem was chronic excess capacity. It was less clear how to deal with this problem, however, and the topic was discussed at length within the industry. Out of these talks the JSA adopted the position that it needed concrete measures to somehow control the unregulated expansion of capacity. As early as the end of 1951, the industry leadership had called for the government to intervene to help restrict such expansion.[19] The association now pursued a long-term political solution: it sought the creation of explicit legislation to help curb excessive capacity growth. The resulting law, known as the Textile Law of 1956, was one of Japan's first legislative actions designed specifically for a troubled industry.

The outline of this bill was based directly on proposals presented by the JSA leadership. In early August 1955, JSA chairman Hara Yoshihira presented a private memorandum to the government summarizing the industry's position.[20] Hara argued that the fundamental cause of the industry's excess capacity arose out of unplanned and unregulated investments by the new entrants after the Korean War. He noted that in the five years following the lifting of capacity restrictions in June 1950, the industry's capacity had more than doubled to 8.1 million spindles. But while capacity in the Big 10 increased only slightly, that in the smaller firms increased nearly ten-fold. The fragmented nature of the industry, Hara contended, exacerbated its tendency toward chronic excess capacity, or what in Japan is known as "excessive competition" (*katō kyōsō*).[21]

It must be stressed that "excessive competition" is not a uniquely Japanese concept. Michael Porter, for instance, discusses at length the special problems a fragmented industry faces. According to Porter, such an in-

---

[18] Tsūshō Sangyōshō 1972, pp. 348–349.

[19] *Asahi Shimbun*, Nov. 16, 1951. The association argued that if prices and profits were to be stabilized over the long haul, the expansion of production and capacity had to be somehow slowed.

[20] Hara was the president of Japan's largest cotton spinning firm, Nihon Bōseki. See MITI's official history of its textile industry policy for the full text of this Hara memorandum, which was entitled "Memorandum on dealing with the cotton spinning industry's excess capacity" (Tsūshō Sangyōshō 1972, pp. 356–357).

[21] Komiya 1988; Itoh et al. 1988; Yamamura 1982; Okimoto 1989. To an economist, of course, "excessive competition" is an oxymoron; from the point of view of firms, however, *any* competition is likely to be seen as "excessive."

dustry is doomed to excess capacity, overproduction, and cutthroat competition—in many ways, it faces the worst of all competitive situations. Given its bleak prospect for future profits, Porter's advice for firms in such an industry is to head for the exits as fast as possible. But exit to where? Firms in the cotton spinning industry perceived a huge gap between the costs and benefits of exit. First, the industry was not able to easily convert its physical capital to other uses. Second, exit was limited by emotional barriers, such as the lack of mobility of owners or their personal attachment to the industry. Third, firms found exit costly because they lacked access to financial and other resources needed to successfully convert to new lines of work. As a result, firms saw few attainable adjustment alternatives; exit was not as simple or as easy as an economist would predict.

Many firms thus found no alternatives to remaining in the industry and doing whatever was necessary to survive. In economic terms, these firms chose to "fight" rather than "flee." This was especially true for the smallest firms. Because they had nowhere to go, they demonstrated considerable staying power even in the face of serious recessions. Porter points out that the least desirable situation is where weak firms have a strong commitment to remain in the business: "Their weaknesses force them to attempt to improve their position by desperate actions, like price cuts, that threaten the entire industry. Their staying power forces other firms to respond." This is obviously undesirable from the industry's standpoint, since "a war of attrition is costly to the victor and vanquished alike, and is best avoided."[22] This description fits the cotton spinning industry in Japan to a tee. Hara described the perennial problem clearly: "during downturns, the financially weak small firms continue to produce and then dump their excess production at very low prices, since they need to maintain current income. This leads to an even deeper recession, and makes achieving a balance between supply and demand even more difficult."[23]

In theory, the market mechanism should take care of the problems of excess competition and capacity, but the industry feared that the market mechanism would lead to perverse incentives. Although from a collective standpoint it made sense for the industry to cut capacity, each firm had strong incentives to cheat by expanding capacity. This was especially true for the weaker, less competitive firms. Porter's analysis cited above focuses on what firms can do to stabilize competition through their individual market behavior; significantly, however, he notes that such a strategy "may well involve treating government as an actor to be influ-

---

[22] Porter 1980, pp. 92, 266–267.

[23] From the transcript of Hara's Diet testimony of November 9, 1962, in *Nihon Bōseki Geppō*, no. 191 (Nov. 1962), p. 6; also discussed in *Nihon Bōseki Geppō*, no. 390 (June 1979), pp. 3–4. Hara argued that most new entrants were not efficient in terms of economies of scale and therefore tended to weaken the industry as a whole.

enced."[24] This advice is something that the Japanese cotton spinning industry understood clearly.

The JSA called on government policy makers to help the industry control, and preferably dispose of, its excess capacity. First, the industry wanted some way to slow the entry of new firms, which it saw as the original source of the problem, even though it realized that such curbs would be too late, since (from their viewpoint) the floodgates had already been held open too long. Second, they called for measures to prevent existing firms from increasing capacity in an unregulated, "excessively competitive" fashion. Finally, they proposed that the government should provide direct financial assistance to the industry.

The Policy-Making Environment

MITI bureaucrats remained reluctant to grant the industry new regulations to help it stabilize itself. MITI saw little future promise in this industry and did not want to see a non-strategic industry become a drain on scarce government resources or, worse, to divert resources from higher priority industries. In particular, MITI worried that regulation to stabilize the cotton spinners would slow the expansion of the man-made fiber industries.

In fact, the cotton spinners were already requesting that capacity regulations also be placed on the man-made fibers, since they realized that efforts to control its own capacity expansion would be fruitless if man-made fibers were left unregulated and free to expand. The chemical and synthetic fiber firms naturally resisted these demands. They had their own industry association, the Nihon Kagaku Sen'i Kyōkai (Kasen Kyōkai), which then consisted of the six chemical fiber firms and two synthetic fiber makers. The Kasen Kyōkai claimed that cotton spinning was a doomed sector and that the consolidation and demise of the industry should be left to the market. Resisting capacity regulations on their own products, the Kasen Kyōkai argued that private investment decisions should be determined solely by the market. MITI officials were entirely sympathetic to the arguments made by the Kasen Kyōkai. By 1955 MITI was convinced that if any part of the textile industry deserved support, it was synthetic fibers, which had shown themselves to be superior to natural fibers in every way. If MITI had had its way, it would have given its policy support only to the man-made fibers.

MITI officials had yet another reason to want the cotton spinning industry to shrink or disappear: growing trade friction with the United States. The Japanese government, and MITI in particular, was extremely

---

[24] Porter 1980, p. 29. This is Porter's sole reference to public policy.

sensitive to the trade friction that Japan's natural textile industry as a whole was causing.[25] This growing political outcry for protection stemmed from the lowering of U.S. tariffs against Japanese textiles in the mid-1950s, combined with Japan's private and public efforts to expand exports. The Japanese textile producers and the textile trading companies had made concerted efforts to penetrate the U.S. market to make up for the loss of Asian textile markets; during the first half of the 1950s the value of all finished textiles to the United States increased by a factor of five. The initial outcry from Japan's trading partners came from the cotton producers in the United Kingdom, but it was the reaction of the American textile producers that particularly worried Japan. By 1955 the U.S. industry had begun to petition the Congress to impede the flow of Japanese textiles, an action that culminated in the request by the Eisenhower administration for Japan to voluntarily restrain its exports, particularly of the so-called "dollar blouses." The government of Japan agreed and, in December, made the formal announcement of the first voluntary export restraint, to take effect on the first of January.[26]

Thus by 1955, MITI bureaucrats had many incentives to let the cotton spinning industry adjust to changing economic realities on its own without government regulation. Denying regulation to the cotton spinners would leave man-made fibers free to expand. And a shrinking cotton textile industry would decrease economic friction with Japan's most important trading partners.

Yet MITI also realized that the cotton spinning industry was not likely to accept the costs of adjustment without putting up a major political fight. MITI thus found itself in a dilemma: while its overall conception of industrial policy made it reluctant to stabilize a troubled cotton spinning industry, it was equally reluctant to take strong measures to force the industry to bear the burden of adjustment. This was a dilemma that would continue to plague MITI's policy choices over the subsequent four decades.

[25] An unpublished MITI document on the cotton spinning industry dated October 1, 1955, shows the extent to which MITI was preoccupied with trade friction (Tsūshō Sangyōshō, Sen'i Kyoku 1955). Friction was also due partly to export incentives the government had given to the textile firms (Tsūshō Sangyōshō 1972, p. 352; Seiji Keizai Kenkyūjo 1958, p. 103).

MITI's official history discusses the textile restraints in some detail. See Tsūshō Sangyōshō 1972, pp. 354–355. John Lynch (1968, 59–126) presents a superb analysis of the negotiating positions of all sides. Aggarwal (1985, pp. 44–54), relying on Lynch's analysis, provides a useful summary of the negotiating process.

[26] U.S. calls for protection continued unabated, however, even as the voluntary restrictions went into effect. In March 1956 the South Carolina legislature passed a law restricting cotton imports from Japan, and other states prepared similar bills (Tsūshō Sangyōshō 1972, p. 355). Pressures from the advanced nations to curb Japanese textiles continued into the 1960s, eventually resulting in the negotiation of the Short-Term Arrangement on Cotton Textiles (STA) in July 1961 and the Long-Term Arrangement (LTA) in February 1962 (Aggarwal 1985).

Although the cotton spinners opposed the export restraint agreement, they also realized that they had no choice but to acquiesce. The American market was far too important for Japan's economy, and the political and military backing of the U.S. government was far too important for Japan's national security. The industry realized that no matter how strongly it pressed its objections it would probably not overcome broader and more compelling national interests. It also realized that informal restrictions were preferable to the formal and more restrictive legislation then pending in the U.S. Congress. As one analyst put it, the industry came to the "sensible realization that a small piece of pie is better than no pie at all."[27] However, if the cotton spinners could not resist these external pressures, they could at least obtain adequate compensation at home. The industry protested that its acceptance of export restraints should be offset by increased public policy support and, in particular, regulation of capacity expansion.[28]

The industry used two mechanisms to realize these policy demands: internal organization and political pressure. First, the industry association, the JSA, played a critical role in building consensus, mediating the conflicting interests between the large and small spinners, and enhancing the industry's lobbying power. While the large firms have tended to dominate the association, the JSA has been careful to consider the interests of all spinners when it has formulated its policy positions. Given the large number of firms in the industry, the diversity of their interests, and inevitable conflicts between them, the association was essential in order to gain even a semblance of an industry-wide consensus. Second, the cotton spinning industry also relied on its political connections to press its policy demands. For instance, one of the early politicians with close ties to the industry was Kato Masato, first elected in 1950 to the House of Councillors with the backing of the JSA; over the next decade Kato tirelessly lobbied for the industry's interests. Industry pressures on the conservative politicians were particularly strong in the Diet debates in May and June 1955.[29]

In direct response to these pressures, the cabinet in August created a public-private advisory group for the textile industry, the Sen'i Sangyō Sōgō Taisaku Shingikai.[30] The Shingikai members based their discussions directly on the JSA's proposal and the Hara memorandum; they paid special attention to the industry's desire to control its excess capacity. The ad-

---

[27] Lynch 1968, p. 149.

[28] See, as one example, All Japan Cotton Spinners' Association et al. (1957, pp. 26–27).

[29] Tsūshō Sangyōshō 1972, pp. 357–358. Kato was president of Daiwabo before his election in 1950 and received the unified backing of the JSA. Four months after leaving the Diet in 1963, he was named chairman of the JSA (Nihon Bōseki Kyōkai 1982, p. 87).

[30] *Sen'i Geppō*, 1956, no. 5, p. 7; Tsūshō Sangyōshō 1972, p. 357. This group was under the chairmanship of Inagaki Heitaro, an ex-industrialist and politician who had the distinction of being the first minister of MITI (Johnson 1982, p. 193).

visory group needed only three months before presenting its recommendations to MITI at the end of November.

The final legislation came very close to the industry's original proposals. It instituted a capacity registration system that included both cotton spinning and man-made fibers. The system required firms to register their spindles with MITI and to use these spindles only in approved categories. Firms that wanted to expand their capacity first had to gain the explicit approval of MITI; this requirement would provide at least a degree of restraint on excessive capacity expansion. Finally, the government made a commitment in principle to supporting capacity reduction. The new textile law authorized the government to estimate excess capacity and then to instruct all members of the industry to cooperate in scrapping or mothballing spindles.

Two of the Shingikai's other recommendations were eventually withdrawn after running into opposition from the FTC: a call for automatically exempting production curtailments from antitrust legislation, and a recommendation for "strong enforcement measures" to be written into the bill to compel compliance. The FTC opposed the compulsory nature of these recommendations, arguing that such measures were illegal. Throughout the 1950s the FTC had suffered a series of antitrust defeats, and now it saw the 1956 Textile Bill as yet another dilution of antitrust principles. With FTC influence over MITI at its lowest, it nevertheless had enough legal clout to restrict the more egregious MITI proposals. MITI itself was lukewarm about requiring all firms to participate because it doubted its own ability to force the small firms to reduce capacity. So, MITI added a carrot: governmental financial assistance to entice firms to reduce capacity.[31]

The bill was also modified, albeit cosmetically, because of opposition from the industry's labor unions. Zensen Dōmei was naturally concerned that cutbacks in production or capacity would entail reductions of the labor force. Already, between 1951 and 1955, the labor force had been reduced by more than 30,000 workers, or about one-quarter of the labor force, this despite earlier pledges from management that it would not fire workers due to production curtailments. Labor argued that the industry's claims of excess capacity were self-serving and that workers should not bear the burden of the past mistakes of the firms, so it pressed its case to the MITI Shingikai but made little headway. Incensed by the Shingikai's draft, Zensen turned instead to the politicians. Zensen in 1955 was still affiliated with the Socialist Party (although its supporters would later split to form the Democratic Socialist Party), which had earlier formed its own

[31] Tsūshō Sangyōshō 1972, p. 370. Between 1956 and 1964, the cotton textile industry was provided with subsidies totaling ¥1.58 billion, or U.S. $4.4 million, not an insubstantial figure at the time (Tsūshō Sangyōshō 1988, p. 19).

textile policy committee, the Sen'i Sangyō Tokubetsu Taisaku Iinkai. This group now became the focus of Zensen's efforts to revise the proposed law. Zensen eventually got only cosmetic changes in the draft, however. The final bill, for instance, mentioned only that the government would do its best not to cause unemployment or other labor sacrifices due to production curtailments. These pledges, while ostensibly protecting labor interests, were not binding. The one real gain for Zensen was that MITI agreed to allow labor representatives to be a part of its textile Shingikai. This episode was the first postwar instance in which labor became directly involved in the industrial policy process.[32]

These various objections to the draft legislation eventually forced MITI and the industry to accept a somewhat weaker version. Both the industry and MITI realized that the process of negotiating away these objections would have taken considerable time, and it was becoming clear that knowledge of the impending restrictions on capacity was exacerbating the problem: throughout 1956 firms were breaking ranks in their efforts to increase capacity before the restrictions went into effect. In the nine months from January to October 1956, industry capacity rose by 11 percent. This rush to increase capacity (*kakekomi zōsetsu*) worried both MITI and the industry alike, and so they wanted the legislation to take effect as soon as possible. As a result, they readily agreed to drop the objectionable clauses from the bill.

The 1956 Textile Bill came very close to meeting the demands of the cotton spinning firms. The industry in 1955 already perceived growing economic constraints: stagnating demand, in part secular and in part induced by foreign trade restrictions; the rise of a competitive substitute, man-made fibers; and the "excessively" competitive nature of the industry. Rather than pursuing economic adjustment, the industry sought some policy means to regulate output relative to demand, in this case a cartel-like solution to the problem of excess capacity. This is essentially what the 1956 legislation provided. Although the automatic antitrust exemption was removed from the bill, analysts characterized the legislation as a *sōtan* bill—that is, one that gave the industry a mechanism to manage supply-side conditions in the face of falling demand. In retrospect, MITI itself characterized the bill in similar terms: "The 1956 Law . . . was little more than a short-term measure for the industry to curtail its operations (*sōgyō*

---

[32] Labor's position is discussed in Zensen Dōmei 1966, p. 652. MITI itself takes credit for this decision to include labor in the Shingikai—evidence, perhaps, that MITI was able to determine which groups were given access to policy making (Tsūshō Sangyōshō 1972, p. 359). Zensen tells a different story, however; angered by the resumption of *kankoku sōtan* in 1955, labor leaders protested strongly to MITI, the Ministry of Labor, and the FTC. Zensen reports that MITI Minister Ishibashi, in response to sharp criticisms by a Socialist Party Diet member, meekly apologized and offered that MITI was now considering adding labor representatives to its Shingikai (Zensen Dōmei 1966, p. 516).

tanshuku)."[33] The industry did not receive everything it wanted: it would have preferred explicit restrictions on entry, and wanted stronger enforcement measures. Nonetheless, it is significant that the legislative process reflected the agenda that the industry—not the government—had put on the table, and that the provisions of the final bill matched the main components of the industry's original proposal.

Thus, industry preferences played the fundamental role in determining Japan's policy choices even in the policy environment of the 1950s, an era in which bureaucratic power should have been at its peak. The industry was still dependent on policy makers in a number of respects, particularly because MITI was able to control access to foreign exchange. Constraints on MITI's numerous policy tools, which were to grow in importance in subsequent decades, had not yet appeared. Yet even in this period when "bureaucratic dominance" arguments should be most applicable, policy outcomes fundamentally reflected the preferences of industry actors.

PRESSURES FOR ECONOMIC LIBERALIZATION, 1960–1964

The response of the larger firms to the decade of adverse economic trends was not limited to the political realm. A few firms were able to diversify into man-made fibers. Three firms, Kanebo, Toyobo, and Nittobo, were able to diversify into the principal chemical fiber, rayon, while the industry's two largest firms, Kanebo and Toyobo, also began production of the more promising synthetic fibers. Some of the Big 10 also made efforts to shift their operations overseas—first to Brazil in order to take advantage of cheaper cotton and later to Southeast Asia for cheaper labor. Between 1953 and 1963, cotton spinners entered into 56 overseas investments valued at US$44.5 million.[34] In addition, most of the large firms tried to become integrated vertically by establishing ties to smaller spinners, to the downstream weaving and processing sectors, and to the textile trading companies. The most successful were, again, the three largest ones, though most of the large firms were able to gain a degree of control over final markets by establishing their own weaving sections or by consolidating ties to downstream firms.

It was, nevertheless, only those firms with access to sufficient resources that were able to pursue these economic adjustment measures, which they carried out without any public policy incentives. For the firms that had the resources, these steps made clear economic sense—they allowed them to

[33] Tanaka 1965, p. 118, Fujii (1971, pp. 389–90) refers to the bill as creating a "national cartel," allowing the industry to manipulate production. MITI's current attitude toward the bill appears in Tsūshō Sangyōshō 1988, p. 14.

[34] Fujii 1971, p. 279.

move into higher value-added products and to diversify their market risk by lowering their dependence on a single mature commodity. The rest of the firms in the industry, lacking access to critical resources, were unable to take even these modest adjustment steps. These smaller firms had enough trouble financing their domestic operations, especially after reconstruction bank loans disappeared, so more ambitious measures were out of the question. These firms also lacked other critical resources such as access to information on market trends at home and abroad and access to new technologies. With these disadvantages, the smaller firms were unable to take aggressive economic steps, and so remained entirely dependent on domestic operations.

During the 1960s Japan came under strong international pressures to liberalize its domestic economy. Over the course of the 1960s the Japanese government opened up numerous sectors of the economy to international competition. This included the cotton spinning industry. Surprisingly, this industry was not overly concerned with the possibility of import competition, though it was extremely alarmed by the government's attempt to wean it away from the domestic regulatory support it had won the previous decade. Throughout the 1960s the cotton spinning industry responded to these attempts by applying strong pressure on both bureaucrats and politicians, and in the end it was able to resist moves toward domestic deregulation.

Market liberalization was a condition for Japan's integration into the international economic organizations. As one Japanese policy maker put it, "by the early 1960s, trade liberalization and the shift to Article 8 status in the IMF had become unavoidable prerequisites to Japan's entry into the advanced nation's club."[35] Japan's key ally, the United States, was especially insistent that Japan liberalize its market to trade and investment. These external pressures found a receptive audience among certain economic policy makers, particularly Ikeda Hayato, who, first as MITI minister and then as Prime Minister, pushed for economic growth and a more open economy. Trade liberalization became one of the pillars of his economic policy along with the income-doubling plan. However, Ikeda's liberalization policy was highly selective: liberalization was to occur first in the raw materials industries, as this would benefit other industrial users, followed by sectors that were already competitive internationally; liberalization of infant industries was to be delayed as long as feasible. Raw cotton and cotton textiles were thus targeted for early liberalization.

[35] Uchino 1983, p. 117–118. By 1959 Japan was the only industrial nation not to have achieved Article 8 status in the IMF, which required governments to eliminate subsidies for exports. At that time, the United States was becoming concerned with its deteriorating balance of payments situation; in 1959 Japan ran its very first balance of payments surplus with the United States.

The groundwork for the liberalization of raw cotton imports was laid in October 1958, when the government established an informal discussion group, the Sen'i Sōgō Taisaku Kondankai, to discuss policy directions. This 15-member group was led by Horie Shigeo, a Keidanren official and a staunch supporter of liberalization, and it included industry officials as well as academics. Among the textile industry officials on the panel were Sakurada Takeshi of Nisshinbo, Hara Yoshihira from Nihon Bōseki, and Oya Jinzō from Teijin and Tashiro Shigeki from Toray. Labor was represented by Takita Minoru, the head of Zensen Dōmei.[36] Based on the recommendations of this group MITI announced a year later first steps to open up the market to imports of raw cotton and finished textile goods.

The cotton spinning industry was not overly concerned with the decision to open the domestic market to imports of cotton yarn or finished cotton products. The trade threat to the industry at that point was not foreign imports but rather exclusion from export markets either because of growing protectionism or because of growing competition from other Asian textile industries. The Japanese industry was unconcerned about opening the domestic market to finished imports because it remained relatively competitive in international terms—indeed, this is one reason cotton textiles was selected for liberalization in the first place. In any case, the JSA had succeeded in maintaining 5-percent tariffs on cotton yarn imports and 10-percent tariffs on cotton fabrics. The industry felt that these tariff rates, which were then comparable to those of the E.C. countries, would be sufficient to protect themselves from the world's lowest cost producers, the Indians and Pakistanis.[37] Imports during the 1960s remained minuscule.

The cotton spinners were more deeply divided over the effect of liberalizing the import of raw cotton. Firms were concerned about liberalization, not because of its trade implications, but rather because it would affect the industry's ability to regulate domestic competition. Japan at that time had a system in which raw cotton imports were allocated to each firm according to its market share. The larger, more competitive firms saw this system as one cause of overcapacity, since it gave firms an incentive to increase their capacity in order to maximize their quota share.[38] These firms thus favored the liberalization of cotton imports. The smaller firms pre-

---

[36] *Ekonomisuto*, Sept. 14, 1976, p. 79; Nihon Kagaku Sen'i Kyōkai 1979, p. 136. Teijin and Toray were two of the larger synthetic fiber firms and will be discussed in Chapter 6.

[37] One factor behind this success was that Hara was then a member of the government's tariff advisory council, the Kanzei Shingikai (Tresize and Suzuki 1976, p. 801).

[38] Johnson reports that MITI wanted to remove the quota system because it worried that its regulatory system was creating the distortion of "superficially risk-free overinvestment." This was clearly also the perception of the main firms in the industry. It is interesting that Johnson should mention only the members of the *kondankai* not connected with the cotton textile industry (Horie and Inaba) but should fail to mention that key representatives of the cotton textile industry were also prominent members: Sakurada and Hara of the JSA, and Takita of Zensen (Johnson 1982, p. 249; *Ekonomisuto*, Sept. 14, 1976, p. 79).

ferred to see this import quota system retained, since it guaranteed access to imports for even the least competitive of them. Without this automatic access to cotton imports, they would be forced to compete head-to-head with the large firms, a fight they could not hope to win. The small firms thus put up a strong fight to delay liberalization. According to Imai Zen'ei, a MITI official who was a strong supporter of liberalization, political pressures forced the postponement of liberalization for over two years (to April 1961) to give the small firms more time to prepare themselves. Imai mentions, for instance, that a prominent member of the LDP's Policy Affairs Research Council pleaded with him to "do something" to help out the industry, as his electoral base was in an area of Osaka dominated by small textile firms.[39]

The industry was more concerned with the government's efforts to weaken existing regulation of its domestic capacity. It had grown accustomed to domestic regulation and managed competition provided by the 1956 Textile Bill. Government efforts to expose the industry to more market-oriented principles set policy makers and the industry on a course for direct political confrontation. This episode marks one of the few times in this case study in which government policy makers tried to ignore the position taken by the textile firms. Only after a seven-year political struggle by the industry was it able to reinstate the domestic regulatory cocoon it had previously enjoyed.

Deregulation was also pushed strongly by MITI. MITI's skepticism regarding the industry's future had grown stronger with the passage of time. It continued to worry that existing regulations, by weakening market pressures, only created incentives for overinvestment. MITI believed that a bloated textile sector represented a drain on foreign exchange. The textile industry as a whole took a disproportionately large share of the foreign exchange budget (20 percent in the late 1950s) and, as Chalmers Johnson put it, "this situation had to change."[40] MITI preferred that foreign exchange be released from the natural textile sector so that it could be put to more productive uses. It felt more strongly than ever that the cotton spinning industry should be phased out in favor of the more promising synthetic fibers.[41]

The preferred mechanism was free market competition—between 1960 and 1964 the government attempted to pass legislation that would weaken the regulatory support the industry had won the previous decade. Pressures for deregulation were first signaled in September 1961, during a meeting of the textile *kondankai* when Tsuchiya Kiyoshi, a member of the

[39] *Ekonomisuto*, Sept. 14, 1976, p. 80.

[40] Johnson 1982, p. 250.

[41] Already, synthetic fibers were closing in on cotton spinning, and they would pass it in value in 1962 (Iwata 1984, pp. 20–21; Tsūshō Sangyōshō 1988, p. 7).

committee from the *Asahi Shimbun*, called for the revision of the 1956 law. Tsuchiya stressed the need for bolstering the industry's competitiveness by loosening regulation at home, or what was labeled a "free competition" system (*jiyū kyōsō taisei*).

The Push for Continued Regulation by the Industry

This push for deregulation was at odds with the preferences of most of the industry's firms. The JSA quickly denounced the idea of deregulation: "The proposal put forward by Mr. Tsuchiya is rife with contradictions and problems . . . in that it . . . is based on a preconceived and abstract notion that the industry should be left to fend for itself after the liberalization of raw cotton and textile imports. It reveals the extremely unsophisticated attitude of a bystander who does not understand the Japanese textile industry."[42]

The JSA argued that regulations should not only be continued, but that they should also be strengthened. The large firms wanted regulation to continue but also wanted government policy to be more aggressive in helping the industry tackle the problem of excess capacity. Many felt that the 1956 Bill did not go far enough in helping the industry deal with its structural problem of excess capacity or curb excessive competition. Although some spindles were temporarily taken out of operation under the 1956 legislation, no capacity had actually been scrapped. These spindles were still being held by the firms and could easily be brought back into operation. In addition, MITI found itself unable to monitor the behavior of all firms, and reports of firms operating unregistered spindles were widespread.[43] As a result, the industry had not been able to reduce its capacity. As seen in Table 4-1, between 1956 and 1964 the industry's total capacity had declined only marginally, by 787,000 spindles. But this decrease had been undertaken entirely by the Big 10; the smaller firms had the same number of spindles in 1964 as they did in 1956.

Especially because economic conditions had continued to deteriorate after 1956, the industry felt that merely continuing the capacity restrictions would not be enough to solve their long-term problems. The JSA instead called for stronger public policy measures to help the industry reduce its excess capacity; in particular, the JSA sought policy that would help coordinate industry-wide efforts to reduce capacity. Only by curbing excess capacity and excessive competition could the industry hope to reverse declining prices and thus stabilize industry profits. Far from endors-

[42] Nihon Bōseki Kyōkai 1969, pp. 164–173.
[43] Cheating was especially prevalent among the small firms. The large firms used a more prosaic phrase to express the sucker's payoff: "honest men suffer" (*Nihon Keizai Shimbun*, July 22, 1965).

ing free competition, then, the JSA called for more active and stronger regulation.

The dynamics of reducing excess capacity are similar to those of production cartels and restraining capacity expansion, except that the incentives to cheat are even greater. This is because the decision to scrap capacity is a permanent one. In theory, the market mechanism will force a reduction in capacity, as the least competitive firms gradually shut down. But in actual practice the industry understood that, if left to the market, each firm would have strong incentives to wait, hoping that others would reduce capacity first. Of particular concern was that the uncompetitive firms would not exit but, instead, hang on by maintaining operating rates just high enough to cover variable costs, even if this meant producing and selling below full costs.[44] The industry worried that sufficient exiting would occur only after a prolonged period of cutthroat and debilitating competition, at a point where all were at the brink of exhaustion. In the meantime, the industry would have to deal with continuing excess production and depressed prices. The long-term market solution thus entailed unacceptable short-term costs in terms of depressed profits.

The smaller firms agreed that the industry's excess capacity had to be controlled somehow but wanted to make sure that they were not forced to bear the burden of adjustment costs. They were the most vociferous opponents of free competition to achieve capacity reductions—after all, in a free-for-all of cutthroat competition it was their throats that were more likely to be cut—and the strongest advocates of the political solution of continued regulation. These firms correctly perceived that existing government regulations, and particularly the capacity registration system, served to insure their existence. As one analyst put it, the registration system provided the small cotton spinners with an "economic property right" (*keizai-teki kenri*).[45] The existing regulatory environment minimized the risk to small firms.

---

[44] Economists provide some theoretical support for this concern. Itoh et al. (1988), for instance, argue that production and capacity cutbacks involve a collective action problem, since all have an incentive to wait for others to make the needed sacrifice. Their point is that this has made government intervention justified to avoid market failure; my point is that the industry had an incentive to seek government intervention in order to overcome its negotiating dilemma.

Similarly, McMillan (1994) argues that small firms may have the incentive to wait for their larger counterparts to exit or reduce capacity. His argument is that large firms benefit more from a shrinkage in the industry and so have stronger incentives to reduce their own capacity. The lower capacity-maintenance costs of the small firm gives them the ability to wait for the large firms to shrink.

[45] Nihon Kagaku Sen'i Kyōkai 1979, p. 203. According to one small firm representative, "deregulation will only result in confusion and disorder. It will be we, the smallest firms, that will suffer because of this disorder" (*Nihon Keizai Shimbun*, May 24, 1963). The position taken by the small firms is discussed in *Nihon Bōseki Geppō*, no. 199 (July 1963), pp. 8–17, no. 207 (Mar. 1964), pp. 59–60, and no. 209 (May 1964), pp. 74–76.

The small firms were now worried that the industry's efforts to reduce capacity would place too large a burden on them. They preferred that, if any capacity was to be cut, it should be done across-the-board, insuring that cutbacks would not favor the large firms. They wanted to make sure that they were fully compensated for any costs of adjustment. They thus sought direct government "policy support" for any scrapping efforts in the form of direct subsidies and low-interest loans. In essence, the small firms wanted three things: to ensure their own survival, to achieve a stable industry at minimal cost to themselves, and to be compensated for any adjustments they had to make. On all three counts, continued government regulation, not free competition, was in their interest.

JSA unity, however, was weakened somewhat because the handful of larger firms that had already diversified were now less interested in pursuing a political solution to the industry's problems. In 1960, two of them were open advocates of relaxing domestic regulation and introducing more competition to the industry. Sakurada Takeshi of Nisshinbo, an industry maverick and member of the *kondankai*, and Mutoh Itoji of Kanebo argued that free competition was the best way to force a consolidation of the industry. The idea was that an unregulated environment would force the small, less competitive firms to exit. Sakurada was particularly outspoken, criticizing both the rest of the industry and the government for seeking regulation as a means to avoid free competition. As a result, he argued, the industry had lost its vitality and its international competitiveness.[46] These two firms also opposed the idea of extending regulations to the man-made fibers industry, since they had already diversified in that direction. The two firms were joined by some of the other large firms who had also diversified or were planning to do so. These firms were thus not strong backers of efforts to regulate synthetic fibers.

The cotton spinning industry in Japan had long had a reputation for being unruly and fractious. Signs of disunity had been muted during the 1950s but had grown during the 1960s, especially as the larger firms diversified out of the industry. In this environment the JSA served a critical coordinating function. The JSA chairman, Hara Yoshihira, endeavored to forge a single, official JSA position. In particular, Hara was able to mediate the conflicting interests of the large and small firms. Without the association, the voice of the textile industry would have been highly fragmented.[47]

---

[46] *Nihon Bōseki Geppō*, no. 245 (May 1967), p. 44. See also Nisshinbo's company history (Nisshin Bōseki 1969, pp. 921–942) and Kanebo's company history (Kanebo 1988). Dore (1986, pp. 200) notes that Nisshinbo remained an industry maverick into the 1980s. Kanebo's Mutoh was equally supportive of liberalization, arguing that the 1956 Bill was the cause of much of the industry's current excess capacity. See *Asahi Shimbun*, Feb. 19, 1963, and *Nihon Keizai Shimbun*, May 24, 1963.

[47] *Asahi Shimbun*, June 15, 1963. Hara at one point threatened to stop representing the industry in the Shingikai meetings if the JSA did not come to a compromise position.

The eventual JSA position reflected a compromise that favored the preferences of the less competitive firms in the industry. It called for continued government regulation of capacity, more active government assistance to help the industry control (and dispose of) excess capacity, and measures to help firms increase their size and to modernize their facilities through concentration.[48] These positions were consistent in that the industry attempted to avoid a purely competitive situation, attempting instead to utilize public policy to stabilize itself through the management of capacity and production. In all cases the goal was the stabilization of prices and ultimately profits. These positions would eventually become the basis for government policy—but only after a protracted political struggle with policy makers.

The Policy Process: The Politics of Compromise

In February 1963 MITI created a committee to draft the new legislation. Significantly, this committee was limited to the four members of the *kondankai* who had no direct ties to the textile industry and who favored deregulation.[49] The committee's initial discussions of the new textile legislation reflected this sympathy and essentially ignored the JSA's stated position. Four main points were to become issues between the government and the industry. First, the committee called for a bill to create "a freely competitive industry that no longer relies on a registration system or on production curtailments." By the time the new legislation expired after three years, the industry was to be completely deregulated. Second, the committee called for the immediate abolishment of the registration system. Third, their initial proposals carefully excluded the chemical and synthetic fiber firms. And fourth, the committee introduced a novel idea at the time: the "scrap and build" system, in which a firm seeking to expand its capacity would have to first scrap a specified amount of its existing capacity.

The core JSA firms were not happy. The industry argued that the purpose of the bill should not be to create a freely competitive industry but rather to insure "regulated, stable growth." The JSA called for retaining the registration system and extending it to the other upstream fiber sec-

---

[48] The initial articulation of this position came once again from JSA chairman Hara. In November 1962, Hara presented testimony to the Commerce Committee of the Diet's Lower House and then to that body's Subcommittee on the Textile Industry. Hara's speech would set the tone of the policy debate for the next two decades. The text of Hara's testimony and the JSA documents presented to the Diet can be found in *Nihon Bōseki Geppō*, no. 191, (Nov. 1962), pp. 2–37.

[49] The four were Horie Shigeo, a Bank of Tokyo official and advocate of liberalization, Inaba Hidezō, an economic analyst closely associated with MITI, Tsuchiya Kiyoshi from the *Asahi Shimbun*, and Fukura Toshiyuki from the *Tokyo Shimbun*.

tors, including the man-made fibers. The one committee proposal welcomed by the industry was the idea of "scrap and build," as this fit with its goal of reducing excess capacity. The industry demanded, however, that the government provide direct funding to purchase the smaller firms' facilities and subsidies to encourage these firms to convert to other lines of business. The industry also asked that the bill include stronger measures to help adjust supply and demand, although it did not mention specific measures.

The industry association now began a lobbying campaign to persuade the committee to tone down its emphasis on free competition and to retain current regulatory mechanisms. In doing so, it utilized its direct ties with MITI bureaucrats and also openly sought the support of the party politicians. Throughout the spring of 1963 JSA representatives met with the textile shingikai and with MITI's Textile Bureau to press their position. In July the JSA leadership held meetings with the Textile Subcommittee of the Lower House of the Diet and in the following month also met with a Socialist Party Diet caucus. The small firms also began lobbying. Representatives of the small firms arranged for separate meetings with the MITI Textile Bureau chief and with Inaba and Tsuchiya of the drafting committee. They stressed their opposition to liberalization and also criticized the draft for implying that the burden of adjustment should be borne by the small firms. But the small firms were especially angered that the drafting committee did not even mention how the government should provide financial support for them. These firms presented a list of financial measures the government should take, including direct subsidies for scrapping, stronger tax breaks, and the easing of existing loan conditions.[50]

These lobbying efforts to tone down the government's push towards deregulation paid off, but only partially. The early drafts of the new legislation reinstated a modified form of the registration system and also mentioned financial support for the scrapping efforts of the smaller firms. On the other hand, the JSA remained dissatisfied because the man-made fiber producers were not directly included in the bill and because the industry wanted more concrete pledges of financial support from government.

At the end of 1963 the cotton spinners launched a second lobbying campaign to address these remaining objections to the draft legislation. In November and December the JSA focused its lobbying efforts on the bu-

---

[50] *Nihon Bōseki Geppō*, no. 207 (Mar. 1964), pp. 59–60; *Nihon Keizai Shimbun*, May 8, 1963. The smaller firms had their own organizations to mediate conflicting interests among themselves. Two informal discussion groups, the Shinbō/Shin-shinbō Renkakukai, and the Shinbō Konwakai, had been established as a part of the JSA in 1952. Membership in these groups, both based in Osaka, was limited to small firms (Nihon Bōseki Kyōkai 1982, pp. 91–92; Nihon Bōseki Kyōkai 1969, p. 182).

reaucrats and the politicians. JSA officials met almost daily with the drafting committee or with MITI officials. In addition, the small firms met separately with the same officials, making a special appeal for subsidies and tax breaks for scrapping operations. The JSA's dissatisfaction with the bureaucracy's draft also led them directly to the politicians. In a key session on December 9, the JSA leadership met with the LDP members of the Textile Subcommittee of the Lower House and handed over a written statement of the JSA position.

Both large and small firms were in complete agreement on the need to increase government financial aid for the industry's scrapping efforts. When it became known that MITI was having trouble getting Ministry of Finance (MOF) approval for increased Fiscal and Investment Loan Program (FILP) funds to be directed to the textile industry, industry lobbyists blitzed the Diet and the bureaucracy. On December 25 the chairman of the JSA and representatives of the smaller firms met in succession with the Ministers of MOF and MITI and with the Directors General of the Bank of Japan and the Japan Development Bank (JDB). These representatives then went to the Diet, where they met with the Commerce Committee and the Textile Subcommittee of the Lower House. The message they carried was consistent and clear: the industry needed more financial support. These efforts paid off. On December 29 a special cabinet meeting instructed the JDB to offer ¥1 billion in financing and also instructed the Chūshō Kigyō Kōko to begin making low-interest loans available for the textile industry. Over the next two years the Japanese government provided subsidies totaling ¥6.3 billion (U.S. $17.3 million), four times the amount provided under the 1956 Bill.[51]

The eventual Textile Bill of 1964 represented a compromise between the government's push for liberalization and the industry's attempts to hold on to its regulatory cocoon. By pushing liberalization and deregulation, MITI clearly favored market-driven mechanisms for the cotton spinning industry. In addition, sympathetic to the interests of the synthetic fiber firms, MITI tried to exempt them from capacity regulations. However, faced with strong pressures from the cotton spinners, MITI chose the path of least political resistance, compromise. Policy makers gave in to the demands of the cotton spinners by extending the registration system to one type of synthetic fiber production.[52]

The industry utilized its direct ties with government bureaucrats and party politicians to make the bill more acceptable. The cumulative lobbying efforts by the cotton spinners resulted in a bill that was consistent with

---

[51] Tsūshō Sangyōshō 1988, p. 19.

[52] These regulations covered spun yarn made from synthetic staple; synthetic filament production was exempted from the registration system. Technical details of these regulations can be found in Uriu 1993, pp. 130–137, and Nihon Bōseki Kyōkai 1969, p. 195.

the industry's fundamental goals. It succeeded in maintaining the regulatory framework—the registration system was continued in a modified form. Also, the scrap and build system was welcomed as a mechanism for promoting the scrapping of excess capacity. (In fact, the JSA had early on criticized the 1956 bill precisely because it lacked such a mechanism.) Finally, the industry lobbied for and received extra government funds to help compensate for the costs of scrapping.

This was one of few episodes of policy making in which MITI openly tried to ignore the position taken by one of its industries. In this sense, MITI demonstrated at least a degree of autonomy from the industry's preferences. In the end, however, MITI bureaucrats found themselves unable to accomplish the goal of removing regulation from the industry. They were unable to force the industry very far towards bearing the costs of liberalization. MITI's initiatives were constrained by industrial politics—both the constraints imposed by industry actors and those imposed by the party politicians.

Even so, some analysts at the time described the new legislation as a defeat for the cotton spinners. The *Nihon Keizai Shimbun*, for instance, reported somewhat gleefully that the new bill represented a move toward free competition or, as its headline proclaimed, "the end of the era of *sōtan*." This victory for the advocates of liberalization, however, was a very short-lived one. Within a year after the law was passed the industry's preference for continued regulation was to prevail, and the same newspaper was forced to admit that "the era of *sōtan* has returned."[53] In 1965, MITI approved a formal recession cartel in the industry. Then in 1967, as described in the next section, the Japanese government passed a new textile bill that both reinstated domestic regulation and went much further in supporting the industry's efforts to control its excess capacity problems.

THE RETURN TO REGULATION, 1964–1970

A new recession hit the textile industry shortly after the passage of the 1964 bill. This recession, known simply as the "Textile Recession" (*Sen'i Fukyō*), saw the highest number of textile bankruptcies in the postwar era.

The industry again turned to a traditional response, curtailments of operations through a recession cartel, only this time it was the small firms that took the initiative in cutting back on production, while the large firms were initially reluctant to cooperate. Opposition to curtailment was led by the two mavericks, Nisshinbo and Kanebo, which had become fully convinced that regulation would not solve the industry's problems. Nisshinbo's Saku-

[53] *Nihon Keizai Shimbun*, Feb. 11, 1964, July 22, 1965.

rada attacked those in favor of restrictions, stating that the industry's situation "will never improve if we run crying to the government for *sōtan* whenever we run into the slightest of problems."[54] In addition, many of the large firms had learned from past experience that those cooperating with cutbacks most often ended up in a worse position, as many firms cheated. The small firms, nevertheless, were able to overcome this resistance through hard lobbying, and the JSA on August 25 formally decided to request a formal cartel. Despite criticisms in the media, the cartel was approved by MITI and by the FTC and went into effect in October 1965.

The simmering conflict between Nisshinbo and the rest of the industry, however, came to a head in December 1965 when cartel supporters attempted to extend the cartel for three more months. Now Nisshinbo refused to participate, arguing that it had been willing to cooperate with short-term curtailments but would not tolerate longer-term restrictions. The press took to labeling Nisshinbo's defiance of the rest of the industry as the "Second Sumitomo Metals Incident." As in the Sumitomo Incident, firms participating in the cartel appealed to MITI to pressure a recalcitrant firm. This appeal came initially from the small spinners, but all of the participating firms had an interest in restraining a strong outsider like Nisshinbo. The same MITI official that cracked down on Sumitomo Metals, Vice Minister Sahashi Shigeru, criticized Nisshinbo for not participating in the cartel. However, unlike in the steel industry, MITI had no "trump card," such as restricting Nisshinbo's access to imports, since the import quota system for raw cotton had been abolished in 1961. Still, Nisshinbo eventually agreed to cooperate with the cartel, or at least to not actively break it. It is not clear if MITI or the rest of the industry used any sort of leverage to persuade Nisshinbo to cooperate. It may be, as Dore argues, that Nisshinbo was motivated by some sense of obligation to the rest of the industry not to take advantage of their situation.[55] More likely, Nisshinbo felt that the costs of open defiance of the industry and of MITI were not worth the benefits. What is important here, however, is that it was the rest of the industry that appealed to MITI to apply pressure on Nisshinbo to compel it to cooperate with the cartel.

The Industry's Pursuit of Structural Adjustment

The 1965 recession convinced the industry that only a drastic change in the industry's structure would solve the problem of excessive competition. It was becoming clear that the scrap and build system was having the opposite effect than intended: MITI reported that total spindles actually increased

[54] *Asahi Shimbun*, Dec. 26, 1965.
[55] Dore 1986, pp. 200–201.

during the first three years of the bill.[56] The JSA and especially the larger firms now began to discuss more drastic means to restructure the industry, or as they put it, pursue *kōzō kaizen* (literally, "structural improvement"). The JSA noted that the European and American textile industries were pursuing restructuring strategies, and that the Japanese industry had to rationalize if it was to stay competitive. The JSA now proposed that restructuring proceed along two tracks: more active scrapping efforts and concentration through tie-ups or mergers. The main elements of the JSA policy proposal, presented to the government in October 1965, were to become the basis of the 1967 Textile Industry Structural Improvement Law (Tokusenhō).[57]

First, the JSA called for the creation of a new government-funded agency that would oversee the scrapping of excess spindles. As the industry envisioned it, this agency was to provide funding to, in effect, buy up its unwanted capacity. In pushing for increased government support for scrapping, the JSA was blatantly self-serving: it criticized past government regulatory policy as a main cause of the industry's overcapacity and argued that the government should therefore buy up half of the excess spindles.

Second, the industry called for more active measures to promote concentration. Here, the interests of the large and small firms were in direct conflict. Ideally, the large firms wanted to see the industry reorganized around them—that is, they wanted to absorb the capacity of the smaller firms. On the other hand, the smaller firms wanted to ensure that they were not swallowed up.

The JSA was again able to mediate and come to a compromise that took into account the concerns of the most vulnerable group, the small firms. The JSA now suggested that the industry consolidate itself not through merger but rather through "business tie-ups" among the small firms. This conception, which was also backed by MITI, called for the formation of small informal groups composed of three to four firms each. This would help the small firms take advantage of economies of scale and would provide them with greater financial strength and profitability. The small firms supported this concept, which they hoped would both stabilize the industry and enhance their bargaining power.[58] All were inwardly confident that tie-ups among themselves would make them less vulnerable to bankruptcy

---

[56] MITI reported that 1.8 million spindles were scrapped between 1964 and 1967, but that 2.6 million spindles, either new or newly released from mothball, were put into operation (Tsūshō Sangyōshō 1988, p. 14).

[57] This position paper was entitled "The Future Vision of the Textile Industry." See Nihon Bōseki Kyōkai 1969, pp. 218–220, for the text of this paper. JSA chairman Hara Yoshihira had issued the first call for restructuring in November 1962; Hara's position papers in 1955 and in 1962 were thus to serve as the basis of two major textile industry laws.

[58] Each group would thus operate between 150,000 to 200,000 spindles. See *Chūshō Kigyō Kin'yū Kōkō Geppō* 13, no. 9 (Sept. 1966), pp. 16–33, for a discussion of these conceptions and the industry reaction. MITI also suggested an alternative that small cotton spinners form

or to being absorbed by the large firms. They therefore did not see the JSA's push for restructuring as a threat to their own independence. In addition, the JSA called for the extension of the capacity registration system for three more years, thus further ensuring stability for the small firms.

The Zensen Dōmei supported the industry's *kōzō kaizen* efforts. This is not what we might expect from labor if firms were trying to force labor to adjust rapidly. But in this case, with the firms pursuing a strategy of trying to stabilize the industry with a minimum amount of disorder, labor leaders found that their interests coincided.[59] Zensen's official textile policy, published in conjunction with the Democratic Socialist Party, was notable not only for its support for restructuring but also for its lack of ideology and stridency. Zensen's moderate stance also reflected the fact that it was a moderate union committed to cooperative relations between management and labor. Another reason that Zensen could take a relatively relaxed position was that the industry at that point had too few workers. Specifically, the industry was having trouble finding enough female workers as more and more female middle-school graduates, the industry's main source of labor, were now going on to high school. Thus, the jobs of the core Zensen members, the full-time male workers, were not at great risk.

The Policy-Making Environment: MITI's Abrupt About-Face

If the industry's preference for stabilization through regulation remained consistent, MITI's behavior did not. In fact, MITI now did an about-face compared to the 1960–1964 period and began to support the return to regulation of the industry. In part, this turnaround reflects the persistent lobbying efforts of the textile industry. In particular, the contentiousness of the 1964 bill had shown MITI that the industry could muster considerable political weight when its interests were not addressed.

MITI's turnaround also resulted from a power struggle within MITI between the "international faction" and the more domestically oriented "industrial policy bureaucrats." Johnson provides a superb analysis of this split within MITI, tracing the careers of Imai Zen'ei and Sahashi Shigeru, who respectively represent these two factions.[60] Imai was commit-

---

tie-ups with the larger spinners, man-made fiber firms, textile *shōsha*, or with smaller weavers and knitters. But the most attractive option for the small firms was to form groups among themselves: according to a survey by MITI, only a handful of small firms, with 3.5 percent of the industry's spindles, eventually tied themselves to larger firms. The representative of the small producers stated, "we have no intention of losing our identities as firms." *Nihon Keizai Shimbun*, Sept. 18, 1966.

[59] Kume notes that in other distressed industries, such as coal and steel, industry-management relations were cooperative to the extent that management did not pursue excessive rationalization (Kume 1993, pp. 167–168).

[60] Johnson 1982, pp. 243–252, 262–268.

ted to liberalization and disliked heavy government regulation; as head of the Textile Bureau from 1958 to 1961, he had pushed for liberalization of textiles, and he continued this policy line once he became MITI vice-minister in 1963. In contrast, Sahashi Shigeru is described by Johnson as a "domestic-use-only bureaucrat," a traditionalist who held a more reserved position on liberalization. Sahashi succeeded Imai as MITI vice-minister in October 1964, immediately after the passage of the Textile Bill. During his tenure, which lasted until mid-1966, MITI backed the industry's recession cartel and supported the stabilization efforts of the large firms.

Sahashi argued that exposing the industry to competition would only cause disorder and would prevent the "healthy restructuring" of the industry. He echoed the industry's long-standing position almost to the letter: "If the industry is left to the market, the result will be excess production and falling prices. Under free competition, the small firms will not be forced to exit, but will instead use the spindles they are secretly hiding to better compete with the large firms. The end result will be disorderly competition and falling profits. Those who propose leaving the industry to fend for itself offer no way to prevent this sort of disorder."[61]

The legislative process surrounding this bill was notable for its lack of controversy. This was mostly because the industry was satisfied with the bill, having proposed it in the first place. The only organized opposition to the bill came from the synthetic fiber industry, which continued to argue that the fate of the natural textiles should be left to the market. This time, however, the opposition from the synthetic fiber firms was muted, as they were then running into their own problem of excess capacity (for details, see Chapter 6).

The one contentious issue involved money, in particular how to finance the bill, and how to create the new scrapping agency. Originally, the Shingikai mentioned only a modest amount of financial support, whereas the JSA was pressing the government for substantial assistance. The small firms were especially vocal, arguing that their lack of resources made them unable to undertake any economic adjustments.[62] Throughout 1966 both small and large firms in the JSA lobbied MITI and the politicians. In a rare show of solidarity, the JSA held a joint conference with the association representing the downstream weaving sector, the Menkōren (Mensufu Orimono Kōgyō Rengōkai). The joint resolution of these associations,

---

[61] *Nihon Keizai Shimbun*, Feb. 18, 1966. Sahashi used the term *doro-numa no kyōsō* ("the quagmire of competition") to describe the likely outcome. Sahashi turned out to be one of the last of the traditional industrial policy bureaucrats, as the internationalists began to dominate the ministry once he left (Johnson 1982, pp. 275–280).

[62] In particular, the small firms wanted the government to raise the price it was offering for the buyout of excess spindles. At that time the government was offering ¥7,000 per spindle if the firm exited the industry but only half that if the firm remained. See *Chusho Kigyo Kin'yū Kōkō Geppō* 13, no. 9 (Sept. 1, 1966), pp. 31–32.

presented to the LDP on December 16, 1966, called for immediate action on implementing structural improvement policies, for increased financial assistance, and for the creation of a new government-funded agency to promote the scrapping of capacity.[63]

These concerns were taken very seriously by the politicians, both in the LDP and the opposition parties. The LDP faced conflicting pressures, since not all in the textile industry supported the bill—in particular, the synthetic fiber firms had made their objections known. Still, the party was reluctant to ignore the political demands of the cotton spinners. The LDP was also concerned because both the JSP and the DSP were using this issue to raise harsh attacks on the government. The JSP was especially vocal, arguing that current policy did not do enough to help the industry and that, in any case, LDP policy favored the larger firms. The LDP was especially sensitive to these attacks because Japan was then going through its most serious postwar recession to date, the 1964–1965 "structural" recession. As an indication of its concern, the LDP in November 1966 established a special Textile Committee in its Policy Affairs Research Council. Forty LDP members joined this committee, and Fukuda Hajime, a former MITI minister from Fukui, a key textile region, was named chairman.[64]

This new LDP textile committee now took an active role on behalf of the industry. Three days after the JSA's resolution, the committee responded with a resolution of its own that stressed the importance of the textile industry to the Japanese economy and endorsed the industry's need for public policy to encourage structural improvement. The LDP committee specifically endorsed the JSA's proposal that MITI create the new scrapping agency.

The struggle over how to finance the textile legislation also involved the Ministry of Finance. After the LDP tripled MITI's original budget request of ¥13.5 billion (U.S. $37.5 million) in subsidies for the textile industry, the Ministry of Finance (MOF) attempted to cut this budget request down.[65] In February 1967 MOF called for budget commitments of only

[63] Nihon Bōseki Kyōkai 1969, pp. 225–239, discusses the industry's lobbying efforts in detail. The emergency textile conference and subsequent lobbying efforts are discussed in *Nihon Bōseki Geppō*, no. 241 (Jan. 1967), pp. 53–55. The conference was attended by MITI minister Kanno, various politicians, and representatives of all sectors of the textile industry.

[64] See Nihon Shakaito Seisaku Shingikai 1968 for the JSP position. The JSP issued a policy paper criticizing the LDP on August 11, 1966. The LDP's subsequent decision to subsidize the textile industry would fit well with Kent Calder's thesis that the LDP has been especially responsive to societal demands during political and economic crisis periods, except that Calder (1988, pp. 102–103) labels the 1964–1971 period an "interlude of stability." The list of the top leaders of the Textile Committee can be found in *Seisaku Geppō* (Feb. 1968). Takeshita Noboru was a member of this committee from the start. Two other future prime ministers, Kaifu Toshiki and Uno Sosuke, later joined it.

[65] The LDP called for ¥36.5 billion to be allocated to the textile industry. The text of this policy statement can be found in the LDP's journal, *Seisaku Geppō*, no. 135 (Apr. 1967). MITI's original request called for ¥800 million from general budget and ¥12.7 billion from the FILP budget (*Nihon Keizai Shimbun*, Dec. 20, 1966).

¥547 million. After another round of lobbying from the industry, the cabinet restored the textile budget to ¥16.9 billion, slightly above the amount MITI had originally proposed. MOF also opposed the creation of the scrapping agency, but again the industry prevailed. The new law, which took effect in July 1967, created the Textile Industry Rationalization Agency (Sen'i Kōgyō Kōzō Kaizen Jigyō Kyōkai) as a special agency attached to MITI.

To the extent that the deregulatory nature of the 1964 Textile Bill was seen as a victory for those in favor of liberalization, it was a short-lived one. By 1967, the industry had succeeded in beating back the effort to expose it to "free competition." At least for the moment the industry had held on to, and in some ways had strengthened, domestic regulations that helped it manage competition. Most significantly, the financial resources of the government were now available to the industry to help it achieve its stabilization goals. Inaba Hidezō, one of the original backers of the liberalization policy, later commented that the 1964 legislation had been designed to provide the industry with a "new direction" from the preservationist government policy that had existed up to then; however, he added somewhat wistfully that by 1965 the industry had "reverted to its traditional ways."[66]

The 1970s and 1980s: Regulation Continues, Imports Rise

Throughout the 1970s and into the 1980s, the largest firms in the industry continued to try to diversify their operations with varying degrees of success, moving mainly into the more lucrative synthetic fiber sector. Toyobo and Unitika (formerly Nihon Boseki) were the first to move into synthetic fibers; during the 1964–1965 recession Kanebo, Kureha, Toyobo, and Kurashiki followed suit. Diversification out of the textile industry, however, was more difficult. Kanebo was the sole exception, transforming itself from a cotton spinner into a chemical and cosmetics firm. In 1965, 84 percent of its sales came from the textile industry, but by 1981 this figure had dropped to 36 percent; cotton products accounted for less than 10 percent of its sales. Nisshinbo also made strong efforts to expand its non-textile divisions.[67] Beginning in the 1960s, other large firms had expanded overseas through direct investment, but investments by the cotton spinners began to decrease after the 1970s mostly because labor costs in

[66] Tsūshō Sangyōshō, Seikatsu Sangyō Kyoku and Sen'i Kōgyō Kōzō Kaizen Jigyō Kyōkai 1977, p. v.
[67] Nisshinbo has been able to diversify into a variety of products, including brake linings, paper, rubber and synthetic foams, machine tools, plastics, and printing machinery. In 1972, 16 percent of Nisshinbo's sales came in non-textile areas, by 1980, the firm had increased this to 25 percent. See Dore 1986, pp. 215–216. Iwata (1984, p. 60–63) discusses Kanebo's diversification efforts.

Asia were no longer as cheap as they once were. Thus, even in a fragmented industry like cotton spinning, a handful of firms were able to pursue economic adjustment options.

The list of diversified, competitive firms is a very short one, however.
The other large spinning firms have made only limited progress. Dore,
for instance, notes that in 1973, 12 percent of the total sales of the
largest firms were in non-textile fields; at the end of the decade, this figure had only increased to 16 percent.[68] And for the smaller firms, which
lacked the necessary financial and other resources, adjustment through
diversification or overseas investment has not even been an option. Similarly, the labor force has not enjoyed attractive exit opportunities. Because many workers were relatively low-skilled, finding new jobs has been
difficult.

Not surprisingly, both firms and labor continued to pursue the alternate
route of politics. Throughout the 1970s and 1980s the JSA lobbied for
government regulation to shield the industry from market pressures.
Zensen has tended to support efforts by the firms to preserve and stabilize
the industry, as this suited labor's goal of minimizing labor displacement.
As before, no one in the industry wanted to see regulation removed completely, since a competitive free-for-all would result in disorder and chaos.
Also, the industry continued to rely on implicit cartel arrangements to regulate production and to manage reductions in capacity. The industry's
policy demands and lobbying behavior also remained basically the same as
in the 1960s: when faced with economic distress, the industry continued
to rely on government regulation to stabilize and manage competition,
production levels, and coordinate the reduction of capacity.

The cotton spinners continued to coordinate production cutbacks in
order to cope with depressed prices. They were able to maintain cutback
agreements for virtually the entire decade of the 1970s, either in the form
of official recession cartels or though voluntary efforts at "self-regulation."
In June 1974, the industry agreed to self-imposed restrictions on output;
six months later this informal curtailment was transformed into an official
recession cartel. After the cartel expired, the industry again resorted to
unofficial, industry-wide curtailments of production. By April of 1977, the
industry again requested the formation of an official recession cartel. This
cartel was extended a total of four times, finally expiring in June 1978,
when the industry was allowed to form an indicative cartel after being designated as "structurally depressed" under MITI's new depressed industry
legislation, the Tokuanhō (for a detailed discussion of this legislation, see
Chapter 5). In 1981, as the Tokuanhō cartel was about to expire, the industry formed a new recession cartel for a total of five months; again after

---

[68] Dore 1986, p. 216.

the cartel ended, the industry entered into a period of "self-restraint" in which the majors cut back production by 10 percent, while the smaller firms cut back by 3 percent. Unlike earlier decades, these cartel agreements did not arouse the strong opposition of maverick firms. The JSA reports that in the 1975 cartel, for instance, 97 firms representing 9.8 million spindles participated in the cartel. The old maverick firm, Nisshinbo, proved to be less of a maverick in the 1980s. As mentioned, Ronald Dore explains this as reflecting the value the firm placed on consensus and cooperation. More likely, its cooperation in the 1970s and 1980s was due to its ability to decrease its dependence on cotton spinning, thus giving the firm less intense stakes in opposing the cartel.

However, the industry was finding that the effectiveness of the recession cartels was being gradually undermined by rising yarn imports (discussed in the next section). Unless imports can be effectively blocked, forming a cartel makes little sense—any cutbacks in output designed to stabilize the domestic market will simply be canceled out by rising imports. With imports rising steadily, the industry after 1982 no longer attempted to form recession cartels to try to raise prices. In addition, as discussed in Chapter 6, foreign criticisms that the recession cartels represented an implicit barrier to imports also made policy makers less willing to use this policy tool.

Second, the industry continued to seek government regulation to help it deal with its chronic problem of excess capacity. It had high hopes for the newly created Rationalization Agency and, in particular, hoped that the government would finance the needed cutbacks in capacity. However, cutting capacity was proving to be even more difficult than cutting production had been. In part this was because the smaller firms were finding it difficult to make cutbacks. They insisted that the large firms, who they argued could better afford it, should bear more of the burden of adjustment. As a result, the agency carried out cutbacks on a pro rata basis (and sometimes called for even greater cuts by the larger firms). This was done in the name of "fairness," but in reality it reflected the refusal of the smaller firms to bear too much of the burden. Pro rata cutbacks were a great advantage to the least competitive firms: otherwise, market pressures would have forced the less efficient firms to cut back more than efficient ones.

The textile industry as a whole also continued to seek explicit legislation to regulate competition. In 1974, when the 1967 law was about to expire, the industry and relevant policy makers agreed to have the legislation extended. Again in 1978, 1983, and 1988, a new textile bill was written to take the place of an expiring one. The politics of extending these bills was essentially similar in each of the episodes, although each of the pieces of legislation differed somewhat in the details. Therefore there is no need to provide a full analysis of the policy making process after 1970. Suffice it to say that although the stated purpose of each law differed slightly, and each contained new policy measures, the underlying purpose of the bills remained the same—to shield the industry from pure market forces and help it deal with its problems of excess capacity through coordinated, managed cutbacks. On the surface, each piece of legislation was touted as new and path-breaking. The 1974 law, for instance, called for a more "knowledge-intensive" industry and a shift to "higher value-added production." Yet few truly believed that computerization would dramatically increase competitiveness or that the value of "higher value-added production" would be all that high. In 1978 the cotton spinners were designated as "structurally depressed" under the Tokuanhō, and were allowed to form an indicative cartel in order to more effectively reduce capacity. None of the provisions of this legislation departed significantly from what the cotton spinners had been doing for the past 30 years. The 1983 textile industry law, entitled a "Vision for the Textile Industry in a New Age," contained very little substance, as its title suggests.

Finally, policy makers continued to be highly responsive to the cotton textile industry's call for financial assistance. The government continued its generous grants to the industry, and particularly to the small firms: special tax treatment, subsidies for further consolidation of the industry through vertical integration, loans for scrapping capacity, interest-free loans, and so on. For instance, under the 1967 Textile Bill direct government financial assistance given to the cotton textile industry totaled ¥204.3 billion (U.S. $567.5 million) in the form of up-front subsidies and government-sponsored loans.[69] To put this figure into perspective, the government in the 1960s provided the computer industry with approximately the same amount (U.S. $542.0 million). During the 1970s the Japanese government would end up channeling even greater financial assistance to the cotton textile industry: between 1973 and 1977, for instance, the government provided the industry with U.S. $1,036.7 million (comparable to the U.S. $1,702.3 million given to the computer industry during this time).[70] If Japan's industrial policy makers were involved in picking and supporting winner industries, they at the same time remained involved in subsidizing a distressed but highly organized one.

---

[69] Tsūshō Sangyōshō 1988, p. 19.

[70] Anchordoguy (1989) calculates government financial assistance given to the more strategic computer sector. She goes to great lengths to track down all direct and indirect financial assistance given to the entire computer industry, including tax and depreciation benefits, and a whole range of government-funded activities including numerous market and technology surveys. The numbers presented here for the cotton textile industry include only direct subsidies and low-interest loans.

The Politics of (Denying) Import Protection

Policy toward the cotton spinning industry in the 1970s and 1980s was not an exact replay of the preceding decades. The major change that occurred in the 1970s was the steady rise in imports of cotton yarn, which began to enter the Japanese market in 1971 (see Chart 4-1). Between 1971 and 1973, imports increased by some 240 percent, with imports of cotton yarn surpassing the industry's total exports for the first time in 1972. Imports surged again in 1978, spurred on by the appreciation of the yen and the Japanese government's efforts to reflate the domestic economy. Imports continued to climb steadily throughout the 1980s, and then jumped dramatically after 1985, due to the appreciation of the yen following the Plaza Accord and further government efforts to boost domestic demand. During the 1980s, imports of cotton yarn nearly tripled, and by the end of the decade had surpassed domestic production.

The cotton spinners were not the only part of the textile industry that faced rising import competition. Textile imports as a whole also grew rapidly in the late 1970s and 1980s, especially in the downstream weaving and knitting sectors. In 1987, for the first time, Japan became a net importer of all textile products. Not surprisingly, the Japanese textile industry has focused its political efforts on trying to slow or stop imports since the mid-1970s.[71] The JSA was the first textile industry association to express an interest in receiving protection—its first appeal to policy makers came in 1974. In the mid-1970s the spinners were joined by the downstream sectors of the textile industry as well as the upstream synthetic fiber producers. One of the industry's central policy demands called on the Japanese government to change Japan's status under the MFA from a *supplier* country, subject to trade restraints imposed by others, to an *importing* country. This would have allowed the Japanese government to formally—and legally—impose temporary restrictions on imports, either in the form of bilateral agreements with exporting countries to restrain the level of trade, or through unilateral restrictions if such agreements were not possible. The industry argued that Japan remained the only OECD country facing rapidly rising textile imports that was not categorized as an importing country. In fact, since Japan was still listed as a supplier country, it remained bound by MFA restraints negotiated with the United States and Canada.[72]

Import protection has been the only major policy concession that the cotton spinners and the rest of the textile industry have not won from gov-

---

[71] Tracing the politics of import protection thus must go beyond the boundaries of the cotton spinners to include much of the textile industry. The argument I make in this section is based on the analyses of Friman 1990, Dore 1986, and Yamazawa 1988.

[72] OECD 1983b, p. 163.

Chart 4-1. Supply and demand for cotton yarn, 1957–1988

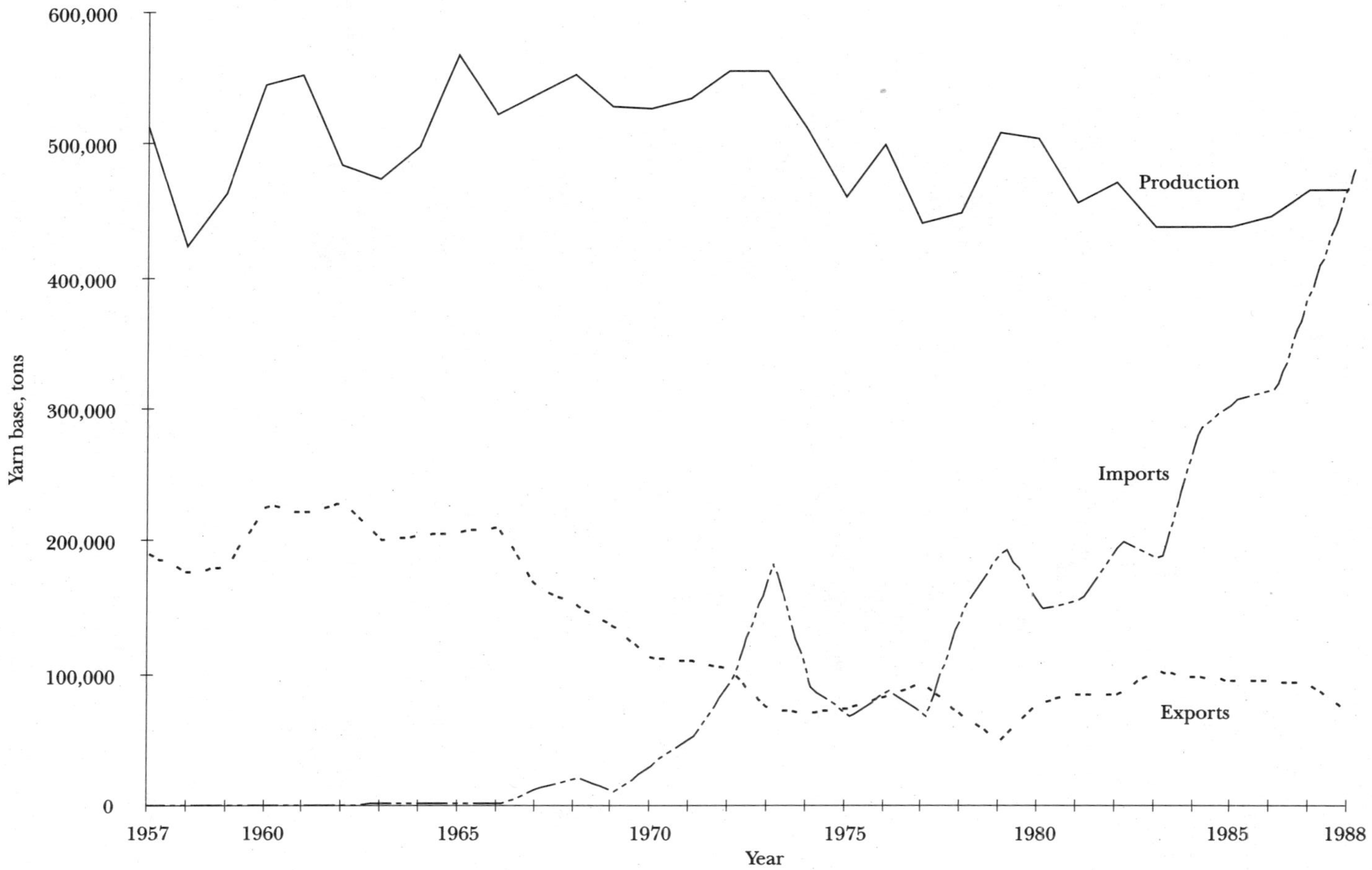

Source: Year Book of Textile Statistics, various years.

ernment policy makers, at least not through 1995. Given the formidable obstacles that the industry faced, both in terms of international constraints and domestic politics, this outcome is not surprising.

International constraints alone can explain the Japanese government's refusal to grant trade protection to the textile industry. As Richard Friman puts it, "the absence of more overt protectionist policies [through the mid-1980s] . . . reflected strong international constraints on Japanese state policy makers against the use of such measures."[73] The question of protecting the textile industry from imports arose at the height of friction with Japan's trading partners. In this period these countries made concerted efforts to pry open the domestic Japanese market. Any attempt by Japanese political leaders to try to close the market further would have met with strong international criticism. Policy makers expressed concern that any effort to impose new trade restrictions would detract from Japan's efforts to open its markets.

In particular, Japanese policy makers feared that its trading partners would retaliate if Japan attempted to institute any new protectionist barriers. As David Lake, Richard Rosecrance, and Jennifer Taw have correctly pointed out, Japan's economic interests in maintaining access to the international market were high and continued to grow throughout the 1980s.[74] Although Japan's dependency on exports has remained lower than that of the continental European states, its dependence on trade has been concentrated among certain key industrial sectors, such as automobiles and electronics, which have relied on external trade and investment markets for a great deal of their profits. In addition, the potential costs of retaliation have been heightened by the deeply-held conviction that the Japanese economy is highly vulnerable to cutoffs of imports of raw materials, energy, and food. Clearly, any cutoff of trade would have been highly disruptive to the Japanese economy. Japan's heavy economic stake in maintaining access to the economies of the West has made such an outcome too costly to risk.[75] Like the small, trade-dependent nations of Europe described by Peter Katzenstein, policy makers in Japan have felt that protecting any single industry would lead to unacceptable risks of retaliation.

---

[73] Friman 1990, p. 125. Friman also reports that the JSA has lobbied to have cotton textiles removed from the list of items covered under the GSP. MITI rejected these demands initially, but by 1981 the preferential tariff on cotton yarn and fabric had been suspended. According to Friman, despite strong international constraints, Japanese "state policy makers were unable to prevent a policy concession more overt than those granted in the past" (1990, p. 131).

[74] Lake 1983, pp. 538–542, and Rosecrance and Taw 1990, pp. 193–200.

[75] This policy line is reiterated by every LDP politician and MITI official one speaks with. For just a few examples of such statements appearing in print see *Japan Economic Journal*, Mar. 21, 1987 and Sept. 10, 1988, and *The Japan Times*, Oct. 21, 1988.

The possibility that any attempt to introduce new protectionist barriers in Japan would lead to foreign retaliation has also brought other key Japanese industries into the domestic policy process. Foreign retaliation would have damaged the core interests of many of these industries, ranging from steel to electronics, all of which have high stakes in maintaining access to international markets. Although these industries normally are not concerned with policy dealing with the textile industry, the question of protection is a different matter. They feared that if foreign partners retaliated against new protectionist barriers, this retaliation would jeopardize their own access to international markets. They have been highly organized and politically influential and have made sure that policy makers heard their interests loud and clear.

Given these formidable obstacles, it is not surprising that the textile industry as a whole has met with a very cool reaction from both the party politicians and the MITI bureaucrats. To make matters worse for the industry, the various textile sectors have not been unified on this issue. For instance, although the weaving firms wanted protection, they worried that protecting the upstream cotton spinning sector would result in higher input costs for themselves.[76] And as will be argued more fully in Chapter 6, the synthetic fiber firms were only half-heartedly interested in protection, since they had already taken steps to diversify out of the industry and since many of them had developed strong overseas stakes in trade and investments. Even within the cotton spinning industry, the various actors were not unified. On the one hand, small firms and labor had the highest and most intense interest in achieving protection. On the other hand, the larger firms that were able to diversify at home or abroad were less avid in their pursuit of protectionism.

For those who see a "strong state" in Japan, it is tempting to portray MITI's autonomy from industry preferences as the main reason that protection was not given to this industry. But this outcome is overdetermined—that is, given the intensity of international constraints, as well as the domestic industrial politics involved, it is highly doubtful that any industry could have convinced policy makers to raise new import barriers. In these circumstances even a "weak state" might have refrained from granting protection to the textile industry.

Although the cards were thus stacked against it, the industry was able to achieve a high level of support from policy makers in trying to restrain imports through informal means. During the mid-1970s, it worked to convince MITI to use its administrative guidance powers to somehow impose restraints on the business practices of the textile trading companies. The Textile Industry Council, acting on a request from the textile industry, rec-

[76] Dore 1986, pp. 158–178; Friman 1990, pp. 115–141.

ommended in 1976 that the Japanese government create a system of "import surveillance" for MITI to use to monitor the import of cotton yarn. Dore describes an elaborate system in which MITI conducted periodic surveys of the textile trading companies and then expressed its "concern" when imports increased too rapidly. That these efforts have had little effect in stopping imports even in the 1990s is not surprising, since MITI has been simply unable to coerce Japanese importers to abide by its "expressions of concern."[77]

The Japanese industry was more effective in utilizing a mechanism more common to American industries: negotiated voluntary export restraints with its major foreign suppliers. In fact, what the Japanese industry was able to achieve through these measures—informal, quantitative export restraints—is roughly what the industry would have received had Japan changed its status under the MFA. The difference is that such restraints under the MFA would have been overt and legally binding; as it was, these agreements were implicit and enforced through tacit threats. In Japan's case, orderly market agreements were negotiated not between governments, but rather directly between the concerned industries. However, because MITI did not object to these arrangements, it gave its tacit stamp of approval.[78]

The textile industry as a whole concentrated its efforts on the two largest suppliers to the Japanese market, Korea and China. It was involved in regular, ongoing "discussions" with its Asian neighbors, and negotiated restraint agreements in the weaving and knitting sectors. The cotton spinners also negotiated their own industry-to-industry trade restraints agreements with their main competitors, Korea and Pakistan. In the case of Korea, unofficial talks between the Korean and Japanese cotton spinners began in 1974, when a JSA representative visited Korea to convey the association's desire for export restraints. In 1975 the JSA and the Korean industry began a series of annual meetings between representatives of both industries. Especially after the yen began to appreciate in 1977, the in-

---

[77] In this system MITI monitors the amount of goods imported by the members of the Cotton Yarn Council of the Japan Textile Importers' Association. MITI tries to apply informal pressure on these importers when imports rise significantly. These pressures, however, are of the weakest sort, taking the form of letters or telephone calls from MITI's Consumer Goods Industries Bureau to the importers association; however, MITI cannot mention specific import numbers and cannot ask them to cancel existing contracts. In rare cases, MITI will invite firms for "hearings," in which firms are asked to explain their import plans. MITI's ability to constrain cotton yarn imports is further weakened because numerous textile importers are not members of the Importer's Association and thus are beyond MITI pressures. The share of imports accounted for by these numerous "outsider" firms has grown over time, from 10 percent in the mid-1970s to nearly 50 percent by 1980. MITI has tried in vain to influence these importers as well, but without meaningful sanctions, MITI's expressions of concern have not been effective. See Yamazawa 1988, pp. 417–419, Friman 1990, pp. 124–125, and Dore 1986, pp. 203–205.

[78] Friman 1990, p. 135.

dustry sought other means to increase pressures on the Korean industry. In 1978 MITI Minister Komoto Toshio asked Korea to voluntarily restrict its exports.[79] And in 1981 the head of MITI's Spinning division was sent to Korea to officially ask for self-restraint. Finally, in December 1982 the JSA filed an antidumping suit against the Korean cotton spinning industry. The suit had its intended effect: in June 1983 the Korean industry announced that it would voluntarily restrain its exports to Japan. Similarly, since 1975 the JSA has held regular talks with their counterparts in Pakistan. At the same time that the JSA filed its antidumping suit against Korea, it also filed a countervailing duty suit against the Pakistani industry. In August of that year, the Pakistani government canceled its subsidies programs for its cotton spinners; two years later the Pakistani industry agreed to introduce a "check price system" to prevent a flood of underpriced cotton yarn. In return, the Japanese industry agreed to drop its legal action.[80]

Japan's record on textile trade is thus a spotty one. On the one hand, for nearly 20 years the Japanese government, to its credit, has refrained from joining the MFA as an importing country. On the other hand, Japan was not so reluctant to pass on adjustment costs to its weaker trading partners. When faced with growing imports from neighbors such as Korea and Pakistan, the Japanese government was willing to endorse the industry's efforts to restrain imports on an industry-to-industry basis. Thus, Japan took the same approach with its importing countries as the United States took with Japan. And Japan's weaker partners in Asia found themselves in the same position that Japanese firms faced vis-à-vis the West, being forced either to voluntarily restrict their exports, or else to risk even greater market closure.

However, these informal means to restrain imports did not prevent the rapid increase in textile products coming into the country (although it is impossible to say how much higher imports would have been in the absence of these restraints). What is important is that policy makers were not able to ignore completely the calls for help coming from the cotton spinners and the other parts of the textile industry. Although the government did not grant explicit protection, it bowed to the political influence of the industry and at least tacitly implemented informal protectionist measures.

The government's opposition to granting overt protection has weakened in the 1990s. As imports continued to rise and as the textile industry's calls for protection became more strident, the Japanese government,

---

[79] *Nihon Bōseki Geppō*, no. 431 (Nov. 1982), pp. 2–12; Friman 1990, p. 128.

[80] *Nihon Bōseki Geppō*, no. 500 (Oct. 1988), pp. 86–94. The industry has held a series of meetings with the officials of the Chinese textile industry as well. The first reported contacts between the two industries occurred in May 1982, when a group of representatives of the Chinese industry visited Japan. However, the Chinese industry was able to resist export restraints throughout the 1980s.

beginning in 1993, signaled a greater willingness to either join the MFA as an importing country or at least to impose stronger and more overt import restrictions. In part, this new stance was meant to increase pressures on Japan's textile trading partners to restrain their exports. This was especially true for China, which since 1985 has been Japan's largest supplier of all textile products but which has been reluctant to enter into restraint agreements.

In May 1994, the Textile Industry Council announced a set of conditions under which the textile industry can expect to receive import protection. These guidelines are extremely close to the MFA's guidelines, calling for import restrictions when a sharp increase in imports causes serious damage to the industry. In language that strongly resembles the policy debates of the 1960s, the MITI panel argued that such protection would "help the domestic textile industry secure time to carry out restructuring measures and avoid employment adjustment." Conversely, if imports are not curbed, this "could offset the restructuring efforts by the Japanese textile industry."[81] Whether or not the government capitulates to this final industry demand, it seems clear that the industry today continues to face much the same problems that it has confronted since the 1950s.

IMPLICATIONS OF THE COTTON SPINNING CASE

The economic and political behavior of industry actors in this case study of cotton spinning in Japan has been consistent with the structural hypotheses laid out in Chapter 2. The majority of small firms in this fragmented industry have lacked the capital and technological resources to pursue economic adjustment options. For these firms the only form of adjustment has been exit, either through bankruptcy or through merger. Without attractive adjustment options, firms faced a stark choice: they could pay the costs of adjustment, or they could organize to pursue political solutions to preserve themselves. Workers, also, perceived limited adjustment options, both because the small firms were unable to retain them through intra-firm transfers and because most of them were not highly skilled. Again, without attractive economic alternatives, labor had strong incentives to resist adjustment and pursue political solutions. As detailed in this case study, for more than forty years industry actors chose the political route, focusing their energies on seeking stability through government regulation.

---

[81] *Yomiuri Shimbun,* May 18, 1994; *Nikkei Weekly,* May 23, 1994; *Nihon Keizai Shimbun,* June 2, 1994.

Not all industry actors, however, have been able to avoid significant adjustment. It turns out that patterns of incidence, which identify those actors forced to bear the burden of adjustment, have differed dramatically between firms and labor. As shown in Table 4-2, labor has been forced to bear a major part of the adjustment burden: between 1965 and 1985, total employment fell by some 65 percent.

Despite this, however, the labor unions have not come into open conflict with management over the displacement of workers. Five factors help to explain this. First, firms in this industry have consistently pursued stabilization rather than rapid adjustment. As a result, the fundamental interests of firms and labor have coincided. Second, much of the adjustment burden has fallen on women workers, most of whom were not full-fledged members of the labor unions. Between 1965 and 1985, more than 72 percent of the female workers left the industry, as compared to 33 percent of male workers. Female workers thus accounted for more than 90 percent of overall labor adjustment. I have found only anecdotal evidence as to the fate of these workers, mostly indicating that they returned to their homes and did not go on the unemployment rolls. (In the economist's somewhat antiseptic phrasing, exit barriers for these workers were relatively low.) As a result, the core of the union's members, the full-time male workers, has not been greatly affected by the industry's decline. The fact that the majority of fired workers were women working part-time made the costs of adjustment—while no less important in human terms—less salient in terms of Japan's political realities. Third, the excellent performance of the overall Japanese economy during this period lowered the costs of labor adjustment. While not documented in this case study, the re-employment costs to labor in a growth economy are certainly lower than in a stagnant one. Overall rates of unemployment in this period in Japan were consistently lower than in other industrialized countries. With a few exceptions such as coal mining, textiles, and paper, most industries in Japan were still expanding through the 1970s. Industry officials often claim that fired textile workers were soon able to find employment elsewhere, particularly in the automobile industry. In fact, the cotton spinning industry has at times worried more about *shortages* of labor, than about oversupply. Fourth, the lack of labor strife reflects the nature of the labor union Zensen. Since its founding in 1946, this union has been known as a right-of-center union, willing to cooperate with management at the shop level. This union has consistently cooperated with management in their effort to streamline and rationalize the industry. Fifth and finally, the labor unions could not prevent rapid worker adjustment because they lacked political power outside of the individual enterprise unions.[82] The Japanese system of enter-

---

[82] Pempel and Tsunekawa 1979.

Table 4-2. Japan's cotton spinning industry, 1965–1985

Year	Number of firms		Number of spindles			Employment		
	Big Ten	Other firms	Total spindles	Big Ten (percent of total)	Other firms (percent of total)	Total	Male	Female
1965	9	116	9,447	4,544 (48.1)	4,903 (51.9)	107,727	19,089	88,638
1970	9	94	9,278	4,630 (49.9)	4,648 (50.1)	96,029	20,916	75,113
1975	9	84	9,713	4,623 (47.6)	5,090 (52.4)	70,975	20,193	50,782
1980	9	75	8,683	4,229 (48.7)	4,454 (51.3)	50,254	15,745	34,509
1985	9	62	7,888	3,810 (48.3)	4,078 (51.7)	38,255	13,030	25,225

SOURCES: *Bōseki Jijō Sankōsho* 1985, p. 67; *Bōseki Jijō Sankōsho* 1986, p. 63.

prise unions divides labor into separate unions for each firm. This system tends to encourage cooperation between labor and management at the shop-floor level, but at the same time, it makes industry-wide solidarity more difficult to achieve. The issue is not one of institutional access to the policy-making process: the textile unions have been represented and involved in every policy debate. But the influence of labor in Japan is undermined by its relative lack of organization at the industry level.

In comparison to labor, firms in this industry have not adjusted much at all. Chart 4-2 shows the overall effects of four decades of capacity regulation on the cotton spinning industry: the industry's overall capacity remained remarkably stable between 1955 and 1985.[83] Capacity in 1970 remained roughly equal to its 1955 level and by 1985 had declined by less than 20 percent. Thus, over the 30-year period in which the industry was considered "troubled," capacity declined by less than 1 percent a year. Given the industry's long-term economic turmoil and distress, this is a considerably slower rate of adjustment than market pressures would have dictated. Chart 4-2 also shows that the Big 10 and the smaller firms have decreased their capacity in a uniform fashion. Between 1965 and 1985, capacity held by the large firms declined by 16.1 percent, while capacity held by the smaller firms declined by 16.8 percent. This uniformity was the result of the industry's use of pro rata, across-the-board reductions in capacity. Finally, the chart shows that the capacity share of the smaller firms was practically the same in 1965 (51.9 percent of total spindles) as it was in 1985 (51.7 percent). Thus, even though the number of small firms declined rapidly after 1965, this consolidation of the industry did little to speed up the scrapping of excess capacity. These figures indicate that the small firms that remained in the industry were now larger in scale. Either these firms merged with other small firms or were able to buy up the spindles of the firms that went bankrupt. In either case, the industry did not take advantage of the consolidation of the industry to decrease its overall capacity.[84]

This lack of capacity reduction indicates that the pace of adjustment in this industry has been dictated not by market forces but rather by the industry's political efforts and the acquiescence of government policy makers. For the last 40 years, policy makers have provided the industry with

---

[83] This conclusion is at odds with the findings of many other analysts who tend to stress the flexibility of all sectors in the textile industry. See Dore 1986, passim, OECD 1983b, and Yamazawa 1988, pp. 409–421. Authors acknowledging the relatively slow pace of adjustment in Japanese textiles include Uryu 1990 and Yamawaki 1989. It should also be noted that the Japanese textile industry measures its capacity in terms of operable spindles rather than potential output. Because of the increase in efficiency of facilities and production processes over the years, capacity measured in terms of potential output may be even higher.

[84] Iwata 1984, p. 45. It is interesting to note that the industry's Herfindahl index has remained virtually unchanged: it was 364 in 1958, 357 in 1970, and 356 in 1980.

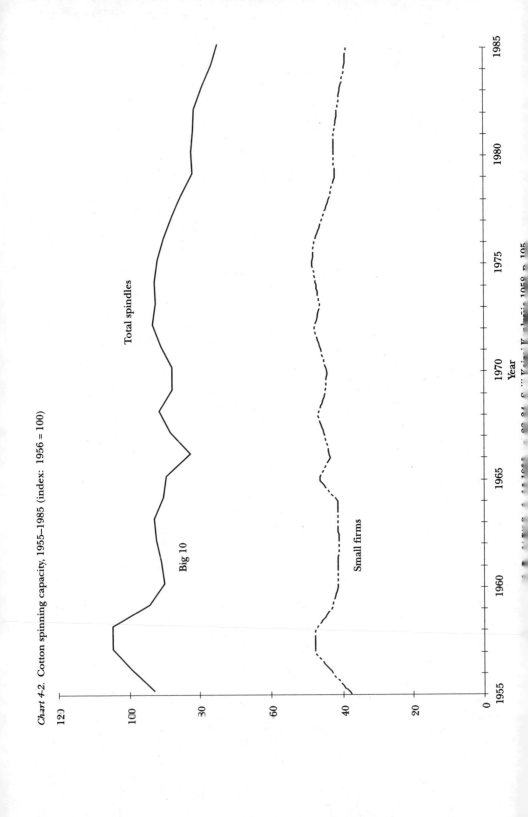

Chart 4-2. Cotton spinning capacity, 1955–1985 (index: 1956 = 100)

formal and informal policy tools through which the industry has been able to regulate competition. Although the government has not given the industry outright protection from imports, it has used a variety of other means to shield the industry from pressures for adjustment. Government support of the industry's implicit cartels has helped to alleviate market pressures and has passed the costs of adjustment on to others—to consumers in the form of higher prices and to the taxpayer to the extent that subsidies were given to the industry. MITI's policy actions, from *kankoku sōtan* in 1952 to the long series of textile industry bills, have slowed down the adjustment process.

The cotton spinning industry has thus received far more policy support than we would have expected of a low-tech industry that is not economically strategic. Nor was the industry particularly powerful in terms of political influence. Although firms in the industry cultivated ties to the ruling LDP, they were never core members of the LDP's support base nor a major source of political contributions. Furthermore, the textile labor unions were tied to the DSP, a small centrist opposition party. As the number of workers in the industry has declined over time, so too has the voting power of the industry.

According to the logic of the "developmental state," we should expect very little policy support for this sort of industry. The state should have tried to "preempt the costs of change" by anticipating decline and working to phase out the industry in favor of new ones.[85] And indeed, MITI's policy statements have been consistent with these goals; it continually claimed to be encouraging the industry to adjust to economic change. Furthermore, MITI has shown no interest in seeing this industry supported, either through regulation or through trade protection, and it has been reluctant to allow the industry to stabilize or preserve itself through anti-competitive schemes, as this only perpetuated inefficiency and risked creating a permanent political ward.

Yet, MITI's behavior has not followed its rhetoric. Japanese policy makers have found themselves heavily involved in propping up this industry. These policy choices have reflected the logic of industrial politics rather than the logic of economic development. First and foremost, the cotton spinning industry was effectively organized. Faced with economic decline compounded by the lack of attractive economic alternatives, firms had extremely high incentives to try to influence industrial policy choices. The industry's association, the JSA, has played a central role in helping the industry maximize its influence over the policy process. In particular, the association has been instrumental in mediating the conflicting interests of

[85] Tresize and Suzuki (1976, p. 801) argue that "the cotton textile and apparel industries perhaps can be considered as proxies for the low-productivity-low-wage manufacturing sectors that industry policy presumably should have discouraged in Japan."

the large and small firms. Second, although the cotton spinners have not been a core constituent of the ruling LDP, their high level of organization increased their political influence. The industry has consistently been able to mobilize its allies and use the threat of politicization and political controversy to increase pressures on the MITI bureaucrats. The political turmoil, for instance, surrounding the 1960 controversy over deregulation was a clear sign that politicians were able and willing to interfere in the policy process on behalf of the industry. The politicians have served as an important resource for the industry when it was not satisfied with its treatment by the bureaucracy.

Far from being impervious to outside influences, MITI has shown itself to be highly responsive to industry preferences and demands for regulation. When faced with strong pressures from the cotton spinners, MITI has chosen policies that limited political controversy over policies that would maximize economic development.

Japan's policy choices have for the most part reflected the agenda that the cotton spinning industry itself brought to the table. This was true even in the 1950s and 1960s—when MITI was at the height of its power. Far from being "responsively dependent" on MITI, then, firms and the industry association have been intimately involved in every phase of the formulation of industrial policy. It was the industry that sought government regulation to manage domestic competition. Over time, as the industry continued to decline, it sought progressively stronger policy measures— from controlling production and capacity growth to efforts to dispose of excess capacity to efforts to restructure the industry. The underlying goal of these measures has been the same: to stabilize the industry through management of the supply side. The cotton spinners have consistently sought to utilize government regulation as a means to avoid unfettered market competition and to alleviate pressures to adjust.

The fact that the industry has consistently pushed for stronger regulation than the government was prepared to give—at first a seeming paradox—implies that MITI regulation was in fact not designed to force the industry to adjust, but rather just the opposite. MITI itself now recognizes, at least in private, that its past regulatory policies have served to retard adjustment. An unpublished internal MITI report, written in 1988, argues that MITI policy failed in the sense that it did not encourage the reduction in capacity. On the contrary, MITI's regulation of the industry in fact encouraged firms to hold on to capacity, and thus served to prop up the least competitive firms.[86]

Although MITI has been basically responsive to the demands of the cotton spinners, it has not been a mere pawn of these interests. Policy makers

---

[86] Tsūshō Sangyōshō 1988, p. 14.

have not given the industry everything it has wanted. The industry has often pushed for stronger regulation or more generous compensation than policy makers were prepared to give. Bureaucratic actors have at times displayed a degree of autonomy, especially in the early 1960s when governmental actors, led by MITI, tried to remove regulatory support. And when faced with conflicting pressures from more than one industry under its jurisdiction, MITI has been a mediator. When the more competitive manmade fiber producers opposed policy that favored the cotton industry, MITI tended to side with them. In refusing to grant trade protection to the textile industry, government policy makers took into account the interests of the many Japanese industries dependent on access to the international economy.

Even when MITI bureaucrats rejected the more extreme demands of the cotton spinners, however, they were constrained by political pressures. In its attempt to remove regulation from the industry in 1960, MITI quickly succumbed to political pressures to reinstate that regulation. When the industry was forced to accept export restraints beginning in the 1950s, the government offered compensation. And although policy makers did not grant import protection to the industry, bureaucrats allowed it informal protection through voluntary restraint agreements with its competitors in Asia.

THE COAL MINING INDUSTRY

The coal mining industry in Japan is a second example of a Type IV industry. The industry at its height was highly fragmented, consisting of over 1,000 mining concerns; its labor force at its peak in 1957 was nearly 400,000 workers.[87]

The coal mining industry faced an unmistakable and irresistible loss of competitiveness early in the postwar period. The main problem was that petroleum, a substitute resource, was cheaper, more plentiful, and more efficient. The development of foreign sources of coal, especially steel-grade coking coal, led to rising imports from the mid-1960s onwards. In addition, the mining industry was saddled with mounting operating costs, rising labor costs and, by the 1970s, growing concerns over pollution. Given these negative economic forces, the coal mining industry faced enormous pressures to adjust.

What is surprising is the extent to which the industry was able to *avoid* adjustment for so long. As Hayden Lesbirel puts it, the central question

---

[87] The industry's 3-digit JSIC number is 111. The main sources for this supplementary case study are Samuels 1986, Lesbirel 1988 and 1991, and Kume 1993.

Table 4-3. The coal mining industry, 1954–1986

Year	Production	Imports	Exports	Mines	Labor
1954	43,223	3,167	291	1,049	321,315
1957	55,734	6,119	64	1,070	340,904
1960	57,459	8,704	14	885	308,433
1963	54,885	11,903	67	645	197,361
1966	56,032	20,796	30	548	149,685
1969	46,389	43,260	21	391	107,718
1972	28,083	50,506	8	221	56,454
1975	18,597	62,339	33	157	37,756
1978	19,285	52,858	56	144	36,442
1981	18,928	78,893	20	154	30,552
1986	15,200	89,463	0	165	26,653

SOURCES: *Historical Statistics of Japan*, 1987, p. 8; Japan Fair Trade Commission 1976 and 1987; *Enerugi Tokei*, 1983, pp. 8–127; *Yearbook of Production, Supply and Demand of Petroleum, Coal and Coke*, 1992, pp. 128, 210–211.

in this case is "why policy did not reflect market forces and terminate [coal mining] more quickly."[88] As shown in Table 4-3, the industry's demise was delayed and spread out over a period of thirty years. For the first fifteen years after the onset of decline in the late 1950s, domestic coal production remained remarkably stable with output hovering around the 55,000-ton-per-year level. In spite of steadily growing coal imports, it was not until the first half of the 1970s that domestic output began to decline dramatically. Since 1975, however, output has again held relatively constant, albeit at the much lower level of 15,000 to 20,000 tons per year.

The story of coal is a political one. The combination of industry pressures and strong political backing forced MITI officials to adopt a series of policy measures that allowed the industry to avoid the most extreme adjustment pressures. Like the cotton spinning case, the coal mining industry has benefited from long-term and pervasive government policy support that has retarded, rather than promoted, economic adjustment.

The coal industry in Japan, like cotton spinning, is bifurcated into large and small firms. There are a handful of relatively large firms that have made concerted efforts to exit the industry. These large firms, led by Mitsui Mining, Mitsubishi, and Sumitomo Coal Mining, were all members of one of Japan's industrial conglomerates, the *keiretsu*. These firms also enjoyed ties to many of the smaller coal mining firms. The large firms were quick to recognize the industry's bleak future outlook and by

[88] Lesbirel 1991, p. 1080.

the 1960s were already trying to exit the industry. They demonstrated at least some ability to adjust through diversification into non-coal-related operations, and by investing in developing overseas coal mining operations.[89]

The vast majority of firms in the industry, however, were small; many of these were independent, owner-operated mines. These firms found it very difficult to adjust economically. They lacked the resources to move toward more capital-intensive production processes and so had no choice but to decrease costs by rationalizing their work forces. The option of diversification or overseas investment was also closed to the small firms. At best, the small firms could hope to stay alive only by merging with other firms. More likely, these firms faced imminent bankruptcy. Not surprisingly, these small firms followed the same route taken by the cotton spinners—political action—in order to alleviate economic pressures or to force private costs into the public realm.

The labor force in the coal mining industry also faced extremely high adjustment costs. First, the small size of most firms meant that retraining or reabsorbing labor within the firm was impossible. Second, the industry was heavily concentrated in two regions of the country that were already underdeveloped—Kyushu and Hokkaido. The lack of alternative employment opportunities in these regions made labor adjustment that much more painful. Third, unlike the cotton spinning industry, in which females and part-time workers accounted for the bulk of the labor force, labor in the coal mining industry has been predominantly male and full time.[90] It is not surprising that labor also took the route of protest and politics to try to alleviate their adjustment burdens.

The coal industry's initial response to postwar market downturns was remarkably similar to the cotton spinning case. The industry's first recession came in 1953 during the general recession following the end of the Korean War. It responded to depressed prices by entering into industry-wide efforts to reduce production relative to existing demand. However, the industry association, the Japan Coal Association (Nihon Sekitan Kyōkai), was unable to prevent cheating by member firms. Because many small firms had to continue to sell coal in order to survive, the industry's production agreements were doomed to fail. The industry quickly realized that its eco-

[89] As early as 1954, according to Samuels (1986, pp. 107, 127) the large firms were attempting to draw down their investments in coal. Over time, these large firms have invested in areas such as cement, real estate, tourism, and amusement parks. Later, when the government and industry discussed capacity reduction targets for the industry as a whole, these firms consistently overshot their targets. Thus, it was the private sector, not the state, that was anticipating decline.

[90] In addition, the coal miners were relatively old, and so the costs of retraining and finding new employment were relatively high (Lesbirel 1991, p. 1085; Kume 1993, p. 165).

nomic problems were structural and that political solutions were required.[91]

By 1953 it was becoming clear to public and private industry officials alike that coal did not make much sense in terms of Japan's long-term developmental goals. All had come to the conclusion that petroleum was a better energy source to fuel Japan's industrialization. Many manufacturing industries and the electric power producers recognized that petroleum was a more cost effective and efficient energy resource and that imported oil was cheap and plentiful. These industries openly advocated policies to spur the switch to petroleum. By the mid-1960s petroleum had clearly demonstrated its cost advantages over coal, and the signs of coal's loss of competitiveness had become unmistakable.

Government policy toward coal can best be described as inconsistent. Immediately after the war the government had designated and supported coal mining as a "priority industry" because of its importance as a basic energy resource for a variety of other industries. Yet by the late 1950s MITI had switched to the promotion of petroleum and heavy oil as the keys to future industrial growth. MITI policy thus shifted to support for rationalizing and downsizing the coal industry. Even after the oil crisis raised concerns about Japan's energy dependence, MITI did very little to try to revive the industry. Given coal mining's clear lack of competitiveness vis-à-vis petroleum, there was little that could have been done to make the industry competitive again. Domestic coal was simply too inefficient and too costly to serve as Japan's main industrial energy source. With a clearly uncompetitive industry on its hands, MITI had strong incentives to insure that the industry adjust rapidly, lest it become a drain on the overall economy.

Of course, the coal mining industry was not about to exit as quietly as policy makers hoped. Like the cotton spinners, the coal mining firms pushed for public policies to stabilize competition and retard the adjustment process. They were also unwilling to pay the full costs of economic adjustment. The owners of both the large and small coal mining firms believed that the costs of exit should be borne by the public treasury, rather than by the firms themselves, and demanded that "the state purchase the mines, urging MITI to adopt a mine-scrapping policy."[92]

The coal mining firms were able to use their strong political influence, especially with the conservative party politicians, to put these demands

---

[91] Samuels 1986, pp. 104–106. Samuels reports that the rift between small and large firms led the former to break away from the nationwide association and set up their own regional associations—the Nihon Sekitan Kōgyō Rengōkai. Like the cotton spinning industry, industry-wide efforts to limit production in order to stabilize markets predated World War II. See Samuels 1986, pp. 75–81.

[92] Samuels 1986, p. 108.

into effect. Early in the postwar period these firms were strong financial backers of the conservative parties. And because coal was regionally concentrated, financial backing was particularly important for a relatively small number of Dietmen, especially from Kyushu. These politicians were very active in their support of the coal industry and dominated the LDP's Special Coal Policy Committee in PARC, which was created in the early 1960s to protect the interests of the coal mining industry.[93]

The coal industry's influence over policy makers was also enhanced by the voice of the labor unions. Tanrō (Federated Coal Miners Union), a Sōhyō-affiliated union, was associated mainly with the JSP and to a lesser extent with the Democratic Socialist Party and the Japan Communist Party. But it was the series of highly visible miner's strikes during the 1950s that raised the plight of the coal miners to a pressing social and political problem. The struggle between the firms and their miners proved to be the most contentious episode of labor relations in Japan's postwar history. Beginning in 1952, the coal mining labor unions were involved in a series of extremely confrontational labor disputes, usually concerning attempts by the firms to fire their excess workers. The most antagonistic of these strikes occurred in 1959 at Mitsui's Miike mine. Although Tanrō was eventually forced to back down from its demands, the enormous political and social controversy it stirred made government policy makers highly sensitive to these demands. As Samuels puts it, from the time of Miike onward, "unemployed miners were a social problem that could not be ignored."[94]

After the Miike strike, labor and management came to the slow realization that they shared a common interest in trying to save their industry. Slowly, they became more cooperative in their efforts to apply pressure on politicians and policy makers. Soon after the collapse of the Miike strike, for instance, the coal unions took their case directly to Tokyo, where they demonstrated in front of the Diet building and the Prime Minister's residence. Their efforts were joined by the strong lobbying of the mine owners as well.[95]

The political influence of the industry made MITI sympathetic to the industry's demands. In particular, the experience of the socially disruptive and highly politicized Miike strikes made government policy makers reluctant to force the industry to adjust too rapidly. Over the next 30 years the coal industry lobbied for and attained coal policies that slowed down the adjustment process, subsidized existing coal production, and passed the costs of adjustment onto others—the petroleum industry, the coal-consuming industries, and the Japanese taxpayer.

[93] Lesbirel 1991, p. 1089.
[94] Samuels 1986, p. 108.
[95] Kume 1993, p. 168.

Government programs dealing with the labor force helped to alleviate some of the adjustment costs borne by labor. These programs provided subsidies to firms that retrain their workers and to firms that hired unemployed coal miners. Although these subsidies may have marginally helped alleviate labor's adjustment burden, organized labor was not able to avoid massive layoffs. In the five years following the Miike strike the industry's labor force was cut by more than one-half. By 1972 the labor force was only one-sixth of its peak 1957 size.

The 1954 Coal Mining Rationalization Special Measures—Japan's first postwar industry-specific law—fulfilled the industry's desire to stabilize competition and slow down the adjustment process. It called for a 20 percent reduction in production, in essence ratifying the industry's earlier attempts to manage the supply side through their informal cartel. Future production and price cartels were explicitly exempted from the Anti-Monopoly Law. Also, the new law established a public agency "to purchase inefficient mines and to restrict the opening of new ones," transferring the costs of exit from the private realm to the public treasury.[96]

The essential features of the 1954 law were extended in what became known as the "Coal Programs." The first of these government programs was established in 1962; since then these programs have been extended a total of eight times.[97] In addition to stabilizing competition in the industry, these programs have helped keep the industry afloat through massive financial subsidies and measures to stabilize domestic demand.

One element of the coal programs has been the taxing of the petroleum refining industry to help subsidize the domestic coal industry. In 1955 the government instituted an import tax on heavy crude oil and redistributed these funds to the coal industry—to help defray the costs of closing mines, to spur rationalization of industry, to improve production systems, and to develop coal-related-technologies.[98] Thus, the petroleum refining industry has been forced to help subsidize and stabilize its main competitor.

Furthermore, the coal programs stabilized demand for coal by requiring coal-consuming industries to purchase domestically produced coal, of-

---

[96] Samuels 1986, p. 109. The only significant industry demand that was not met was their demand for import restrictions to block the inflow of foreign petroleum and coal. Given that most industries already preferred cheap petroleum over expensive domestic coal, it is not surprising that this demand was rejected.

[97] The rationale for these programs was definitely political. According to Samuels (1986, p. 114), the first of these coal programs was a response to the social and political unrest stemming from the 1959 Miike strike: "Under great pressure the cabinet responded by forming the first coal industry task force (Sekitan Kōgyō Chōsadan) to develop a policy response to rationalization and unemployment. That response is now known as the First Coal Program."

[98] Lesbirel 1991, p. 1081. Prior to 1967 the import taxes went through the General Account Budget; subsequently the government set up what were known as the "Special Coal Accounts." Between 1968 and 1983 between 83 and 92 percent of petroleum import taxes were channeled to the coal industry (Lesbirel 1988, p. 15).

ten at prices higher than international ones. The steel industry and the electric power industry were the two main industries that helped stabilize demand for the coal industry. Up through the early 1970s both were evidently willing to help subsidize the coal industry: in 1968, for instance, steel and electric power firms accounted for more than 70 percent of the 50-million-ton domestic production target called for by the coal program.[99]

These industries have grown increasingly unwilling to help prop up domestic coal, however. In fact, it was their growing opposition that eventually led to coal's demise. First, the steel industry in the late 1960s began to import massive quantities of coking coal to replace less efficient and more costly domestic sources. The steel industry, concerned with its international competitiveness and facing recession periods of its own, found itself with little choice but to switch to more economic sources of energy. As shown in Table 4-3, during the 1960s, coal imports increased by nearly five times. Approximately 90 percent of this was accounted for by the steel industry. Second, the electric power industry also abandoned coal in the late 1960s by switching to cheaper and cleaner oil imports. In the span of only five years, between 1967 and 1971, the electric power industry cut its consumption of domestic coal by nearly 50 percent. By the early 1970s both steel and electric power were openly resisting further coal purchases.[100]

MITI thus found itself caught between the interests of three politically powerful industries—coal, steel, and electric power. It showed itself to be highly responsive to the policy demands advanced by the coal miners, yet at the same time it had to consider the interests of the consuming industries. This situation served as a brake on how far MITI was willing to grant coal's demands for subsidization. The opposition from the steel and electric power industries was a major factor in the 1973 decision to reduce domestic production targets to a more realistic 20 million tons per year. Yet even then, MITI found that it could not abandon the coal mining industry. Not until the late 1980s did the vehement opposition of electric power and steel result in the final decision to pull the plug on the coal industry.

If one sees Japan as a "developmental state," it is hard to explain why the government would remain so heavily involved in propping up a clearly uncompetitive industry for such a long period of time. One might argue that MITI was concerned about energy self-sufficiency, and that this concern

[99] Samuels 1986, pp. 114–115; Lesbirel 1988, pp. 14–15. According to Lesbirel (1991, p. 1087), in the mid-1980s these two industries were still providing some 27 percent of the total financial assistance flowing to the coal industry.

[100] In fact, as early as the Korean war, coal producing and coal consuming sectors clashed over price and quantity agreements (Samuels 1986, p. 105). Consumption by the electric power industry went from 26.2 million tons in 1968 to just 13.9 million tons in 1971 (*Enerugi Tokei*, 1976, pp. 248–251). The shift from coal to oil is also noted in Samuels 1986, pp. 113, 133–134.

caused it to support the coal industry. But this was not a major motivation in the 1950s and 1960s when government policy clearly favored imported petroleum over domestic coal. It was only in the aftermath of the oil shocks, when one might have expected the developmental state to want to hold on to domestic coal, that MITI finally began to push for more rapid adjustment.

The decades of continuous public policy support for coal mining were clearly the result of industrial politics. Given the strong political ties enjoyed by the firms in the industry and the strong voice of labor, policy makers were compelled to capitulate to the industry's political demands. As Samuels sums up, "the political benefits of providing unlimited state subsidies to coal producers seemed always to outweigh the staggering economic costs."[101]

---

[101] Samuels 1986, p. 134.

Marginalized Industries:
Steel Minimills and Paper (Type III)

Type III industries are similar to industries such as cotton spinning and coal mining in that firms tend to be small, which means that the majority of firms probably lack access to resources needed to diversify or to pursue other economic adjustment options, such as overseas investment. Faced with a choice of adjustment through exit versus stabilization via politics, these firms are likely to favor the latter. On the other hand, Type III industries have a relatively small labor force, which suggests that the problems of adjusting labor will be less central to the outcome. More important, the political influence of this industry is likely to be lower than that of Type IV industries as it will not have the voting power of a large labor force. Although industry actors may have incentives to pursue political options, their lack of political power means that they may have difficulty in achieving them.

The electric furnace steel industry is an example of a Type III industry. In this industry, steel makers use small-scale electric furnaces to produce regular steel products (excluding specialty steels) and thus have come to be called "minimills." All of the firms in this industry are small and approximately of equal size. The industry's labor force at its peak in 1964 was about 73,000 workers.[1]

---

[1] Japan's industrial classification system lumps together minimills with open-hearth steelmakers (JSIC #3133). The latter declined in Japan beginning in the late 1950s. The industry's Herfindahl-index number was 294 in 1964 and declined to 209 in 1975 (Japan Fair Trade Commission 1987, p. 96). Because of the public policy controversy it engendered, the minimill case in Japan has received more coverage than many other industries (Yamamura 1982; Peck et al. 1987; Noble 1988 and 1989; Uriu 1988; and Yonekura 1994).

The minimill industry in Japan is often described as a typical example of an excessively competitive industry, prone to cutthroat competition, price wars, and wildly fluctuating prices. The industry's competitive nature is due to its low barriers to market entry. Minimills are relatively inexpensive to startup in comparison to an integrated steel firm. The minimills are essentially scrap recyclers, using electricity to melt steel scrap in order to produce final products. The minimills are thus able to bypass the first stages of the integrated process and so do not require massive capital facilities such as coke ovens, blast furnaces, and basic oxygen furnaces. Also, electric furnace technology requires much smaller furnaces than its integrated counterpart. The minimum efficient scale for electric furnaces can be as low as 100,000 tons of hot metal per year (in comparison to 1.5 million tons per year for a blast furnace).[2] As a result, capital costs for a minimill are 75 percent lower than for an integrated plant. In addition, Japanese minimills require only about half the man-hours to produce a ton of steel that their integrated counterparts need. Finally, minimills have traditionally limited their output to a narrow range of simple, standardized products. By far the most important minimill product is bar steel, used by the construction industry to reinforce concrete. As bar steel does not require high levels of quality, product differentiation is difficult. Competition is thus based mainly on price, and users can acquire products easily from a large number of producers and steel traders.[3]

Demand for minimill goods is highly cyclical in nature. Between 1970 and 1990 the industry went through three major cycles of boom and bust, each tied to swings in domestic construction demand (see Chart 5-1). First, the industry underwent a recession between 1970 and 1972 that was followed by a brief boom caused by the massive public-works spending of the Tanaka administration. Second, the industry experienced a five-year slump following the first oil crisis; this recession was followed by a period of moderate recovery resulting from the Fukuda administration's reflationary policies in the late 1970s. Third, the minimills had to cope with depressed prices throughout much of the 1980s. This third phase ended, at least temporarily, with the boost in domestic spending stemming from the 1987 Maekawa Report.

[2] Findlay 1988. In Japan in 1980 40 of the industry's 57 plants had a capacity of under 400,000 tons per year, and only three firms had a total capacity of over 1 million tons per year. In contrast, Japan's integrated steel producers average more than 7 million tons per year (Barnett and Crandall 1986, p. 3). These figures are remarkably similar to those for the U.S. minimill industry. For capital and operating cost comparisons, see Brown 1980, p. 8, Barnett and Crandall 1986, passim, and Millan 1980, p. 61.

[3] Okamoto 1984. Small bars are often referred to as "market goods" (*shikyō hinshu*), since they follow market supply and demand swings so closely. In 1985 bar steel accounted for 62 percent of the industry's output.

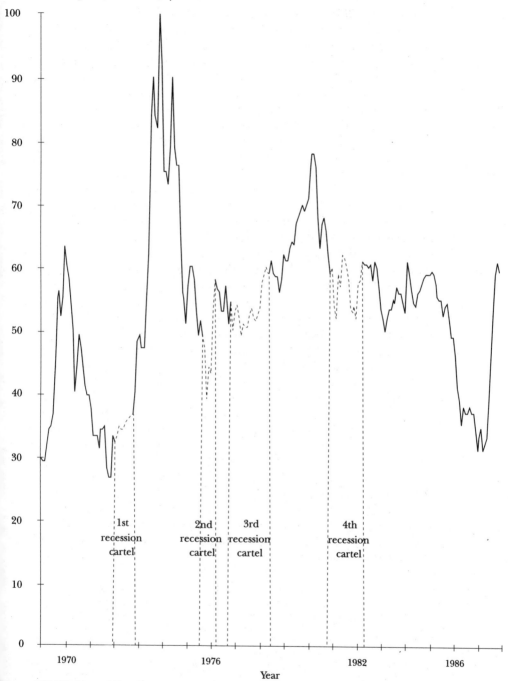

art 5-1. Bar steel prices, 1969–1988, by month

100
90
80
70
60
50
40
30
20

1st
recession
cartel

2nd
recession
cartel

3rd
recession
cartel

4th
recession
cartel

10
0

1970   1976   1982   1986

Year

ources: Tekkō Nenkan and *Futsūkō Denro,* various issues.
Jote: Bar steel prices are for 19 mm bar (SD 30), Tokyo market, monthly lows, current prices.

During periods of depressed demand the minimills faced the same dilemma that the cotton spinners had to deal with: should they let the market operate to eventually reduce excess production and capacity, or should they utilize public policy to try to manage competition in the domestic market? The industry as a whole saw the same drawbacks to market-driven change as the cotton spinners did: it would entail unacceptable costs in terms of depressed prices and financial losses. Of particular concern were the smallest and most vulnerable firms, most of which operated only a single plant and were completely dependent on bar steel production. Industry actors recognized that these firms, rather than exiting, would try to hang on by maintaining operating rates just high enough to cover variable costs.[4] Furthermore, like the small cotton spinners, these firms could persist for a considerable length of time, and if they ever exited it would only be after a prolonged and serious recession. In the meantime, overproduction by small firms would continue to depress prices and drive down profits for all involved.

Rather than leaving its fate to the unregulated market, the minimill industry turned to the same mechanism that the cotton spinners had used: industry-wide, collective efforts to stabilize supply-side conditions. Throughout the 1970s and into the 1980s, the industry lobbied for cartel solutions to control excess production in the short term and excess capacity in the longer term. These organizational efforts were pushed most strongly by a group of minimills that became known as the industry "insiders." At the beginning of the 1970s the insiders were relatively large, were well supported financially through their ties to the trading companies or steel majors, and were relatively, but not overwhelmingly, competitive. It is important to note that these firms sought cooperative cutbacks, not because they wanted the industry to shrink, rather because they were motivated by the same goal as that of the cotton spinners (indeed, of any cartel arrangement), the collective benefits of stabilized selling prices and stabilized profits.

Like the cotton spinners, the minimills had to worry about the enforcement of industry-wide agreements that involved large numbers of firms. One problem was that many of the small firms felt that they could not afford to cut back their production and thus were prone to cheat on industry-wide cartels. Another problem was that the minimills accounted for only about two-thirds of bar steel production: the five major integrated steel makers accounted for about 12 percent of the market, while some 200 smaller bar steel producers accounted for about 19 percent of total production.

[4] See, for instance, Bethlehem Steel's report (1983, p. 11) on government policy toward the Japanese steel industry. Of the 50 minimills in Japan in 1980, only six possessed more than one plant—the rest operated single, stand-alone plants. See table in Uriu (1988, p. 7).

By far the most intractable obstacle to a collective solution in the mini-mill case, however, was the existence of about ten firms known as the industry "outsiders." These firms, which in 1980 accounted for 25 percent of the industry's capacity, preferred free competition over cooperation. They were more competitive than the insiders and had more confidence that they could prosper without stabilization efforts. They were not only unwilling to *cut* production, they wanted to *increase* production at the expense of firms cooperating with the cartel.

The industry insiders recognized the need to coerce the mavericks into cooperating. This was the goal that the insiders, with the support of MITI, pursued throughout the 1970s.

The 1970s: The Industry Seeks Cartelization

The industry's first significant recession period began in 1970. The minimills, which up until that time had enjoyed twenty years of relatively stable growth, were faced with depressed prices that lasted for about three years. Chart 5-1 shows that between early 1970 and late 1971 bar prices fell by more than half, from a high of ¥63,000 per ton to below ¥27,000.

The industry's initial reaction was to seek some sort of coordinated, political solution to stabilize the industry. In October 1971 the industry requested that MITI intervene with the same administrative guidance tool that it had used for the cotton spinners: *kankoku sōtan*, recommendations to curtail operations.

Given the daunting obstacles to successful collective action, it is somewhat surprising that the minimills even attempted collective solutions. The fact that the industry actually achieved this goal for much of the 1970s was due to the industry's political organization and leadership and to the government's willingness to help the industry enforce these efforts. The industry insiders were strong leaders, tirelessly lobbying and persuading their fellow firms to reach and then comply with industry-wide agreements. The industry's association, the Electric Furnace Regular Steel Association (Futsūkō Denkiro Kōgyōkai), was also important in overcoming organizational obstacles.[5] The Electric Furnace Association in the 1970s was led by the insider firms that favored collective solutions. The association provided a forum for bargaining, allowing member firms to convene to exchange information, hammer out agreements,

[5] The association, which represents all non-integrated regular steel producers, was created in 1966 as Heidenro Futsūkōgyō (Open Hearth and Electric Furnace Regular Steel Association). Its name was changed in 1978, since the last of Japan's open hearths had been shut down the year before. The association is affiliated with Japan's most influential steel organization, the Tekkō Renmei, an organization dominated by the integrated majors.

and most significantly, communicate interests, intentions, and commitments. Regularized contact in an institutional setting assured that interactions would be iterative, and that firms' activities would be watched and monitored by others, a function vital for the enforcement of agreements.

It soon became clear, however, that the enforcement of industry-wide agreements was beyond the association's means. Besides regularized contact and informal pressures, it had few tools to deter cheating and to hold firms to their commitments. The association by itself lacked the private enforcement powers even to prevent cheating among the insiders, let alone rein in the determined outsiders. If collective action was to be feasible, a retaliatory capability far beyond the association's means was essential. The minimills would have to appeal to a higher authority for help in enforcing their agreements. That authority was MITI.

MITI officials had no compelling reasons to give regulatory support to the minimill industry. Most policy makers believed the minimills had little strategic importance for Japan's industrial development and disregarded the industry's own argument that it was strategic because Japan needed to retain the ability to recycle scrap.[6] And the minimills, given the small size of their labor force and the fact that they were spread throughout the country, had even less political clout than the cotton spinning industry did.

Non-strategic, marginal industries such as the minimills are logical candidates for "industrial euthanasia." We should expect a "developmental state" to try to downsize the industry and transfer its resources to more productive uses. At the very least, the bureaucracy, being autonomous from particularistic pressures, should be able to resist industry calls for protection and subsidization, thereby leaving the industry to its market fate.

MITI also had organizational reasons to avoid becoming too involved in propping up the minimill industry. First, *kankoku sōtan* was the same policy tool that MITI had used in 1965 which had led to the politically embarrassing Sumitomo Metals Incident. That incident occurred during the 1965 recession when the integrated steel firms, faced with a market downturn, tried to cut production by 10 percent, and appealed to MITI to help enforce these cutbacks through its administrative guidance powers. Sumitomo Metals was originally a party to this implicit cartel but became dissatisfied when the industry tried to extend the curtailments. Sumitomo refused to abide by the new agreement. With the prodding of the other steel majors, MITI cracked down, using its powers under the Foreign Exchange and Control Law to threaten to limit Sumitomo's im-

[6] The argument the industry put forward referred to Japan's experience before World War II when the U.S. embargo of scrap iron threatened the Japanese economy. I find no evidence that policy makers ever took this argument seriously.

ports of coking coal.[7] MITI came under heavy criticism for its actions, particularly from the FTC, and the public furor over what was deemed inappropriate behavior was a political embarrassment that made MITI more cautious than usual. By 1970, *kankoku sōtan* had become politically controversial, and MITI was willing to use this policy tool only in extreme situations.

MITI's experience with the steel industry, as well as its long struggles to help the cotton spinners try to enforce their industry-wide production curtailments, had led it to realize that administrative guidance is effective only when the industry wants to be guided. That is, unless MITI actions are consonant with a clear consensus within the industry, there is a danger of being embroiled in politically controversial situations where the risk of policy failure is high. MITI's apprehensions were compounded in the case of the minimill industry, which had already earned a reputation as uncooperative and difficult to control.[8]

MITI also worried about the growing activism of Japan's FTC. During the late 1960s the FTC had begun to assert itself in a number of confrontations with MITI, in the Sumitomo Incident, for instance, or in its opposition to the Yawata-Fuji merger in 1969. In addition, the FTC had mounted a growing number of challenges to the use of recession cartels in the early 1970s, including a key challenge to a cartel created in 1972 by the synthetic fiber firms in the wake of the Textile Wrangle. The FTC chairman, Tanimura, had already made clear his opposition to *kankoku sōtan* on the grounds that it was not consistent with a free economy. Tanimura argued that if something had to be done, a legally recognized recession cartel was preferable.

For these reasons the consensus within MITI, which included Heavy Industries Bureau Director Yajima, favored a formal recession cartel over administrative guidance. Yajima argued to the minimills that the cartel, since it would allow limitations on production, was the effective equivalent of *kankoku sōtan*.[9] From MITI's point of view, the cartel solution would allow the industry to regain stability while at the same time avoiding another confrontation with the FTC.

The industry leadership eventually abandoned its quest for *kankoku sōtan* and accepted the cartel. In fact, the minimills had realized from the beginning that their request for *kankoku sōtan* would likely be rejected since the integrated majors had a year earlier made the same request, only to be con-

---

[7] See Johnson 1982 and Upham 1986, pp. 281–285. Sumitomo Metals backed down in January 1966. This episode is often cited as an example of MITI's ability to control industries under its jurisdiction, but it is important to remember that it was the steel industry that initiated the production curtailments and that pressured MITI to rein in the outsider, Sumitomo.

[8] *Tekkō Jukyū no Ugoki*, Jan. 1972, p. 19; *Nihon Keizai Shimbun*, Nov. 17, 1971.

[9] *Nihon Keizai Shimbun*, Nov. 17, 1971.

vinced by MITI to accept a recession cartel. The insiders were basically content with this. Although they preferred administrative guidance, which they thought would be more effective, the cartel did give the minimills what they sought: a degree of control over production in order to prop up sagging prices and profits. The industry's application to the FTC for the recession cartel, the first in its history, was approved in February 1972.[10]

This first cartel initially had few problems with the outsider firms. Although up to 17 firms originally refused to join, all of these were small. Still, the industry leadership felt that it had to maintain industry-wide unity. The fear was that, since not all members were happy with the cartel, even the existence of very small outsiders might destroy the agreement. By April 1972, after six months of strenuous lobbying, 10 of the 17 had agreed to enter, and the cartel covered 94.4 percent of minimill capacity.[11]

The cartel was only marginally effective in stabilizing prices, which rose from ¥33,000 per ton at the start of the cartel to ¥40,000 per ton at its end. The industry's fortunes began to improve dramatically, however, thanks to the massive increase in public expenditures associated with Prime Minister Tanaka's ambitious Plan to Rebuild the Japanese Archipelago (Rettō Kaizō Keikaku). This sudden infusion of public finance caused a rapid rise in domestic demand for minimill products. Bar steel prices exploded in 1973: from ¥40,000 at the end of 1972, prices doubled in the first half of 1973, reaching their all-time high in December at ¥100,000 per ton (see Chart 5-1). Suddenly, the future of the industry was looking extremely bright. In mid-1973, at the height of the minimill boom, MITI was confidently predicting that bar steel demand would double in the five years between 1972 and 1977 from 8.3 to 16.2 million tons. MITI therefore calculated that minimill capacity would have to increase by more than a million tons per year over that period.[12] The minimills rushed to increase their capacity. Between 1973 and 1976 the industry began an "investment war" (*tōshi gassen*)

---

[10] The cartel was chaired by Uchinami Yoshitomo, president of Otani Jukogyo, an affiliate of Nippon Steel. The cartel was run by a steering committee composed of the presidents of five insider minimills. Production limits were determined by a cartel steering committee, based on production rates over the previous two years. The cartel was extended in October 1971 to run until the end of the year.

By 1972, therefore, Japan's entire steel industry had been allowed official cartels: the six integrated majors and the six specialty steel makers (both in 1971), the nine structural alloy producers (in 1972), and the minimills. All together, 97 percent of Japan's crude steel production was cartelized (*Nihon Keizai Shimbun*, July 7, 1972).

[11] Chairman Uchinami was given credit for successfully lobbying and persuading all significant minimills to participate (*Nihon Keizai Shimbun*, July 7, 1972). This first cartel, however, did run into problems with uncooperative firms, foreshadowing later, more serious problems. As the recession wore on, the cartel organizers tried to lower the total output level by a further 10 percent in May 1972. At that point Tokyo Seitetsu, led by Taro Iketani, and Tosa Denki Seikojo, headed by Iketani's son, Masanari, broke ranks and remained outside of the cartel for the remainder of its duration. This was the first indication of the Iketani family adopting the role of industry outsider.

[12] Tsūshō Sangyōshō, Kiso Sangyō Kyoku 1973, pp. 234–237.

in which it increased total capacity by nearly one-third. This investment boom would later have deleterious effects, as most of the new capacity came on line just as the industry entered its most serious recession.[13]

This boom period for the minimills disappeared as quickly as it had arrived. By 1975 the temporary and artificial period of optimism was at an end. The minimills were hit by rising costs for its two main inputs, scrap and electricity. Of greater concern for the industry was a tremendous drop in domestic demand for bar steel in 1974. Falling domestic demand, especially in the construction and housing sectors, led to a strikingly rapid fall in bar steel prices. From ¥100,000 per ton at the end of 1973, bar prices plunged to ¥55,000 at the end of 1974 before bottoming out at ¥39,000 in late 1975. With prices falling by over 60 percent in less than two years, the industry's profit picture also darkened: nearly all firms showed negative profits between 1975 and 1977, with the larger firms averaging more than ¥2 billion in losses for the three-year period. With its financial conditions in desperate straits, the industry could not avoid a spate of plant closings and bankruptcies.

The industry's response to this second crisis was the same as its reaction to the first: collective efforts to hold production to "reasonable" levels in order to control the excessive production that was driving prices downward. Beginning in late 1974 the industry insiders began to unilaterally cut back on production. When it became clear that other firms were not following suit, these firms attempted to persuade the rest of the industry of the need for stabilization measures. Lacking any mechanism to enforce production curtailments, however, these efforts were doomed to fail. The insiders soon were lobbying for the same external enforcement mechanisms that they had used before—from mid-1975 until the end of 1978, the industry petitioned for and received permission to form recession cartels.

Two men were the driving force behind the industry's efforts to organize collective stabilization: Uchinami Yoshitomo, president of Otani Jukogyo and the head of the industry association, and Yasuda Yasujiro, president of Toshin Seiko. They argued strenuously that the minimills should take advantage of the legally permitted "shelter" in times of difficulty, the recession cartel. The acknowledged goal of the cartel was to cut production far enough so that bar steel prices would recover to the industry's "break-even level" of ¥60,000 to ¥65,000 per ton.[14]

---

[13] The trading companies and integrated majors provided much of the capital to fund this increase in capacity. Work on 23 new plants totaling 3.8 million tons of capacity was begun in this boom period. All of this capacity came on line between 1974 and 1976, the industry's low point. See Okamoto 1984 and Heidenro Kihon Mondai Kenkyūkai 1977.

[14] The industry's "break-even line" (*saisan sen*) was widely reported in the press and industry journals. See, for example, *Nihon Keizai Shimbun*, Aug. 25, 1975, and Mar. 5, 1977. Costs at that point were estimated to be ¥60,000 to ¥62,000 per ton (*Jiyū Minshu*, Aug. 1978). These figures are most likely applicable to the average insider firm—the more competitive outsiders probably had lower "break-even levels."

This time around, however, a number of minimills refused to cooperate. In the end 13 bar-producing firms, led by Japan's largest, Tosa Denki Seikojo, refused to join the cartel. The other 12 minimills were small single-plant firms, all but two of which had no ties either to the majors or to the trading companies. Despite these differences, all 13 firms felt they could compete effectively without stabilization efforts.

These outsiders were led by the young president of Tosa Denki Seikojo, Iketani Masanari, who was to become the central figure in the minimill story. In 1970 at the age of 25, Iketani had been sent by his father, then president of Tokyo Seitetsu, to become Tosa Denki's president. By 1975 the junior Iketani had transformed Tosa Denki into Japan's largest bar steel producer. Tosa Denki and Tokyo Seitetsu merged in December 1975, soon after the cartel was formed, with the junior Iketani becoming president. He and Tokyo Seitetsu then embarked on a decade-long confrontation with the insider minimills and, eventually, with the government.

Tokyo Seitetsu was already recognized as the industry's most competitive firm. Its competitive edge can be seen first in its growing market share: in 1965, the combined output of Tokyo Seitetsu and Tosa Denki was 4.3 percent of the industry's total output; ten years later this figure had more than doubled to 9.4 percent. Similarly, their combined share of bar steel nearly tripled in this period. Second, Tokyo Seitetsu had remained remarkably free of external borrowing. Whereas the rest of the minimills by 1977 had borrowed nearly ¥500 billion, mostly from the trading companies and banks, Tokyo Seitetsu had been able to use internal resources to fund its expansion efforts.

Tokyo Seitetsu's underlying competitiveness and independent position made Iketani a fervent believer in the free market and an absolute opponent of recession cartels and other cooperative efforts to manipulate supply and demand. He had no intention of curbing his firm's future growth plans for the sake of stabilizing the market or rescuing ailing minimills. He lambasted the rest of the industry for attempting cooperative solutions, arguing that such arrangements would allow the less competitive firms to survive without having to lower costs or improve technology. In short, such arrangements would hurt the more competitive firms and sap the industry's longer-term vitality, domestically as well as internationally.

A second obstacle to the formation of the cartel was the changing domestic antitrust environment. The key turning point had come in 1974 when the FTC prosecuted what became known as the petroleum cartel case. In that episode MITI, under pressure from petroleum importers, agreed to help the industry form a cartel. This was later challenged by the FTC on antitrust grounds and eventually determined to be illegal. The industry defended itself by arguing that the cartel had been formed with MITI's knowledge and guidance, and so the firms themselves should be exempt from prosecution. The final verdict—that even the approval of MITI did not legitimize behavior otherwise considered illegal—was not handed down until 1980. Nevertheless, the FTC's legal challenge hung over MITI's head throughout the 1970s and served as a constraint on MITI's powers (both informal and statutory) to guide industry behavior.[15] MITI and industry had thus been warned that the FTC would no longer automatically approve MITI decisions when antitrust principles were involved. In so far as the FTC had jurisdiction over controversial policy decisions, its acquiescence could no longer be taken for granted.

Thus, despite evidence that a sizable group of firms would not cooperate with any sort of collective solution, and despite evidence that antitrust authorities would try to discourage such efforts, the minimill leaders pushed ahead with their cartel plans. The first application was completed and presented to the FTC for approval in August 1975. Takahashi Toshihide, the new chairman of the FTC, expressed his reservations to the cartel since the minimills had not had a lot of bankruptcies. And recession cartels, he argued, had been granted too readily in the past.[16]

MITI, by contrast, preferred the formal cartel to controversial administrative guidance. In addition, MITI stated its goals in more overtly political terms, expressing the need to avoid further instability in the industry. The head of MITI's steel division, for instance, spoke in favor of the cartel, saying that "we are talking about structural depression, not just the need to regulate production. . . . Without a cartel, there is a good chance the industry will collapse."[17] MITI's backing proved crucial in persuading the FTC to approve the cartel.

The industry's second recession cartel was approved in September 1975 and extended a number of times before expiring the following April. Within a half year of this the industry applied for its third cartel, which lasted until September 1977. MITI further bolstered the effectiveness of the cartel by holding separate supply-and-demand-outlook (*jikyū mitoshi*) hearings in which firms reported their recent production levels. Firms who went over the agreed upon limits were put in the uncomfortable position of explaining to the industry association and to MITI why they had done so and what their future plans were. MITI, however, had no way to impose sanctions on recalcitrant firms either formally through the cartel or informally through its administrative guidance.

---

[15] See Upham 1986 for the legal ramifications of this case. Upham argues that because MITI's petroleum policy was carried out under specific legislation, namely the 1962 Petroleum Industry Law, the High Court's findings constrained MITI's latitude even in areas where it had obtained explicit legal authority.

[16] *Nihon Keizai Shimbun*, Sept. 10, 1975.

[17] *Nihon Keizai Shimbun*, Aug. 25, 1975.

From the beginning, the cartel operated under a severe handicap: participants in the cartel represented only about 65 percent of total production in 1975. Of the producers that were not covered by the cartel Tokyo Seitetsu and the other outsiders accounted for about 15 percent of production. The integrated steel firms produced about 12 percent, and the small steel processors turned out 8 percent. As expected, the cartel's biggest headaches were caused by the outsider minimills, which continued to produce at their previous levels. Most of the industry's anger was directed at Tokyo Seitetsu, the most vocal and most prominent of the defectors, but there were other important outsiders, including the industry's third largest producer, Ito Seitetsujo, which joined the ranks of the defectors in early 1977 despite strenuous lobbying by the industry leaders and MITI.[18] During the course of the cartel a number of minimills also complained to the government that the integrated steel firms were overproducing and underselling the cartel. Although the majors denied doing so, MITI responded to the minimill demands by requesting that the majors go along with the cartel arrangements. Kobe Steel, the largest bar steel producer among the majors, was singled out.

With such a large portion of the industry not abiding by the agreement, cartel members felt strong incentives to defect, since by continuing to cooperate with the cartel, they faced the possibility of losing their market share to the outsiders and had no guarantee that the cartel would succeed in raising prices. These fears of being exploited by the outsiders were fanned by strategic behavior and cheating within the cartel. There were widespread reports that cartel participants boosted their production just before the cartel went into effect, either in the hopes of increasing their production allotment or to raise capital to make later production cuts more palatable. According to one minimill executive, a number of firms agreed to curtail operations of their furnaces under the cartel agreement but then went ahead and operated them in secret. Even monitoring by the industry association proved ineffective: monitoring seals placed on idled facilities proved to be easily removed and replaced.

As the recession cartel provided no provisions for reining in the outsiders, or even to effectively deter cheating from within, compliance was unenforceable. Not surprisingly, the effects of these cartels were negligible; prices in summer and fall 1977 hovered around ¥50,000, well below the industry's goal of ¥65,000 per ton. The leaders of the industry association insisted that overproduction by the outsiders, including the integrated majors, was to blame. They rarely mentioned insider cheating. As the minimill recession entered its third year, industry leaders recognized the need for more effective enforcement mechanisms. The solution advo-

---

[18] *Nihon Keizai Shimbun,* Dec. 11, 1976; Nov. 11, 1975.

cated by Iketani and Tokyo Seitetsu—the market mechanism and survival of the fittest—was not yet considered an attractive one.

The Industry's Long-Range Goal: Control over Capacity

Faced with its most serious recession ever, the minimill insiders continued to try to stabilize the industry through regulation of the supply side. The industry continued to look for ways to make the production curtailments more effective. More important, the industry insiders were coming to realize that its fundamental structural problem was excess capacity, which in 1977 the industry estimated to be 20 percent of its total capacity. The insiders now began to pursue a second policy goal: attaining regulatory support to help them control or reduce their excess facilities.

Industry association chairman Uchinami and cartel chairman Yasuda again took the lead in organizing the minimills in this new direction. In December 1975 they created a Discussion Group on Basic Problems (Kihon Mondai Kanjikai), with Kondo Hajime, president of Nakayama Kogyo, a Nippon Kokan affiliate, serving as chairman. Membership in this group was limited to representatives of the insider minimill firms; if any of the outsiders were invited to participate, none decided to do so.

Subsequent government policy toward the industry was based directly on the recommendations of the Kondo discussion group. The group recognized that even the formal recession cartel was not sufficient to enforce the industry's stabilization efforts. The group acknowledged that if the industry were to try to control capacity, they would face even more difficult collective action problems. As with efforts to limit output, the long-term objective of capacity reductions was a collective good—stabilized prices—and thus susceptible to free riding or exploitation if the outsiders took over the market shares vacated by cooperators. And because capacity limitations are both costlier and more permanent than production cutbacks, the potential costs of being exploited are also much higher, increasing the disincentives to cooperate.

Rather than give up on stabilization efforts, however, the insiders focused on how to coerce the outsiders into cooperating. They understood very well that controlling the outsiders required much stronger enforcement mechanisms than the industry possessed. The direct enforcement powers of the government would also be necessary. The specific proposals of the Kondo discussion group, presented to the industry as a whole in April 1976, called for a change in the legislative basis of the recession cartel that would put more teeth into the production limitations.[19] In partic-

---

[19] Kondo 1976.

ular, this would give the industry a mechanism to control the outsiders. This proposal would embroil MITI in one of its most controversial industrial policy actions of the 1970s.

The Kondo discussion group also recommended measures to help enforce long-term capacity cutbacks. The group called for the establishment of a special industry committee to monitor capacity by checking on actual operating rates, production levels, idled facilities, and the like. The group further proposed that a government advisory body be created to deal with problems of new capacity and draw up regulations governing replacement investment. According to this proposal, current capacity would be registered, and all new investment would be subject to the advisory body's approval. In essence, the industry group was asking the government to establish regulation to curb the industry's excessively competitive nature.

The industry's labor force was basically content with the policies pursued by the firms. Because the insiders were seeking to stabilize the industry and retard adjustment, there would be less need for further labor cuts. Alleviating adjustment pressures was consonant with organized labor's goal of maintaining employment. At the same time, however, the minimills were also employing various labor-shedding schemes, notably calling for voluntary retirement, through which some 3,000 workers were shed in 1975 and 1976. Still, the industry estimated that 10 percent of its work force was redundant. If workers were to be forced into unemployment, the union wanted to make sure that they were adequately compensated for their losses. By early 1977 the unions, in cooperation with the industry insiders, had established a labor-management body (Heidenrō Rōshi Renkakukai) within the industry association that exerted pressure on government officials to make the minimill labor force eligible for special government unemployment programs. The group sought designation as a depressed industry so that workers could take advantage of extra unemployment benefits under the Employment Stabilization Fund (Kōyō Antei Shikin Seido).[20]

Two questions complicated the industry's attempts to limit capacity: how should cutbacks be allocated? and how should they be paid for? Pro rata capacity cuts were not feasible even aside from the refusal of the outsiders to share in these cuts. The cotton spinning industry was able to do this because each firm could mothball a small portion of its spindles and still remain in operation. But the electric furnaces were larger discrete units, so that the only way to reduce capacity was to close down entire plants. For many of the smaller firms operating single plants, cutting capacity meant exiting from the industry. Also, the weakened financial situation of many of these firms made capacity cuts even more difficult. Some of these firms were on the brink of collapse, and they all were already hav-

[20] *Tekkō Jūkyū no Ugoki*, Aug. 1977.

ing enough trouble reducing production to the levels set by the cartel. Their financial problems were made even more complicated by the fact that most of their facilities had also been used as collateral for existing loans, so these would have to be taken out of collateral before they could be scrapped. For these firms considerable financial support would be required to enable them to scrap any capacity.

Dealing with these financial problems went beyond the limits of the minimills' financial capabilities. The industry insiders had adopted the principle that "survivors should bear the burden of adjustment" (*jūekisha futan*), since firms that remained in the industry could expect higher prices and stabilized profits. Therefore, survivors were called upon to encourage the exit of weaker firms by shouldering a portion of their scrapping costs. Although the industry leadership had taken this principle to heart, their hearts were more willing than their pocketbooks. For one thing, it was not clear that the industry would recover even if some of the firms were to exit, so survivors were therefore reluctant to help others exit. In any case, most firms were in no position to provide compensation, since they were themselves battling for survival.

Funds to support production cuts and capacity reductions would have to come from other sources. The minimills concentrated their pressures on the trading companies and the commercial banks. The trading companies and the banks had helped finance the rapid minimill expansion in the early 1970s so had an interest in protecting these particular investments. The trading companies had an additional reason to support minimill stabilization: they had shareholding relationships with several insider minimills that represented 18 percent of total production.

The trading companies and banks, however, were increasingly frustrated with the turmoil and squabbling in the industry and were running out of patience with their minimills. Warnings that they would cut the minimills off cold increased as the recession wore on. Both the trading companies and the banks therefore were supportive of the insider's attempts to stabilize supply-side conditions, since the resulting stability in the industry would reduce the risk of bankruptcies and corporate reorganizations and permit them to decrease their financial commitments to the industry. The banks and trading companies thus had an interest in seeing the industry somehow regain its stability through collective efforts—so long as someone else would pay for it.

The steel majors also supported the minimills' stabilization efforts, but for conflicting reasons. First, the steel majors maintained corporate ties with many of the minimill insiders, which together accounted for 38 percent of total minimill output in 1980.[21] Cooperative efforts to stabilize

---

[21] Yonekura (1994) provides a table listing all minimill affiliations.

prices and profits would also improve the health of their affiliates, so the majors had at least an indirect interest in seeing the minimills regain stability. On the other hand, the minimills are a potential rival to the integrated majors, at least in the lower end of the steel market. Throughout the 1970s, however, the majors were not overly alarmed about competition from the minimills. The minimills had been content to concentrate on bar steel, so the majors were free to dominate all other product lines.[22] Also, the steel majors had an almost arrogant attitude toward the minimills, which they described as "no more than a recycling industry." Throughout the 1970s the minimill share of total steel production showed no signs of rising above 20 percent.

By the mid-1970s, however, the integrated firms were beginning to wake up to the threat posed by the minimills. In 1978 the minimills' share of national steel output broke the 20-percent barrier for the first time. The majors were more alarmed by the competitive outsiders, which were showing that they could move beyond bar steel production and make inroads into the more lucrative steel markets. On this score, the majors did not have to worry about the insider minimills, especially those that were its affiliates. But the competitive outsiders were completely independent of either the trading companies or the majors, and so their market behavior was less predictable. The majors now began to see that if regulations on capacity were applied equally to all minimills, this would prevent the outsiders from expanding too rapidly.

Another organized actor with some stake in policy choices for the minimills was the construction industry. Normally, the minimills' competitive nature meant that the construction firms enjoyed an ample supply of low-cost bar steel, their main steel inputs. Because successful stabilization agreements would translate into higher prices for construction-grade steel, the construction industry opposed a political solution that would raise prices. However, the construction industry only occasionally grumbled about subsidized bar prices. Especially considering their close ties to the LDP, one might have expected the construction firms to more actively oppose a policy that required them to bear a part of the costs of adjustment. There are three reasons why this did not happen. First, the industry faced organizational barriers of its own because thousands of construction firms were spread throughout the country. Second, steel is only a small part of its production costs, so it had a relatively small stake in the minimills. Third, the construction industry in Japan is somewhat insulated from market pres-

[22] Okamoto (1984) alludes to MITI's administrative guidance in the 1960s as a factor in this division of product lines. This is correct to a degree, but there is also a more fundamental technological reason. Because the scrap that electric furnaces use contains impurities, minimills until only recently have been unable to meet the metallurgical requirements to produce higher quality steel goods (Brown 1980).

sures, with relationships between firms that are often described as collusive. The construction industry has thus been able to use cost pricing to simply pass on the costs of higher inputs to final consumers.

It was the minimills themselves, or at least the insider minimills, that had the highest incentives to push their concerns onto government policy makers. Industry insiders now tried to place the blame for their current problems squarely on MITI by blaming their excessive capacity investments on the government's optimistic forecasts of 1973. Speaking to an LDP forum, Yasuda in 1977 argued as follows: "Who published those optimistic growth outlooks? The government did. The industry was 'taken in' by those forecasts. So it is not only the industry that bears responsibility for today's problems of excess capacity."[23]

MITI was still torn in its attitude toward the minimills. On the one hand, MITI was reluctant to become too deeply involved in the industry. It realized very clearly that given its existing enforcement powers, it would be difficult to coerce the recalcitrant outsiders into cooperating with the industry's stabilization schemes. Even if the industry insiders could agree on how to cut capacity, they would still have to ensure that the outsiders would not swamp these efforts by increasing their output. Already heavily involved in the unruly cotton spinning industry, MITI was not keen on increasing its regulation of the minimills. Yet MITI was sensitive to the pressures emanating from the minimill insiders and their supporters. The industry's sense of crisis had been fully conveyed to MITI, through direct contact and indirect forums such as the Kondo group. Also, minimill policy had already aroused considerable political attention—far beyond the industry's economic importance. MITI was conscious that it needed to avoid further instability in the industry, since further economic dislocations might exacerbate politicization and controversy.

MITI eventually decided to implement the policy recommendations that the industry's Kondo group had put on the table in April 1976. That fall MITI convened a private study group in its Industrial Structure Council to discuss minimill problems. This group, the Heidenrō Kihon Mondai Kenkyūkai, was chaired by Ueno Hiroya, a professor of economics at Seikei University, and was composed of representatives from all interested parties.[24] This group's recommendations, published in February, stated that the industry would not be given a free bailout. In the words of one com-

---

[23] *Jiyū Minshu*, Aug. 1978. The industry also criticized MITI for its policy about-face in 1973, when the minimills were strongly encouraged to increase production in the face of what proved to be only temporary shortages and inflation.

[24] The nine members included representatives from two insider minimills (including Kondo Hajime, the head of the industry's discussion group), Nippon Steel, Mitsui Bussan, the Industrial Bank of Japan, the Japan Steel Distributors' Association, and the Japan Construction Association, as well as two academics. The Ueno group's report appears in Heidenro Kihon Mondai Kenkyūkai 1977.

mentator, "the minimills should not expect the national subsidies given to the textile industry."[25]

However, the Ueno Report went on to echo the industry's concern over excess capacity and called for measures to help the industry manage its supply-side conditions. The Ueno Report endorsed almost every concrete proposal that the industry had called for.[26] First, it recommended that the industry draw up regulations to restrict capacity expansion and new investments, which would then be applied through the steel subcommittee of the Industrial Structure Council. Second, the group suggested that total bar steel capacity be reduced by 3.9 million tons by mid-1978. Third, the group recommended that the industry be allowed to form a trade association cartel (shōkō kumiai), as called for by the industry's Kondo group. This proposal was attractive to the industry because MITI could approve this cartel without having to gain FTC approval and because it provided MITI with compulsory powers to force the outsiders to abide by the cartel's decisions. MITI would thus have legal authority to issue so-called "outsider restrictions" against firms not participating in the cartel.

Not surprisingly, the reaction of most of the minimills was overwhelmingly positive. The industry association endorsed the report at an ad hoc meeting convened soon after the Ueno proposals were presented to the government. Also not surprisingly, Tokyo Seitetsu was the only one of the 51 firms in attendance that refused to endorse the report. Iketani's most pointed criticisms were reserved for the industry insiders who had sought to blame the government for their own problems; he argued that although "the government did push Tanaka's plan, it never used administrative guidance to force the industry to expand capacity. It was the firms themselves who decided to invest. It is a bit odd to say now that the government should come to our aid just because its forecasts were incorrect."[27] Iketani openly stated that he would not participate in any capacity cuts.

The provisions of the Ueno Report were rapidly implemented. In June MITI created a special minimill subcommittee in the Industrial Structure Council to draw up rules for new investments. The subcommittee was composed of representatives from the industry, the trading companies, and private banks, and a few academics. Industry insiders created a subcommittee within the industry association to deal with capacity reductions. The capacity committee soon announced that 14 minimills had agree to seal 1.13 million tons of capacity, about one-third of the Ueno group's recommendations. All 14 firms were industry insiders, led by Toshin,

[25] Heidenro Kihon Mondai Kenkyūkai, 1977.
[26] The only proposal that was rejected was the idea of allowing the industry to register existing capacity with the government.
[27] *Zaikai*, Oct. 15, 1977. Tokyo Seitetsu and Tosa Denki, under the junior Iketani's leadership, were among the few firms that had refrained from expanding capacity in that period.

Nakayama, and Funabashi. MITI was also responsive to demands that the government help with funding for scrapping efforts—one of the few points on which the minimills, the trading companies, and the banks had agreed upon. In December MITI set up a "structural adjustment promotion association," strictly for use by the minimills, to guarantee loans for the purpose of scrapping capacity. The association, chaired by Yasuda, was funded at ¥7 billion (U.S. $21 million); one-half of the necessary capitalization came from the government and one-half from private institutions.[28]

MITI was responsive on other counts as well. First, it applied informal pressures on the trading companies and the private banks to support the minimills' efforts to cut production. This pressure included a formal request by MITI Basic Industries Bureau director Amaya Naohiro of various banking associations to continue to supply funding for minimills that had reduced production. In a somewhat tense meeting between MITI and 18 trading company representatives, MITI urged cooperation with the production cutbacks. The trading companies agreed, but with the understanding that the government would provide future financial support for scrapping efforts. Second, in an unusual move, MITI convinced the Ministry of Finance to set aside funds to purchase small amounts of bar steel for commodity aid to other countries, notably Pakistan, Sri Lanka, and Egypt. Third, the government agreed to help with the industry's problems of excess labor by making the minimill labor force eligible for additional unemployment benefits under the Employment Stabilization fund. Finally, MITI agreed to implement the industry's strongest demand—the creation of the trade association cartel with its attendant outsider restrictions. It was this act that would embroil MITI in a direct confrontation with the industry outsiders.

MITI Cracks Down on the Outsiders

The summer and fall of 1977 proved to be the minimill's most serious crisis. Prices for bar steel had hovered around ¥50,000 per ton for more than three years, well under the ¥65,000 mark considered to be the break-even point for the average minimill. As a result, in 1977 the industry as a whole reported negative profits for the third consecutive year.

With no end to the crisis in sight, drastic measures were required. The minimill leadership took just such a bold step in July by applying to the FTC for a price stabilization cartel. This step was seen as an indication of how serious the minimill situation had become since price cartels had

---

[28] Yonekura 1994, p. 206. A number of minimills were in debt to the Japan Development Bank and asked for these debt payments to be postponed or for their terms to be softened.

been approved only three times in the postwar period. The cartel ran into immediate resistance on two fronts. First, the outsiders refused to participate in the cartel, now joined by as many as 15 former insiders, who felt that price controls went too far in terms of government intervention into the industry's affairs. Second, the FTC's new chairman, Sawada Yasushi, expressed his extreme opposition to the cartel, arguing that prices should be determined by the market and that while other choices still existed, the industry should not resort to a cartel. With the FTC's increasingly assertive opposition to cartelization in general, its approval of the price cartel seemed unlikely. In a speech to the Diet at the beginning of August, Prime Minister Fukuda Takeo explicitly called on the FTC to approve the cartel. This direct intervention by the prime minister eventually persuaded the FTC to grant the minimill request.

It is surprising that the minimills were the beneficiaries of such high-level political intervention. The minimill industry was certainly not a critical constituency of the LDP, and with a labor force of less than 40,000, it did not carry much weight with any party at the national level. Minimills have had some influence over regional Dietmen, particularly those from areas in general economic distress, but their national-level influence has not been significant.

Bowing to pressures from the industry and the LDP, the FTC approved the cartel, and set a price floor for bar steel at ¥52,000 per ton, just above the existing market price of ¥50,500. The minimill insiders considered this an important symbolic victory, since the government had finally acknowledged how serious the minimill plight had become.

This new cartel arrangement, however, still did nothing to curb the outsiders, who continued to defy the production limits set by the cartel. MITI bureaucrats were vexed that they could not force outsider firms to cooperate. It is not that MITI had not tried—it had held countless private meetings and hearings with outsider representatives. The problem was that MITI's informal powers of persuasion were useless against firms that refused to be persuaded. And the independent status of the outsiders—their lack of ties to the integrated majors, trading companies, or banks—meant that indirect forms of pressure were also ineffective.

The problem for MITI was that it still lacked the legal authority to restrict the outsiders. Administrative guidance through *kankoku sōtan* was a possibility, but would be politically difficult given the changes in the antitrust environment. Even then, administrative guidance still would not give MITI the legal means to curb the outsiders, so the industry and MITI now turned to the legal recourse that had already been suggested by the Kondo and Ueno groups: the formation of a trade association cartel.

The industry submitted its application to create a Bar Steel Trade Association cartel (Zenkoku Kogata Bōkō Kumiai) on August 4, 1977, two weeks after the price cartel application. The same 50 participants in the price cartel joined the association, together representing about 75 percent of the industry's capacity. Although the FTC again opposed the creation of this cartel, approval was out of its direct jurisdiction; circumventing FTC opposition was, after all, one of the reasons that the industry, and MITI, wanted the change in legal status.

At the strong urging of the industry insiders, MITI approved the Trade Association cartel on October 7. Its motivations were more political than economic. The minimills were not a critical industry, and no one in policy circles considered it vital in terms of Japan's economic security. But in the face of determined lobbying pressures and the possibility of even greater controversy down the road, MITI agreed to step in.

The creation of this cartel was a great victory for the insiders. Now MITI's full enforcement powers could be used to ensure industry-wide cooperation. The outsider restrictions were expected to allow the industry to finally realize its goal of stabilized production and prices. Although the penalty was a fine of only ¥300,000, it was believed that even Tokyo Seitetsu would not dare defy MITI so blatantly.

Now that a legal enforcement mechanism existed, the industry was quick to request it. On October 21, the trade association formally appealed to MITI to impose sanctions on firms that were not participating in the cartel. The aim of the industry, they stated, was not to control the outsiders, but to "crush them."[29]

The outsiders were understandably outraged. Iketani led the charge, criticizing the bureaucracy for its preference for a "controlled economy" (*tōsei keizai*). He also argued: "The government has spent billions of yen on the textile industry without improving its competitiveness—a good example of how a regulatory approach does not work. Cartels are not effective because artificial efforts to raise prices are not sustainable in the long run. To force all firms into the same mold leads eventually to death for all. If your legs are weak you can strengthen them by running. It is a mistake to instead ask for a wheelchair. If you are provided a wheelchair, you will next ask for someone to push you, and so on without end."[30]

The other major outsiders were Ito Seitetsujo and Toyo Seiko. The president of the former argued that the minimills were "becoming a 'second textile industry'—to be protected is one thing, but to be overprotected is not welcome." And the president of Toyo Seiko, a former insider, expressed his complete frustration over cartel arrangements: "Cartels over the past ten years have not shown any results. They have been a waste of time and money."[31]

[29] *Asahi Shimbun*, Oct. 22, 1977.
[30] *Nihon Keizai Shimbun*, Nov. 21, 1977.
[31] *Nihon Keizai Shimbun*, Nov. 21, 1977.

After a month of public hearings, MITI agreed to the association's request and issued outsider restrictions against 12 firms for a period of six months. Total production levels for the industry were revised accordingly, from 470,000 tons per month for the original 52 firms to 570,000 tons for the 64 firms.

The day the restrictions went into effect, Iketani announced that he was filing an administrative suit against MITI on the grounds that such orders were unconstitutional.[32] At the same time, he felt he had no choice but to comply with the restraint orders. Tokyo Seitetsu and the other outsiders agreed to limit production starting in December. The minimill insiders had prevailed, at least for the moment.

Others have portrayed Tokyo Seitetsu as capitulating to the powers of MITI.[33] Judging from its subsequent actions, however, this retreat was merely tactical. Although it did limit its production while the restraints were in effect, it made up for lost ground as soon as production restraints were lifted six months later, so that its total output of bar steel in 1978 increased 15.5 percent over the previous year. In the meantime it pushed ahead with its long-range expansion plans. According to one estimate, Tokyo Seitetsu invested nearly ¥30 billion in 1978 and 1979, a figure that dwarfed the investments made by all other minimills.[34] This allowed it to complete two large electric furnaces at its Okayama plant in April 1978 and add a gigantic bar steel facility at the same plant in January 1979. These expansion efforts left the firm poised to take a larger slice of the market, which it did over the next two years: in 1979 and 1980 Tokyo Seitetsu increased its production of bar steel by nearly 95 percent, raising its market share from under 4 percent to over 7 percent in the process. Tokyo Seitetsu's adherence to the outsider restrictions was thus little more than a temporary retreat. Its outsider status did not end with its decision to adhere to MITI's restrictions.

Long-term Responses: Capacity Cutbacks under the Tokuanhō

Thus far in this case study the LDP politicians have not played a central role. In many instances of policy-making for individual industries the politicians have tended to remain on the sidelines, allowing the industry and MITI to negotiate and implement policy. However, when LDP constituencies have not been satisfied with the policies worked out with the bureaucrats, the LDP politicians have shown themselves to be quite responsive to constituent pressures.

---

[32] This was in the form of an administrative appeal as provided by the Administrative Appeals Law of 1962. See Ogawa (1981, p. 225).

[33] See, as one example, Yamamura (1982).

[34] Yonekura 1994, pp. 206–207.

Such was the case during the economic recession of 1977–1978. Since coming into power in 1976 Fukuda Takeo's cabinet found itself subject to growing criticisms over its handling of the economy. The Fukuda cabinet was beset with a twin economic crisis: a domestic economy in deep recession and a rapid appreciation of the yen (*endaka*). As 1977 wore on and the recession showed no indication of ending, the business community was becoming increasingly restless; business interests argued that this recession, now in its fourth year, was unlike anything in the past, and therefore new policy initiatives were needed.

The strongest criticisms came from a group of industries that were faced with bankruptcies and extensive labor dislocations—the structurally depressed industries. The largest and most politically powerful of these was the textile industry (including both synthetic fibers and cotton spinning), which now blasted Fukuda for his "do-nothing" policy and called for strong action to deal with *endaka*. Other depressed industries included shipbuilding, aluminum, chemical fertilizers, cardboard, and the minimills. These industries throughout 1977 had been calling for emergency relief and were increasingly dissatisfied with what MITI was able to do for them, grumbling openly about MITI Minister Tanaka and his failure to come up with any new policy initiatives. These industries in late 1977 took their problems straight to the chairman of the LDP's Policy Affairs Research Council, Komoto Toshio. Komoto, a businessman and former MITI minister in the Miki cabinet, was seen as an ally of business and someone who sympathized with the problems they faced. According to the business press, it was Komoto who conveyed industry concerns to MITI and the rest of the bureaucracy. Komoto was in an even better position to help the depressed industries when he was again appointed MITI minister in November 1977. In the growing crisis atmosphere the LDP finally decided to act.

The result was the depressed industries legislation, Tokuanhō (Tokutei Sangyō Antei Rinji Sochihō). This new legislation was also supported by MITI. All through 1977 it had been hinting that a more comprehensive approach to the depressed industries was under consideration. MITI had a number of reasons to want the new legislation. First, it was already feeling considerable heat from the depressed industries under its jurisdiction, and it shared the politicians' desire to avoid socially disruptive (and politically complicated) bankruptcies and massive labor dislocations. It feared that unless these industries were stabilized quickly, these pressures would only intensify and become more politically controversial. Second, MITI had no comprehensive policy approach for its declining industries and no apparent vision for their future. Each had been treated in an ad hoc, industry-specific manner, and as seen in the previous two chapters, this often led to controversy and ineffectiveness. The Tokuanhō would enable MITI to deal with all of the troubled (and at times, troublesome) industries generically, with more clearly defined administrative powers and procedures. Third, the Tokuanhō was a response to the recent strengthening of the FTC. It was intended to give MITI autonomy in dealing with designated industries without having to negotiate with the FTC for its approval.

The Tokuanhō was basically aimed at regulating capacity in the designated industries.[35] In this sense it was fully consistent with the regulatory policies that distressed industries such as cotton spinning and the minimills had been pursuing for the previous three decades. Designation carried with it restrictions on new capacity investments. Also, designated industries were exempted from antimonopoly legislation, allowing the industry to meet, discuss, and formulate a "stabilization plan" outlining capacity reduction targets and methods. Industries that could not scrap sufficient capacity could form an indicative cartel for the purpose of capacity rationalization. The law also created a special fund, capitalized by public and private monies, for use by the designated industries to guarantee low-interest loans used for scrapping purposes.

The Tokuanhō was obviously motivated by industry pressures and political interests that went far beyond the interests of the minimills. However, despite the industry's small size and lack of clout, the minimills occupied a central part of MITI's thinking about the new legislation. MITI at that point was more deeply involved in the minimill industry than in any of the other three industries that it designated in its original draft (the others were aluminum, synthetic fibers, and shipbuilding). In March 1977 MITI Minister Tanaka had said that MITI viewed its policy efforts to stabilize the minimills as a "critical test case" for the proposed depressed industry legislation.[36] Most important, the original MITI draft contained provisions giving it powers to require outsiders to cooperate with the capacity agreements, similar to the outsider restrictions that it had used against Tokyo Seitetsu. This portion of the draft was clearly aimed at dealing with the problems of the minimills, since outsiders were not an issue in any of the other original Tokuanhō industries.

MITI's release of the draft of the Tokuanhō, on January 19, 1978, was greeted with praise by the affected industries but also with considerable criticism from certain groups, including the FTC, the opposition parties, consumer groups, assorted academics, and the minimill outsiders. On January 24, Tokyo Seitetsu, Ito Seitetsujo, Toyo Seiko, and six other firms sub-

---

[35] The legislation has been described in detail elsewhere. See for example, Wheeler et al. 1982, Totten 1984, Uriu 1984, Vogel 1985, Anderson 1986, Upham 1986, Young 1986, Yonezawa 1988, Boyd 1989, and Young 1991. See Boyd and Nagamori 1991, passim, for an interesting account of the political background to the passage of this law. The government also passed two related pieces of legislation—the Temporary Measures for the Unemployed Workers in Designated Depressed Industries, and the Temporary Measures for Stabilization of Designated Depressed Regions.

[36] Iwasaki 1977.

mitted a formal objection addressed to MITI Minister Komoto calling for withdrawal of the draft. The group criticized excessive bureaucratic intervention and the semicompulsory nature of the law as inappropriate in a free economy. They warned—with considerable prescience, as it turned out—that restrictions on capacity would only protect inefficiencies and would result in the industry failing to modernize and remain competitive internationally. The group complained most loudly about the outsider restrictions written into the draft, calling them a "major infringement on the principle of private property rights."[37]

Of greater consequence were the objections of the FTC, which was locked in its ongoing battle with MITI. The FTC's opposition prompted MITI to agree to seek FTC approval for the Tokuanhō indicative cartels. Furthermore, it forced MITI, to the chagrin of the minimill insiders, to remove the clause relating to restrictions on outsiders.

Opinions among the minimills on whether to apply for designation under the Tokuanhō were predictably divided along insider-outsider lines. Yasuda, now chairman of the industry association, went ahead with efforts to convince two-thirds of the firms to agree to seek designation (as required by the law). The insiders needed little persuasion. They perceived the Tokuanhō as a supplement to, not a replacement of, current policy support, which they anticipated would continue as before. The Tokuanhō was consonant with the fundamental goal of the insiders—the regulation and prevention of further expansion of capacity. Although there was some dissatisfaction over the removal of the outsider restriction clause, the industry expected the trade association cartel to continue to regulate output, so at least outsiders would be kept in check in terms of production. Finally, the industry was attracted by the government's offer of financial support for capacity reductions.

The stabilization plan, drawn up in the steel committee of the Industrial Structure Council, called for the scrapping of 2.85 million tons of capacity, or 14 percent of the industry's total, by March 1981. Eight firms pledged to dispose of furnaces (one per firm), while 14 firms agreed to idle 18 additional furnaces. Although this amounted to a significant chunk of capacity, the target number reflected only what insider firms were willing to scrap. It was not an objective assessment of what was required to close the excess capacity gap, which was estimated to be nearly 10 million tons. Further, all of the furnaces designated to be scrapped had already been idled for a considerable period, some for as long as seven years, and many had already been pledged to be destroyed in the industry's previous scrapping program. The government was thus paying to scrap facilities the minimills had planned to scrap anyway. Most of these

---

[37] *Asahi Journal,* Feb. 24, 1978; Takeuchi 1978, p. 44.

capacity cuts did not represent new reductions likely to restore balance between supply and demand.

In the meantime the Fukuda cabinet's decision to reflate domestic demand gave an enormous boost to the minimills. As mentioned, the general business community at the time was exerting strong pressures on Fukuda to take this step. Furthermore, these demands were bolstered by external pressures from the Carter administration for more rapid growth in the Japanese economy. Responding to both internal and external concerns, Fukuda promised in a 1977 OECD meeting that the Japanese economy would grow by 7 percent in 1978.[38]

The effect of the Fukuda reflation policy on the minimills in particular was immense as increased public-works spending gave a huge boost to domestic demand. Domestic shipments of bar steel increased by nearly 50 percent between 1977 and 1979. In addition, the industry's export picture also improved in 1979 as a result of surging domestic demand in the OPEC countries. Total production for the industry thus hit an all-time high in 1979: 14.7 million tons. Prices stabilized around ¥60,000 per ton throughout 1978, then began to boom in 1979, rising to ¥78,000 per ton in March 1980, its highest point since the first oil crisis. Average industry profits turned positive in 1978 and rose further in 1979. It was clearly Fukuda's policy of fiscal reflation that was the main cause of this significant turnaround in minimill fortunes. Although capacity cuts and other collective schemes may have had marginal effects, the recovery in production, prices, and profits was due mostly to the boom in construction demand. In any case, the minimills' recovery was underway well before the Tokuanhō was even passed.

The industry clearly had not anticipated this sudden turnaround. In a replay of the 1973 recovery, the industry now seemed to forget the crisis it had just gone through. In an effort to recoup losses suffered during the long recession, firms scrambled to expand production and capacity. Under these circumstances MITI could not justify continued regulation of the industry. The price cartel was therefore not renewed after April 1978, and outsider restrictions were allowed to lapse that June. For MITI these were welcome developments, since both the confrontation with the FTC over the price cartel and with Tokyo Seitetsu over outsider restrictions were publicly embarrassing. Having the industry perform well without having to expend valuable political assets was MITI's preferred outcome.

As had happened before, however, the 1979 boom disappeared as quickly as it had appeared. Again, depressed domestic demand was the cause: in 1980, following the government's effort to return to fiscal restraint under administrative reform, public expenditures stagnated, while

---

[38] Putnam 1988; Suzuki 1995.

private housing expenditures dropped by 10 percent. As a result, domestic shipments of bar steel fell by a third between 1979 and 1983, and bar prices plummeted from a high of ¥78,000 per ton in 1979 to ¥52,000 in 1981. By 1982 the industry as a whole was again showing negative profits.

Once again alarmed over excess capacity, the industry scrapped or idled 2.72 million tons, 95 percent of the target called for by the stabilization plan. Total capacity that year, however, reached 22.5 million tons, indicating that other firms had increased capacity by 4.2 million tons. And capacity expansion continued over the next four years, reaching 26.7 million tons in 1982, a jump of one-third over four years. The minimills were the only Tokuanhō industry which actually increased its capacity during the period of designation. MITI and industry officials insist that this expansion was due, not to new investments, but rather to improvements in technology (especially oxy-fuel burners and ultra-high power technology) leading to greater furnace capacity.[39] Regardless of the cause, however, the Tokuanhō failed in its objectives in the case of the minimills: the problem of excess capacity had worsened dramatically.

The 1980s: The Outsiders Prevail

As the 1970s came to a close, the industry was still grappling with the problems of excess capacity and depressed prices. It found itself in no better shape than before regulation had begun. In February 1980 an industry association report on progress under the Tokuanhō found that the industry still had an estimated 5 million tons of excess capacity, about 20 percent of the industry's total. A year later the industry drafted a revised stabilization plan calling for previously idled capacity to be scrapped. The plan set a new target of June 1983, the date the Tokuanhō was to expire.

The Tokuanhō was originally designed to be in force for only five years. MITI officials argue that were it not for the Second Oil Shock, the bill's goals would have been attained during the Tokuanhō's original tenure. By 1981, however, it was clear that none of the originally designated industries was yet ready to graduate. In fact a number of new industries, including certain chemical and petrochemical sectors, were now in need of restructuring. MITI therefore sought to extend the Tokuanhō. This follow-on legislation, the Structural Improvement Law, Sankōhō (Tokutei Sangyō Kōzō Kaizen Rinji Sochihō), was approved with little controversy. It did not represent a major departure from the Tokuanhō in the sense that both

---

[39] At least part of the growth, however, can be attributed to the actions of Tokyo Seitetsu, which in April 1978 completed a plant in Okayama with two very large (100-ton) electric furnaces and an 88-ton continuous caster just before restrictions on new facilities went into effect.

were aimed at encouraging capacity cutbacks in order to help stabilize designated industries.

The insiders had little trouble in mustering enough support to continue its designation under the Sankōhō. The minimills were again one of the original industries designated under the legislation. The new bill extended restrictions on new investments to June 1988. The industry drew up a new structural improvement plan, this time calling for capacity cuts of 3.8 million tons, 15 percent of existing capacity, to be completed by March 1987. The industry ended up scrapping 2.4 million tons, 63 percent of its target. Total minimill capacity, however, again increased while the industry was designated as structurally depressed. As the Sankōhō drew to an end in 1988, there had been no improvement in the problem of unutilized capacity; excess capacity was now over 5 million tons, a situation even worse than in 1977.[40]

The Sankōhō's only new provisions were additional antitrust exemptions to encourage industries to enter into so-called "joint business activities"—mergers, business tie-ups, joint marketing agreements, and the like. These new provisions were designed to help concentrate production and distribution.[41] The industry did try to take advantage of these new provisions but found consolidation as difficult as the cotton spinners had previously. Earlier, Nippon Steel had merged three of its affiliates to create Godo Seitetsu; Godo then went on to absorb five more minimills. Under the Sankōhō, however, only one merger occurred: in 1986, two large Nippon Kokan affiliates joined to form Toa Steel. These efforts, however, were not substantial enough to improve the industry's conditions.

In the face of the recession of the 1980s the industry also continued to pursue short-term production cutbacks. It applied for a recession cartel in December 1980, which was approved two months later. As in previous cartels, the major outsiders did not participate, so only 31 minimills and 20 processors joined. This time around, however, direct confrontation between MITI and the outsiders was avoided due to restraint practiced by both sides. First, Tokyo Seitetsu did not grossly violate the cartel limitations, although a number of cartel members still complained to MITI. MITI never issued outsider restraints, but it did informally request Tokyo Seitetsu to abide by the cartel. As in 1977, Tokyo Seitetsu only retreated tactically, and within two years after the cartel had ended, it expanded its output by a third, while the rest of the minimills kept their production steady, allowing Tokyo Seitetsu's share of the bar steel market to rise from 7.5 percent to over 9 percent.

[40] Ohashi 1988; Sekiguchi 1991.

[41] The Sankōhō is discussed in detail in Tsūshō Sangyōshō, Sangyō Seisaku Kyoku 1983. Sekiguchi (1991) and Upham (1986) provide comprehensive overviews of both the Tokuanhō and the Sankōhō.

The cartel was allowed to lapse after a year with bar prices at approximately the same level as when the cartel began.

Tokyo Seitetsu Challenges the Majors

The relationship between Tokyo Seitetsu and the industry insiders appeared to change in the early 1980s. In particular, Iketani surprised observers by agreeing to join the industry association. This occurred in 1982, when the new head of the association, Ohashi Fujio, president of Godo Seitetsu, offered Iketani the chairmanship. Iketani declined but eventually agreed to accept a vice-chairmanship along with the presidents of two other leading outsiders, Toyo and Ito. Much has been made of this change of heart on the part of Iketani and the other outsiders, with some analysts claiming that they were beaten into submission and "co-opted" into joining their former foes.[42] However, if Godo and Nippon Steel thought they were co-opting Iketani, they were wrong.

In the early 1980s Tokyo Seitetsu was in the process of shifting its focus to a more lucrative part of the steel business: structural steel shapes, and especially H-beams. A handful of the other outsiders, notably Yamato Kogyo, followed suit. This move set it on a direct collision course with Nippon Steel, which then dominated this market segment. No one guessed at the time that it would be the upstarts that would win the so-called "H-beam war."

Ironically, the outsiders' decision to move into high value-added areas was a natural consequence of MITI's regulatory policies, although a completely unintended one. The Tokuanhō and Sankōhō had placed restrictions on the building of new electric furnaces but not on new rolling facilities. And because MITI was also restricting the industry's production of bar steel, this gave the outsiders strong incentives to shift to other products. Tokyo Seitetsu was in the best position to challenge the majors. In 1984 it had just completed a major expansion program in which it introduced the latest in minimill technology. In contrast, the rest of the industry had not made comparable investments, either because of a lack of capital or because the industry's push for regulation of capacity prevented them from doing so. Throughout the 1980s Tokyo Seitetsu thus enjoyed the luxury of operating newer and more advanced facilities than any of its competitors.[43]

As Tokyo Seitetsu and the other outsiders began to gain market share, the majors finally reacted. Nippon Steel had been largely complacent

---

[42] Yamamura 1982; Noble 1988.
[43] During the late 1970s it had installed H-beam facilities at three of its plants (Okayama, Senju, and Kochi), all financed through internal resources (*Tekkō Gyōkai no Keiei Hikaku*, 1980, pp. 52–53). In 1984 it built a new rolling facility in its Kyushu plant. In addition, it installed a universal roller capable of producing plates, in the late 1980s (Yonekura 1994, passim).

throughout the 1970s but finally went on the attack in late 1982 when it drastically cut its H-beam prices by nearly one-fourth, to ¥56,000 per ton. Again in 1984 Tokyo Seitetsu and the other outsiders went head-to-head with Nippon Steel in a price-cutting battle. Observers expected the minimills to be crushed in this battle, but the minimills steadily gained market share. Against all odds, the minimills increased their share of H-beam production from 24.3 percent in 1977 to 59.1 percent by 1987. It was only later that industry analysts recognized that the minimills were much better suited to H-beam production than the majors. Not until 1987, for instance, did the Industrial Bank of Japan indicate that the minimills could produce H-beams at costs one-third lower than the integrated firms. By 1993, both Tokyo Seitetsu and Yamato Kogyo passed Nippon Steel in H-beam market share.[44]

The market behavior of Tokyo Seitetsu and the other outsiders finally succeeded in derailing attempts by the industry insiders to continue to manipulate market forces. Thus, the 1981–1982 bar steel cartel was the last time that the industry resorted to collective production cuts. Although the minimills continued to regulate capacity growth under the Tokuanhō and Sankōhō, the industry abandoned its more controversial efforts to use government regulation to directly control production levels. The outsiders' opposition to government regulation had prevailed.

By 1984, the insiders finally recognized that they simply did not have the strength, unity, or backing to organize and enforce cooperative stabilization efforts. Controlling the outsiders was an impossible task, even with the help of MITI's enforcement powers. Any new cooperative effort was doomed. Industry leaders expressed frustration over their long and fruitless efforts to bring the entire group to a consensus. Yasuda, citing the unfairness of insiders cooperating while outsiders did not, said that "it has proven impossible to reorganize or concentrate the industry, or to dispose of excess capacity, on an industry-wide basis."[45] From this point on, Yasuda said, scrapping and production decisions would be left to the individual firms.

MITI was also ready to abandon its efforts to regulate the industry. MITI bureaucrats by 1984 were publicly voicing their frustration with the unruly outsiders. In discussing the new Sankōhō in a Diet debate in March 1983, MITI minister Yamanaka blamed the outsiders for the increase in capacity, but then went on to add "it is *possible* for MITI to issue orders or recom-

---

[44] The "H-beam war" is discussed in Industrial Bank of Japan 1988, p. 45, Yagi 1989, pp. 86–88, and *Nihon Keizai Shimbun*, Jan. 13, 1983. Tokyo Seitetsu's share of the H-beam market was 18.3 percent in 1984. Other producers included Yamato Kogyo at 11.5 percent, and Tupy Kogyo, Toshin Seiko, Godo Seitetsu, and Osaka Seitetsu, all with 4 to 7 percent shares.
[45] *Asahi Shimbun*, Jan. 12, 1983. Yasuda, of course, failed to mention the problem of insider cheating.

mendations to restrict the outsiders. But the government has tried to take care of this industry for five years now. . . . Industrial policy should avoid such extreme intervention, so in my opinion, we should not again issue these orders and should let the industry go on its own. . . . If this means the industry disappears, then so be it."[46] The minister overstated both the consequences of ending policy support for the minimills, as well as MITI's ability to rein in the outsiders. By 1984 it was clear that there was nothing that MITI could do to coerce Tokyo Seitetsu into cooperation.

MITI's new stance reflected first and foremost its realization that it was powerless to control the outsiders, especially Tokyo Seitetsu. At the same time, there were other reasons for MITI to give up on its heavy-handed regulation of the industry. First, the integrated majors no longer favored it. They had previously supported minimill stabilization not only to support their affiliates but also because they hoped that regulation of the industry would slow overall capacity growth and thus curb the growth of the more dynamic outsiders. Now that it had become clear that government regulations could not control the outsiders, and in fact had the reverse effects, making them more aggressive in new areas, the majors preferred that regulation be ended.

Second, MITI's reluctance to continue regulation of the minimills also reflected changes in the industrial-policy-making environment in Japan. The FTC's challenge to MITI's administrative guidance powers had exerted a growing constraint on MITI's policy instruments. As mentioned, the FTC had become increasingly assertive during the 1970s and into the 1980s. The turning point was the legal decision on the petroleum cartel case, handed down in 1980. MITI still retained considerable powers and could still convene recession cartels for troubled industries, but it was put on notice that it must take more fully into account antimonopoly considerations. It would have to pick and choose its intervention more carefully and always factor in possible opposition from the FTC. In this sense, MITI was now less likely to intervene in what it considered lost causes.[47]

Third, the external environment facing Japan had also undergone an important change by the 1980s. As Japan's position as an economic power grew, so too did international criticisms and scrutiny of its domestic regulatory practices. Japanese policy makers were constrained by the growing criticisms of the OECD and the U.S. government against the use of cartels as well as the anticompetitive provisions of Japan's depressed industry legislation. The United States was particularly concerned that cartel-like solutions were at least implicitly protectionist, in the sense that some restraint on imports was necessary if domestic cartels were to be effective.

---

[46] Tsūshō Sangyōshō, Sangyō Seisaku Kyoku 1983, pp. 49–50.
[47] A memorandum by MITI recognized these limits on the use of administrative guidance. See Shiono 1984, p. 212.

The Japanese government found that traditional responses, such as the recession cartels, carried with them increasing political costs.

Changes in the industry's position and in the broader policy environment were demonstrated in 1986, when the industry, already facing a domestic recession, was further devastated by the rapid appreciation of the yen. Exports completely disappeared, falling from 3 million tons in 1985 to only 130,000 tons in 1987.[48] Domestic demand, although growing slightly, was more than offset by this drop in exports, and prices plunged again, hitting a low of ¥31,000 per ton in January 1987, its lowest level since 1971.

In addition, the industry now had to worry about rising imports. Imports jumped in late 1987, then leveled off in 1988, although still at relatively low levels.[49] The industry again found itself divided, this time on the desirability of protection. No clear call for restrictions emerged. Iketani issued a warning very similar to his opposition to the Tokuanhō: protection from competition would doom the industry. He argued that each firm needed to cut costs and rationalize itself. In particular, Iketani argued that firms should move to larger furnaces and invest in the refurbishing of rolling equipment. This time his suggestions were heeded.

Although recession cartels were not granted to the industry after 1982, the government remained willing to continue to help the industry try to regulate its excess capacity problem. The minimills were one of the industries originally designated in the draft of the 1988 Adjustment Facilitation Law (Enkotsukahō), the follow-on legislation to the Tokuanhō and Sankōhō.[50] Unforeseen events intervened, however: demand for minimill products was boosted again, this time by the explosion in domestic construction demand following the 1987 Maekawa Report and the govern-

[48] In the 1970s the minimills had found new markets among the newly rich OPEC nations. But during the early 1980s, the OPEC nations, faced with falling oil revenues, were cutting back on domestic development projects. Japanese exports then shifted to the PRC, which took more than 70 percent of small bar exports by 1985. China's balance of payments problems, combined with the appreciating yen, caused this source of demand to disappear.

[49] In the minimills' case, imports became an issue only after 1985. The *Nihon Keizai Shimbun* (July 25, 1988) reported that bar steel imports grew from 537 tons in the first half of 1986 to 156,000 tons in the first half of 1987. This was still only 2 percent of domestic production.

Bar steel is a standardized, low quality good, so Korean and Taiwanese makers should have no problems meeting JIS standards. However, a number of factors offer a degree of natural protection to the Japanese minimills. First, even after *endaka*, the cost advantage for Taiwanese and Korean producers is not overwhelming. One estimate shows that Japanese production costs (at 1987 prices and exchange rates) are only slightly higher for bar steel and are lower for H-beams (Industrial Bank of Japan 1988, p. 49). Second, the localized nature of scrap, the importance of ties to consumers (especially the ability to respond flexibly to local demand), and high transportation costs relative to selling prices, reduce the cost advantages to the Koreans and Taiwanese.

[50] Tokyo Seitetsu's Iketani did not oppose this bill strongly, finding the new law less objectionable in that it encouraged uncompetitive firms to diversify.

ment's subsequent steps to reflate the domestic economy. The consequent recovery of the minimills made them ineligible under the 1988 legislation. As the industry noted, the Maekawa reflation was the latest in a series of "divine winds" that rescued the minimills—prices soared in 1987, production was close to its historic high, and the industry as a whole enjoyed its most profitable year ever. With conditions far from depressed, the minimills withdrew their Enkotsukahō application in March 1988.

Epilogue: The Unrepentant Outsider

The direct confrontation between Iketani and the integrated steel firms continues into the 1990s. If anything, the confrontation is now more direct and intense. Tokyo Seitetsu has continued to invest heavily in the newest technology and to expand its production capacity. In 1989, for instance, it introduced in its Kyushu plant the largest electric furnace in the world that uses direct current. This new technology promised to cut its production costs in half and also allowed Tokyo Seitetsu to become the first minimill in Japan with a capacity of over 2 million tons.[51] More significantly, after winning the H-Beam war, Iketani continued to move beyond the old boundaries of the traditional minimills and into niche markets that were dominated by the majors. In 1988 the firm began to produce steel plate and sheet. In 1991 it was the first minimill to install a hot-strip mill, and the following year it became the first to produce hot-rolled coils. In 1994 it began to manufacture sheet piles used in large infrastructure projects. If it can maintain adequate levels of quality in these products, it stands to make significant inroads into these lucrative markets once monopolized by the steel majors.

Tokyo Seitetsu's competitiveness also stems from its lean management style. For instance, the firm employs a staff of only 60 in its head office (as compared to over 7,000 for Nippon Steel). Iketani also prides himself on the firm's flexible philosophy and willingness to make hard, pragmatic business decisions—the very traits that have made minimills so successful in the United States. These moves have made Tokyo Seitetsu the most profitable steel maker in Japan. In 1992 and 1993, its profits surpassed those of Nippon Steel, a firm that is nearly 15 times larger in terms of capital and employs more than three times as many workers. Iketani continues to be confident in his firm's ability to master the majors and unrepentant over his status as industry maverick. As he stated in late 1992, "cooperation is not our basic principle. It is competition. In the free market we will not be beaten."[52]

---

[51] *Nihon Keizai Shimbun,* Aug. 31, 1989.
[52] *The Nikkei Weekly,* Nov. 16, 1992; Yonekura 1994, p. 195.

Since the mid-1980s the steel majors have tried to keep up with Tokyo Seitetsu and the other minimills. The majors have continued to consolidate their minimill affiliates through mergers, but analysts believe that more drastic consolidation is necessary. It was not until 1994 that some of the majors began to consider adding electric furnaces to their existing plants. Since much of the steel scrap used by the minimills comes from the majors, this move seems to be a logical step. The majors still reveal a lingering arrogance, believing that only blast furnaces make real steel. According to one analyst, when Kawasaki Steel became the first major to install an electric furnace it had "to put aside its pride as a major steelmaker and come down to the level of the minimills."[53] Finally, the majors have tried to unseat Tokyo Seitetsu by buying up and exporting steel scrap. Their hope, evidently, is that if Tokyo Seitetsu's access to domestic steel scrap is choked off, its production costs will rise. One Nippon Steel executive boasted, "We are going to collect and export steel scrap to China and other countries to disturb Tokyo Steel's operations." Iketani admitted that this move "could create a lot of trouble for us."[54] But given his firm's underlying competitive strengths, such annoyance tactics are not likely to stop, or even slow, Tokyo Seitetsu.

In a revealing comment, an executive at Nippon Steel compared Tokyo Seitetsu's plan to expand into hot-rolled sheet steel to "someone with a full stomach snatching a hungry man's food." An industry analyst put it more directly: Nippon Steel executives simply "do not understand capitalism."[55]

IMPLICATIONS OF THE MINIMILL CASE

Aside from a handful of outsiders, the minimill firms were unable to take any steps to diversify or otherwise adjust economically. This is understandable given the industry's structure. The small scale of the average minimill and their limited capital bases prevented most firms from pursuing adjustment options. Diversification into other steel products would put the minimills into direct confrontation with the majors, a confrontation most could not hope to win. And diversification into non-steel products requires capital and R&D capabilities far beyond what most minimills possess.[56] For the majority of firms the diversification option has not been

[53] Nihon Keizai Shimbun, Jan. 21, 1994.

[54] The Nikkei Weekly, Mar. 28, 1994.

[55] Japan Economic Journal, Sept. 15, 1990; The Nikkei Weekly, Nov. 16, 1992.

[56] Also, there have been only a few attempts to diversify into the U.S. market. Most notably, Tokyo Seitetsu has established a joint venture with Tamco and has entered into talks with Nucor, the largest minimill in the United States and also somewhat of an industry maverick. Yamato Kogyo entered into two joint overseas ventures, one with Nucor and one with a Thai producer. In addition, Kyoei Seiko has tied up with Auburn Steel (Barnett and Crandall 1986, p. 69).

a viable one. In fact, the trend in the industry has been in the opposite direction: most firms have actually increased their reliance on bar steel, which remains a highly cyclical and low value-added product. Lacking viable adjustment alternatives, firms have been left with the same choice open to the cotton spinners: either bearing the costs of adjustment or seeking political solutions to avoid those costs.

The labor force, which ended up bearing a large part of the adjustment burden, has joined the firms in pursuing political solutions. Between 1978 and 1987 the industry's work force was cut by 50 percent. Although labor has at times been able to prevent plant closings, unions have had a difficult time organizing on an industry-wide basis. Labor has been compensated through a number of special government unemployment schemes dating back to 1975 and under special provisions of the Tokuanhō and Sankōhō; however, they have not been able to avoid significant reductions in the work force.

Even more clearly than in the cotton spinning and coal mining cases, two decades of government regulation of the minimills has preserved the status quo and retarded the adjustment process. Economic efficiency arguments suggest than an industry like the minimills would do better by responding to market forces, allowing the least competitive firms to exit and be replaced with newer, more competitive facilities.[57] In Japan's case, policy makers have chosen a different route: regulation. Government regulation of the supply side has effectively insulated the industry from market forces and the need to adjust. Although a few insider minimills have merged, turnover in the industry has been slight.[58] Furthermore, the industry's total capacity actually increased during the years that it was designated as "structurally depressed"—the exact opposite of what the Tokuanhō and Sankōhō intended. These policy efforts to stabilize the industry have particularly benefited the least competitive producers, which otherwise would have had no choice but to bear the burden of adjustment.

Over the long-term, however, government policy to freeze or restrict capacity has robbed the industry of the one main advantage it should enjoy over the integrated firms: flexibility. One of the key advantages of the minimills is their low capital costs that allow them to modernize quickly. At least in the United States, it is not unusual for minimills to replace or rebuild furnaces after only a few years of use.[59] In contrast, as shown in Table 5-1, furnaces in the Japanese industry have aged dramatically. In 1976, at

[57] Barnett and Crandall (1986) make these points in discussing what optimal U.S. policy should be toward American minimills.

[58] Three small minimills exited in the 1975–1977 crisis. There have also been a number of corporate resuscitations, the largest of which was Kokko Seiko, in August 1986. There has been one new entrant into the industry.

[59] Barnett and Crandall 1986, p. 6.

Table 5-1. Age structure of Japan's electric furnaces (percent of total furnaces)

Year	20 years or older	15 to 20 years old	Less than 14 years old
1976	3	17	80
1978	7	25	68
1983	20	6	73
1987	20	37	43
1993	57	25	18

SOURCES: 1976 figures from Heidenro Kihon Mondai Kenkyūkai 1977; all other figures from Tekkōkai, various issues.

the beginning of efforts to control capacity, 80 percent of the furnaces were younger than their 14-year depreciation period. By 1987, this figure had dropped to only 43 percent. In the late 1980s the industry understood that this trend would continue to intensify unless it embarked on a concerted modernization campaign. No such campaign occurred.

Those firms that followed the insiders and cooperated with government regulation have gotten the worst of both worlds. They have remained dependent on bar steel production and are still at the mercy of future fluctuations in construction demand. They are beset with problems of aging facilities, excess capacity and production, and depressed profits. Rather than becoming lean and competitive, the industry insiders have become fatter and more complacent. The net result of government regulation has been a less vibrant, less competitive industry. Although it is not my purpose to judge the effectiveness of MITI's industrial policy, this case, judged by any rational criteria, has been a clear policy failure.

The outsiders now enjoy a stronger competitive position than they ever have, but only because they were willing to defy the MITI bureaucrats and the rest of the industry. Tokyo Seitetsu in particular resisted all industry-wide "stabilization" schemes and at the same time diversified into more lucrative market niches.

"Developmental state" approaches have even greater trouble explaining MITI's behavior in the minimill case than in cotton spinning and coal mining. MITI had no economic or developmental reason to intervene so deeply in this industry. Its policy actions have certainly not been motivated by efficiency, or even effectiveness. Its policy has not helped the industry anticipate economic decline, nor has it been designed to "preempt the costs of change" by encouraging the industry to undergo needed rationalization. Even if one makes the argument that the minimills are somehow a strategic industry—which no one outside the minimill industry association even tries to do—MITI's policies have followed no discernible economic rationale. Its actions were not designed to increase the industry's competitiveness. In fact, the opposite was the case; it was precisely the most vibrant and competitive firms that MITI's regulatory approach tried to rein in. The only firms that have done well have succeeded in spite of MITI regulations, not because of them.

MITI was clearly not able to "simply ignore the non-strategic sectors of the society."[60] Rather, it was highly sensitive to the shifting preferences of the minimills themselves. During the 1970s, when the insiders still dominated the industry association, MITI agreed to help the industry stabilize itself, and subsequently found itself embroiled in one of its messiest and most controversial episodes of regulation. MITI's industrial policy is a creature shaped by politics as much as economics.

In explaining policy outcomes in this case, we cannot completely ignore the policy making environment. That a fragmented industry like the minimills even tried to pursue collective stabilization for most of the 1970s was in part due to MITI's ability and willingness to use its regulatory powers to enforce industry agreements. Given high obstacles to organization, it is doubtful that the industry would even have tried to manage its supply-side situation on its own. In this sense, the policy environment, while not defining the industry's interests, did help to define what the industry could and could not achieve. Also, environmental constraints on MITI's use of informal administrative guidance and the more formal recession cartels grew in the 1980s. By 1985 it was politically more difficult to implement policies that were under attack by the antitrust authorities and Japan's trading partners.

But the real story of the minimill case centers around the outsiders. In particular, Tokyo Seitetsu's stubbornness as a maverick and its subsequent triumph in the market place made attempts to manipulate supply-side conditions completely futile. The defiant behavior of the outsiders moved industrial policy out of the realm of government regulation and into the realm of the markets.

THE PAPER INDUSTRY

The paper industry is a second example of a Type III industry. The industry is a fragmented one: in the early 1980s it consisted of about 500 firms, 426 of which were classified as small- or medium-sized firms.[61] The industry at its peak in 1953 had a labor force of around 82,000 workers.

---

[60] Johnson 1982, p. 316.
[61] This industry is usually divided into pulp, paper, and paperboard producers. The paper industry's JSIC number is 2421. Within these groups analysts often treat separately the producers of particular products: high-quality paper (for use in newsprint and publishing), craft paper (used in industrial packaging), and cardboard (Tokutei Fukyō Sangyō Shinyō Kikin 1982, p. 100; Japan Development Bank 1983, p. 2).

The industry's structure makes it a classic example of "excessive competition." With no firm dominant enough to exercise market leadership, the industry has been faced with a cycle of overproduction and drastic price declines whenever demand has declined. The industry has also been prone to investment wars in which firms tried to outdo each other by adding new capacity whenever market conditions picked up; the fundamental problem of excess capacity has made cyclical downturns even more difficult to weather.

The paper industry first encountered significant economic distress following the oil shocks of the 1970s. Like the minimills, paper firms attempted to adjust in the face of economic distress, but these efforts were largely ineffectual. Consequently, the industry began pursuing stabilization policies, seeking cartelization and other cooperative efforts to control output and later capacity. Unlike the minimills, however, the paper industry faced a significant external constraint: since the early 1980s American trade officials began to press Japan for greater access to the paper market. These external pressures had a great impact on the policy process in Japan, making it difficult to implement cartels and other policies to manage domestic competition.

Domestic Recession, 1975–1988

The domestic recession that followed the First Oil Shock led to a drastic fall in domestic demand for paper products. On the economic front, the industry did what it could to adjust to economic distress. In particular, it tried to shift away from expensive imported crude oil and locate cheaper foreign sources of its main raw materials, pulp and wood chips. The industry also tried to rationalize its labor force: between 1975 and 1980 the labor force declined by more than 17 percent.[62]

However, the industry in the 1970s and 1980s was by and large unable to pursue other more significant economic adjustment strategies. Firms made no progress in diversifying out of paper-related production. A handful of the largest firms had already ventured into overseas production, but all of these investments had been completed by the 1960s before the Oil Shocks. The vast majority of firms remained tied to the domestic market and completely dependent on the production of paper.

Two separate sectors of the paper industry, cardboard and paper, were affected by declining demand following the Oil Shocks. Economic distress hit the producers of cardboard first. This product sector, which ac-

---

[62] The oil shock caused production costs to rise especially because the industry relied heavily on oil for its energy needs. Firms thus attempted to use domestic coal to replace imported oil. Through concerted conservation efforts, the industry was able to reduce its dependence on oil from 76.2 percent in 1973 to 71.4 percent in 1979. *Business Japan*, April 1981, p. 99.

counted for some 20 percent of the industry's total output, was highly diffuse: of the 88 firms in this sector at the end of the 1970s, 65 were considered to be small or medium, and the largest three firms accounted for only 30 percent of total production. Firms in this sector were also widely known as "unruly" and prone to excessive competition and excessive investment. In 1973 alone, just prior to the First Oil Shock, this sector entered into an investment race in which firms increased capacity by 40 percent. The sudden rise in oil prices thus caught the cardboard producers at a particularly vulnerable moment. With demand falling, operating rates plummeted from 95 percent in 1973 to a mere 57 percent in 1975, and prices fell from ¥24.1 to ¥9.1 per kilogram. Over the next three years operating rates remained below 66 percent, and prices also remained depressed. Seventeen firms went bankrupt between 1974 and 1978.[63]

The cardboard producers found themselves in the same dilemma faced by other fragmented industries: whether to allow the market to weed out the least competitive firms or to attempt to manage competition through the use of cartels and other cooperative solutions. The cardboard producers chose the latter.

In late 1974, firms in the sector initiated internal discussions on the need to cooperatively cut back on production.[64] By July of 1975 firms had agreed to pursue "voluntary curtailments" of production (*jishu sōtan*) in order to stabilize prices. Cardboard firms reduced their operating rates to between 60 and 70 percent during that summer. The paper industry's *gyōkai*, the Japan Paper Association, then appealed to MITI for help in monitoring these efforts.[65] In response, MITI in March 1976 agreed to issue guidelines to help producers in their efforts to manage supply and demand.

With market conditions still stagnant, the Japan Paper Association in July 1977 set up an internal committee to discuss structural improvement for the cardboard industry.[66] The committee advised the firms to seek a formal recession cartel. The cardboard manufacturers were quick to follow this advice and formally requested cartels to cover linerboard and corrugating medium. These cartels were approved in September for a period of three months and then were extended until February 1979 when prices showed no signs of recovering. Subsequently the cardboard sector was designated under the Tokuanhō, which allowed the firms to extend their cartel agreements.

[63] Tokutei Fukyō Sangyō Shinyō Kikin 1982, p. 103.

[64] *Industrial Review of Japan*, 1976, p. 110; 1977, p. 115; *Japan Economic Almanac* 1985, p. 136.

[65] Japan Development Bank 1983, p. 4.

[66] *Business Japan*, Apr. 1979, p. 93; Japan Development Bank 1983, p. 4.

Soon after being designated as a depressed industry, it became clear that MITI and the firms disagreed on the severity of the problem. Since 1977 the industry's structural improvement committee had been advocating a plan to freeze 17 percent of capacity; in contrast, MITI officials felt that the sector needed to cut up to 25 percent of total capacity in order to regain its viability. The final capacity reduction plan was even below the industry's suggestion, calling for a cut of 15.2 percent. In the end, firms reduced capacity by only 14 percent.[67]

As in the previously discussed case studies, most firms were in favor of the coordinated capacity cutbacks. This was particularly true for the small and less competitive firms, since they would have been the first to exit in the absence of any stabilization scheme. There were exceptions, however. In particular, Settsu Paperboard refused to participate and, like Tokyo Seitetsu, set out to expand its output and capacity. Unlike Tokyo Seitetsu, however, this firm did not have the market power to upset the cartel arrangement and so was allowed to defect. The other cardboard producers, however, were well aware of the potential problem of outsiders: in January 1978 the cardboard firms requested that MITI retain outsider restrictions in the Tokuanhō.[68]

A second segment of the paper industry, which included craft and high-quality paper, was hurt more by the Second Oil Shock. Again, the problem was excess capacity investment. Even though domestic demand was stagnant throughout the 1970s, these paper producers found themselves locked in a series of investment races: between 1975 and 1980 capacity increased by 33 percent in high-quality paper and by 30 percent in craft paper.[69] The industry thus created an unstable situation. As soon as demand fell, the industry faced the inevitable cycle of overcapacity, excessive output, falling prices, and reduced profits.

The sector reacted to falling prices by trying to cooperatively cut back on production with the help of MITI's administrative guidance. However, with operating rates falling below 70 percent in 1980, the industry realized that it could not "cope with . . . slow demand by voluntarily curtailing production alone."[70] It thus decided to seek more extensive cartelization and in May 1981 received approval for separate cartels for high-quality paper, coated paper, and craft paper. Even after the formal cartels ended in

[67] *Industrial Review of Japan,* 1978, p. 117; *Business Japan,* Apr. 1979, p. 94; *Japan Economic Institute (JEI) Report,* Nov. 26, 1993, p. 4; Peck et al. 1987, p. 96. In all, 66 cardboard producers representing 95 percent of capacity participated in this plan.

[68] The minimill insiders had also made this request but were turned down because of the strong opposition of the FTC (*Nihon Keizai Shimbun,* Jan. 31 1978). In 1983 Settsu again refused to cooperate with the cardboard sector's plan to cut capacity under the Sankōhō (*Industrial Review of Japan,* 1984, p. 125).

[69] Tokutei Fukyō Sangyō Shinyō Kikin 1982, p. 107.

[70] *Industrial Review of Japan,* 1982, p. 114.

early 1982, however, the industry benefited from new MITI guidelines to help enforce the industry's voluntary production curtailments.[71] These guidelines remained in effect for the next five years.

The industry's long-term difficulties were not lost on the industry itself. In June 1981 the Japan Paper Association convened a "special study group" to discuss the fundamental problem of excess capacity. This group, which consisted of the 16 main firms in the industry, estimated that 50 percent of craft paper capacity was excessive, while other product segments were deemed to have about 20 percent excess capacity.[72]

In September 1981, MITI accepted the advice of the Industrial Structure Council and announced that it was using its administrative guidance powers to freeze capacity expansion. Although the FTC objected immediately, MITI went ahead and froze capacity for two years. Under this guidance firms submitted biannual reports on their investment plans to MITI.

This action was clearly welcomed by the industry itself. Two months later the industry's special study group passed a resolution endorsing this managed approach to cutting capacity and called for inclusion of the paper industry in the new Sankōhō. This designation enabled the industry to make significant capacity cutbacks.[73]

The paper industry seemed on the verge of recovery in the mid-1980s, due mostly to a significant expansion of domestic demand, spurred on in part by the Japanese government's efforts to reflate the domestic economy. In addition, the appreciation of the yen helped to lower production costs in the industry since the paper firms relied heavily on imported materials. Because the industry was on the road to recovery it no longer qualified under the depressed industry laws. Consequently, the paper industry was not designated under the Enkotsukahō, the successor to the Sankōhō. And because MITI no longer enforced even informal restrictions on capacity, the industry was not covered by any capacity or output regulations for the first time in more than a decade.

The paper producers soon showed that they had not learned much from their earlier experience: immediately after restrictions were lifted, firms quickly entered into yet another period of unrestrained capacity expansion, or what was termed an "investment free-for-all." Between 1988

---

[71] *Industrial Review of Japan*, 1983, p. 112. Under the cartel, output for all three products was limited to 50 percent of total capacity. With prices recovering, the craft paper cartel ended in December 1981, while the cartels for high-quality and coated paper were extended until February 1982 (Tsūshō Sangyōshō 1984, p. 222; *Industrial Review of Japan*, 1982, p. 114). Initially, the third largest firm, Toyo Pulp, did not join the cartel. See Sekiguchi 1991, pp. 428–429, and 1994, pp. 183–184.

[72] The group was chaired by Tanaka Fumio, chairman of the industry's largest firm, Oji Paper (*Industrial Review of Japan*, 1982, p. 115).

[73] The paper firms eventually cut capacity by 10 percent, while the cardboard firms were able to reduce capacity by 11 percent (Peck et al. 1987, p. 117; *JEI Report*, Nov. 26, 1993, p. 5).

and 1992 more than 20 firms built new paper-making facilities, increasing capacity by 4 million tons. Overall, capacity rose by 7.9 percent in this period. In comparison, between 1983 and 1988, while the industry was designated under the Sankōhō, its capacity increased by a mere 0.3 percent.[74]

The industry's timing could not have been worse: the majority of this capacity came on line just as the Japanese economy entered its most serious recession since World War II. This time around, however, Japan's external environment had changed, and the industry found that it was now unable to manage competition at home.

External Constraints Increase: 1983 to the Present

As has been noted earlier, domestic stabilization efforts can only succeed if imports are somehow prevented from increasing. This was not an issue before 1978, since imports of paper products into Japan were just over 2 percent of domestic demand. However, the appreciation of the yen beginning in 1986 and the industry's attempts to raise prices at home opened a gap between domestic and international prices. American and Canadian firms were particularly competitive, since the industries in those countries enjoyed cost advantages in the basic inputs needed to make paper—wood, water, and energy. These cost advantages allowed the American and Canadian industries to produce paper and paperboard at prices 5 to 30 percent lower than in Japan.[75]

The issue of market access soon became a focus of trade negotiations between the United States and Japan. The U.S. government first tried to lower Japan's tariffs on cardboard and paperboard imports.[76] Then the U.S. government complained that the recession cartels provided the industry with at least implicit protection. These criticisms of the paper industry were later extended to include Japan's structurally depressed industry laws in general; both the recession cartels and the industry laws were widely perceived to slow imports.[77] In response, the Japanese government agreed to lower tariffs on craft paper and paperboard in 1983 and again in 1984. The paper industry was not able to prevent these concessions. The chairman of the Japan Paper Association, Oji's President

[74] *Japan Economic Almanac,* 1989, p. 183; 1992, p. 136; *Far Eastern Economic Review,* Oct. 29, 1992, p. 77; *JEI Report,* Nov. 26, 1993, p. 6.

[75] North American firms have been able to rely on cheap and plentiful supplies of hydroelectricity (*Japan Economic Almanac,* 1989, p. 183; 1990, p. 173; and *Business Japan,* April 1981, p. 99).

[76] At least one analyst argues that these tariffs were actually rising in this period, leading the Japan Economic Institute to argue that "MITI was attempting to down-size and simultaneously protect an important component of the paper industry" (*JEI Report,* Nov. 26, 1993, p. 5). U.S. negotiators were still trying to lower tariffs on paper products in Japan well into the 1990s (*Nihon Keizai Shimbun,* Jan. 24, 1991).

[77] *Japan Economic Journal,* Jan. 1, 1988; *Nihon Keizai Shimbun,* Jan. 30, 1988.

Tanaka, argued that these tariff cuts put the Japanese industry in a more difficult position. In an appeal that only underscored the industry's insular attitude, Tanaka argued, "we have consented to cut our tariffs and turn over a considerable market share to imported paper and paperboard and borne the pain caused by an increase in imports so far, but . . . any more drastic tariff concession may endanger the very foundation of the pulp and paper industry in this country."[78]

Despite the industry's gloomy forecast, paper imports by December 1990 still accounted for only 4 percent of domestic consumption. (In contrast, U.S. firms held a 30 percent share of the paper market in Europe.) Thus, in 1991 the issue of access to Japan's paper market was again on the trade agenda of the United States. In January 1991 a new committee, the US-Japan Paper Experts Working Group convened to discuss the access issue. The 1992 visit of President Bush to Tokyo gave a further impetus to these negotiations: one of the few positive results of this trip was a commitment by the Japanese government to encourage paper imports. In subsequent negotiations, the Japanese side implicitly agreed to raise the market share of foreign firms to 10 percent by 1997, up from between 3 and 4 percent in 1991.[79]

These external pressures exerted a clear constraint on the domestic policy options open to the Japanese industry and to MITI. Tariffs had already been reduced substantially. In addition, growing international pressures and criticisms made the use of recession cartels increasingly unacceptable.

The extent of these constraints became clear in 1991 as the economy moved deeper into recession. With demand drying up, industry analysts estimated that existing capacity exceeded current demand by 20 percent.[80] In previous periods, the industry would have immediately appealed to MITI for help in forming some sort of collective stabilization scheme. This time, however, support from industrial policy makers was not forthcoming. Analysts attribute this mostly to the growing external criticisms and pressures. The Nikkei Weekly observed: "Until recently, when the industry got itself in . . . trouble, the government would extend a helping hand in the form of administrative guidance, such as 'suggesting' that major firms form a cartel to allot production ratios. But these days, the government has tied its hands out of a desire to avoid arousing the U.S. In the Structural Impediments Initiative talks, the Americans have criticized administrative guidance as a form of protectionism that works to block foreign firms out of the Japanese market."[81]

---

[78] *Keidanren Review*, no. 94, (Aug. 1985), p. 12.
[79] *Nihon Keizai Shimbun*, Dec. 21, 1990; *JEI Report*, Nov. 26, 1993, pp. 7–9.
[80] *Japan Economic Almanac*, 1993, p. 124.
[81] *Nikkei Weekly*, Sept. 21, 1991. See also *JEI Report*, Nov. 26, 1993, p. 6. The *Far Eastern Economic Review* (Oct. 29, 1992, p. 77) put it more succinctly: "in the past, there would have been a MITI-led cartel that would have restored prices. . . . [Now, however], MITI feels impelled to stand aside."

The industry went ahead with its own voluntary efforts to cut production in May 1991. But without a formal mechanism to enforce these cutbacks the industry was unable to deal with free riding. Rather, the industry found itself locked in a price-cutting competition, with prices of some products falling by 30 percent or more in this period.[82] Industry officials now openly lamented their own unrestrained capacity expansion after 1988. One industry source lamented, "if someone could have regulated the industry's investments, or taken the leadership in price negotiations, this slump might not have been so serious." A MITI official made a different point: "It may seem that the Japanese paper companies are doing stupid things by selling more and making more losses, but it has been their nature for several years."[83]

The industry now found itself in real trouble. Unable to manage competition at home, and with imports certain to increase in the future, the major firms in the industry now saw no choice but to turn to more drastic economic adjustment efforts. First, a handful of the industry's largest firms stepped up their efforts to enter into joint ventures with North American producers. In 1979, for instance, Jujo Paper tied up with Weyerhaeuser, and Japan's largest producer, Oji Paper, entered into a joint venture with International Paper the following year. In 1987 Oji Paper agreed to a tie-up with a major Canadian producer, Canfor, while Daishowa Paper purchased a major paper mill in Washington State in 1988 and another large mill in Virginia the following year. Second, the industry turned to domestic mergers as the most direct means to restructure the industry.[84] In August 1992, the second and fourth largest Japanese firms, Jujo Paper and Sanyo-Kokusaku Pulp, agreed to merge; this new firm, Nippon Paper Industries, is now Japan's largest producer of paper. In January 1993 Oji Paper entered into a merger of its own, tying up with Japan's ninth largest firm, Kanzaki Paper. These adjustment strategies, however, have been limited to the largest firms in the industry. Choices have been more difficult for the industry's smaller firms, which have been limited to bankruptcy or absorbtion through merger. Furthermore, analysts view these efforts as unlikely to lead to a recovery of the industry any time soon. A MITI-sponsored panel in June 1994 estimated that 14.7 percent of the industry's 33 million tons of capacity was excessive and that the industry would continue to suffer from excessive capacity until the end of the century. Other than possibly exporting

---

[82] Operating rates fell from 94 percent in 1989 to 74 percent in 1991 (*Japan Economic Almanac*, 1992, p. 137; 1993, p. 124; *Far Eastern Economic Review*, Oct. 29, 1992, p. 77).

[83] *Nikkei Weekly*, July 18, 1992; *Far Eastern Economic Review*, Oct. 29, 1992, p. 77.

[84] Throughout the 1970s and 1980s the main firms had sporadically absorbed the smaller, less prosperous mills. But it was not until the 1990s that the industry saw its first serious mergers (*Japan Economic Almanac*, 1989, p. 182; *Industrial Review of Japan*, 1983, p. 113).

more to other Asian markets or waiting for another upturn in domestic demand, an industry leader admitted that "we don't have any plan for helping the industry to achieve a quick recovery."[85]

[85] *Far Eastern Economic Review* Oct. 29, 1992, p. 78. See also *Nihon Keizai Shimbun,* June 16, 1994; *Nikkei Weekly* June 20, 1994; *Japan 21st* , Apr. 1994.

CHAPTER SIX

Flexible Industries: Synthetic
Fibers and Aluminum (Type I)

The cases discussed in this chapter, the Type I industries, are highly concentrated (tending to have a small number of relatively large firms) and have a small labor force. Concentration is the key difference between these industries and those in the first two case studies. Type I firms are, on average, larger compared to firms in fragmented industries and have greater access to critical resources, including capital and technology. They are therefore more likely to be able to pursue a strategy of economic adjustment, both at home and abroad. As in industries such as the minimills and paper, the labor force is relatively small, but because of the large size of the firms, it should be easier to absorb redundant workers in other parts of the organization or to shift them to related firms. The barriers to labor adjustment should be the lowest of all industry types. With the cost of adjustment relatively low for both labor and capital, we should expect Type I industries to pursue strategies of economic adjustment. Although these industries, as with all declining industries, will also seek stabilization strategies, these efforts should be more temporary and less intense than in any of the other industry types.

Japan's synthetic fiber industry is a representative Type I industry. In the mid-1970s the industry consisted of nine firms, with the top three accounting for more than 50 percent of output.[1] At its peak, in 1971 the labor force consisted of 53,871 workers.

The synthetic fiber industry and the cotton spinning industry occupy the upstream portion of textile production but otherwise there is little

---

[1] The JSIC number for the synthetic fiber industry is 2643.

overlap between the two; it is thus important to keep the industries analytically distinct. The usual image of a textile firm is of a small, labor-intensive operation with unsophisticated machinery. While this description may fit natural fiber producers such as the cotton spinners or the downstream weavers and textile processors, it does not characterize the synthetic fiber firms. Rather, these firms are more accurately classified as industrial conglomerates that use sophisticated production processes to transform petroleum-based chemicals into one of three main synthetic fibers—nylon, polyester, and acrylics. The industry's structure is also quite different from cotton spinning. As shown in Table 6-1, all nine synthetic fiber firms are large and capital intensive. Six of the main firms are core members of the *keiretsu* groupings; all of the others enjoy close ties to the *keiretsu* through their main bank relationships.

THE INDUSTRY'S EARLY PERIOD OF ECONOMIC DISTRESS

The industry's concentration is the result of high barriers to market entry. Until the early 1960s, synthetic fiber production was dominated by a handful of firms that had been able to obtain foreign technology. As shown in Table 6-2, Toray and Nippon Rayon were the pacesetters in the original synthetic fiber, nylon. In the early 1950s Toray obtained nylon technology through a tie-up with Du Pont, at that time the world's dominant nylon producer, while Nippon Rayon obtained its nylon technology from a Swiss firm, Inventa.[2] Toray, along with Teijin, also led the way in the polyester field. In 1953 the two firms were able to obtain technology from the world leader, Britain's ICI (Imperial Chemical Industries). Asahi Kasei, Mitsubishi Rayon, and Toyobo were the early entrants in the industry's third field, acrylics.

The Japanese government provided important support for these early private efforts, including tax exemptions, depreciation allowances, and import protection. Furthermore, the government arranged for loans from the Japan Development Bank and other government subsidies. Between 1949 and 1955, government finance accounted for 20.3 percent of the industry's total capacity investments. The government also helped domestic firms obtain foreign technology. In the case of polyester, for instance, when Toray and Teijin felt that ICI's original conditions were too stringent, MITI's mediation in these negotiations helped to soften the terms.[3] MITI poured most of its efforts into promoting vinylon, a product that

---

[2] The industry's development is discussed in Uriu 1993, Sakota 1987, Fujii 1971, Nihon Kagaku Sen'i Kyōkai 1974, Japan Development Bank 1974, and Sangyō Seisaku Shi Kenkyūjo 1977.
[3] Hiwatari 1989, p. 173.

Table 6-1. Structure of the synthetic fiber sector, 1979

	Capital (billion yen)	Labor force	Capacity (tons per day)				Principal banking relationships	Keiretsu group
			Total	Polyester	Nylon	Acrylic		
Toray	54.8	14,052	866	441	296	129	Mitsui	Mitsui
Asahi Kasei	48.7	13,733	473	65	164	244	Sumitomo, DKB, Fuji	Dai-ichi
Teijin	34.4	7,446	587	460	127	—	Sanwa, Fuji	Sanwa
Toyobo	30.4	12,171	476	218	72	186	DKB, Mitsubishi	Sanwa
Unitika (formerly Nippon Rayon)	23.8	6,943	177	22	155	—	Sanwa, Tokai, Kyowa	—
Kanebo	19.0	5,522	241	90	76	75	Mitsui, Fuji, Tokai	—
Mitsubishi Rayon	16.4	3,464	336	97	—	239	Mitsubishi Bank, Mitsubishi Trust, DKB	Mitsubishi
Kuraray	10.4	5,133	186	186	—	—	Industrial Bank of Japan, Fuji, Sumitomo	—
Toho Rayon	0.3	2,020	141	—	—	141	Fuji, Mitsubishi, DKB	Fuyo
Nihon Ester (joint venture between Unitika, Kanebo, and Mitsubishi Rayon)			239	239	—	—		

SOURCES: Nihon Keizai Shimbun 1979, pp. 23, 46; Gerlach 1989, pp. 146–147.

Table 6-2. Early development of Japan's synthetic fiber industry

	Technology obtained	Began full-scale production	Foreign technology source	Capacity (tons/day) 1963	1967
NYLON					
Original entrants					
Toray	1951	1952	Du Pont (US)	161	260
Nippon Rayon (Unitika)	1954	1955	Inveta AG (Switzerland)	74	138
Late entrants					
Teijin	1961	1963	Allied Chemical (US)	14	72
Kanebo	1961	1963	SNIA Viscosa (Italy)	22	72
Toyobo	1961	1964	Zimmer (West Germany)	14	72
Asahi Kasei	1962	1964	Zimmer (West Germany); Firestone (US)	6	72
POLYESTER					
Original entrants					
Toray	1957	1958	ICI (UK)	86	197
Teijin	1957	1958	ICI (UK)	86	195
Late entrants					
Nippon Rayon (Unitika)	1961	1964	Inventa AG and Emser Werke AG (Switzerland)	15	76
Toyobo	1961	1964	Chemtex (US)	15	88
Kurary	1962	1964	Monsanto (US)	15	80
"Late-late entrants"					
Kanebo	1967	1969	SNIA Viscosa (Italy)	0	10
Asahi Kasei	1967	1969	Rhodiaceta (France)	0	10
Mitsubishi Rayon	1968	1969	Glanzstoff (West Germany) and AKZO (Holland)	0	10

SOURCES: Nihon Kagaku Sen'i Kyōkai 1974, p. 919; Fujii 1971, pp. 259–261, 402; Japan Development Bank 1974, p. 10.

eventually proved a commercial failure; at the same time, it failed to provide early funding for polyester, a product that would become the most profitable of the synthetic fibers.[4]

Until the early 1960s the original entrants were able to use their exclusive control over synthetic fiber technology to deter the entry of new firms. However, the expiration of the original patents for both nylon and polyester opened the door for a spate of new entrants (see Table 6-2). In 1961 and 1962 four new firms were able to gain access to nylon technology and three new firms were able to enter the polyester field. The most important of these late entrants was Asahi Kasei, which was able to integrate forward into nylon from its strong base in chemical production. In addition, two of the larger cotton spinning firms, Kanebo and Toyobo, had the technological and financial resources to diversify into synthetic fibers.

This flood of new entry, later known as the *gōsen rasshu*, or "rush into synthetic fibers," led to a period of intense expansion in which total capacity increased by 166 percent. As a result, the late entrants were able to erode the dominant position the original entrants had enjoyed. In 1962 Toray and Nippon Rayon accounted for all of the nylon produced in Japan, and Toray and Teijin produced all domestic polyester; by 1967, just five years later, the late entrants accounted for 41 percent of both nylon and polyester capacity.

Unfortunately for the industry, this expansion race coincided with a slowdown in domestic demand, the first such slowdown it had encountered in its short history. Declining demand was soon exacerbated by a price-cutting war, with each firm increasing production and slashing prices in order to expand domestic market share. The result was drastically falling prices and declining profits for all. Competition was particularly fierce in nylon, where prices were cut in half during 1964.[5]

The Industry's Early Attempts at Regulation

The industry soon began to consider ways to restrain price cutting and to stabilize market prices. As an immediate step they chose the same mechanism employed by the cotton spinners and minimills: temporary, voluntary production cutbacks. The original entrants, Toray and Nippon Rayon, began unilateral production cuts at the end of 1964. Industry analysts note that these firms had incentives to unilaterally stabilize the market because depressed prices were hurting them more, since their market share was so much larger than the late entrants. Although the newcomers were

---

[4] Sangyō Seisaku Shi Kenkyūjo 1977, p. 118; Nihon Kagaku Sen'i Kyokai 1974, pp. 481–484, 490–492.

[5] Nihon Kagaku Sen'i Kyōkai 1974, pp. 846–849; Sakota 1987, p. 21.

initially reluctant to cut back their own production so soon after entering the industry, they followed suit, and prices soon recovered.[6]

The industry also began to discuss a more fundamental problem: excessive capacity expansion. The original entrants blamed the newcomers for being too aggressive in their efforts to expand capacity. This, they argued, had led to a situation of excessive competition. They were now convinced that some regulation to curb capacity expansion was necessary and desirable. The newcomers also shared this conviction, although to a lesser degree, because they had already completed their immediate expansion plans and had become established in the industry. Now, they too stood to benefit from a regulated, stabilized, and less risky economic environment.

In 1964 the synthetic fiber firms discussed three regulatory mechanisms: the 1964 Textile Bill; new legislation then being proposed by MITI, the Tokushinhō; and the possibility of self-regulation under "public-private cooperation" (*kanmin kyōchō*).[7] The focal point of the industry's discussions was the Kasen Kyōkai (Nihon Kagaku Sen'i Kyōkai, or Chemical Fiber Industry Association). This body was to serve as a central forum for the mediation of industry conflicts and as a body to mobilize and exert political pressure.

As discussed in Chapter 4, the synthetic fiber firms did not want to be included in the 1964 Textile Bill, which they saw as an attempt by the cotton spinners to stifle the growth of synthetic fibers. This was not the sort of regulation the Kasen Kyōkai had in mind. The industry was interested in regulating its capacity expansion but not at the cost of surrendering its autonomy to a competing industry.

The industry next discussed MITI's new and controversial proposed legislation, the Tokushinhō (Special Measures Law for the Promotion of Designated Industries). To the synthetic fiber firms the most attractive feature of this bill was that it allowed designated industries to form a cartel to regulate surplus capacity and control excessive investment.

The Tokushinhō, however, died in Diet committee in 1964. Chalmers Johnson attributes the bill's demise mostly to the strained personal relations between the director of MITI's Enterprises Bureau, Sahashi Shigeru, and the Kansai-area businessmen and politicians. But Japan's business circles, and in particular the Keidanren and financial interests, were more worried that the Tokushinhō would give MITI excessive power to intervene in the economy. A number of industries complained that they would

---

[6] Sakota 1987, p. 21; Dokusen Bunseki Kenkyūkai 1970, p. 191. I have found no evidence of pressures put on the new entrants to cooperate in cutting production; the Kasen Kyōkai states that the four new entrants went along for the purpose of "solidarity" (Nihon Kagaku Sen'i Kyōkai 1974, p. 848).

[7] Johnson 1982, pp. 256–257.

lose a substantial degree of autonomy if MITI succeeded in its attempt to increase its bureaucratic control (*kanryō tōsei*).[8]

The synthetic fiber industry was one of the few industries that favored the passage of the Tokushinhō. The synthetic fiber firms were willing to tolerate a degree of bureaucratic influence in order to achieve their main goal of curbing the industry's capacity-expansion race by allowing them to discuss and set appropriate investment levels. The Kasen Kyōkai lobbied for the passage of the bill, but in the end was unable to overcome the opposition of stronger industrial and financial interests.[9]

When the bill failed to pass the Diet, the synthetic fiber firms decided to follow the guidelines of the bill informally, through the public-private cooperation system. As one industry analyst put it: "[The Kasen Kyōkai] was by no means in favor of complete laissez-faire. . . . The idea of utilizing regulation under *kanmin kyōchō* to curb our excess capacity was consonant with our own desire to establish 'industrial order' [*sangyō chitsujo*]. . . . The firms felt that some industrial order was necessary, and so began industry-wide discussions in July 1964, [a month after the Tokushinhō had failed] . . . and decided to follow the Tokushinhō in principle."[10]

From the point of view of the industry, this stabilization mechanism was the best way to ensure orderly expansion and to ensure that the industry's status quo was not altered too drastically by an all-out investment race. From the point of view of newcomers as well, controlling excessive competition would lead to a stabilized, less risky economic environment. More simply put, this cooperative system allowed the industry to form an informal capacity-investment cartel.[11]

Following industry-wide discussions during July and August, the industry decided to petition MITI for the formation of a public-private consultative body. In mid-October the industry submitted its formal petition to MITI Minister Sakurauchi Yoshio, who approved the request two weeks later. The eventual discussion group, the Chemical Fiber Discussion Group (Kagaku Sen'i Kyōchō Kondankai), consisted of representatives from the synthetic fiber firms, the industry association, MITI, and independent academics and commentators. The group set up special subcommittees to discuss particular products and drew up informal guidelines on new entry and capacity expansion. In both nylon and polyester, for example, yearly capacity expansion was limited to 15 tons per day per firm. The discussion group system also allowed the industry and MITI to discuss future supply and demand trends.

---

[8] Nihon Rōdō Kyōkai 1988, p. 85.

[9] Sakota 1987, p. 16; Nihon Rōdō Kyōkai 1988, p. 84. The Kasen Kyōkai's public appeal in favor of the bill appears in Nihon Kagaku Sen'i Kyokai 1974, pp. 841–842.

[10] Sakota 1987, pp. 15, 17.

[11] Sakota 1987, p. 18.

Johnson describes this eventual adoption of the *kanmin kyōchō* system as one of Sahashi's "greatest satisfactions," making up for the rejection of his Tokushinhō proposal. But if Sahashi and MITI were satisfied with this outcome, so too were the synthetic fiber firms themselves. In a sense the industry got the best of both worlds. On the one hand, it was now able to cooperatively regulate excessive expansion and receive explicit government sanction for this. At the same time, because the industry was relying on self-regulation, it did not have to sacrifice any of its autonomy to governmental interference.

The FTC was the one institutional actor that was conspicuously absent from deliberations on the formation of the discussion group. Following a month of discussions between MITI Vice Minister Yamamoto and FTC Director Takenaka, the FTC quietly approved this new form of government-industry cooperation. In a public memorandum issued in late November 1965, the FTC noted that it considered the discussion groups to be consistent with antimonopoly principles; it reasoned that firms were allowed to restrict investment activity so long as this did not interfere with short-term supply and demand trends. This choice of rationales is curious, since interfering with supply and demand trends was exactly what the industry had in mind.

By the late 1960s, however, the industry had discovered that demand at home and abroad was again beginning to boom. This period of renewed optimism led to a change in attitudes within the Kasen Kyōkai. Now early and late entrants alike were finding the investment cartel system to be a drag on desired expansion. The discussion group dealt with two issues in the late 1960s. First was the question of new entry into polyester. In particular, Kanebo and Asahi Kasei, both of which had become established nylon producers, now wanted to diversify into this more lucrative field. Although the existing polyester producers saw additional entry as destabilizing, they had no means to prevent it. Kanebo, Asahi Kasei, and Mitsubishi Rayon began polyester production in 1969; within a decade these firms, known as the "late-late entrants," accounted for 14 percent of polyester capacity. The second issue was the need to ease restrictions on capacity expansion. Both the original and late entrants called for looser regulations, but it was the late-late entrants who were most vocal. Kanebo was the most strident proponent and became the first to call for the abolition of the *kanmin kyōchō* system. The discussion group in October 1969 responded by doubling the limit on yearly capacity expansion in nylon, polyester, and acrylic, from 15 to 30 tons per day. Total capacity increased rapidly in all three products between 1969 and 1971: up 31 percent in nylon, 56 percent in acrylic, and 78 percent in polyester.[12]

[12] Japan Development Bank 1974, p. 12; Sakota 1987, pp. 23–25.

Early Economic Adjustment Efforts

The synthetic fiber firms took these early economic problems as a sign that the industry was nearing economic maturity. Most of the firms now took steps to adjust economically, either through vertical integration or through the expansion of their international operations.[13]

Most of the synthetic fiber firms had already built up stable relationships with downstream textile producers—weavers, textile processors, and distributors. For example, by 1964 Toray's "vertical *keiretsu*" included more than 300 small textile processors. In addition, Toray was reported to have formed ties to over 1,000 textile distributors (although most of its sales were still handled by four major trading companies, Chori, Mitsui Bussan, Marubeni, and Itochu). By the early 1970s all of the synthetic fiber firms had developed significant relationships with the downstream sectors.

The synthetic fiber firms also took steps to integrate upstream by either acquiring or entering into business tie-ups with suppliers of petrochemical inputs. As these inputs accounted for 50 percent of total production costs, the fiber firms hoped to increase their cost competitiveness by gaining direct control over their suppliers. (This was an advantage already enjoyed by most of the synthetic fiber firms in the United States and Europe, as well as by Asahi Kasei and Mitsubishi Rayon.)[14] Toray took the most direct route. In the mid-1960s it began to build its own chemical facilities and also entered into a business tie-up with Nihon Sekiyu Kagaku to produce nylon's main raw material. By the early 1970s, Toray had become completely self-sufficient in all of the three main nylon inputs. Following Toray's example, the rest of the firms entered into joint ventures with their chemical suppliers or established their own subsidiaries to supply their material needs.[15]

The synthetic fiber firms also responded to economic maturity by expanding their operations overseas. In terms of exports, the industry cooperated with their main textile trading companies to capitalize on growing

[13] These early diversification efforts are described in Nihon Kagaku Sen'i Kyōkai 1974, pp. 835–869, 948–1007, 1036–1054, Sakota 1987, pp. 21–27, Nihon Rōdō Kyōkai 1988, pp. 162–163, and Dokusen Bunseki Kenkyūkai 1970, pp. 185–186.

[14] In the West, synthetic fiber firms such as Du Pont, Monsanto, ICI, Bayer, and Rhone-Poulenc were originally chemical producers and so were already integrated upstream. In contrast, most of the Japanese firms were textile firms that had diversified into what was for them a new technological field (Sakota 1987, p. 23).

[15] Dokusen Bunseki Kenkyūkai 1970, pp. 194–199; Japan Development Bank 1974, p. 16. In similar fashion Toray built its own facilities to supply the main inputs for polyester production and relied on a fellow Mitsui *keiretsu* firm, Mitsui Sekiyu Kagaku, for its other needed materials. Teijin entered into a joint venture with a U.S. firm, Hercules, and in addition established a subsidiary, Teijin Petrochemicals. In the nylon field Teijin has relied on Ube Kosan for its raw material supplies. Both firms are main members of the Sanwa *keiretsu* (Iwata 1984, p. 85). The efforts of the other synthetic fiber firms to establish a presence in raw material production are described in Toyobo Keizai Kenkyūjo 1975, pp. 109–110.

demand in both the United States and Europe. At the same time, six firms created a joint venture enterprise, the Nylon Fabric Export Promotion Association, to buy up and export excess inventories of nylon products. This association was created in August 1965 with the approval of both MITI and the FTC. These export promotion efforts resulted in a steady increase in the industry's dependency on exports: in 1962 the industry exported 16.5 percent of its total production (in volume terms); by 1971 this figure reached 53.6 percent.[16]

The final economic measure pursued by the synthetic fiber majors was expansion overseas through direct investments. Again, Toray and Teijin led the way. By 1974 Toray had formed relationships with 46 companies overseas, with investments totaling ¥2.9 trillion; this amount made Toray the sixth largest overseas investor among all Japanese firms. Teijin was also active, entering into investment relationships with more than 20 firms. The rest of the synthetic fiber firms expanded overseas as well, especially in Asia. By 1978 the industry had invested U.S. $161 million in 84 different firms; most of these investments (50) were in Asia, followed by Latin America (16) and Africa (10). The industry's early investments centered mostly around downstream sectors (weaving, processing, and finishing) rather than upstream fiber production. Evidently, these firms were seeking to develop stable markets for their fiber exports rather than moving their own production facilities overseas. The Japan Development Bank reported that in 1973 overseas synthetic fiber production in Japan-affiliated firms amounted to only 7.5 percent of domestic sales in Japan. Thus by the early 1970s, many of the synthetic fiber firms had already established strong international ties. Toray and Teijin in particular were full-fledged multinational firms, with a strong investment presence in Asia as well as strong export ties to the rest of the world.[17]

The Textile Wrangle of 1969–1971

The contentious textile trade dispute between the United States and Japan that began in 1969 was in part the result of the Japanese industry's attempt to deal with its domestic problems by expanding exports. These negotiations, which became known as the Textile Wrangle, resulted in a formal bilateral agreement limiting Japan's textile exports to the United States. This trade dispute was also part of a broader attempt by the Western industrialized nations, in particular the United States, to extend the international regime of managed textile trade beyond cotton textiles (cov-

[16] Export figures include both synthetic fibers as well as finished synthetic textiles or apparel (Sakota 1987, p. 23).

[17] Statistics are from Japan Development Bank 1974, p. 36, Tran 1985, p. 55, Toyobo Keizai Kenkyūjo 1977, pp. 51–52, and Export-Import Bank of Japan 1984, p. 176.

ered in the Long-Term Arrangement on Cotton Textiles) to include synthetic fibers and textiles.[18]

The reaction within the Japanese textile industry was much stronger and more intense than the cotton spinners' reaction to the first U.S. demand for voluntary export restraints back in 1955. Now 20 textile-related associations cooperated to form a policy association (the Taibei Sen'i Yushutsu Taisaku Kyōgikai). This group, including the industry's labor association, the Zensen Dōmei, put intense pressures on the politicians, who responded with a series of resolutions opposing efforts to manage textile trade. Within the synthetic fiber industry opposition was led by the president of Asahi Kasei, Miyazaki Kagayaki, who helped to organize the industry in an effort to block the proposed agreements. In January 1970 Miyazaki was instrumental in founding the Japan Textile Federation (JTF), composed of 26 textile-related associations representing all parts of the Japanese textile industry. The JTF embarked on a year-long confrontation with the Japanese government, sporting the slogan of "breaking the textile negotiations with the United States" (*taibei kōsho o uchikire*). The JTF's broad-based membership, and the common interests of all textile sectors in avoiding managed trade solutions, gave it an influential voice.

In spite of industry's determined opposition, Japan was not in a position to block some sort of agreement. In addition to its heavy reliance on the United States as a political ally and as an economic market, an additional factor became intertwined in the textile negotiations: the reversion of U.S.-occupied Okinawa. By early 1971 the Japanese government was ready to accede to U.S. pressures.

But if the industry was unable to dissuade the government from bowing to external pressures, it could at least extract domestic compensation. As a result of strong industry lobbying, the Japanese government announced in May 1971 that it would provide direct subsidies and credit guarantees to the industry to compensate for economic dislocations caused by the agreement. In particular, the government passed the Temporary Special Measures for the Textile Industry, in which some ¥202.9 billion (U.S. $563.6 million) was provided to help purchase or scrap facilities made redundant by the decline in exports. Most of these subsidies went to the natural textile spinners and weavers, rather than to the synthetic fiber firms.[19]

For Japan's synthetic fiber industry the Textile Wrangle marks a clear dividing line between the industry's first 15 years of rapid growth and the

[18] Still the best and most comprehensive account of these negotiations is Destler et al. 1979. The position of the Japanese synthetic fiber industry is discussed in better detail in Sakota 1987, pp. 28–31.

[19] The industry's labor arm, the Zensen Dōmei, was not completely satisfied, however, and in October 1971 filed an administrative suit against MITI, in February of the following year the Kasen Kyōkai also filed suit. Both suits were eventually dropped following the formal conclusion of the Multi-Fiber Arrangement in 1974.

subsequent 15 years of economic distress and restructuring. So far, the industry had followed the classic product cycle: initial growth based on domestic demand, followed by efforts to expand exports, and then by efforts to expand overseas through direct investments. Over the next two decades the industry struggled with how to respond to the final phase of the product cycle—economic maturity and growing economic distress at home. One strategy, however, was now no longer viable; due to the Textile Wrangle, the industry could no longer get rid of surplus domestic production through concentrated exports.

THE INDUSTRY'S CRISIS PERIOD, 1974–1979

The industry's worst period of economic distress was ushered in by the First Oil Shock. Rising oil prices hit synthetic fibers particularly hard, first because the industry is a heavy user of crude oil and electricity, and second because its petrochemical inputs are also highly oil-intensive. Furthermore, domestic demand plunged during the next two years, as the economy entered its post–Oil Shock Recession. Between January 1974 and August 1977, stagnant demand caused synthetic fiber prices to fall by more than 30 percent. Stagnant demand also led to significant surplus capacity. Idle facilities increased sharply in 1974, and the industry's operating rate declined to about two-thirds of capacity. Unlike in the 1965 downturn, however, the industry could not hope to increase its exports. First, Japanese exports were now less attractive due to rising production costs and the appreciation of the yen. In addition, the external constraint resulting from the Textile Wrangle now prevented the industry from exporting its way out of this recession. Solutions, if any existed, would have to come at home.

Predictably, the net result was significant operating losses for the entire industry. The industry recorded losses for the first time in its history in 1974. Negative profits for the industry peaked in 1975, when the nine firms recorded total ordinary losses of ¥8.27 billion, and continued through 1978. In the words of industry participants, the industry had "fallen from heaven into hell" in the space of two years.[20] The industry was now clearly mature, if not declining.

The Industry's Efforts to Adjust

Over the next two decades the synthetic fiber firms responded to economic maturity by trying to lessen their dependence on synthetic fiber

---

[20] Sakota 1987, p. 34.

production. As noted earlier, firms had begun their economic adjustment efforts in the 1960s, especially through vertical integration and overseas expansion. These adjustment efforts were continued and intensified in the context of economic distress in the 1970s and early 1980s. Now the industry focused on three strategies—solidifying their overseas investments, diversifying production at home, and trimming the labor force.

First, firms continued to expand their overseas investments. In particular, they began to invest heavily in fiber production rather than in downstream processing as had been their practice in the 1960s. By 1976, the industry had invested a total of U.S. $175 million in 30 firms producing synthetic fibers; of these, 22 were in Asia. Toray and Teijin were again the two dominant investors. One analyst calculates that by 1978 Toray and Teijin accounted for 91 percent of the total fiber capacity of Japanese-affiliated firms in Southeast Asia.[21]

Second, firms made concerted efforts to diversify their operations into non-textile-related areas. As shown in Chart 6-1, textile-related sales fluctuated over time, while non-textile sales increased steadily. In 1972, textile-related sales accounted for 83 percent of the total sales of the nine firms. By 1978, the industry had lowered this percentage to 70 percent, and further to 52 percent by 1987. At the firm level, Table 6-3 shows that all of the industry's firms have made steady progress in lowering their dependence on synthetic fiber production. The diversification efforts of the two chemical firms, Asahi Kasei and Mitsubishi Rayon, were particularly effective: both were able to use their background in chemicals to diversify into related areas such as plastics, resins, and a variety of other products. By 1987 only 23 percent of Asahi Kasei's sales were related to textiles. Mitsubishi Rayon in 1971 was one of the firms most reliant on textile production; by 1987, more than 62 percent of its sales were in non-textile areas. Similarly, Kanebo cut its commitment to textiles by expanding its well-known line of cosmetic products and by moving into other areas. And the industry's largest firms, Toray and Teijin, have been able to shift production away from synthetic fibers into plastics, chemicals, pharmaceuticals, and other products.

These diversification efforts were made possible by the large resources these firms had at their disposal. Most especially, the synthetic fiber firms

---

[21] Tran 1985, p. 72. The industry's overseas investment activities in this period are discussed in Toyobo Keizai Kenkyūjo 1977, pp. 51–52, Export-Import Bank of Japan 1984, p. 176, and Tran 1985, pp. 72–73. Foreign firms affiliated with Toray or Teijin had a total capacity of 1,182 tons per day, representing 44 percent of Japan's total domestic capacity of 2,708 tons per day. Japanese-affiliated firms altogether accounted for 48 percent of synthetic fibers produced in those countries. Tran Van Tho finds that Japanese-affiliated firms accounted for all of the synthetic fiber production in Malaysia and Indonesia, 79 percent in the Philippines, 62 percent in Korea, 61 percent in Thailand, and 26 percent in Taiwan (1985 pp. 72–73).

art 6-1. Diversification efforts in the synthetic fiber industry, 1972–1987

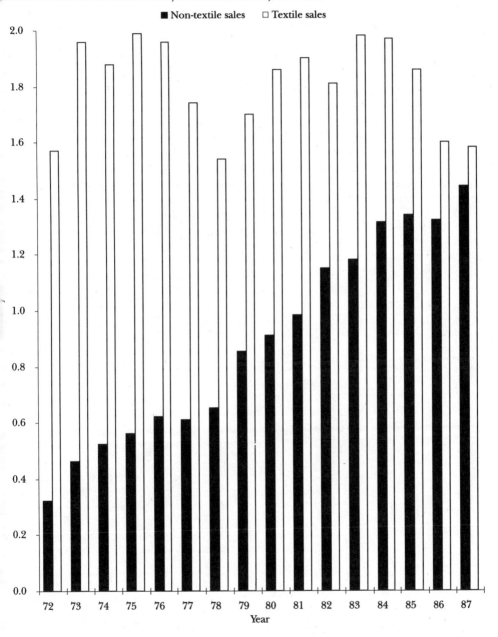

■ Non-textile sales □ Textile sales

Table 6-3. Diversification efforts of synthetic fiber firms, 1971–1987

	Textile-related production (percent of total sales)				Main non-textile related production (percent of total sales, 1987)
	1971	1978	1981	1987	
Asahi Kasei	70.1	45.9	35.7	22.8	Plastics and resins (32), chemicals (18), construction (18), food products (4), other, including electronics, pharmaceuticals, real estate (5)
Mitsubishi Rayon	90.3	72.6	57.6	37.8	Resins and plastics (46), other, including optical and carbon fibers, electronics, and real estate (16)
Kanebo	82.1	77.9	63.7	52.0	Cosmetics (35), pharmaceuticals (4), other, including plastics, food products, and real estate (9)
Toray	90.0	79.7	71.8	58.5	Plastics (25), chemicals (7), carbon fibers (4), other, including pharmaceuticals, ceramics, construction and real estate (5)
Kurary	85.6	75.8	74.1	62.7	Plastics and chemicals (23), other, including pharmaceuticals, real estate, and food products (14)
Teijin	92.6	73.1	72.2	68.2	Chemicals (21), pharmaceuticals (4), other, including plastics and real estate (7)
Unitika	88.6	77.5	79.7	70.9	Engineering (8), plastics and resins (7), other, including real estate and food products (14)
Toyobo	100.0	94.6	88.9	79.1	Plastics and resins (16), other, including chemicals, carbon fibers, and pharmaceuticals (5)
Toho Rayon	100.0	99.0	99.0	86.3	Carbon fibers (14)

SOURCES: Nihon Kagaku Sen'i Kyōkai 1974, p. 1105; Iwata 1984, pp. 56, 60; Tanaka 1989, p. 192; Japan Development Bank 1986, pp. 30, 32; Toray 1988.

had adequate access to financial capital. Toshihiro Horiuchi argues that the main bank relationship enjoyed by the synthetic fiber firms was critical for two reasons: first, the main banks helped to rescue firms when they were in trouble; second, the main banks were willing to lend enough money to allow the more competitive firms to diversify out of synthetic fibers.[22] In addition, the synthetic fiber firms all had access to other resources such as research and development capabilities and a technically skilled labor force. Just as important, all of these firms found alternative opportunities open to them in major growth sectors: resins and plastics (all firms), cosmetics (Kanebo), and chemicals (Asahi Kasei and Mitsubishi Rayon).

The ability to pursue the option of adjustment through diversification sets this industry apart from the first two case studies, the minimills and cotton spinners. With alternatives available, and the resources to attain them, firms have steadily decreased their dependence on the troubled synthetic fiber industry.

The third mechanism for adjustment involved cutting the labor force. Between 1971 and 1987 the industry trimmed its work force by more than two-thirds. In this sense, the behavior of the synthetic fiber firms was similar to that of the cotton spinners and minimills. A critical difference, however, is that adjustment costs for labor were lower in the synthetic fiber industry. The number of workers was relatively small, and the work force was more highly skilled and thus more flexible in terms of finding new jobs. Also, the firms were able to retain many, if not most, of their workers and then transfer them to other sections or to related firms. Since the adjustment of labor was relatively easy, labor had little incentive to push for political solutions.

The lack of labor opposition is also related to its relative political weakness. As in other industries in Japan, labor is organized on a company-by-company basis, which tends to tie worker interests to the interests of individual firms. On the national level, synthetic fiber workers are represented by the Zensen Dōmei, where they make up some 15 percent of the total membership. However, as discussed in Chapter 4, this union has been more active in supporting the spinners, weavers, and others dominated by small-scale firms. In addition, the Zensen Dōmei has long been known as one of the most moderate unions in Japan and has usually been willing to cooperate with the firms' retrenchment programs.[23]

---

[22] Horiuchi 1985, pp. 12–13, 40.

[23] See Dore 1986, pp. 217–221. In part to increase their influence on the national level, the man-made fiber workers in the Zensen Dōmei also participated in a labor association, the Kagaku Enerugi Rōdō Kyōkai (ICEF-JAF), which brings together workers in 22 separate unions representing chemical and related industries such as petroleum, petrochemicals, and synthetic fibers.

Although organized labor has lacked political power at the national level, company-based unions have had more influence on the shop floor. Management is always careful to discuss rationalization or retrenchment plans with their unions. Analysts speak of numerous incidents in which the company-based unions have been able to prevent or delay plant closings or have successfully negotiated for increased severance compensation. In addition, the unemployed have received retraining and other subsidies through Japan's general unemployment programs and through special legislation enacted specifically for the depressed industries.

Although labor has received some compensation, in the end it has been forced to bear a significant portion of the costs of adjustment. Rationalization of the labor force has been a critical adjustment mechanism used by all of Japan's distressed industries.

Political Responses: The "Warring States" Period, 1977–1978

Although the essence of the synthetic fiber story is economic flexibility and adjustment, the industry also pursued the political solution of supply-side stabilization. Compared to our earlier case studies, however, these efforts were relatively short-term and temporary. However, for a period of two years the synthetic fiber firms did engage in an intense effort to stabilize the industry. As in the other case studies, the industry focused on the regulation of the supply side in an effort to restore a balance between supply and demand and to prop up prices and profits.

In trying to limit overall production and capacity, the industry faced the same obstacles to organization that the cotton spinners and the minimills faced. That is, the industry had to be able to overcome the always present incentives to be a free rider. In theory, a concentrated industry should have had an advantage over a fragmented one, in that its smaller numbers should facilitate cooperation and the enforcement of agreements. However, while private enforcement mechanisms can be used to discourage cheating, it is usually difficult; even highly organized industries often cannot deter cheating within their own ranks. Furthermore, the interests and preferences of the members of even a small group are not necessarily unified. In the case of the synthetic fiber industry, a sense of distrust divided those firms that were original entrants and those that entered later. Although this dividing line has become blurred over time, it was still relatively sharp in the mid-1970s. A more important division separated firms according to their competitive positions. By the 1970s, Toray was clearly in a more competitive position than the other firms. As mentioned, Toray had become vertically integrated and had also expanded its overseas presence dramatically. Especially under the leadership of Fujiyoshi Tsuguhide,

Toray had strengthened its competitive position and had increased its desire to be independent from the rest of the industry.[24]

Toray's more competitive approach was made clear in the fall of 1976, when the firm initiated a price-slashing war that came to be known within industry circles as the "survival game" (*ikinokori gamu*).[25] Toray took its cue from its U.S. ally, Du Pont, which was then in the process of cutting its polyester prices in half in an attempt to drive the less competitive producers out of the market. Du Pont was successful in this attempt to reorganize the U.S. industry, forcing nine of the industry's sixteen firms to exit within a year. After Toray initiated this strategy in Japan, the other large Japanese polyester firm, Teijin, also followed suit by slashing its prices. The aim of this price war was the same as Du Pont's: to force the smaller late entrants to either exit from certain product lines or else leave the industry altogether. Toray, and to a lesser extent Teijin, hoped that its market position, size, and staying power would convince the smaller firms to exit without a fight.

These price cuts, however, were soon matched by the rest of the industry. The late entrants, particularly the former cotton spinning firms, were large and stable enough to withstand a period of low prices and were willing to try to outlast the established firms.[26] The result of this period of "mutual defection" was the exacerbation of depressed prices. Prices in the domestic market fell by 15 percent between August 1976 and August 1977; in May 1977 prices were some 20 percent below average production costs.

The other firms in the industry were not happy with what they considered a destabilizing move by Toray. The two principal antagonists in the industry were the president of Toray, Fujiyoshi, and the president of Asahi Kasei, Miyazaki. In April 1977, when Miyazaki became the chairman of the Kasen Kyōkai, his first priority was to try to arrange an industry truce. He began by initiating formal talks on the formation of a recession cartel in an effort to curb excess production and end the destructive price war.

The industry had once before tried to use production cutbacks to deal with declining prices. This happened in early 1972 in the wake of the Textile Wrangle. In that instance, however, the FTC quickly challenged this

---

[24] Toray's new attitude is discussed in Nihon Keizai Shimbun 1979, pp. 28–30. A further difference dividing the industry was that five of the top six firms were based in Osaka, with only Toray, the original entrant, being Tokyo-based. The tradition of independence of the Osaka-based textile firms is often mentioned, but I have not found it to be a determining variable. The structural characteristics of the industry have been more important than their history of interaction with the government.

[25] The industry's price war is discussed in *Asahi Journal*, Feb. 24, 1978, p. 104, and Nihon Keizai Shimbun 1979, pp. 20–22.

[26] The Asahi Journal (Feb. 24, 1978, p. 104) said that this was "a case of a cornered rat biting the cat."

collusive activity as a violation of the Anti-Monopoly Law. During this period, the FTC was especially vigilant in policing collusive practices by concentrated industries such as synthetic fibers. In November 1972 the FTC advised the Kasen Kyōkai to end their production agreements, and the synthetic fiber makers agreed to do so the following month.[27] That episode, however, made the industry, and MITI, more sensitive than usual to antitrust considerations and FTC objections.

Miyazaki now created an informal organization within the industry association, the Shachōkai, or President's Club. This discussion group, limited to the presidents of the industry's nine firms, served as a semi-official forum for consultations. As one of the industry leaders explicitly charged with forming the illegal cartels in 1972, Miyazaki was careful to include at least one representative from MITI at each of these meetings in order to avoid antitrust complications.[28] The meetings of the Shachōkai were used to negotiate and discuss how the industry as a whole should react to its present difficulties. This semi-formal institution was to play an important role in imposing at least a modicum of cooperation in the industry.

By April 1977, Toray was already close to admitting defeat. It had recognized that its strategy of reorganizing the industry through a price war was not only costly but probably futile as well. The other firms had demonstrated their commitment to remaining in the industry. Because these firms were financially strong or had strong financial backers, forced exit did not seem likely. The only outcome then would be continued instability, depressed prices, and losses for all in the industry. Toray may not have been as enthusiastic about collective solutions as the other members of the Shachōkai, but it did not actively try to block their efforts to stabilize the market.

Still, the industry was unable to reach a consensus on forming the cartel. As this was the industry's first experience with a formal (legal) cartel, it had to overcome a number of disagreements and uncertainties. First were the technical problems of how much each firm should reduce, which products to include, and whether exports should be subject to limitations. Second, relations between firms were still characterized by mutual distrust, as all firms worried that others would cheat by exceeding their allotments. Third, each firm suspected that other firms had been underreporting their actual capacity, which would make them less constrained by

---

[27] The production cutback agreements and the FTC's responses are detailed in Matsushita 1972, pp. 16–19.

[28] Two MITI officials regularly attended these meetings: the director of the Consumer Goods Bureau and the director of the Fiber Spinning Division. Although MITI was solidly in favor of the formation of this group, the FTC was conspicuously silent, at least initially. The debates within the Shachōkai are reported in *Nihon Keizai Shimbun*, May 10, 1977, May 31, 1977, and *Asahi Shimbun*, May 20, 1977.

future capacity regulations. Mutual distrust and fear of being exploited by others were organizational barriers too great to overcome.[29]

The head of MITI's Textile Bureau, Fujiwara Ichiro, favored the formation of the cartel.[30] Fujiwara was concerned about the synthetic fiber firms and about the ripple effects the industry's troubles would cause for the rest of the textile industry. But the main reason that Fujiwara supported the cartel was that the only alternative to the recession cartel, administrative guidance through *kankoku sōtan*, was not attractive for MITI. In fact, *kankoku sōtan* had become so controversial that it was now referred to as a "forbidden phrase." The FTC had for some time been on record as being opposed to MITI's use of *kankoku sōtan*, but it was only in the early 1970s that it was able to impose significant legal constraints. As mentioned in Chapter 5, a critical turning point was the much publicized 1974 FTC challenge to MITI's informal guidance of the petroleum importers. This legal challenge hung over MITI's head throughout the 1970s and served as an important constraint on its willingness to use its informal guidance powers.

The FTC agreed with MITI that some sort of policy action was necessary and argued that the recession cartel was the more desirable one. In fact, the FTC publicly encouraged MITI to form a recession cartel, not because the FTC was in favor of cartelization, but because it was so opposed to the informal alternative.

MITI preferred to avoid an open confrontation with the FTC, with which relations were already strained. Not only was MITI embroiled in the legal battle over the petroleum importer cartel, it was also faced with a legislative attempt to amend and strengthen the Anti-Monopoly Law then pending in the Diet. MITI soon had another reason to avoid antagonizing the FTC: it was in the midst of preparing its structurally depressed industries legislation, the Tokuanhō, and realized it would need FTC cooperation in order to get this law enacted. It wanted to give the FTC as little ammunition as possible and preferred to avoid antagonizing an already strained relationship. When the industry talks in the Shachōkai ended inconclusively at the end of May 1977, therefore, Fujiwara decided against taking action. Since the industry could not come to a unified position in calling for a cartel, MITI took no initiative and left the firms to fend for themselves.

With a consensus on the recession cartel still out of reach, and with MITI unwilling to step in with its administrative guidance powers, the syn-

[29] The industry's internal debates are reported in Sakota 1987, p. 37, *Nihon Keizai Shimbun*, Feb. 18, 1977, May 10, 1977, May 26, 1977, and *Asahi Shimbun*, May 20, 1977. The measurement of capacity used in the synthetic fiber industry—tons per day—is an imprecise one, so it is relatively easy for firms to disguise their true capacity. See, for instance, *Nihon Keizai Shimbun*, Sept. 8, 1975 and *Asahi Shimbun*, May 7, 1977. Toray and Teijin were the worst offenders (Tsunabuchi 1980, p. 95).

[30] Fujiwara's concerns are discussed in Nihon Keizai Shimbun 1979, pp. 12–16, and *Nihon Keizai Shimbun*, Feb. 18, 1977.

thetic fiber industry looked for other ways to stabilize its economic conditions. With the industry's condition continuing to worsen through the summer of 1977, it turned to an alternative route: broadening the debate and turning up the political pressure on policy makers. It was in the context of a deepening textile crisis and rising political pressures that Fujiwara ultimately was compelled to act.

The textile crisis of 1977 was quickly spreading throughout the industry, giving all sectors an interest in restoring a degree of stability. The other upstream fiber sectors, particularly the cotton spinners, were strong supporters of efforts to have the synthetic fiber industry stabilize its prices. Both the cotton and wool spinners had formed recession cartels of their own in April 1977 but were having major difficulties in restoring prices. They suspected that the synthetic fiber firms were continuing to produce at their former levels, thus grabbing market share and keeping prices of all fibers depressed. These other upstream firms, which included firms such as Toyobo, Unitika, and Kanebo that produced both cotton and synthetic fibers, were in favor of having the synthetic fiber industry cooperate with their stabilization efforts. If the synthetic fiber makers could not agree on a cartel, MITI's administrative guidance was the only alternative.

More critical were the problems of the weaving sector, which was concentrated in a few areas such as Aichi and the Hokuriku prefectures of Fukui, Ishikawa, and Toyama. The deepening textile crisis threatened a string of bankruptcies in these regions. The foremost interest of the downstream weavers was therefore the recovery of their own stability. One might expect the weaving firms to object to policies that propped up the price of their principal inputs, but in this case the downstream textile producers were able to pass on higher material input costs to final consumers in the form of higher prices. Depressed fiber prices had a ripple effect, depressing the prices of finished products throughout the textile chain. Thus, weavers called on the synthetic fiber firms to end their domestic "dumping" practices and to stabilize prices.

The summer of 1977 was a period of deepening crisis for the textile industry as a whole. In May alone, for instance, some 60 textile-related firms in the Aichi area failed. More alarming were the threatened bankruptcies of two mid-sized textile trading firms, Ichimura Sangyo and Chori. Finally, two major synthetic fiber firms, Kanebo and Unitika, faced what seemed to be impending bankruptcy in September.

The prospect of a chain reaction of bankruptcies, growing unemployment, and political controversy made inaction increasingly dangerous in the eyes of the political leadership. The cabinet of Fukuda Takeo was already preoccupied with dealing with the domestic recession and so was particularly sensitive to the plight of the textile industry. As discussed in the last chapter, Fukuda was under a rising tide of criticism, both at home and abroad, for not doing enough to deal with the long-running post–Oil Shock recession. One of the strongest and most vocal of these domestic critics was Miyazaki, head of the Kasen Kyōkai. The textile industry now stepped up its pressures on the political leadership. In February 1977 the Japan Textile Federation had created a special committee to lobby for government aid to deal with the recession, the Rinji Fukyō Taisaku Honbu.[31] Further, Miyazaki and Teijin president Oya Jinzō met with Fukuda at the Prime Minister's residence on June 15, 1977, in the first official meeting between a Prime Minister and the industry since the Textile Wrangle.[32] The textile industry's demands were general in scope, reflecting the broad range of industry concerns. Among the demands that pertained to synthetic fibers were government financing for the scrapping of excess capacity, help in easing the financial crisis faced by downstream sectors, and intervention to stabilize the employment situation. A month later the textile industry convened what it called the Conference to Overcome the Textile Crisis (Sen'i Kiki Toppatsu Taikai), consisting of both labor and management from the various textile sectors. The list of demands was similar to the one presented to Fukuda, with one addition: a call on the government to increase MITI's administrative guidance efforts for industries undergoing restructuring. After the conference, Teijin's Oya stated that "the textile industry has gone to the limits of what we can do on our own. Now we can only wait for the government to take action to rescue the structurally depressed industries."[33]

Despite its reluctance to use its *kankoku sōtan* powers, MITI found itself under growing pressure to act. On September 22, 1977, with synthetic fiber prices at a postwar low, Fujiwara announced that he was finally issuing *kankoku sōtan* recommendations. This action, one that MITI had not taken since 1965, was described by analysts as an extraordinary step for MITI. Throughout the downturns of the 1970s MITI had denied similar requests by a number of other industries for this informal enforcement tool, instead forcing industries to form official recession cartels. (This would be the last time that MITI would use this policy instrument.)

A number of sources give MITI, and especially Fujiwara, credit for deciding to issue these recommendations.[34] Fujiwara was certainly responsible for the timing of this action, the decisiveness of which took most

---

[31] Nihon Keizai Shimbun 1979, p. 22.

[32] *Kasen Geppō*, July 1977. Also in attendance were the heads of the Japan Spinners Association, representatives of the wool spinners, and MITI minister Tanaka. Two days later, on June 17, MITI announced new textile policy actions, including increased financial assistance and the extension of the spinning recession cartel.

[33] *Nihon Keizai Shimbun*, July 22, 1977. Also included in the list was import relief, which would have benefited the other textile sectors more than synthetic fibers. The synthetic fiber firms at that time were still only lukewarm in their support for import relief.

[34] See, for instance, *Nihon Keizai Shimbun*, Sept. 21, 1977.

observers by surprise. Taken in isolation, MITI appears to have taken the initiative. But in light of the preceding nine months of intraindustry negotiations and bargaining to achieve exactly this end, it is clear that MITI was giving the industry what it wanted. *Kankoku sōtan*, which was no more than the administrative equivalent of the recession cartel, provided the enforcement and coordination mechanism to achieve collective stabilization.[35] The majority of the synthetic fiber firms expressed satisfaction with MITI's decision. Even Toray, despite its lack of enthusiasm for collective solutions, did not criticize or oppose MITI's action.

The FTC, however, raised strong objections. It noted publicly that although the use of *kankoku sōtan* was not a direct violation of the Anti-Monopoly Law, it amounted to a collusive production agreement and thus violated the spirit of the law. FTC chairman Hashimoto stopped short of directly challenging MITI's action, since as he put it, "we can't deny the need for some sort of emergency measures for the synthetic fiber industry."[36] However, the FTC also warned MITI that it considered *kankoku sōtan* a mere smokescreen hiding illegal cartels. And shortly after MITI announced the extension of *kankoku sōtan* in January 1978, the FTC announced that it was investigating the possibility that the synthetic fiber industry had created an illegal cartel and charged that the Shachōkai meetings had illegally discussed production cutbacks.[37] It also again raised the issue of the legality of MITI's administrative guidance and repeated its long-standing argument that if production cutbacks were necessary, they should be done through an explicit cartel. In response, MITI argued that it had actually preferred a recession cartel, but because the industry could not come to a unified position, emergency measures were needed. It also assured the FTC that it was not considering *kankoku sōtan* for any other industry.

The more aggressive stance taken by the FTC in this period reflects a significant evolution of the antitrust environment in Japan. During this same period MITI was also embroiled in the controversy over its administrative guidance of the minimill industry, including the controversial price cartel and imposition of outsider restrictions. The 1980 court ruling on the petroleum importer cartel case, a decision that went against the in-

---

[35] Fujiwara insists that he bore sole responsibility for this policy decision, although he acknowledges that this was what the industry wanted (Interview with author, March 1990). According to Fujiwara, a key turning point was a meeting with all nine synthetic fiber presidents a week before his decision. At that meeting each firm was forced to admit the extent to which they underreported their capacity. Fujiwara became convinced at this point that the industry could not act together and so decided to intervene. The *Nihon Keizai Shimbun*, Sept. 22, 1977, describes Fujiwara's actions as essentially a response to strong political pressures, including pressure from Prime Minister Fukuda.

[36] *Nihon Keizai Shimbun*, Sept. 22, 1977.

[37] *Asahi Shimbun*, Jan. 7, 1978.

dustry and MITI, proved to be a turning point. After this, MITI's use of its informal administrative guidance powers declined greatly.

Synthetic fiber prices began to recover somewhat following the imposition of *kankoku sōtan*. The industry still wanted to continue limits on production relative to existing demand, however, and so agreed to seek a recession cartel once *kankoku sōtan* ended in April 1978. Almost all of the firms had come to recognize that the benefits of cooperation outweighed those of cutthroat competition. Furthermore, the industry faced strong pressures both from MITI and the FTC to replace *kankoku sōtan* with a recession cartel.[38] With the choice of a cartel or a return to destabilized competition, the industry had little trouble in choosing the former. The recession cartel, the first in the industry's history, was to last for a period of twelve months, expiring in April 1979.

The industry apparently did not have any problems with cheating on the production cutbacks. Although the firms still were not unified or trusting, the risk of being exploited decreased once all had entered into a formal agreement. Enforcement was also easier because only a small number of actors had to be monitored and because the mechanisms of the industry association, in particular the regular meetings of the Shachōkai, helped to facilitate monitoring. In addition, the formal policy actions by MITI, even though they lacked explicit mechanisms to punish non-cooperation, helped to decrease the likelihood of defection.

Long-Term Solutions: Structural Adjustment

After the short period of open industry conflict had evolved into uneasy cooperation, the industry turned to a long-term solution to its difficulties: controlling and eventually reducing excess capacity. The Shachōkai had informally discussed the need to scrap capacity for a number of years, but discussions intensified in 1978. Although all firms agreed that excess capacity was a problem, there was no agreement as to which firms should make cuts, or by how much. In addition, firms were undecided on how these cuts should be financed. Like the minimills, the Shachōkai agreed that, in principle, "survivors should bear the burden of adjustment." And like the minimills, the industry called for government support in financing capacity cutbacks. Miyazaki estimated that the industry would need to spend some ¥200 billion in scrapping costs and other allowances; in order to raise these funds the industry would need some sort of assistance from the administration. Throughout the fall of 1977 Miyazaki kept up his criticisms of the Fukuda administration, calling for more active government

---

[38] *Asahi Shimbun,* Jan. 19, 1978.

support. In particular, Miyazaki pressed for government involvement in helping the industry to restructure and reorganize itself.[39]

During 1977 the Kasen Kyōkai tried to restructure the industry on its own through tie-ups and mergers. The first of these efforts came in May 1977, shortly after the cartel discussions had failed, when Miyazaki called for the formation of joint selling companies. Miyazaki hoped that limiting the number of sales points would create a more concentrated industry and would make it easier to coordinate production limitations. His plan called for the three main firms, Toray, Teijin, and his own Asahi Kasei, to form the basis of the groups. The industry attempted to implement Miyazaki's plan, but due to conflicts between firms, ranging from technological differences to personality differences, most of these talks ended in failure.

A more ambitious plan was announced in December by one of the "elder statesmen" of the industry, Teijin's President Oya. The so-called Oya plan envisioned a series of mergers in which the three original entrants, Teijin, Toray, and Asahi Kasei, would absorb the late entrants. Oya recalled, somewhat wistfully, the old days, when his firm together with Toray had enjoyed a duopoly in polyester. Back then, industry discussions went smoothly, whereas now there were too many firms, and coordination was too difficult. Oya's strategy was clear: because the industry's problems were the fault of the late entrants, "in order for the industry to recover, the late entrants and those with no competitive power should exit."[40] In direct talks with Miyazaki of Asahi Kasei and Fujiyoshi of Toray, Oya argued that there were three logical groupings in the industry: Toyobo and Mitsubishi Rayon, since they had just formed a joint selling company; Asahi Kasei and Kanebo, which were then negotiating a joint selling firm of their own; and Teijin and Unitika, because they were both in the Sanwa *keiretsu*. Oya then proposed that the two remaining firms, Toray and Kuraray, should merge.

The presidents of the other two main firms refused to endorse the plan. Miyazaki told Oya that he was already having problems in reaching agreement with Kanebo on a mere tie-up, let alone full merger. Toray had already shown itself to be less than enthusiastic about negotiated solutions, preferring to "go it alone." Although Toray was willing to comply with the industry's efforts to stabilize itself, it would do so only so long as these efforts were not too intrusive on its independence. Now, Oya's proposal left Toray's Fujiyoshi incredulous: why should Toray tie up with Kuraray simply because they were the two firms left over?[41] The Oya Plan never proceeded beyond the proposal stage.

[39] Nihon Keizai Shimbun 1979, pp. 17–18, 32–33.
[40] Oya's thinking, and the intraindustry negotiations that lay behind his plan, is described in detail in Nihon Keizai Shimbun 1979, pp. 47–52. See also Horiuchi 1985, pp. 26–28.
[41] Nihon Keizai Shimbun 1979, pp. 48–50; Tsunabuchi 1980, pp. 94–98.

With these talks on restructuring at a standstill, the industry had little trouble in deciding to seek designation as a depressed industry under the Tokuanhō. Again, Toray was the one firm that was less than wholly supportive of collective capacity cutbacks. As already described, Toray had been lukewarm to the industry's earlier stabilization efforts. Now it felt that existing self-regulation and curbs on capacity expansion would be sufficient, and in addition, it was reluctant to see even more government interference in the industry.[42] Toray felt that economic conditions were already improving, and that it could get along without major scrapping programs.

The industry's stabilization plan under the Tokuanhō included restrictions on the building of new capacity. In terms of reducing capacity, the industry decided that it would be sufficient to simply idle, rather than actually scrap, excess facilities. Beginning in July 1978 the industry held a series of meetings to discuss the industry's scrapping program. These meetings involved representatives of the industry and MITI, as well as a number of independent scholars and analysts. The industry's resulting stabilization plan called for the idling of an average of 15 percent of facilities.[43]

The Second Oil Shock exacerbated the industry's excess capacity problem, however. The industry thus revised its stabilization plan, eventually calling for the scrapping of most of the previously idled facilities. To help finance these efforts the synthetic fiber firms took advantage of the Tokuanhō's special credit fund to guarantee loans for the scrapping of capacity. The industry, nevertheless, saw this fund as far from adequate. The entire Tokuanhō fund was capitalized at ¥100 billion, about half of what Miyazaki had argued would be necessary for the synthetic fiber industry alone. Firms that undertook these cuts eventually received only a small fraction of compensation in low-interest loan guarantees.[44]

THE 1980S: THE INDUSTRY FORGOES REGULATION

The synthetic fiber firms continued to regulate their capacity under the new Sankōhō, after the expiration of the Tokuanhō. Again, the industry negotiated an industry-wide scrapping program, and agreed to continue

---

[42] Nihon Keizai Shimbun 1979, pp. 56–57. At this point the industry, through the old Chemical Fiber Discussion Group (Kagaku Sen'i Kyōchō Kondankai), had drafted a proposal calling on MITI to provide "supply and demand outlooks." Although MITI and the industry would discuss and come to a consensus about likely demand trends, it would be up to each individual firm to decide on appropriate production levels. The FTC never challenged this informal regulation (Horiuchi 1985, p. 45).

[43] The industry's stabilization plan is discussed in Sakota 1987, pp. 37–39, and Dore 1986, pp. 234–236.

[44] Sekiguchi 1991, p. 436; Nihon Keizai Shimbun 1979, pp. 56–60.

restrictions on investments for new or expanded facilities until June 1986. It also attempted to form additional business tie-ups and joint marketing agreements. Certain firms in the industry, notably Toray, argued that the industry had already dealt with its excess capacity problems and should therefore graduate after the Sankōhō expired.[45]

When the industry's coverage under the Sankōhō expired in June of 1986 it followed Toray's advice and decided not to try to extend its period of designation. Already the industry had seen a dramatic improvement in its profit picture. In essence, the synthetic fiber industry no longer fit the criteria of a structurally depressed industry: it had curbed its excess capacity and had improved its economic performance. For the first time in eight years, capacity restrictions were to end, and the synthetic fiber industry was to become MITI's first graduate of the depressed industry legislation.

Although the industry was no longer to be covered by formal regulations, the industry association still did not leave everything up to the market. MITI continued to use its "supply and demand outlooks" to help the industry regulate production. Under this system, the industry and MITI discussed likely future demand trends. Although production decisions were left to the discretion of individual firms, these discussions made the behavior of firms more transparent to others. Further, one month before the industry's designation under the Sankōhō was to expire, the Kasen Kyōkai convened all of the firms to hammer out a new capacity agreement. The industry decided that after the Sankōhō had expired, firms would still publicly announce all capacity expansion plans to the association and to MITI. The association gave assurances that this was not a new investment cartel, but, nonetheless it made sure that this "declaration" system had the approval of both MITI and the FTC.[46]

The industry's decision no longer to pursue formal capacity regulations was in part motivated by external considerations. Since the early 1980s foreign criticisms of Japan's declining industry policies had begun to focus on the trade implications of capacity and other cartels. During regular consultations between 1984 and 1986, U.S. officials repeatedly raised the issue of cartels for declining industries in general and for the synthetic fiber industry in particular. Analysts cited these complaints as one reason that capacity regulations were not extended past 1986.[47]

---

[45] The industry's stabilization plans under the Sankōhō are discussed in Endo 1986, pp. 17–19, and Sakota 1987, p. 39.

[46] *Nihon Keizai Shimbun*, Feb. 7, 1986; *Asahi Shimbun*, Feb. 7, 1986; *Japan Economic Journal*, Apr. 23, 1988; Sangyō Nenpō 1987, p. 88.

[47] *Japan Economic Journal*, Jan. 17, 1984, and Mar. 22, 1986. In 1982, U.S. Trade Representative William Brock raised pointed criticisms of the impending Sankōhō bill. These and other American complaints were taken very seriously by Japanese officials and were later incorporated into the new legislation. Tsūshō Sangyōshō, Sangyō Seisaku Kyoku 1983, pp. 28–31.

At the same time, the industry itself was becoming less interested in continuing regulations. As already discussed, by the mid-1980s all the synthetic fiber firms had made good progress in diversifying out of the industry and thus lowering their dependence on synthetic fiber production. This critical development decreased their incentives to preserve the industry's status quo through regulation.

Moreover, the firms were coming to realize that government regulation of synthetic fiber capacity was having unintended negative consequences—capacity restrictions at home were causing the industry to lose competitiveness abroad. The industry now realized that its stabilization efforts had prevented a needed reorganization of the industry. Even after two decades of economic distress, the structure of the Japanese industry had remained essentially static: the same number of firms still maintained their presence in the same product lines. There were no cases in which a Japanese firm had ceased production of any of the three main synthetic fibers. In stark contrast, between 1980 and 1986 four American firms and seven European firms had withdrawn partially or entirely from the synthetic fiber industry.[48] In addition, the restructuring of the European and American markets allowed the remaining firms to specialize on particular products; by 1985 only two firms, Du Pont and Italy's SNIA, produced all three of the main synthetic fibers. In contrast, four of Japan's nine firms, Toray, Asahi Kasei, Kanebo, and Toyobo, still produced the full range of the synthetic fibers. It is not clear if the U.S. and European method of adjustment was superior, but analysts criticized the Japanese industry for not making more fundamental structural changes.

Table 6-4 points to another indicator of the lack of restructuring within the Japanese industry: since 1971, there has been almost no change in the capacity shares for each of the three main products. This is particularly true for the top producers in each field, where market shares have remained virtually constant, despite 15 years of "structural depression." These figures indicate that, even while firms had made efforts to diversify *outside* of the synthetic fiber industry, *within* the industry capacity levels have been effectively managed.[49]

[48] The four American firms were Du Pont, Celanese, Monsanto, and Eastman. In Europe, Bayer and Courtalds withdrew from both nylon and polyester; Montedison and Hoechst, from nylon; Rhone-Poulenc, from polyester; and SNIA Viscosa and AKZO, from acrylic (Sangyō Nenpō 1987, pp. 86–87; Sakota 1987, pp. 39–42). This exit in the early 1980s is in addition to the numerous exits seen in the United States and Europe during the 1970s, particularly following Du Pont's price-slashing war. In a single year (1976–1977) as many as nine U.S. firms left the polyester field.

[49] The industry's Herfindahl index also declined only slightly: from 1,127 in 1970, to 1,106 in 1975, 1,057 in 1980, and 1,016 in 1984 (Japan Fair Trade Commission 1976, p. 75; 1987, pp. 62–63).

Table 6-4. Synthetic fiber capacity share trends, 1971–1985 (percent)

Fiber	1971	1975	1980	1985
POLYESTER				
Teijin	25.6	24.7	25.2	25.0
Toray	25.6	24.7	24.2	24.0
Toyobo	13.7	14.3	13.4	13.0
Kuraray	12.9	12.4	9.6	9.6
Asahi Kasei	3.7	3.5	3.7	4.0
Mitsubishi Rayon	2.8	4.6	5.2	5.0
Other*	15.7	15.9	18.7	19.4
NYLON				
Toray	33.0	31.7	31.3	31.3
Teijin	12.9	13.4	14.9	14.4
Unitika	19.1	19.1	16.1	16.4
Asahi Kasei	12.3	13.9	18.8	20.2
Kanebo	12.3	12.3	10.3	9.0
Toyobo	10.5	9.5	8.5	8.7
ACRYLIC				
Asahi Kasei	21.3	20.4	23.9	21.9
Mitsubishi Rayon	21.9	20.4	21.9	21.7
Toyobo	22.5	20.4	17.5	17.5
Toho Rayon	15.3	14.4	12.8	12.2
Toray	14.0	14.3	12.0	11.0
Kanebo	5.1	10.1	11.9	15.8

SOURCES: Annual stock market reports.

*"Other" polyester producers include Unitika, Kanebo, and their joint venture firm, Nihon Ester.

The industry now realized that its past regulatory cocoon, while helpful in overcoming temporary instability, was having the unwelcome effect of preventing restructuring over the long term. The net result was the same as that in the minimill case: older, less competitive facilities. The industry could not stand still if it hoped to remain competitive. This was especially true in the international context, for while the industry was restricting itself from making new investments, its international competitors were increasing theirs. In particular, the industries in Taiwan and South Korea were introducing the most advanced product and process technologies and were becoming significant competitive threats. By 1986, Taiwan had passed Japan in terms of total synthetic fiber capacity.

As detailed in Chapter 4, the surge of textile imports in the late 1970s led to growing pressures for domestic protection. In particular, the textile industry asked the government to change Japan's coverage under the MFA from a supplier country to an importing country. As most of these imports were in natural fibers and textiles, however, the synthetic fiber industry remained lukewarm to import restraints throughout the 1970s and 1980s. Its interest in import protection was tempered by a number of economic factors. First, the synthetic fiber firms retained some degree of export competitiveness, particularly relative to the U.S. and European producers, and still depended heavily on exports. During this period these firms were trying to prevent the closure of their critical overseas markets; to raise import barriers in the Japanese market would have undermined these efforts. Second, the industry had made heavy investments abroad, especially in Southeast Asia, and thus had an interest in avoiding retaliation. In particular, Toray and Teijin had increased their international stakes and had become, in effect, multinational firms; their interests in protecting the domestic market were thus somewhat muted. Compared to the cotton spinners and weavers, the synthetic fiber firms had more of an interest in keeping markets open overseas and less of an interest in seeking protection at home.[50] On the other hand, the industry also resorted to non-tariff means to slow the pace of imports. In particular, firms held regular and direct talks with synthetic fiber producers in both Korea and Taiwan in an effort to achieve "orderly markets." These industry-to-industry talks led to tactit "understandings" but no formal agreement on orderly marketing arrangements.

How the industry reacts to probable increased imports in the future remains to be seen. If the industry continues to follow Toray's lead, calls for protection from the synthetic fiber firms will continue to be muted. Toray continues to advocate a strategy of economic adjustment at home and increased investment overseas.[51] By the late 1980s it was becoming clear that this sort of approach was the only way the industry could hope to remain competitive with its Asian rivals. Today, Toray and most in the industry remain relatively optimistic—not so much about their future as synthetic fiber producers, but rather about their future as diversified, internationalized firms.

IMPLICATIONS OF THE SYNTHETIC FIBER CASE

The essential story of the synthetic fiber case is successful economic adjustment. The industry has been relatively flexible in its treatment of both capital and labor. This ability to adjust has been an important factor in explaining why the industry has not pursued collective stabilization schemes to the extent seen in our first two case studies. In other words, the industry has exercised the exit option rather than fighting to preserve the status quo.

[50] This is consistent with Milner 1988. The Kasen Kyōkai, despite its ambivalent position on import protection, did show its solidarity with the rest of the industry by cosponsoring most of the resolutions that appealed to the Japanese government for protection.

[51] The industry's thinking is outlined in Sangyō Nenpō 1987 and *Asahi Shimbun*, Mar. 11, 1985. In particular, Toray's strategy is discussed in *Asahi Shimbun*, Feb. 7, 1986 and *The Japan Times*, July 11, 1988.

At the same time, this case study contains an undercurrent of industrial politics, as the industry tried, at least temporarily, to collectively stabilize its economic situation. At critical junctures the industry appealed for government support for its stabilization efforts, the implicit and explicit cartels to help enforce production and capacity cuts. In addition, the industry received some compensation for economic adjustment, although public subsidies and loans played only a small role.

Compared to the cotton spinning and minimill cases, these collective efforts were neither long-lasting nor far-reaching. The industry did ask for temporary support for its stabilization efforts in the late 1970s but has not pressed strongly for more overt measures to resist industrial change or preserve the status quo. Instead, firms for the most part followed economic incentives, pursuing economic adjustment rather than lobbying for political stabilization or protectionism. The movement of the industry away from the collective stabilization schemes of the 1980s can be attributed to the firms' gradual shift away from dependence on a single industry, synthetic fibers. Because the industry was able to adjust economically, its demands for preservation of the status quo were muted.

As in the first two cases, I have found very little evidence that MITI behaved like a "developmental state." Nowhere did MITI play a strong role, following a clear "vision." MITI certainly did not anticipate decline and did not push the industry into making economic adjustments. On the contrary, the effect of MITI intervention has, if anything, been to slow down adjustment and protect the less competitive firms in the industry—certainly not the goal of a "developmental state."

Furthermore, the bureaucracy was unable to resist pressures to help the industry stabilize itself. During the crisis of the mid-1970s MITI stepped in to rescue the industry from its own excessive competition, and helped the industry to stabilize prices and profits, first through administrative guidance and then through a recession cartel. Although MITI officials may have determined the timing of the policy actions, I argue that they were basically responding to the industry's expressed preferences.

THE ALUMINUM INDUSTRY

Of all of Japan's troubled industries, the aluminum smelting industry was the clearest case of an industry that adjusted rapidly to changing market conditions.[52] Prior to the Oil Shocks of the 1970s the Japanese aluminum industry was the world's second largest with an annual capacity of

---

[52] The aluminum smelting industry's JSIC number is 3216. The aluminum case is discussed by Samuels 1983, Sheard 1987, Tanaka 1988, Goto 1988, Sheard 1992, and Rajan and Brahm 1994.

1.64 million tons. In the subsequent fifteen years the industry cut over 98 percent of its domestic capacity; by 1990 only a single smelter, with a capacity of only 64,000 tons, remained in operation. In the process, the industry essentially shifted itself overseas by moving its operation to regions which offered cheaper resources or energy.

Analysts who credit Japan for pursuing a smooth and effective approach to industrial adjustment invariably highlight the case of aluminum. However, the experience of this industry is not at all typical of Japan's general adjustment experience. No other troubled industry in Japan adjusted as smoothly or as quickly as this one did; even the synthetic fiber industry was more resistant to adjustment. Furthermore, the adjustment process was initiated by the industry itself; public policy tended to merely ratify the actions that the private firms were pursuing on their own. If anything, public policy tended to slow down adjustment rather than speed it up.

A number of features of the Japanese aluminum industry facilitated adjustment. First, the industry's structure made adjustment costs very low. Aluminum is an extreme example of a Type I industry: it is by far the most concentrated of any of Japan's troubled industries and has the smallest labor force (in 1970 its H-index score was over 2,500 while its labor force totaled less than 14,000 workers). Also, the industry's six firms all benefited from their ties to the main *keiretsu* in Japan. As Paul Sheard has argued, *keiretsu* members helped by providing financial and technology assistance and by absorbing a portion of the industry's excess labor.[53] These structural advantages made the costs of adjustment very low, especially for labor. Second, access to these resources also opened up some adjustment alternatives for the industry. In particular, capital in the aluminum industry was mobile in that capacity could be shifted overseas through the creation of joint ventures. Third, the industry had compelling incentives to pursue economic adjustment since its loss of competitiveness was so apparent and extreme. Aluminum is a highly energy-intensive commodity, often referred to as "canned electricity." The Japanese industry was at a competitive disadvantage because it relied on petroleum-based electricity rather than cheaper hydroelectricity. The drastic increase in oil prices following the Oil Shocks made it simply unfeasible to produce aluminum in Japan. According to one analyst, Japan's aluminum firms simply had "no

[53] Sheard 1987; Sheard 1992, passim. Paul Sheard's various articles on the aluminum industry stress the common theme that the firms' affiliation with the *keiretsu* helped to cushion the costs of adjustment. I agree. However, Sheard's argument is weakened because he focuses on the "easiest" case—as I have argued, the tiny number of workers in this concentrated industry made adjustment easy to achieve. Sheard needs to look at other industries in which the adjustment of labor was more difficult. In these cases, there were clear limits to the ability of *keiretsu* firms to absorb excess labor. Furthermore, the majority of firms in most troubled industries did not enjoy such *keiretsu* ties.

real incentive . . . to maintain any domestic smelting capacity."[54] In short, the aluminum firms themselves had a strong economic incentive to exit from the industry—the complete collapse of their competitiveness—and also had the resources to pursue alternatives.

In addition, even if the aluminum industry had wanted to preserve itself, it would have faced strong opposition both at home and abroad. Domestically, the industrial consumers of aluminum ingots adamantly opposed attempts to subsidize the domestic smelters. These consumer industries—the aluminum rollers that produced sheet and the fabricators that created final products—were themselves faced with strong domestic and international competitors and so had strong inducements to obtain the lowest-priced ingots. After 1978, when the London Metals Exchange began to trade aluminum ingots, aluminum became an international commodity, freely available at international market prices. From that moment on, the aluminum smelters had no hope of maintaining higher domestic prices.[55] Especially as the smelting firms began to draw down their domestic capacity, the aluminum fabricators "gradually replac[ed] the smelters as the central figures in the aluminum industry." And given the fabricators' strong desire for access to cheap aluminum, "to protect smelters at the expense of fabricators was not politically possible."[56] In addition, the Japanese government was subjected to pressures from the United States to forgo protection of the aluminum industry. In the 1980s the United States pushed Japan to lower its tariff on aluminum imports, which then stood at 9 percent, and warned Japan not to use other measures to block imports of lower-priced aluminum ingots.[57]

---

[54] Rajan and Brahm 1994, p. 418. The Japanese industry relied on petroleum for more than three-fourths of its total energy needs. Hydroelectricity accounted for only 11 percent of the industry's energy needs. In contrast, 100 percent of the Canadian industry's energy needs came from hydroelectric sources (Tanaka 1988, p. 453). Although the Japanese industry had become the most energy-efficient one (requiring the lowest number of kilowatt hours to produce a ton of aluminum), they could not overcome the huge differential in the price of energy: in 1980, Japanese costs were nine times those of Canadian firms and three times those of American firms (Samuels 1983, p. 496).

[55] Tanaka 1988, p. 458. Sheard argues that *keiretsu* members helped to cushion the blow to the aluminum smelters by continuing to purchase their higher-priced ingots. Actually, the major rolling firms had begun to rely on imported ingots even before the Oil Shocks (Tanaka 1988, p. 459). This trend accelerated after the Oil Shocks. As Goto Akira (1988, p. 105) notes, "apparently there was a limit to the protection provided by the quasi-vertical integration or group membership." Richard Samuels (1983, p. 498) also cites the industry's "lack of internal group discipline" and notes that other end users such as the automobile industry and wire and cable producers also had a voice in the political process.

[56] Goto 1988, pp. 116–117.

[57] Goto 1988, pp. 117–118; Rajan and Brahm 1994, p. 403. According to *Business Japan*, these pressures were led by America's largest aluminum producer, Alcoa. The U.S. government subsequently considered aluminum as a possible 301 case. *Business Japan* (1985, p. 85) opined that "it is deplorable that Alcoa has picked as its scapegoat Japan's aluminum refining industry which is in its death throes."

Thus, economic adjustment became inevitable because of the aluminum industry's own economic incentives, combined with the opposition of domestic consumers and Japan's international partners. The aluminum industry at no point seriously considered seeking an overtly protectionist or preservationist strategy. The only issue was how—not whether—firms would exit the industry. The best that the firms could hope for was that exit would be orderly and that they could receive compensation for their adjustment efforts.

The aluminum firms initiated the market adjustment process in 1976. In that year the three major firms demonstrated their desire to exit the industry by "hiving off" their aluminum smelting operations into separate firms. This unilateral restructuring effort, an attempt by the firms to minimize their own losses, was the first step in a long-term strategy of exit.[58]

At the same time, the industry sought public policies that would help to temporarily stabilize economic conditions. These lobbying efforts were led by the industry association, the Japan Aluminum Federation. As Richard Samuels portrays it, the industry association was the central actor in the subsequent discussions held between the industry and bureaucrats, which took place in the Aluminum Industry Committee of MITI's Industrial Structure Council. Samuels argues that the industry was well represented in these talks and that eventual policy decisions fully reflected the interests and positions taken by the industry. Furthermore, in this case "seldom have final legislative, administrative, or LDP programs strayed far from the proposals resulting from these *shingikai* deliberations."[59]

In January 1976, as a result of these deliberations, MITI issued its first demand and supply guidelines to the aluminum industry. The industry had already been struggling with production cuts, but these efforts were voluntary and uncoordinated. The industry did not apply for a traditional recession cartel because, as one analyst argues, "MITI guidance, in effect, acted as a production control cartel."[60]

However, these pressures from the industry for policies to stabilize it were limited in scope and duration. Unlike the other industries we have

---

[58] Sheard 1987, pp. 15–18; Tanaka 1988, p. 462. The three main firms were Mitsubishi Chemical, Sumitomo Chemical, and Showa Denko; the firms they created were Mitsubishi Light Metal, Sumitomo Aluminum, and Showa Light Metals.

[59] Of the 29 members of the two aluminum-related committees in 1981, nine represented the aluminum industry and one came from the aluminum labor federation. In addition, there were nine representatives of aluminum-consuming industries, two from electric power, four from government banks, and one newspaper reporter. The committees were headed by two academics, one of whom was Ueno Hiroya, the same Seikei University professor who headed the minimill committee described in Chapter 5 (Sheard 1987, pp. 48–49; Samuels 1983, p. 501).

[60] Tanaka 1988, p. 462. Production cutbacks under these guidelines reached 40 percent. The industry considered these informal guidelines to be less binding than either the recession cartel or informal administrative guidance (*kankoku sōtan*), but they were evidently strong enough.

studied thus far, the industry made no repeated calls for the formation of formal or informal cartels. And the industry never demanded that the government help it by regulating competition. This is not surprising given the industry's drastic economic condition—rather than looking for ways to stabilize the status quo, firms were searching for the most graceful means of exit. Firms in the industry quickly turned their attention to coordinating capacity cutbacks and convincing the government to compensate them for these efforts.

Again, public-private discussions centered on the Aluminum Industry Committee. In the fall of 1977 the committee recommended that the industry seek designation under the Tokuanhō. The industry's dire straits made it a clear candidate for designation; in fact, as mentioned in Chapter 5, aluminum was one of the four industries designated in the original draft of the bill. It faced almost no internal controversy in seeking designation and then negotiating a Basic Stabilization Plan. Nor was there any controversy in implementing the stabilization plan worked out in the Aluminum Industry Committee, which called for a reduction in capacity from 1.64 million tons to 1.1 million tons. In the end, the industry scrapped 97 percent of this target.[61]

The Tokuanhō program fit in well with the industry's objectives in that it helped the industry coordinate capacity reductions and promised to be a source of compensation for these efforts. Since the industry was already heading for the exits, the Tokuanhō enabled firms to overtly coordinate industry-wide capacity cuts and also compensated them for the adjustment efforts they had already planned to make.

The industry also pursued another government policy tool to help defray the costs of capacity reductions. On the recommendation of the Aluminum Industry Committee, the government in 1978 adopted a "tariff-quota system," in which a portion of the 9 percent tariff on imported aluminum ingots was channeled to the firms to help subsidize capacity reductions. These proceeds went to the industry's Structural Improvement Association, which then passed these funds on to individual firms.[62] In the end, the industry received ¥83 billion from government sources, about 20 percent of its total adjustment costs.[63]

---

[61] Peck et al. 1987, p. 96.

[62] The tariff-quota system is described in detail in Goto 1988, pp. 110–111, Tanaka 1988, pp. 462–463, and Samuels 1983, p. 502. Specifically, about one-half of the tariff on imported aluminum ingots was channeled to the aluminum industry. Most analysts praise the Japanese government for using this system as a means to encourage exit. I agree that this policy tool was "positive" in the sense that it did not prevent adjustment. However, I argue that this tool served to compensate firms for actions they were planning to take on their own.

[63] Sheard 1992, p. 129. Sheard uses these figures to indicate that the private sector bore most of the costs of adjustment. Although this is true, the figures also indicated that a sizable chunk of adjustment costs were in fact subsidized through the public treasury.

Thus far, the process of adjustment had led to significant capacity cutbacks and had remained orderly. The onset of the Second Oil Shock in 1979, however, signaled the death knell for the domestic industry and touched off a mad scramble for the exits.

Over the next seven years the industry continued to take the initiative in eliminating its domestic capacity. This drastic slashing of domestic capacity was the result of individual firms following their own incentives rather than the guidelines provided by public policy. In fact, the capacity reduction targets worked out in MITI's *shingikai* called for a much *slower* rate of reduction than the private sector desired. Instead of following MITI's lead, firms in the industry consistently reduced their capacity at a much faster pace than public policy recommended.

In 1981, for instance, the Aluminum Industry Committee recommended that the industry should reduce its capacity to around 700,000 tons over the next four years. Yet, the industry understood that even this level was not sustainable, since domestic output in 1981, a mere 665,000 tons, was already well under the new capacity target. In the subsequent year output dropped to only 295,000 tons, and operating rates fell to as low as 36 percent in the first half of 1983. In addition, imports were growing rapidly and had more than tripled since 1976, so that by 1983 they accounted for over 75 percent of domestic demand. Given these conditions it is not surprising that firms scrapped or shut down their capacity at a much faster pace than the Aluminum Committee's plan called for. Changing market pressures overwhelmed any hopes of hanging on to this level of domestic capacity; Samuels noted that "within six months, these targets were meaningless."[64]

Subsequent capacity reduction targets set by the Aluminum Committee also lagged behind what the private sector was already doing. In 1985 it called for the reduction of domestic capacity from 700,000 to 350,000 tons per year by 1988. But again industry analysts criticized this new target as being out of date even before it was announced; in 1985, for instance, output was already at the 227,000 ton level, and the next year dropped to a mere 140,000 tons.[65] In February 1985 Showa Aluminum led the way out by shutting down its aluminum smelting operations altogether. The

---

[64] Samuels 1983, p. 503. It is not clear which parties pushed the hardest for the maintenance of some capacity at home. Samuels (1983, p. 502) implies that it was some of the firms themselves that wanted to maintain some domestic capacity, perhaps in the hope of gaining further public policy support. Others, such as Rajan and Brahm (1994, p. 418) and Tanaka (1988, pp. 463–467), argue that policy makers, particularly the MITI bureaucrats, feared becoming completely dependent on foreign sources. Of all of the industries I have examined, this was the only case in which government officials expressed significant concerns for economic security (Goto 1988, p. 116; *Japan Economic Journal*, Sept. 11, 1984; *Analysis of Japanese Industries for Investors 1987*, p. 208).

[65] *Business Japan*, Nov. 1985, p. 33; *Analysis of Japanese Industries for Investors 1992*, p. 178.

following year three other firms, Sumitomo Aluminum Smelting, Mitsui Aluminum, and Ryoka Light Metal Industries also closed their remaining plants. This left Nippon Light Metal's Kanbara plant, with an annual capacity of only 64,000 tons, as Japan's sole remaining aluminum smelter.[66]

In sum, Samuels is entirely correct when he argues that "the unanticipated pace of industrial transformation [was] much more a response to the exigencies of the market than due to the foresightedness of MITI planners."[67] MITI policy was not responsible for pushing the industry to adjust. If anything, public policy followed behind what the private sector was already doing and ended up slowing rather than speeding up adjustment.

The industry's drastic adjustment was made possible by three structural advantages—advantages that no other troubled industry in Japan enjoyed. First, the costs of labor adjustment in this industry were the lowest of all of Japan's troubled industries. The industry started off with a very small labor force (a mere 8,557 workers in 1977); by 1983 this number was down to 3,715, a decline of 56.6 percent.[68] The adjustment of labor was further facilitated by the depressed industry employment legislation, which provided subsidies for workers fired from the industry. Goto Akira reports that about one-half of the workers that left the aluminum industry were hired by affiliated firms. This outlet for absorbing redundant workers made labor adjustment the easiest and least controversial of all of the industries I have examined.[69]

Second, the aluminum firms also had a viable economic alternative: diversification into aluminum rolling. The aluminum smelters had not made concerted efforts to diversify prior to the Oil Shocks, but afterward they found that their survival depended on being able to move downstream. As an example, Nippon Light Metals between 1975 and 1985 increased its output of rolled and fabricated aluminum products by some 150 percent; these new sales more than offset its withdrawal from aluminum smelting. As a result, the firm increased its dependence on fabricated aluminum products from 43 percent to 66 percent.[70]

Third, capital in the industry was mobile enough to shift overseas. Beginning in the mid-1970s the aluminum firms entered into a series of overseas joint ventures to produce aluminum ingots. The industry invested mostly in regions such as Canada, the United States, New Zealand, Australia, Venezuela, Indonesia, and Brazil, all of which offered low elec-

---

[66] *Japan Economic Journal*, 1987, p. 189. Significantly, the Kanbara plant was the only smelter in Japan that relied on hydroelectric power rather than oil (Rajan and Brahm 1994, p. 403; Goto 1988, pp. 104–105).

[67] Samuels 1983, p. 497; Tanaka 1988, pp. 466–467.

[68] Peck et al. 1987, p. 101.

[69] Goto 1988, pp. 99, 117.

[70] *Japan Company Handbook*, various years; Goto 1988, p. 98. The main firms diversified by acquiring smaller aluminum rollers and fabricators (*Business Japan*, Aug. 1989, p. 111).

tricity costs or cheap sources of raw materials. By 1977 the industry had established overseas facilities with an annual capacity of 1.24 million tons; of this amount, Japan's share was 750,000 tons. Samuels reports that by 1986 the industry had entered into an additional ten projects, with an annual capacity of 2.06 million tons of aluminum per year—considerably more than the capacity that the industry had cut at home.[71] In essence, the industry had succeeded in relocating itself from Japan to sites abroad.

[71] The industry's overseas investment efforts in this period are discussed in Goto 1988, p. 109, *Business Japan*, Aug. 1978, p. 89, Samuels 1983, pp. 506–507, and *Business Japan*, Aug. 1981, p. 97. Goto reports that imports from these overseas projects accounted for 34 percent of all imports by 1983. Samuels also notes that three more projects, with another 465,000 tons of annual capacity, were under negotiation in 1986.

CHAPTER SEVEN

Mixed-Incentive Industries:
Shipbuilding and Integrated Steel (Type II)

Type II industries are those that are concentrated and have large labor forces. Because this industry type consists of a small number of large firms, we can expect firms to be able to respond to distress through economic adjustment strategies. Like those in the synthetic fiber industry, firms should have incentives to pursue economic adjustment options such as diversification into higher value-added products or out of the industry altogether. This should decrease a firm's stakes in maintaining the status quo. On the other hand, the large size of the labor force pulls the industry in the opposite direction. Compared to the Type I industries, firms must deal with larger numbers of redundant workers and will thus have greater incentives to resist adjustment by pursuing political solutions. This industry type thus occupies the middle ground between Type I and Type IV industries.

Given the larger number of workers involved, labor adjustment should be more difficult than was the case in the synthetic fiber industry. On the other hand, adjustment costs should be lower than in the cotton spinning case since the large size of the firms gives them a greater absorptive capacity—the ability to shift workers to other divisions within the firm or to related companies. Labor will resist attempts by firms to pursue strategies that will result in the loss of jobs but support attempts to preserve the industry's status quo.

The Japanese shipbuilding industry is an example of a Type II industry. In 1973, just before the onset of economic distress, the industry had a Herfindahl-index number of 1,041, just above the usual cutoff point be-

Table 7-1. Structure of the shipbuilding industry, 1975

	Number of firms	Berths or docks	Capacity (1,000 CGRT)*	Employment (shipbuilding only)
Major firms	7	55	5,720	87,639
Quasi-major firms	17	38	2,900	46,367
Small firms	37	45	1,190	22,252
Industry total	61	138	9,810	156,258

SOURCES: *Zosen*, Apr. 1981, pp. 66–71; Nihon Zōsen Shinkō Zaidan 1983, pp. 68–69.
*Compensated gross registered tonnage

tween concentrated and fragmented industries.[1] The industry's labor force numbered over 274,000 workers in 1975.

The most salient structural feature of the shipbuilding industry is its dual structure. As shown in Table 7-1, the industry in the mid-1970s was dominated by seven major firms. These firms accounted for close to 60 percent of the industry's total capacity and employed 56 percent of the industry's labor force. At the same time, there were 54 smaller firms, classified into two groups—the 17 quasi-majors, which accounted for 29 percent of capacity, and the 37 small shipbuilders, which accounted for the remaining 12 percent.

Table 7-2 provides further details on the disparity between the majors and the rest of the industry. The majors were gigantic industrial conglomerates, already highly diversified before the First Oil Shock. The largest of the majors, Mitsubishi Heavy Industries and Ishikawajima-Harima Heavy Industries, had annual capacities of over 1 million tons. All of the majors operated numerous docks or berths. Most striking is that all were already highly diversified in 1975: only 32 percent of the total sales of the seven majors were accounted for by shipbuilding or ship repair. The two largest firms, Mitsubishi Heavy and Ishikawajima-Harima, each relied on shipbuilding for less than 40 percent of their sales. Even the most dedicated majors, Mitsui Zosen and Hitachi Zosen, depended on shipbuilding sales for only 76 and 63 percent of their total sales, respectively. Another characteristic of the majors is that all were closely tied to the *keiretsu*: all were members of the presidents' clubs, symbols of core status in Japan's industrial conglomerates. This implies that, all else being equal, the majors could count on not only their own broad

[1] The H-index later fell below the 1,000-level. Thus, Peck et al. (1987) classified the industry in 1978 as "unconcentrated." Japan's shipbuilding industry (*zōsengyō*) generally includes only ships of 2,500 gross tons or more, the size of ships covered in the 1953 Shipbuilding Law. The shipbuilding industry's JSIC number is 3641.

Table 7-2. Representative shipbuilding firms, 1975

Firm	Berths or docks	Capacity (CGRT)*	Labor force	Shipbuilding as percentage of total sales	Keiretsu affiliation
SEVEN MAJORS					
Mitsubishi Heavy Industries	13	1,326,126	79,828	36	Mitsubishi
Ishikawajima-Harima Heavy Industries	8	1,175,378	36,060	39	Dai-Ichi
Hitachi Zosen	10	889,100	23,517	63	Sanwa
Kawasaki Heavy Industries	6	709,224	33,068	30	Dai-Ichi
Mitsui Zosen	7	623,413	15,909	76	Mitsui
Nippon Kokan	5	539,091	41,333	10	Fuyo
Sumitomo Heavy Industries	4	427,284	12,780	29	Sumitomo
REPRESENTATIVE QUASI-MAJORS					
Sasebo Heavy Industries	3	322,186	6,792	86	
Hakodate Dock	3	309,000	3,408	78	
Namura Shipbuilding	2	177,548	2,524	93	
Sanoyasu Dockyard	2	173,548	2,096	96	
Kanasashi Shipbuilding	2	167,592	480	100	
Oshima Shipbuilding	1	118,763	N.A.	99	
Hashihama Shipbuilding	2	117,857	1,425	99	
REPRESENTATIVE SMALL FIRMS					
Naikai Shipbuilding	2	69,510	1,917	98	
Narasaki Shipbuilding	3	68,401	N.A.	100	
Mie Shipyard	1	51,830	376	99	
Shin-Yamamoto Shipbuilding	1	48,812	248	100	
Tohoku Shipbuilding	1	48,478	N.A.	95	
Miho Shipyard	2	40,324	N.A.	100	
Shikoku Dockyard	1	33,066	N.A.	100	
Shimoda Dockyard	1	31,721	N.A.	100	
Fukuoka Shipbuilding	1	28,346	N.A.	100	
Ujina Shipbuilding	1	24,486	170	98	
Yamanishi Shipbuilding	1	18,764	570	100	
Asakawa Shipbuilding	1	18,456	116	100	
Geibi Shipbuilding	1	16,230	N.A.	99	
Shinhama Zosen	1	13,862	107	100	

SOURCES: *Zosen*, Apr. 1981, pp. 66–71; Nihon Zōsen Shinkō Zaidan 1983, pp. 74–75; Un'yushō, Senpaku Kyoku Zōsenka 1976, pp. 30–31; Gerlach 1989, pp. 148–149.

*Compensated gross registered tonnage.

technological bases but also relatively assured access to financial and other resources.

In stark contrast, the 54 remaining shipbuilders were tiny by comparison. As the table makes clear, the capacity of the quasi-majors averaged about 170,000 tons, while the smallest firms had average capacities of only

37,000 tons, less than 5 percent of that of the majors. In addition, the quasi-majors averaged two berths or docks, while most of the smaller firms operated only a single dock or berth capable of turning out only the smallest class of ships. Furthermore, these firms were entirely dependent on shipbuilding for their income. Of the quasi-majors only the two largest, Sasebo and Hakodate, derived less than 90 percent of their income from shipbuilding. In 1975, over 96 percent of total sales of all small- and medium-sized firms came from shipbuilding and ship repairs. According to industry analysts, these firms had been unable to diversify in the past "because they lacked [the necessary] financial and technological foundations."[2]

The differing economic circumstances of the two parts of the industry led to different reactions to the onset of economic distress in the mid-1970s. On the one hand, because the majors were already diversified, they were able to offset their unprofitable shipbuilding operations by shifting their production efforts to their land-based and engineering-related businesses. On the other hand, the smaller shipbuilders did not enjoy this option. Because they were so dependent on shipbuilding, they lacked the flexibility to smoothly move into other markets. When faced with economic distress these firms had nowhere to turn: their survival depended on the ups and downs of a single product. This economic reality was to be an important part of the policy process in the 1970s and 1980s. The competing interests of these two groups, and the mediation of their demands, proved to be a fundamental part of the policy process described in this case study.

One difference between this case and all of the others is that the shipbuilding industry falls under the jurisdiction of the Ministry of Transport (MOT) rather than MITI. The MOT has been described as more interventionist and more domestically oriented than MITI. This is not surprising given that much of the MOT's activities involve the regulation of domestically oriented sectors. Also, the narrowness of the ministry's jurisdiction suggests that it will be more sensitive to the interests of each industry that it regulates; unlike the situation in MITI with its broad jurisdictional base, MOT bureaucrats would have fewer employment opportunities if one of their industries were to disappear. On the other hand, the MOT is not thoroughly beholden to the shipbuilders. Throughout this case study the MOT has had to mediate between very strong interests: between the majors and the smaller shipbuilders, between the shipbuilding industry and the shipping industry, and between domestic interests and international pressures. Having to reconcile such disparate interests has

---

[2] Chida and Davies 1990, p. 172. Of the 55 small firms, 42 were completely dependent on shipbuilding and ship repair; an additional 10 of these firms relied on shipbuilding for more than 90 percent of their income (Un'yusho, Senpaku Kyoku Zōsenka 1976, p. 29).

been a difficult job, but it has also given the MOT some leeway in choosing between the competing demands that it faces.

Given the strategic nature of shipbuilding to an island trading nation such as Japan, the government has traditionally been more intimately involved in this industry than in any of the industries we have examined thus far. Indeed, three of Japan's largest shipbuilders—Ishikawajima-Harima, Mitsubishi Heavy, and Kawasaki Heavy—got their start as government-owned shipbuilding concerns during the Meiji era. In subsequent decades the Japanese government expended considerable resources in support of both the shipbuilding and shipping industries. Throughout the first half of this century the shipbuilding industry was strategically significant for Japan's military ambitions. During the 1930s and 1940s, the Imperial Navy was the industry's key source of demand for ships.[3]

After the war, the government was quick to designate shipbuilding as a priority industry. Of the various efforts to promote the industry, the most important was the "planned shipbuilding" program (*keikaku zōsen*). Under this program, begun in 1946, the government provided low-interest loans from the Reconstruction Finance Bank (later the Japan Development Bank) for the construction of new ships; these ships were then purchased by a public corporation and leased to Japanese shipping companies. The planned shipbuilding program provided the industry with a stable source of demand and was particularly important in the context of economic instability during the early 1950s.

With the help of government support—but more because of its own efforts—the Japanese industry by the 1960s had established itself as a world-class competitor. In 1956 Japan surpassed the United Kingdom as the world's largest shipbuilder. In 1963 shipbuilding became Japan's second largest export industry, accounting for 8.4 percent of Japan's total exports, ranking just behind the steel industry.[4] As the world's most efficient producer of ships, Japan was able to capture more than 50 percent of the world market by 1968, and maintained this market share for the next two decades. The industry was thus highly dependent on exports: in 1974, 83 percent of Japan's new ship launchings were destined for export markets.

---

[3] For instance, during the 1928–1931 period, demand from the Imperial Navy accounted for nearly one-half of all man-hours worked in the shipbuilding industry (Chida and Davies 1990, p. 46). The early development of the shipbuilding industry is discussed in Nihon Zōsen Kōgyōkai 30–Nenshi Kankō Shōiinkai 1989, Un'yu 50-Nenshi Hensan Kyoku 1989, Blumenthal 1976, Vogel 1985, and Chida and Davies 1990.

[4] Nihon Zōsen Kōgyōkai 30-Nenshi Kankō Shōiinkai 1980, p. 163. The shipbuilders held this position until 1975 when they were surpassed by the automobile industry. Before 1963 the cotton textile industry was the second largest exporter, behind only the steel industry (Chida and Davies 1990, p. 156; U.S. General Accounting Office 1982, p. 59).

On the eve of the Oil Shock, the major Japanese shipbuilders had become particularly dependent on the production of oil supertankers. To meet growing worldwide demand for large tankers the Japanese majors in the 1960s entered into an investment race to expand their supertanker-class facilities. The majors were confident that through aggressive investments they could widen the already huge gap they had opened up between themselves and their international rivals, thus assuring themselves a virtual monopoly on this lucrative market. By the early 1970s Japan's newest dock, in Mitsubishi Heavy's Nagasaki shipyard, was capable of constructing ships of up to 1 million tons. The government also actively encouraged the building of ever-larger facilities. In 1965, for instance, the MOT encouraged the construction of docks capable of producing 500,000-ton ships and later in 1973 encouraged the building of one-million-ton tankers.[5] By 1974 tankers accounted for 76 percent of Japan's shipbuilding output.

The smaller shipbuilders, most of which entered the industry in the mid-1960s, tended to concentrate on smaller, more specialized ships such as cargo carriers. The oil tankers and other large ships were left to the majors, a de facto market segmentation that was also encouraged by the government. By the 1970s, only a handful of the more competitive of the smaller firms had begun to enter the more lucrative tanker market.

INITIAL RESPONSES TO THE WORLD SHIPBUILDING CRISIS, 1974–1977

Global demand for ships collapsed completely following the First Oil Crisis of 1973. The collapse of the shipbuilding industry was a global phenomenon, with worldwide orders dropping from 72.8 million gross tons (GT) to 25.3 million GT between 1973 and 1974. One reason was that the slowdown of global commerce in the mid-1970s reduced significantly the demand for new ships. More important for the Japanese industry, the sudden drop in oil consumption led to a shrinkage of demand for the giant supertankers. By 1978, it was estimated that only two-thirds of the world's existing oil tankers were actually being utilized.[6]

Chart 7–1 illustrates the sudden onset of economic distress in the Japanese industry. Total orders garnered by Japan's shipbuilders plummeted between 1973 and 1974 from a high of 33.8 million GT to 13.0 million GT. In 1978 the industry received only 3.2 million GT in new orders, less than

---

[5] Chida and Davies 1990, pp. 159–160; Vogel 1985, p. 49. Totten (1984, p. 138) notes that by 1974 seven Japanese shipyards had facilities to build ships of over 500,000 tons, which equaled the number of such facilities existing worldwide.

[6] Ekonomisuto Henshūbu 1978, p. 71.

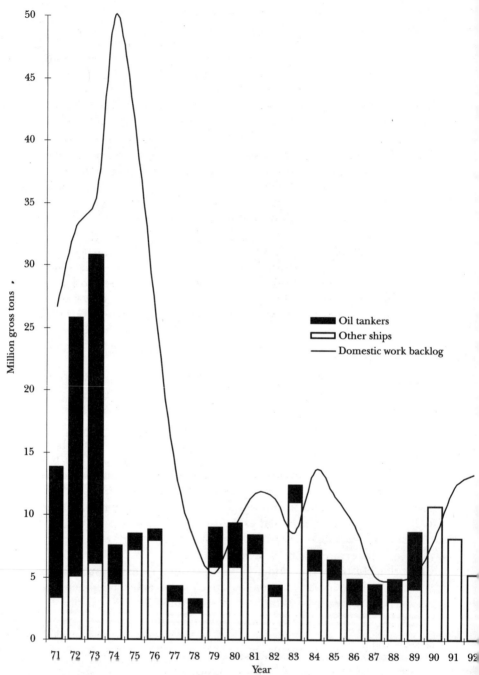

Sources: Un'yu Hakusho, various issues, and Un'yu 50-Nenshi Hensan Kyoku 1989, p. 30.

one-tenth of the orders in the industry's peak year of 1974. More drastic was the fall in orders for oil tankers; as can be seen in the chart, tanker orders declined from a high of 27.6 million GT in 1973 to only 610,000 GT in 1975, 2 percent of the industry's peak production. In particular, demand for supertankers, the types of tankers that Japan's majors had become most proficient at producing, dried up almost overnight. The "shipbuilding crisis" was, according to one analyst, more accurately described as a "tanker crisis": now, the industry's huge capacity to construct these tankers, built up over the previous decade, had become a competitive liability.[7]

The shift of demand away from the giant supertankers to smaller, more specialized ships was to have two critical policy consequences for Japan over the next decade. First, at home, the majors now were forced to compete directly for the one remaining market niche—the smaller ship market—resulting in growing conflicts between the majors and the small shipbuilders. Second, competition between Japanese and European shipbuilders intensified as firms around the world scrambled to maximize their share of a shrinking global market. As competition increased, so too did international criticisms of the actions taken by the Japanese industry and government; Japan came under intense pressures to refrain from taking too much of the world market. These European pressures to create an international cartel became an important constraint on the behavior of the Japanese industry and Japanese policy makers.

The collapse of demand was not felt immediately by the Japanese industry: as it takes two years for ships to be completed, the industry hoped to spread out its existing orders at least through 1977. In fact, as shown in the chart, the industry was at its busiest in 1974 and 1975, as it worked to complete the backlog of ships that had been ordered just prior to the Oil Shock. Beyond that, however, disaster loomed. Because the work backlog would soon be completed, and because new ship orders had all but disappeared, the industry foresaw that 1977 and 1978 would be crisis years. By 1975, no one in the industry could fail to recognize the dire situation Japan was about to face.

The Ban on "Parallel Building": Protecting the Small Firms

The collapse of the tanker market threw the majors and the small shipbuilders into direct conflict. In order that their giant facilities would not

---

[7] *Zaikai*, Aug. 31, 1976, p. 53. At the same time, the industry was beset by a spate of canceled orders (Nihon Zōsen Shinkō Zaidan 1983, p. 3). The industry was also hurt by a dramatic rise in its production costs, in part due to rising steel costs, increasing industry wages, and the revaluation of the yen after 1973. It has been estimated that Japanese ship producers suffered nearly $900 million in exchange rate loses in 1974 alone (*Japan Economic Journal*, July 15, 1975).

lie completely idle, the majors became more aggressive in seeking orders for the smaller cargo and bulk carriers. At times the majors even built ships as small as 10,000 GT in their enormous docks. They also began to use these large docks to construct two small ships at a time, a practice known as "parallel building."[8]

The small firms were quick to criticize the majors for encroaching on the market niche previously considered their own domain and appealed to the MOT for a ban on this practice. The small firms argued that unless there was some sort of orderly marketing arrangement, they would be pushed out of their one remaining market segment. The smaller firms felt that they would be destroyed in a direct confrontation with the majors, since they simply could not compete in terms of finance, technology, and marketing power. Ezra Vogel encapsulates the threat to the smaller firms: "Without some kind of agreement it was likely that the smaller companies would quickly be eliminated and that no company would remain healthy."[9]

The majors did not favor government intervention in this case. Rather, these firms argued that decisions regarding the kind of ships a company produced should be left to the discretion of the company itself. Given their more competitive position, this was a reasonable position for them to take.

Although the majors had the more compelling and economically rational case, the smaller firms had more political influence. The main industry association representing the interests of the smaller firms, the Cooperative Association of Japanese Shipbuilders (CAJS), pressed their interests directly with MOT officials. Their position was also supported by the labor union representing workers in the smaller shipyards, the JSP-affiliated Zenzōsen (Zen Nihon Zōsen Kikai Rōdō Kumiai, or All-Japan Shipbuilding and Engineering Union). This union had only 8,000 members but was a radical and vocal supporter of the small shipbuilders. These smaller firms also used their ties to the politicians. Many analysts have noted the general responsiveness of the ruling LDP to the concerns of small and medium enterprises; in the case of shipbuilding, this responsiveness was magnified by the industry's heavy regional concentration. In many cases the shipbuilders, including their webs of related subcontracting firms and allied industries, were the single most important local industry.[10] Furthermore, shipbuilding centers such as Sasebo and Hiroshima, which were already among the nation's poorer areas, could not withstand the failure of an industry as central as shipbuilding. Regional politicians made sure that the interests of the smaller shipbuilders were al-

---

[8] *Zosen*, Apr. 1976, pp. 6, 14; Totten 1984, p. 139; Nihon Zōsen Shinkō Zaidan 1983, p. 41.
[9] Vogel 1985, p. 51; Boyd 1989, p. 4.
[10] The shipbuilding industry, for instance, accounted for over half of all local commerce in regional cities such as Nagasaki and Sasebo. Shipbuilding in these areas was clearly "the determining factor in these local economies" (Totten 1984, p. 164).

ways taken into account in the policy process.[11] In addition, the local ship-builders also organized themselves into national lobbying groups, the most important of which were four committees representing prefectures or cities that were highly dependent on the shipbuilding industry. These organizations were not at all peripheral to the policy process: their chairman was Nagano Shigeo, who was also chairman of the MOT's shipbuilding *shingikai*.[12]

The MOT responded to these pressures in the fall of 1975, using its administrative guidance powers to restrict the large firms from practicing parallel building. This action clearly favored the interests of the medium and small firms: the MOT's action spread the economic burden around and minimized the dislocations facing the smaller firms.[13]

The MOT's Administrative Guidance: Domestic and International Motivations

As the crisis continued into 1976 and 1977, individual shipbuilders were becoming increasingly desperate to secure whatever new orders they could find. The situation was especially dire for the smaller firms since their very survival depended on their ability to secure a minimum share of new orders. Both the small firms and the majors began to accept orders at well below their break-even prices: prices for new orders in 1977, for instance, were 30 to 40 percent lower than at their peak in 1974.

One result of this price-cutting competition, aside from declining profits, was that the Japanese share of the world shipbuilding market began to increase. In 1976 Japan's share of new ship orders rose to over 55 percent (up from 48 percent in 1973); at the same time, the Europeans saw their share dwindle to 20 percent, down from nearly 40 percent in 1973.

The European industry associations, worried that many of its ship-builders were faced with imminent failure, now began to apply pressures on Japan. European criticisms focused first on Japan's ship-pricing policies. The Europeans charged that the Japanese industry was increasing its market share through dumping—deliberately accepting ship orders at below cost. The Europeans pressed Japan to voluntarily raise its export prices through stricter government regulation and through unofficial exchanges of information on ship order prices.[14] This, it was hoped, would serve to stabilize world market shares.

---

[11] Boyd and Nagamori 1991, p. 184, Vogel 1985, pp. 50–52; Keyser 1990, p. 138. The clearest example of the role of local politicians is the bail-out of Sasebo in 1978.

[12] Nihon Zōsen Shinkō Zaidan 1983, p. 5.

[13] Nihon Zōsen Shinkō Zaidan 1983, p. 41; Vogel 1985, pp. 50–52.

[14] *Ekonomisuto,* Jan. 1977, pp. 30–34. Many of these charges of dumping pertained especially to smaller ships; in particular, West Germany was hard hit.

In addition, the Europeans began to push for an explicit international market-sharing agreement. In June 1976 the Europeans began to discuss a political solution—the formation of an informal international cartel in which Japan and the European Community would share new shipbuilding orders equally.[15] In particular, it was West Germany, whose small shipbuilders were rapidly losing market share to Japan, that was the most insistent that the issue be taken up at the highest political level. The Europeans, as represented by the Association of West European Shipbuilders (AWES), used forums such as the OECD Working Party on Shipbuilding and the Japan-E.C. Shipbuilders Conference (Nichi-Ō Zōsen Kyōgi) to press their demands. In addition, bilateral talks were held in a series of industry-to-industry negotiations and in sporadic high-level E.C.-Japan economic summit meetings.

The Japanese industry was split over how best to respond to the European demands. These conflicting interests were discussed, and eventually mediated, by the industry's main political organization, the Shipbuilders Association of Japan (SAJ, or Nihon Zōsen Kōgyōkai).[16] Because Japan's shipbuilders were still the world's most competitive, they opposed the explicit market-sharing schemes then being proposed. The industry was in the same position as the outsiders in both the cotton spinning and minimill case studies: the most attractive solution for it was to increase its world market share at the expense of the Europeans. Yet, the Japanese shipbuilders were more than aware of the international political realities facing them. After all, the Japanese shipbuilders had for decades tacitly agreed to hold their world market share at around 50 percent. During the tumultuous conditions of the mid-1970s, the Japanese shipbuilders realized that a significant surge in their market share would cause an international political backlash. Judging from comments made at the time, the SAJ appears to have been quite savvy about the realities of Japan's international trade politics. During one round of interviews, for instance, the core SAJ leaders maintained that they were "dead set against" fixing market shares, but then in the same breath they claimed that a 50-percent share would be "appropriate," since taking a larger share would only "invite political interference."[17] In other words,

[15] *Zosen*, Feb. 1977, p. 5; Nihon Zōsen Shinkō Zaidan 1983, p. 10. The process of negotiations between the European and Japanese industries is discussed in detail in Nihon Zōsen Shinkō Zaidan 1983, pp. 6–12.

[16] The SAJ, founded in 1947, represented the majors and quasi-majors. Nihon Zōsen Kōgōkai 30-Nenshi Kankō Shōiinkai 1980 describes the SAJ's organization.

[17] *Zosen*, Apr. 1976, p. 12. Unlike the other industries we have examined so far, the shipbuilding industry felt that it could still capture a larger part of world orders. It is not clear how high Japan's market share would have been in the absence of the international market-sharing agreement, but the industry estimated that it enjoyed a cost advantage over European shipbuilders as high as 30 percent (*Zosen*, Apr. 1976, p. 8).

the shipbuilders, like the synthetic fiber firms, understood that they could not export their domestic problems of surplus capacity.

In addition, the industry, especially its largest firms, had an interest in seeing ship prices stabilized both at home and abroad. It realized that it was trapped in a vicious cycle of depressed prices and depressed profits that led to further desperate efforts to secure new orders at whatever price. All parties realized that this downward spiral was harming their financial viability. Already in the past the industry had hurt itself by competing for orders on unfavorable terms, at times even producing at a net loss; industry officials now warned of the need to avoid the pitfalls of excessive competition, or what they called "prosperity sans profits" (*rieki naki han'ei*).[18] The entire industry stood to gain by curbing its destabilizing cutthroat competition. The shipbuilders perceived the same advantages of market stabilizing arrangements that have been described in the other case studies. Seeing competition stabilized and having ship prices recover to "appropriate" levels became a central concern for the Japanese shipbuilders. For this reason the industry did not object when, in late 1975, the MOT established a floor on export prices; indeed, the Japanese majors welcomed this price guidance, since dumping was more prevalent among the small firms.

Beyond this, however, the industry refused to go. In mid-1976 the SAJ decided to resist the European demands for an explicit market-sharing arrangement. The industry now refused to further reduce Japan's market share, as demanded by the European Community. Rather, it hoped that Japan's cooperation in stabilizing ship prices would be enough to quell international pressures.

The MOT found itself in a difficult position. The ministry did not want to sacrifice the interests of the shipbuilding industry too easily.[19] At the same time, the ministry was already under growing political pressures to do something to placate international criticisms of Japan. The MOT held numerous discussions throughout 1975 and 1976 in order to mediate these conflicting pressures and diffuse the shipbuilding crisis. The most important deliberative forum was the MOT's long-standing *shingikai*, the Shipping and Shipbuilding Rationalization Council (SSRC, or Kaiun Zōsen Gōrika Shingikai). This council became the focus of all deliberations between the shipbuilders, the bureaucrats, and other concerned parties. It consisted of about 45 members, of whom 11 to 13 comprised a separate shipbuilding subcommittee. The industry association and the individual shipbuilding firms were fully represented in the SSRC as were the

[18] *Zosen*, Apr. 1976, p. 8.
[19] Boyd and Nagamori 1991, p. 180. Initially, the MOT endorsed this SAJ position. The MOT even went one step further, demanding that AWES and the other E.C. producers agree to cut back on their surplus capacity in exchange for Japanese cooperation.

unions and other related actors.[20] The SSRC as a whole was under the chairmanship of Nagano Shigeo, one of Japan's leading industrialists. Although Nagano did not have a background in shipbuilding, he did have personal ties to shipbuilders (his brother was president of Ishikawajima-Harima); furthermore, Nagano, as head of the committee of shipbuilding prefectures and cities, was fully involved with the problems of local shipbuilders.

Over the course of these industry-government discussions, the shipbuilding firms focused their attention on the same policy option that we have seen in the other case studies—having the MOT use its administrative guidance powers (*kankoku sōtan*) to enforce cooperative production cutbacks. This policy response would meet the demands of both the Europeans and the Japanese shipbuilders themselves: not only would guidance stabilize world ship prices, it would also help to stabilize competition at home. The SSRC recommended that between 1976 and 1980 the Japanese shipbuilders should aim to produce around 6.5 million GT, or between 54 and 65 percent of world orders.

However, far from quelling international pressures, this report set off a further round of protests from abroad. The European Community complained that if Japan were to follow the *shingikai*'s recommendations, the Europeans' market share would be forced as low as 10 percent. The Europeans portrayed the SSRC report as an attempt to expand Japan's market share, not a call for restraint and cooperation. The Japanese industry in turn reacted angrily, arguing that it had faithfully adhered to the tacit agreement not to expand beyond 50 percent of the world market. In addition, it felt that current MOT efforts to raise export prices were sufficient to prevent further dumping.

The shipbuilding issue, however, was rapidly spreading beyond the boundaries of this single industry and was beginning to affect Japan's broader economic interests. In October 1976 European criticisms of Japanese trade practices came to a head during a two-week visit by the Keidanren president, Doko Toshio, to the United Kingdom, France, and West Germany. During direct talks with high-level trade officials of these nations, the "Doko Mission" turned into a lightning rod for E.C. complaints, especially about the shipbuilding industry, although other sectors, including automobiles and electronics, were also criticized.[21]

---

[20] Totten 1984, p. 161. The unions, for instance were represented by Hokari Naomi, Secretary General of Zenzōsen of Sōhyō. Here, the role played by outside academics was especially visible. Two academics well-known within shipbuilding circles were SSRC members: Wakimura Yoshitaro, professor emeritus of Tokyo University, and Chida Tomohei of Hitotsubashi University. Donna Keyser (1990, p. 196) presents a full list of the affiliations of SSRC members.

[21] Nimura 1976, pp. 25–27. Ironically, Doko was originally a shipbuilder, serving as president of Ishikawajima-Harima from 1950 to the late 1960s.

This rising level of international politicization motivated other domestic actors to become more involved in the issue. Upon Doko's return to Japan the Keidanren initiated discussions between representatives from the key sectors under attack and the relevant ministries and bureaus. Doko made it absolutely clear to the shipbuilders that they would have to solve their trade dispute before it damaged Japan's overall trade relationships. The Keidanren's position reflected the interests of the majority of its members that had a stake in maintaining access to markets abroad.

The shipbuilding issue was also being taken up at the highest levels of the Japanese government.[22] The cabinet in late 1976 entered into an intense round of internal discussions of Japan's position in the upcoming meeting of the OECD Working Party on Shipbuilding, scheduled for January 1977. In a November interministerial meeting, for instance, the Ministry of Foreign Affairs strongly pushed the MOT to concede to the European demands. MITI likewise pressed the MOT and the shipbuilding industry to make sure that the issue did not have a negative impact on Japan's other exporting industries. In addition, politicians from the ruling LDP were now fully engaged in the issue. A special Subcommittee on Shipping and Shipbuilding Policies of the LDP's Policy Affairs Research Council, for instance, became constantly involved in all phases of the policy process.[23] And in a late November meeting involving the industry and the various ministries, Prime Minister Miki Takeo himself took the chair.

Now that shipbuilding policy had become an international issue and a full range of domestic interests had become involved, pressures on the MOT to respond directly to the European Community's demands were becoming irresistible. With the top political leadership now involved, the interests had broadened well beyond the shipbuilding industry. As Richard Boyd and Seiichi Nagamori aptly stated, "control of the problem was surrendered to a macro-political world, to a broader, more uncertain, more weakly and loosely integrated set of actors in pursuit of a wider range of interests and answerable to a multiplicity of different constituencies."[24]

The MOT issued its first *kankoku sōtan* recommendations in November 1976. The ministry, using its authority granted under Article 7 of the 1950 Shipbuilding Law (Zōsenhō), called on the top 40 firms in the industry to curtail their operations to 75 percent of their 1974 peak levels. The ministry also took into account the differing economic situations of the large and small firms: the majors were instructed to make the largest cutbacks, while the smaller firms were allowed slightly higher operating rates. This

---

[22] The industry's lobbying efforts are described in Totten 1984, passim, Boyd and Nagamori 1991, and Nihon Zōsen Shinkō Zaidan 1983.

[23] Totten 1984, p. 162, passim; Boyd and Nagamori 1991, p. 176. This body, under the chairmanship of Tsukahara Toshiro, had been established in August 1975.

[24] Boyd and Nagamori 1991, p. 181.

differential reflected both economic and political realities: simply put, asking the smaller and less stable shipbuilders to make equal cutbacks would have pushed many of them into bankruptcy.

By February 1977 the Japanese government had succeeded in diffusing the international crisis. The head of the MOT's Ship Bureau explained to the OECD Working Party that Japan had committed itself to limiting Japan's market share to around 50 percent of world orders (a commitment that the SAJ had already been maintaining). The MOT promised to take further action in terms of production cuts if Japan's share threatened to rise above this level. In addition, the MOT promised to continue to check export prices in an attempt to prevent further dumping.

Domestic opposition to the production curtailments came not from the shipbuilders but from the FTC and the domestic shipping industry. The FTC's negative response was not surprising. After all, the FTC was at that time attacking MITI for using the same policy instrument and, furthermore, had gone to court to try to curb this practice (in the petroleum cartel case). The FTC informed the MOT that its administrative guidance violated the spirit and philosophy of the Anti-Monopoly Law. At the same time, however, the FTC was fully aware of political necessities both at home and abroad and so decided to "close its eyes."[25] Japan's shipping industry, however, was not pleased with this policy action. As the main domestic consumer of ships, it worried that concerted action by the shipbuilders to stabilize prices would mean that the shipping industry would have to pay higher prices for ships. In the late 1970s the shipping firms were in a situation every bit as unstable as the shipbuilders: the industry argued that it was facing its worst recession since the end of the war and thus could not afford to subsidize the shipbuilders in this way. The Japan Shipowners' Association complained to the FTC and to the MOT concerning the MOT's administrative action.[26]

The shipbuilding industry, on the other hand, welcomed the announcement of *kankoku sōtan*. As already noted, the industry had ample reason to welcome managed competition in the domestic market. First, the industry wanted to put an end to cutthroat competition which was hurting the profitability of every firm in the industry. Second, the MOT was careful to keep its recommended operating rate for the industry above 60 percent, which was then considered break-even. The industry fully realized that, given the total collapse of the shipbuilding market, they would

---

[25] Nihon Zōsen Shinkō Zaidan 1983, pp. 42–43. The FTC argument was that Article 7 of the Zōsenhō allowed the MOT to offer guidance to individual firms but not the industry as a whole. The MOT argued somewhat disingenuously that it was indeed giving guidance to individual firms even if, ultimately, all firms were to be given similar instructions.

[26] Yonezawa 1988, p. 439. The shipping industry argued that, in addition to excess ships, it also had to deal with escalating wages for Japanese seamen (*Business Japan*, Jan. 1976, p. 158; *Business Japan*, July 1979, pp. 92–94).

be lucky to operate even at that level. In other words, they saw the MOT guidelines not as a ceiling on their operating rates, but rather as a "desired target" that the industry could only hope to meet. In fact, it was soon clear that actual operating rates would be at least 15 to 25 percentage points below the MOT's recommendations.[27]

Some accounts of this episode argue that the MOT's decision to use administrative guidance was a response to European criticisms, and they tend to downplay the industry's desire to manage competition at home. The MOT's official history, however, argues that *kankoku sōtan* was aimed at stabilization at home, as it rectified supply and demand imbalances, "prevented excessive competition, and insured that the smaller shipbuilders had adequate orders."[28] A compromise view is taken by Boyd and Nagamori, who argue that the adoption of price guidance was designed to placate the Europeans, while *kankoku sōtan*, much like the ban on parallel building, "was adopted to control excessive competition at home."[29] The industry's desire to stabilize domestic market conditions became clearer in subsequent years, after foreign criticisms of Japan had subsided: from 1978 to 1988, the industry consistently lobbied the MOT to continue, and to strengthen, these production curtailments. Like the other industries we have studied, Japan's shipbuilders clearly desired government regulation as a means to manage competition at home.

LONG-TERM RESPONSES: CAPACITY REDUCTIONS AND DIVERSIFICATION

As had been foreseen by the industry, 1977 and 1978 were its most desperate years. New orders in 1978 amounted to less than 10 percent of those in the peak year of 1973. In addition, the industry's work backlog in 1978 and 1979 was barely above the 5-million-GT level, or about one-tenth that of the industry's best year. And as firms scrambled to grab whatever orders they could, ship prices continued to fall. In addition, the industry now faced a further problem: beginning in the second half of 1977 the yen began to appreciate, rising from ¥290 per dollar to ¥170 per dollar by the middle of 1978. Combined with rising labor and material costs, the appreciation of the yen cut further into Japan's export competitiveness.

However, these harsh economic conditions hurt the smaller firms much more than they did the majors. In fact, the seven majors as a group

[27] *Industrial Review of Japan*, 1976, p. 71; *Industrial Review of Japan*, 1977, p. 76; Totten 1984, p. 144.
[28] Un'yu 50-Nenshi Hensan Kyoku 1989, p. 37.
[29] Boyd and Nagamori 1991, p. 177.

reported positive profits in every year of this case study, even during the industry's crisis period of 1977–1978. The key advantage the majors enjoyed was their highly diversified character: by the early 1970s nearly 70 percent of their income derived from nonshipbuilding sources. Because their other divisions were doing well, the majors were able to maintain a positive income stream in spite of the collapse of their production of supertankers. In contrast, the small shipbuilders lacked alternative sources of income and so could not prevent a disastrous plunge in their profit rates. In 1978 only 11 of the 54 medium and small firms managed to turn a profit; in 1979 only 12 firms had done so. The smaller firms were hit by a spate of bankruptcies: in 1977 alone, 24 small and medium shipbuilders were forced into bankruptcy, including three quasi-majors. The impending failure of two of the larger quasi-majors, Sasebo Heavy Industries and Hakodate Dockyard, sent a clear political signal, spurring more concerted government efforts to stabilize conditions for the small firms.[30]

As the industry's slump continued to worsen, all firms realized that more drastic responses would be necessary. Over the next decade the industry as a whole made efforts to deal with its structural problems of excess capacity and redundant labor. Firms attempted to reduce capacity, diversify out of the industry, and decrease their labor forces. The seven majors had a much easier time in making these economic adjustments.

The Pursuit of Coordinated Capacity Cutbacks

By 1977 the industry realized that it simply could not sustain its current capacity levels. Owing to the permanent falloff of world demand, excess capacity was estimated to be one-quarter to one-third of the industry's total capacity. Although the industry disagreed over how the burden of adjustment should be divided, all shipbuilders agreed that drastic cutbacks were needed if any of them was to remain viable.

The need for dramatic capacity cutbacks was pushed most clearly by the majors. SAJ president Shinto Hisashi expressed the long-standing position of most of the larger firms in favor of government support for "structural reform" of the industry, by which he meant capacity cutbacks. In a June 1977 press conference, Shinto urged the SSRC to come up with policies to help the industry cut its redundant capacity. This desire for capacity cuts was echoed even more strongly by the other majors. Kawasaki Heavy In-

---

[30] The bailout of Sasebo, the nation's eighth largest shipbuilder, is discussed in Vogel 1985, Magaziner and Hout 1980, and Mainichi Shimbunsha 1978. The efforts to resuscitate Hakodate Dockyard are discussed in Nihon Zōsen Shinkō Zaidan 1983, pp. 5–6. Of the 1977 bankruptcies, the largest was Hashihama Shipbuilding (Nihon Zōsen Shinkō Zaidan 1983, pp. 5, 13, 74–75; *Japan Economic Journal*, July 4, 1978).

dustries president Umeda Zenji, for instance, argued that the industry needed to cut capacity by as much as 50 percent.[31]

However, the majors faced the same dilemma as the other industries we have studied: how best to achieve adequate capacity reductions. The majors feared that if the process was left to market forces the smaller shipbuilders would do all they could to resist capacity cutbacks. For these firms, most of which operated only a single dock or berth, to reduce capacity was tantamount to exiting. The likely result would be a continuation of excess capacity and excessive competition.

Although the smaller shipbuilders also saw the collective benefit of coordinated capacity cutbacks, they did not want the burden of these cutbacks to fall on their shoulders. The small firms argued that most of the industry's excess capacity in fact belonged to the majors, since it was the tanker market that had collapsed. In contrast, the facilities held by the smaller firms, more suitable for building the smaller cargo carriers that still enjoyed stable demand, should not be cut back. The small firms argued that it was only fair that the majors bear the burden of capacity cuts. Furthermore, the smaller firms argued that the majors could afford to make larger cutbacks since they were already diversified and thus had an easy "refuge" (*nigeba*). The small firms, on the other hand, had nowhere else to go—their choice was between building ships and bankruptcy.[32]

The SAJ was well aware of the need to ensure the cooperation of the smaller firms. Shinto, for instance, recognized that to ask for any capacity cutbacks by many of the smaller firms would be "like asking them to slit their own throats." He realized that it would be difficult for the industry to come to an agreement on its own. He therefore called on the SSRC, as a "neutral party," to serve as a forum in which the conflicting interests of the industry could be mediated.[33]

Subsequently, the SSRC held numerous hearings on the subject of capacity reductions. Of equal importance was an "informal discussion group" convened by the Director of the MOT's Ship Bureau, Shashiki Muneto, for the purpose of hammering out an industry-wide consensus. (Industry insiders later acknowledged the critical mediating role that Shashiki ended up playing.) And finally, in March 1978, the Diet held a long series of hearings on the shipbuilding crisis, inviting testimony from

[31] SAJ discussions of structural reform are reported in *Business Japan*, Mar. 1973, p. 101, *Zosen*, Feb. 1978, p. 5, Totten 1984, p. 145, *Nihon Keizai Shimbun*, June 16, 1977, and *Japan Economic Journal*, Apr. 8, 1975, Aug. 26, 1975, and June 21, 1977. In fact, the majors had discussed the need for restructuring as early as 1975, when Shinto himself was regarded as the main proponent of rationalization. In January 1978, the top 15 firms agreed on the need to seek government assistance in scrapping excess capacity.

[32] Suzuki 1975, pp. 59–63, and *Tōyō Keizai*, Feb. 26, 1977, pp. 43–45, discuss the position taken by the small firms.

[33] *Nihon Keizai Shimbun*, June 16, 1977.

representatives of the large and small firms, the subcontractors, the unions, and the related financial institutions.[34]

The result of these deliberations was that the industry turned to public policy in order to coordinate industry-wide cutbacks in capacity. As George Totten put it, the "shipbuilders wanted the government to help reduce the 'excessive' or 'cut-throat' competition . . . [through the] government-coordinated collaborative cutback of the shipbuilding industry as a whole, with 'guidance' from the Ministry of Transport."[35] The MOT was largely sympathetic to the industry's requests. Boyd and Nagamori argue that the MOT was interested above all in "good order in the sector." Further, the MOT was in favor of capacity reductions "because this accorded with the preferences of the industry itself."[36]

By mid-1978, the industry had focused its attention on MITI's depressed industry legislation, the Tokuanhō. Although the shipbuilders were not one of the original industries designated in MITI's draft, most analysts assumed that it would be so designated as soon as the industry requested it. (That the shipbuilding industry was not originally mentioned in the bill is not surprising, since MITI drafted the Tokuanhō with its own industries in mind.) The response of the large firms was immediate and favorable; their only amendment was that the industry be allowed to form a cartel to enforce production curtailments.[37] The initial reaction of the smaller firms, however, was more restrained. The small firms were reluctant to endorse the bill because it did not resolve the questions of how cutbacks were to be apportioned or to what extent the government would provide financial compensation. The small firms insisted that they needed adequate compensation if they were to be able to make any cutbacks at all. As a result, the SAJ pushed for increased funding for the scrapping association proposed in the Tokuanhō. In discussions with the MOT and the JDB in July 1978, the SAJ proposed that the excess facilities of the 54 medium and small firms should be purchased by a scrapping association that would be funded by private financial institutions and the government with smaller contributions from the major shipbuilders, the trading companies, and local governments.[38]

The outlines of the scrapping association, the Designated Shipbuilding Enterprise Stabilization Association, came very close to this SAJ proposal. The association was eventually funded jointly by the JDB and the private banks, each of which put up ¥1 billion. In addition, each firm that re-

[34] Totten 1984, p. 149. *Zosen*, Feb. 1978, p. 5, describes the MOT discussion group. Nihon Zōsen Shinkō Zaidan 1983, pp. 139–169, presents a transcript of the Diet debate.

[35] Totten 1984, p. 155.

[36] Boyd and Nagamori 1991, pp. 168, 183.

[37] *Zosen*, June 1978, p. 5.

[38] Nihon Zōsen Shinkō Zaidan 1983, pp. 26–27.

mained in the industry contributed 1.3 percent of the price of new vessel orders to the Stabilization Association. And finally, proceeds from the sale of land were used to repay part of the loans.

The industry, however, still had a difficult time deciding who should scrap how much. Donna Keyser argues that these conflicts were so deep-rooted that the industry ended up submitting three separate stabilization plans to the neutral SSRC—one each from the majors, the quasi-majors, and the smallest firms.[39] The final capacity cutback plans were then hammered out in deliberations between the industry representatives and the SSRC's shipbuilding subcommittee, headed by Wakimura Yoshitaro, professor emeritus of Tokyo University. This subcommittee finished its draft of the industry stabilization plan in June 1978. The subcommittee reported that the industry would have to scrap 35 percent of its current 9.81 million CGRT (Compensated Gross Registered Tonnage) of capacity in order for it to match the level of expected demand (which the SSRC continued to place at 6.4 million CGRT). As shown in Table 7-3, the stabilization plan called for greater cutbacks among the majors.

The capacity cutbacks under the Tokuanhō were extremely successful: within two years, the industry had pared 36.6 percent of its total capacity, even exceeding the goals established in the rationalization plan. As can be seen in the table, the majors bore the lion's share of these cutbacks, accounting for 50 percent of the docks that were closed and 63 percent of the capacity that was cut.

Much attention has been paid to the fact that the majors agreed to trim their capacities by a greater amount than the smaller firms. Different authors have attributed this to various aspects of Japanese society, including altruism and fairness.[40] But the behavior of the large firms seems more "rational" when we consider the economic situations facing the two groups of firms. According to McMillan, "both [large and small] firms benefit if either one reduces its capacity. But the bigger firm benefits more, and so has a stronger incentive to shrink." Conversely, because small firms will have higher incentives to play a waiting game, McMillan argues that "the larger firm [will] bear a disproportionate share of the burden of the industry's shrinkage."[41]

---

[39] Keyser 1990.

[40] Boyd 1989; Vogel 1985, passim; Young 1991, p. 150.

[41] McMillan 1994, p. 31. McMillan also mentions the case of Japanese shipbuilding: "the pattern of shrinkage mandated by the MOT, with the largest firms shrinking the most, was not inconsistent with each firm's perception of its self-interest. Furthermore, although the plan was formally the MOT's, it was initiated by the firms themselves, and at least to some extent, reflected the firms' own wishes" (p. 33). As argued in this case study, the shipbuilding firms played an even more active role than McMillan was aware of. Another concession to the small firms was the extension of the ban on parallel building, instituted at the insistence of the CAJS (*Zosen*, Oct. 1978, p. 7).

Table 7-3. Disposal of excess shipbuilding capacity under the Tokuanhō

	Capacity before disposal			Capacity disposed of			Remaining capacity	
	Docks/ berths	Capacity (1,000 CGRT)	Target (%)	Docks/ berths	Capacity (1,000 CGRT)	Achieved (%)	Docks/ berths	Capacity (1,000 CGRT)
Majors (7)	55	5,690	40	25	2,250	40	30	3,430
Quasi-majors (17)	38	2,890	30	10	1,030	36	28	2,050
Small (16)	23	790	27	9	250	32	14	450
Other (21)	22	400	15	6	50	13	16	260
Total	138	9,770	35	50	3,580	37	88	6,190

SOURCE: Adapted from *Zosen*, Jan. 1981, p. 18.

The majors also benefited by having to shut down only a few of their many dockyards. This allowed them to consolidate their facilities and retain their core workers, thus minimizing the need for massive layoffs. In contrast, for the smaller firms to meet their share of the capacity cuts, some firms would be forced to exit. Some of them thus entered into business tie-ups or outright mergers with other small firms and then jointly scrapped their less competitive dockyards. Most notably, the Kurushima Dockyard Company absorbed 14 small and medium firms, most on the brink of bankruptcy; by 1984, this group had become the largest in the industry. These efforts were encouraged by substantial financial assistance from the government in the form of low-interest loans or loan guarantees. In addition, the Stabilization Association purchased and then scrapped nine shipyards owned by the smaller firms, accounting for 37 percent of the capacity that the smaller firms were able to scrap.[42]

The Industry's Diversification and Employment Adjustment Efforts

The fact that the majors were already diversified, and therefore less dependent on shipbuilding, made their capacity reductions less burdensome. Because these firms had economic alternatives open to them and had the resources to pursue them, the costs of economic adjustment were relatively low. With one foot already out the door in 1973, these firms had the capability and the incentives to take the second step. As shown in Chart 7-2, the majors decreased their dependence on shipbuilding steadily after 1973. Even as early as 1973, only 32 percent of total sales of the majors came from shipbuilding. By 1978 the majors had reduced this to 17 percent and, after a brief increase in shipbuilding sales, reduced it again to under 16 percent in 1985. As a consequence, their non-shipbuilding sales increased steadily. All of the majors were able to raise sales in their land machinery and engineering divisions, while some were also able to specialize in energy production and in defense manufacturing. The majors also stepped up their investments in medium-sized specialty ships, including high-speed freighters and liquefied natural gas carriers. The diversified nature of the majors thus gave them two advantages over

[42] The Stabilization Association provided ¥36.7 million to purchase and scrap a total of 490,000 tons of capacity. (Keyser (1990, pp. 121, 142) reports that the majors received no financial assistance from the Stabilization Association.) In addition, the small shipbuilders received U.S. $57 million in loan guarantees, out of a total of U.S. $93 million for all industries under the Tokuanhō (Peck et al. 1987, p. 106). Between 1978 and 1980, the association channeled a further U.S. $170 million in low-interest loans to help the smaller shipbuilders carry out their scrapping efforts. The industry also requested and received a variety of other financial assistance measures: the "deferral of loan repayments, long-term low-interest loans to facilitate diversification . . . special tax privileges, such as tax exemption on profits from sale of facilities and reduction of the fixed-asset tax on suspended facilities" (Vogel 1985, p. 54; see also Totten 1984, p. 159).

Chart 7-2. Diversification efforts, major firms, 1973–1985

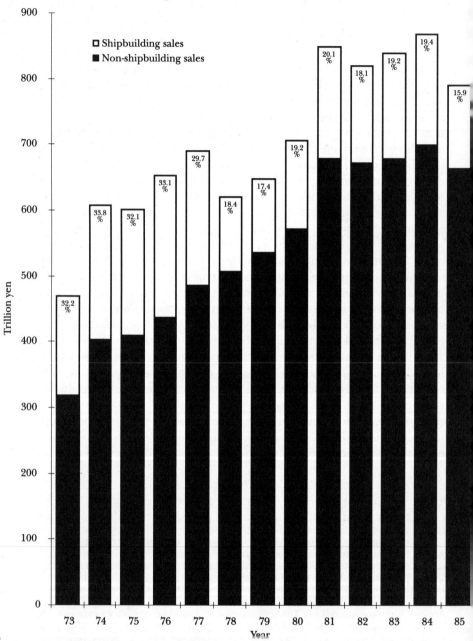

Sources: *Japan Company Handbook,* various issues.
Note: Percentages in white areas represent yearly shipbuilding sales as a proportion of total sales.

the smaller firms: it allowed them to endure shipbuilding downturns by relying on profits made elsewhere and to move up the value-added chain using their broad technological base.[43]

In stark contrast, the industry's other firms lacked the technological and financial resources to pursue a strategy of economic adjustment. As shown in Chart 7-3, the quasi-majors were not able to significantly increase their non-shipbuilding sales. Because these firms depended on shipbuilding sales for 80 to 90 percent of their income, they were highly susceptible to fluctuations in shipbuilding demand. The situation for the industry's smallest firms was even worse. Very few of the smallest firms had significant non-shipbuilding operations to begin with, and none was able to take steps to lower its dependence on shipbuilding.

Dealing with the large number of redundant workers was the industry's most pressing problem. Between 1974 and 1979, the industry reduced its work force from 274,000 employees to 162,000, a 40 percent decrease in the space of five years. All firms tried to trim their labor forces through the least painful means, such as by cutting overtime hours and freezing new hirings. One mechanism that all firms used was voluntary retirement in which workers were offered separation bonuses to retire before the mandatory age. Once these offers were made, however, firms found themselves deluged by three times the number of retirees they had originally sought. In all, 18,551 of the majors' workers chose to retire early between 1978 and 1979, representing 8 percent of their total work force. In the quasi-majors, between 1977 and 1979 fully one-third of the work force chose to retire early. The small firms trimmed 56 percent of their total labor force in this way. Clearly, the shipbuilding labor force recognized the desperate straits the industry was facing. One business journal called these voluntary retirees "rats leaving a sinking ship."[44]

[43] Blumenthal 1976, pp. 147–148, 151–157. On the firm level, Mitsubishi Heavy shifted its sales to such products as nuclear and electric power plants, oil refineries, construction machinery, and defense-related production. Ishikawajima-Harima concentrated on land machinery, electric power plants, LNG plants, and defense-related aircraft engines; in addition, the firm has tried its hand at operating "theme parks." Kawasaki Heavy Industries relied on its train and motorcycle divisions, as well as on the production of an anti-submarine aircraft, the P-3C. Nippon Kokan, Japan's largest producer of steel, was able to shift to its other products for as much as 96 percent of its total sales in 1979 (*Japan Economic Journal*, Aug. 21, 1979; Apr. 2, 1988). Mitsui, the least diversified major, established a new department in its main office in 1988 for the purpose of promoting new businesses. Overall, there were very few cases of overseas investments in shipbuilding capacity, although some of the majors did operate overseas ship repair facilities (*Japan Economic Journal*, Sept. 30, 1975; *Business Japan*, Feb. 1977).

[44] *Japan Economic Journal*, July 4, 1978. Employment adjustment is discussed in Nihon Zōsen Shinkō Zaidan 1983, pp. 70–71, and *Japan Economic Journal*, Apr. 10, 1979 and May 22, 1979.

Chart 7-3. Diversification efforts, medium firms, 1973–1985

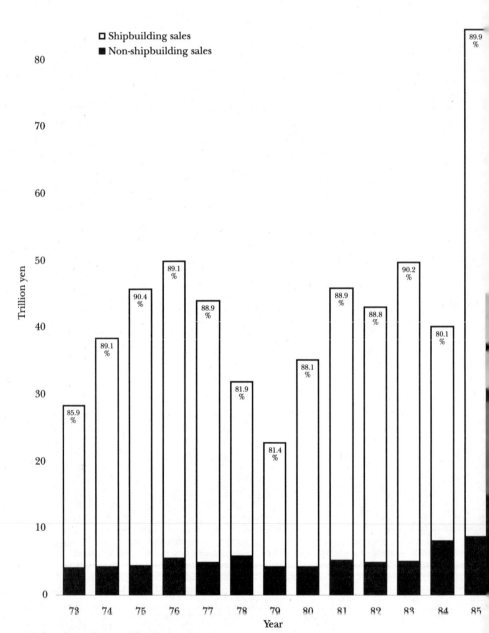

Sources: Japan Company Handbook, various issues.

As the crisis wore on, firms were forced to consider more drastically reducing their core workers. At this point, the major firms enjoyed some key advantages that lowered the costs of labor adjustment for them. They were able to force their subcontractors to bear a large portion of the needed work-force cutbacks. While the main shipbuilders cut their work forces by 35 percent between 1974 and 1979, their subcontractors experienced a larger proportional decrease, 53 percent in the same period. In addition, the majors were able to shift workers to other more prosperous divisions within the same firm and occasionally to other firms within the same *keiretsu* grouping.[45]

The case of Mitsubishi Heavy Industries is representative of the efforts of the major shipbuilding firms to avoid outright dismissal of their redundant workers. Between 1973 and 1983 the firm reduced its labor force by 21,551 workers, a 27 percent decrease, but was able to do so without substantial layoffs.[46] In June 1975 the firm was the first of the major shipbuilders to approach its labor union to request temporary furloughs for 10,000 of its workers. The firm reduced its work force by an additional 5,000 people the following year, including 800 who were transferred to affiliated firms. In June 1978, at the height of the industry's depression, management announced the layoff of 1,365 workers; of these, 861 were reassigned to another Mitsubishi *keiretsu* firm, Mitsubishi Motors. Within a week, the firm announced a plan to cut a further 10,500 employees by October 1980 (9,000 in the shipbuilding division) and used furloughs, transfers to affiliated firms, intra-company relocations, and regular retirements before turning to direct layoffs. Finally, in March 1979, Mitsubishi Heavy approached its union offering "preferential separation allowances" to workers willing to retire voluntarily. However, it had to withdraw this offer within a month because it had already received twice the 1,000 applicants it had originally sought.

In contrast, the smaller firms enjoyed none of these advantages. Overall, between 1974 and 1981 these firms cut their employment by more than 50 percent (as compared to 27.7 percent for the majors). These firms had to rely almost totally on the more onerous practice of outright dismissals to trim their work forces.[47]

[45] Nihon Zōsen Shinkō Zaidan 1983, p. 4; Totten 1984, p. 146. Keyser cites a Ministry of Labor report that the large firms relied mostly on transfers and early retirement, rather than dismissals, to reduce their labor forces (1990, p. 151).

[46] Yasuki 1989, p. 65; *Japan Economic Journal,* Nov. 16, 1976.

[47] Keyser 1990, p. 151. It is difficult to trace the fate of the discharged workers either at the company or the industry level. One analyst notes that as of 1978, of the 44,000 workers released by the shipbuilding industry, 25,000 wound up on the unemployment rolls, in other words, "most did not move directly into new jobs" (Peck et al. 1987, p. 101). The 44,000-person decline in employment is more than that in all of the other ten Tokuanhō industries combined. Keyser (1990, p. 151) estimates that 62 percent of workers fired between 1975 and 1980 ended up on one government welfare roll or another.

Although the main shipbuilding labor union, the Jūki Rōren (Zenkoku Zōsen Jūki Rōdō Kumiai Rengōkai, or Japan Federation of Shipbuilding and Engineering Workers' Unions), was in principle opposed to layoffs and other sacrifices borne by its workers, it also proved willing to cooperate with the retrenchment efforts of the firms. In part, this cooperative stance can be attributed to the fact that it was affiliated with Dōmei, the more moderate of the two national labor unions. But it also reflected the hopelessness of its situation: Jūki Rōren, most of whose 230,000 members were employed by the majors, was concerned first and foremost that their firms did not fold. Labor's dilemma is neatly summarized by one union leader's justification for accepting his firm's restructuring plan: "we have only two choices. That is, to reject the plans, which would ruin the company, or to accept them to protect the jobs of the remaining employees."[48] Although the company unions were always consulted by management before work-force reduction programs were instituted, there is little evidence to suggest that the unions were able to significantly alter the plans put forth by the company. In most cases the unions had no choice but to approve these plans.

In assessing the role played by the labor unions, one might praise Jūki Rōren's cooperative stance—because it cooperated with management, the union did what was necessary for the firm's survival and thus minimized the loss of jobs. On the other hand, the Jūki Rōren has been heavily criticized by the more radical shipbuilding union, the smaller JSP-affiliated Zenzōsen, for being too cooperative with management and sacrificing the interests of its members.[49]

Management and labor found themselves able to fully agree on at least one point: the need to pressure the government to extend unemployment assistance to the shipbuilding industry. These efforts paid substantial dividends. In 1977, for instance, shipbuilding workers were made eligible under the Temporary Measures for Unemployed Workers in Designated Depressed Industries (Tokutei Fukyō Gyōshu Rishokushahō). This law provided special Ministry of Labor funds to workers affected by capacity reductions, including provisions paid to firms that retrain or help relocate employees. In addition, the government granted extra assistance to small firms. Finally, in 1978 a number of shipbuilding regions were designated as depressed under MITI's Depressed District Act, which provided additional assistance for workers and firms.

Industry Pressure for Government Demand Stimulus

The shipbuilders and the labor unions also applied pressures on the government to bolster demand for new ships. The industry called for the

---

[48] *Japan Economic Journal*, Nov. 1, 1986; Totten 1984, pp. 145–146.
[49] Rōdōsha Chōsa Kenkyūkai 1984, pp. 233–234.

revival of a scrap-and-build program for domestically owned ships that would force Japan's shipping industry to speed up the replacement of its older ships. However, the Shipowners' Association, the Senshu Kyōkai, opposed this proposal, arguing that similar programs in the past had unfairly benefited the shipbuilders. The shipping firms in this period were also in serious financial difficulties and in fact were grappling with their own problem of excess capacity. The shippers thus welcomed government assistance to help scrap their older ships but had no desire to buy new ones—they preferred to reduce their fleets without replacements. The MOT was again forced to mediate the conflicting interests of two powerful industries. The end result was a compromise in which the MOT set aside funds to scrap 4 million tons of domestic ships.[50] At the same time, the MOT offered "side payments" to the shipping industry, including an agreement to charter 20 idle tankers to store crude oil.

Second, the industry asked that various government agencies increase their purchase of ships. Unlike the other industries we have studied, in which government spending has only an indirect effect on demand, in the shipbuilding industry the government can affect demand directly by buying new ships. The SAJ asked the Maritime Safety Agency and the Japan Defense Agency to scrap all of their ships over 15 years of age. In addition, the SAJ pushed for an increase in planned shipbuilding, which had declined up until 1977. In the 1978 budget process the SAJ achieved its goal: in the next three years, the Japanese government provided funding for 5.3 million GT of new ships, representing 15 percent of the industry's new orders. This revival of planned shipbuilding was later cited as a main cause of the industry's temporary rebound in the early 1980s.[51]

Third, the SAJ asked for government help in spurring exports, as international frictions had subsided after 1979. Specifically, the SAJ wanted the Export-Import Bank to help finance the export of vessels. The Export-Import Bank responded with ¥190 million for export finance loans, which, although a fraction of what the SAJ originally had asked for, was still enough to subsidize a sizable 2.8 million GT of ship exports.[52]

---

[50] The director of the MOT's Ship Bureau requested the public corporation that bought these ships to give priority to the smaller firms (Nihon Zōsen Shinkō Zaidan 1983, p. 39). The discussions between the shipbuilders and the shipping industry are summarized in Ekonomisuto Henshūbu 1978, pp. 116–117, *Business Japan*, July 1979, p. 94, Totten 1984, pp. 150–151, and Vogel 1985, p. 54.

[51] Nihon Zōsen Shinkō Zaidan 1983, iii. According to Totten (1984, p. 143), the SAJ estimated that 80 percent of their budget demands had been met. The industry also requested that the government take measures for "promotion of remodeling of tankers to prevent marine pollution . . . active donation of ships to developing nations as part of the economic assistance program . . . [and] promotion of construction of offshore structures including oil stockpiling facilities" (Totten 1984, p. 159). Finally, the SAJ supported the proposed New Kansai International airport, as the majors stood to gain a sizable part of construction and engineering orders.

[52] Totten 1984, pp. 141–142.

Finally, the major shipbuilders benefited from a rise in military spending during the early 1980s. Already, Mitsubishi Heavy and Kawasaki Heavy were the two largest defense contractors in Japan; another major, Ishikawajima-Harima, was the fourth largest. These three firms were able to increase their defense sales by nearly 150 percent between 1979 and 1982, from ¥186 billion to ¥460 billion.[53] Although Japan's decision to increase its defense spending was not directly related to the shipbuilders' economic distress, these firms were clear beneficiaries.

The shipbuilding firms also tried to influence Japanese security policy on the question of arms exports. In February 1978, for instance, Nagano Shigeo, president of the Japan Chambers of Commerce and Industry and head of the SSRC, openly called on the government to allow shipbuilders to provide ships for foreign navies on the grounds that this would provide needed work for the shipbuilding industry. Although the majors as individual firms did not publicly endorse this proposal, "it was clearly something they desired." Even the DSP-affiliated union, the Jūki Rōren, tacitly endorsed this proposal and in addition called on Prime Minister Fukuda to build up Japan's production of warships and other defense systems.[54]

THE 1980s: THE CONTINUING SHIPBUILDING CRISIS

The industry's efforts to reduce capacity put it in a good position to benefit from a brief recovery in global shipbuilding that began in 1980. New orders for the Japanese industry more than doubled in 1979, although at considerably lower levels than during the industry's heyday prior to 1973. This upturn was due to a spurt in demand for supertankers as well as to the increase in orders from the government's "planned shipbuilding" program. As a result, the industry's operating rate improved dramatically: with total capacity down to the 6 million CGRT level, the operating rate increased to 64 percent in 1980 and then to 79 percent in 1981. In addition, the extension of production curtailments helped to raise ship order prices to an all-time high in 1981, so industry profits improved as well.

With the industry seemingly on its way to recovery, it was no longer eligible to renew its designation as a structurally depressed industry under the Sankōhō. The industry hoped that the capacity cuts it had already made would be sufficient to make it a leaner and more competitive indus-

---

[53] As a result, the defense-related sales as a proportion of total sales increased from 7.2 percent to 16.4 percent for Mitsubishi Heavy, from 10 to 14 percent for Kawasaki Heavy, and from 5.5 to 10.6 percent for Ishikawajima-Harima (Rōdōsha Chōsa Kenkyūkai 1984, pp. 240–241). Most of the sales were related, for Mitsubishi Heavy to F-15 fighters and tanks; for Kawasaki Heavy to P 3C anti submarine patrol planes; and for Ishikawajima-Harima to F-15s

[54] Ekonomisuto Henshūbu 1978, p. 118; Totten 1984, p. 149; Ekonomisuto, Mar. 9, 1976, pp. 24–27; Rōdōsha Chōsa Kenkyūkai 1984, pp. 240–241.

try. Compared to the shipbuilding industries in other countries, capacity adjustment in the Japanese industry had thus far been relatively smooth and successful.[55]

This period of relative optimism was an illusory one, however. Demand fluctuated during 1982 and 1983, but then began to fall again after 1984, marking the beginning of a second and more serious cycle of depressed demand. This prolonged slump reached crisis proportions in 1987 and 1988, and touched off another round of restructuring.

The industry's first response to this new period of economic distress was similar to its reaction to the crises of the 1970s: the shipbuilders pushed the MOT to extend its supply and demand regulations in order to help them manage their problem of excessive competition. Some form of supply-side regulation had been in effect since 1976, when the MOT first issued its *kankoku sōtan* recommendations.[56] By 1982, however, income and profits in the industry had temporarily recovered and so the chances for renewing the cartel appeared slim. The shipbuilders were openly worried that the removal of regulation would again lead to a period of cutthroat competition and further turmoil and destabilization. The SAJ now became the most vocal and persistent advocate of having the government continue to regulate the industry's supply and demand situation.[57] In particular, if the industry was not eligible for a formal recession cartel, it wanted the MOT to use its informal powers of administrative guidance.

Significantly it was the industry that was now the most insistent on continuing production regulations. The rationale for regulation was no longer external, since after 1979 the Europeans were basically satisfied that the Japanese industry was adhering to its tacit market-sharing agree-

---

[55] Although the shipbuilders never formally requested designation under the Sankōhō, they did desire it. Because the new law was intended for the basic materials industries, however, an assembly industry like shipbuilding was not considered to be eligible. The fact that the industry as a whole, and especially the smaller firms, were now enjoying strong profits, made the issue moot (*Zosen*, Mar. 1983, p. 5).

[56] In 1978 the industry made a smooth transition from the MOT's administrative guidance to the more formal recession cartel. The FTC approved the cartel with little fanfare, after holding hearings with the industry and its main consumers, notably the Shipowners' Association and the Japan Steel Federation (Tekkō Renmei). The cartel was eventually administered by an "Anti-Recession Cartel Committee" established by the 39 participating firms and located in the SAJ headquarters (Nihon Zōsen Shinkō Zaidan 1983, pp. 41–43). Operating rates were set at 61 percent of current capacity, about the same levels as pertained under the MOT's administrative guidance. Only one of the top 40 firms, Koyo Dockyard, chose to remain outside of the cartel. This firm, however, did not significantly hurt the cohesion of the cartel. With the strong urgings of the shipbuilding industry, the FTC later extended the cartel for another year, to March 1982 (*Zosen*, June 1978, pp. 5–6; *Zosen*, June 1979, pp. 5–6; *Zosen*, Sept. 1979, p. 5; *Zosen*, Nov. 1979, p. 5; *Nikkei Sangyō Shimbun*, Jan. 22, 1982, p. 9). Formal regulation was extended through March 1982, but only after the shipbuilding companies "strongly requested a one-year extension of the recession cartel" (*Industrial Review of Japan*, 1981, p. 71; Totten 1984, p. 157).

[57] *Zosen*, Aug. 1981, pp. 16–17; *Zosen*, May 1982, pp. 3–4.

ment, and international criticisms of Japan's shipbuilders had faded. The fact that the industry still pressed for the MOT's administrative guidance is a clear indication that it valued regulation as a means to manage domestic competition.[58] Regardless of the strength of external pressures, the industry preferred a cartel-like arrangement at home that would help it avoid excessive competition and depressed profits.

The MOT was ambivalent over using its informal regulatory powers. On the one hand, it wanted to stabilize the industry and thus avoid further political controversy. On the other hand, the MOT had reasons to be reluctant about reinstating this form of regulation, since it still had to deal with opposition to administrative guidance. The shipping firms continued to complain that higher ship prices were hurting their own businesses. Also, the FTC stepped up its pressure on the MOT to avoid informal and opaque regulatory mechanisms such as *kankoku sōtan*. The FTC preferred the MOT and the industry to use the more formal and more transparent recession cartel.

Despite these constraints, in March 1983 the MOT followed the advice of an SSRC report and reinstated informal recommendations to curtail operations. The MOT recommendations called for the shipbuilders to reduce their operating rates by 26 percent in fiscal 1983 and 32 percent in fiscal 1984. The shipbuilders openly welcomed this extension of regulation; in fact, the industry's only complaint was that the MOT's curtailments were not strong enough.[59]

This application of *kankoku sōtan* turned out to be the last time that Japan ever implemented this oft-used policy tool. Changes in the policy-making environment had finally eliminated it. Japan's overseas trading partners had become fully aware of the trade effects of Japan's domestic regulations and were quick to apply pressure and criticisms. Also, domestic antitrust restrictions had grown more stringent over time particularly for informal policy tools such as administrative guidance. In this case it was FTC pressures on the MOT, which continued and intensified throughout 1984 and 1985, that caused the MOT to allow its curtailment recommendations to expire in March 1985. In particular, the FTC charged that the use of *kankoku sōtan* was "unduly restricting the freedom of enterprises and depriving them of vitality in the long-term."[60]

To take the place of *kankoku sōtan* the MOT introduced a similar but more amorphous regulatory tool: price guidelines. In this new system, the MOT continued to regulate overall production levels, not through recommendations, but through overall guidelines; in cases in which firms were producing beyond these guidelines, the ministry would ask

---

[58] See, for instance, Nihon Zōsen Shinkō Zaidan 1989, p. 49.

[59] *Nihon Keizai Shimbun*, Mar. 24, 1983, p. 10; *Nikkei Sangyō Shimbun*, Apr. 15, 1983, p. 8.

[60] *Japan Economic Almanac*, 1985, p. 110; *Japan Economic Journal*, Mar. 5, 1985.

them to alter their plans.[61] Although the FTC expressed its unhappiness over this new form of regulation, the industry welcomed it because it would continue to provide at least some restraint on excess production and excess competition. All involved realized that the difference between "recommendations" and "guidelines" was mostly semantic; the MOT had essentially switched to a less overt mechanism to help stabilize market conditions.

As the shipbuilding recession continued unabated in 1985 and 1986, the industry began to feel a growing sense of crisis. New ship orders in 1985 totaled only 6.5 million GT, and fell below 5 million GT in each of the next three years. As a result, the industry's work backlog continued to fall, reaching a low of 5 million GT in 1987.

With the industry facing its most serious crisis since the First Oil Shock, the MOT in November 1985 asked the SSRC to conduct a comprehensive policy review of the industry's problems. Over the next six months the SSRC held a series of discussions and deliberations with industry representatives. As before, the council's deliberations became the focus of the policy-making process for the shipbuilding industry. The SSRC's discussions centered on a by-now familiar agenda of policy proposals: first, the possibility of production curtailments through a formal recession cartel; second, ways to encourage even further cuts in capacity; and third, methods of reorganizing and consolidating the industry's structure.

Instituting the recession cartel was not difficult. With the industry again in dire straits the FTC had no grounds on which to reject the formal cartel. In December 1986 the industry received approval for a recession cartel to begin the following April that set an overall production target of 3 million CGRT for 1987. As the industry's conditions did not improve even after the cartel was instituted, it asked for and received extensions of the cartel in 1988 and 1989.

As was the case in the late 1970s, the industry was more concerned with the structural problem of excess capacity. The SSRC's forecast of future demand indicated that about 20 percent of the industry's capacity would remain excessive, so it recommended a 20-percent cut. This recommendation was not only heartily endorsed by the majors. All of the major shipbuilders were prepared to go well beyond the SSRC's recommendations, since they had come to the conclusion that radical cutbacks were necessary. Like the aluminum smelting firms, the shipbuilders pursued far more decisive adjustment measures than were called for by public policy. Ishikawajima-Harima, for instance, announced plans to cut its capacity by 60 percent, while Kawasaki Heavy cut its capacity by 40 percent, and Hitachi Zōsen began a

---

[61] *Japan Economic Journal,* Mar. 5, 1985, p. 10; *Nihon Keizai Shimbun,* Feb. 26, 1985, p. 5; *Japan Economic Almanac,* 1985, p. 110.

drastic restructuring program with the goal of reducing its reliance on ship-building from 35 percent of total sales to just 20 percent. If the SSRC and the MOT foresaw the need to cut capacity, the industry's majors saw it even more clearly—and acted on their own to achieve it.[62]

The industry faced the same problem it faced in 1978, however: how best to encourage the smaller firms in the industry also to cut capacity. This was even more difficult now than it had been in the past since 31 of the industry's 37 remaining small firms operated just one dock each. The SSRC's recommendation of a 20-percent cutback in capacity was clearly problematic for these smaller firms. They had but two choices: to leave the industry altogether, or to make even more drastic attempts to merge with other small firms and carry out joint scrapping efforts.

The SAJ now turned to a more overtly political solution for the indus-try's structural problems: in April 1986, during discussions in the SSRC, SAJ chairman Maeda requested that the government pass a new industry-specific law designed solely for the shipbuilding industry.[63] Maeda argued that a new shipbuilding law, which was to be modeled on the earlier Tokuanhō and Sankōhō programs, was needed if the industry was to carry out the recommended restructuring efforts. This law would provide the industry with an automatic exemption from antitrust considerations, which meant that the industry's stabilization plan would be approved by the SSRC rather than the less sympathetic FTC. In addition, the new law would include generous financial assistance. This assistance was to be tar-geted to the smaller firms, who continued to insist that they required mas-sive aid to make any capacity cuts at all. As one smaller shipbuilder put it, "without any financial assistance from the Government, the reduction in capacity is tantamount to [a] declaration of death for smaller compa-nies."[64] The industry called for the creation of an agency similar to the Tokuanhō Stabilization Association that would provide outright subsidies, credit guarantees, and loans. The industry called for financial assistance to buy up land and facilities owned by the shipbuilders, to finance "group ac-tivities," to help firms convert to new businesses, and to help firms in mak-ing further employment adjustments.

The SSRC and the MOT eventually agreed with the position taken by the SAJ: the new industry-specific legislation, the "Stabilization Law for the Shipbuilding Industry" (Tokutei Senpaku Seizōgyō Keiei Antei Rinji Sochihō), followed directly from the SAJ's proposals. Under the new law the government provided funds to the industry to scrap excess capacity ac-cording to a stabilization plan that was to be approved by the SSRC. As

---

[62] The industry's efforts are described in *Japan Economic Almanac*, 1988, p. 140, and *Japan Economic Journal*, Sept. 13, 1986, Sept. 27, 1986, and Nov. 1, 1986.

[63] *Zosenkai*, no. 154 (May 1986).

[64] *Japan Economic Journal*, July 19, 1986.

with the Tokuanhō, the MOT set up a government-financed agency to purchase equipment and land from the shipbuilders. In the end, this association provided ¥30 billion for the direct purchases of land or equipment, and an additional ¥50 billion in loan guarantees.[65]

Despite all of these efforts, it had become clear to the majors that continued regulation would not lead to sufficient reductions of capacity. They argued that the industry's past efforts at cooperative capacity cutbacks had not forced it to undergo a meaningful restructuring. On the contrary, regulation had allowed the least competitive firms to avoid market competition and had in fact slowed their exit. As a result the Japanese industry remained excessively competitive, at least by worldwide standards. For instance, in contrast to Korea, which had four firms, and Europe, which had one firm per country, Japan still had 44 independent shipbuilding firms. Although the industry was loosely tied into 22 groups, it remained considerably more fragmented than its international competitors.[66]

The majors saw the need for an even more drastic reformation of the industry's underlying structure. If the industry could not achieve restructuring through the exit of the smaller firms, the only remaining solution was to force a restructuring through administrative guidance. The final SSRC report, issued in June 1986, endorsed this position and called for the industry to consolidate itself into ten groups of shipbuilders. These groups were then to act as units to cut capacity and reduce labor forces. The hope was that firms would cooperate in order to reduce capacity without having to actually merge. The major shipbuilders were solidly in favor of this plan—after all, the council's proposal implied that the industry would be consolidated around the majors—and the chairman of the SAJ, Maeda Kazuo, immediately expressed his satisfaction with the proposed restructuring. Later that month, the major shipbuilders again went farther than the SSRC by calling for an even more drastic restructuring: a reorganization of the industry into just three groups.[67] In the end, the industry's new structure consisted of eight shipbuilding groups.

[65] *Japan Times*, May 30, 1987. Keyser (1990, p. 129) estimates that ¥10.7 billion was spent on direct purchases of land and facilities. The shipbuilding bill is also discussed in Saito 1990, pp. 31–35, Sangyō Seisaku Kenkyūjo 1987, pp. 204–205, Chida and Davies 1990, p. 183, and *Zosenkai*, no. 154 (May 1986).

[66] *Nikkei Weekly*, May 16, 1994. In Europe, only the West German industry had more than a single firm. The Japanese industry's H-index number was 850 in 1985 (*Japan Economic Journal*, July 5, 1986; *Nihon Keizai Shimbun*, May 16, 1994; *Japan Economic Almanac*, 1988, p. 140).

[67] This suggestion was made by Kanamori Masao, chairman of Mitsubishi Heavy and a former chairman of the SAJ (*Japan Economic Journal*, July 26, 1986). In January 1987, the MOT compromised by calling for a reorganization of the industry into five groups. Under this plan, four of the majors would coalesce to form two groups, with the other three majors remaining independent. The rest of the industry's firms would be encouraged to join one of these groups. It turned out, however, that only two of the majors, Kawasaki Heavy and Nippon Kokan, were able to agree to form a single group. The other majors all refused to enter into any such unions.

By 1988 the combined efforts of the shipbuilding majors and the inducements provided by government legislation had resulted in a second major reduction in the industry's capacity. Within two years the industry cut its excess capacity by 24 percent, from 6.0 million to 4.6 million CGRT. As the larger firms had already determined to cut their capacity significantly, the inducements provided by government policy had a greater impact on the smaller firms. As before, the smaller firms were able to cut capacity by forming into groups and then absorbing and consolidating their facilities. The financial assistance provided by the government was channeled almost solely to the industry's smaller firms.[68]

Despite this drastic restructuring the Japanese shipbuilding industry remained much less concentrated than its international counterparts. Even after 1988, the industry consisted of 26 firms. And although these firms were loosely tied in eight groups, they all retained their individual identities and interests. Worse, once prosperity began to return to the industry in 1989, and the industry's sense of crisis began to dissipate, firms began to break ranks, behaving more and more independently. The industry's restructuring efforts resulted in a smaller but not more cohesive industry. Without greater cohesion in the future in these shipbuilding groups, analysts are worried that excessive competition in the industry will continue to remain a problem.[69]

Since the early 1990s, government regulation of the shipbuilding industry has become looser and less direct. In particular, in September 1991, the LDP Minister of Transport, Muraoka Kanezo, suggested that the SSRC should ease up on its efforts to regulate output and capacity in the shipbuilding industry.[70] By implication, Muraoka suggested that the Shipbuilding Stabilization Law should not be extended once it expired in 1992. This easing of regulation can be traced to three factors: the growing competitive threat from the Korean shipbuilding industry, which made cartelization at home more difficult; increasing pressures on Japan from the European Community and the OECD; and especially another economic upturn in the shipbuilding industry that began in 1990.

The competitive threat from the Korean industry had been a problem since the early 1980s when the Korean shipbuilders, prompted by government support, dramatically increased their capacity. By 1982 the Japanese shipbuilders found themselves blaming the Koreans for taking ship orders

[68] According to Keyser (1990, pp. 155–157), 16 docks formerly held by single-dock firms were scrapped in this way.

[69] Even in the case of the tie up between Kawasaki Heavy and Nippon Kokan, analysts assert that there has been no meaningful cooperation. The industry's lack of cohesion is described in *Japan Economic Almanac*, 1989, *Japan Economic Journal*, Aug. 11, 1990, and *Nikkei Weekly*, May 16, 1994.

[70] *Nihon Keizai Shimbun*, Sept. 26, 1991.

at reduced prices and thus "fueling even more confusion in the sagging world shipbuilding market."[71] Thus, in just five years, the Japanese industry had gone from being accused of dumping and unfair competition to being the accuser; the shoe was now clearly on the other foot.

The Japanese industry now found itself allied with an unlikely partner—the European shipbuilders. In December 1982 the Japanese and Europeans initiated direct talks with the Korean industry on the worldwide excess capacity problem. Japanese accounts of these talks speak only in vague terms of the need to restrain the Koreans, using such phrases as "reaching a mutual understanding" and "fostering international cooperation." Privately, however, Japanese shipbuilding executives were more forthright: the executive director of Kawasaki Heavy Industries, for instance, stated that the "Japanese shipbuilders should ask their Korean counterparts not to expand [their] facilities any more in view of [the] critical situation world shipbuilders are facing . . . since market order can hardly be achieved unless the three major centers in the world, namely [Japan], West European countries and South Korea, [cooperate] to that end."[72] The Japanese executives expressed their satisfaction with the Korean response undoubtedly because the Koreans reduced their share of world orders from 19.2 percent in 1983 to just 10.4 percent in 1985. These industry-to-industry talks continued into the 1990s, and they are likely to continue into the indefinite future.

Increasingly, the world shipbuilding industry has come to resemble an international cartel, with output shares determined via negotiation rather than the market. The *Far Eastern Economic Review*, for instance, refers to these international shipbuilding discussions as a "soft cartel," adding that the world shipbuilders have avoided a more explicit arrangement only because they "are wary of publicity for fear of provoking anti-trust charges from the US."[73] This informal international cartel, however, is far from watertight. Although the Koreans have pledged to cooperate with the Japanese and Europeans, there is little that can be done if the Koreans decide to defy the rest of the global industry. This was clearly demonstrated in

---

[71] *Industrial Review of Japan*, 1982, p. 71. *Zosen*, Aug. 1982, pp. 28–35, and *Zosen*, Sept. 1982, pp. 20–21, provide reviews of the Korean industry. The Koreans had increased their capacity by nearly 10 times to 2.4 million GT, between 1973 and 1975, just as the world shipbuilding industry fell into depression. Capacity grew slowly until 1981, when the industry added a further 1.2 million GT in a single year. Two firms, Hyundai Heavy Industries and DaeWoo Shipbuilding, accounted for 80 percent of Korea's total capacity. In 1983 the Koreans, unrestrained by any international cartel agreement, procured more ship orders than all of Western Europe combined. In that year, the Japanese and Koreans together accounted for more than 75 percent of the world's total ship orders (*Industrial Review of Japan*, 1982, p. 71; *Industrial Review of Japan*, 1983, p. 73; *Industrial Review of Japan*, 1984, p. 108).

[72] *Zosen*, March 1984, p. 6. See also *Un'yu Hakusho 1983*, p. 127, and *Un'yu Hakusho 1986*, p. 98.

[73] *Far Eastern Economic Review*, May 25, 1989.

1993, when the Koreans announced new and ambitious plans to expand their capacity. From the Japanese industry's point of view, the inability to rein in the Korean industry makes efforts to regulate supply and demand in the domestic Japanese market increasingly fruitless. In particular, curtailments of production and capacity cutbacks make sense only in a global context of stabilized competition. Like the uncooperative outsiders discussed in the minimill case, an unrestrained Korean industry would nullify attempts to stabilize competition in the global arena. As one Japanese shipbuilding official put it, "we know that no foreign nation can force South Korea to change its ways"; if this is the case, curtailments and domestic cartels will become increasingly futile in the future.[74]

Growing international pressure on the Japanese government to loosen its protective regulation of the shipbuilding industry is a second cause of the easing of domestic regulation. In June 1989 the American shipbuilding industry filed a Section 301 complaint against Japan, charging that the Japanese government had given its industry unfair subsidies, including export subsidies. Although MOT officials argued that the subsidies were only to help the industry restructure itself, the U.S. industry countered that these domestic subsidies had the indirect effect of boosting Japan's competitiveness in export markets. The U.S. government also began to focus its attention on the trade effects of the recession cartels. In particular, the United States urged Japan to review the recession cartel in the shipbuilding industry, which it suspected was hindering "fair international competition," and asked the Japanese government to clarify the relationship between the Anti-Monopoly Law and the recession cartels.[75] The OECD's shipbuilding committee endorsed these efforts to loosen Japan's shipbuilding regulations. In response to American complaints the OECD decided in December 1991 that member nations should gradually abolish all subsidies for their shipbuilding industries. The Japanese government has agreed, albeit reluctantly. Analysts have described the easing of domestic regulation as a "response to the OECD's call for free competition."[76]

The third and most important factor that helps explain the loosening of regulation was yet another boom in the shipbuilding industry that began in 1989 and 1990. The industry estimated that orders for new oil tankers would continue to rise throughout the 1990s, since many of the tankers

---

[74] *Industrial Review of Japan*, 1984, p 108. By the early 1990s, the Japanese and Europeans were joined by an even more unlikely partner, the U.S. shipbuilding industry, in a combined effort to put pressure on Koreans to refrain from further destabilizing the world market (*Nihon Keizai Shimbun*, Feb. 15, 1994).

[75] The United States voiced its suspicions "that Japan and South Korea may have an agreement to share the shipbuilding market" (*Nihon Keizai Shimbun*, Jan. 15, 1990; *Japan Times*, Apr. 3, 1990; *Japan Times*, June 10, 1989).

[76] *Nihon Keizai Shimbun*, Dec. 6, 1991, Feb. 16, 1990, May 10, 1990, Dec. 21, 1991.

built in the 1970s were now due to be replaced.[77] In 1990, with orders booming and the work backlog rising, the Japanese industry found itself in a novel position: it did not have enough workers to operate its facilities at full capacity. The drastic labor cuts of the late 1980s now came back to haunt the industry. Especially hard hit were the smaller firms, since most of the unemployed workers were quickly grabbed by the largest firms. Furthermore, it was increasingly difficult to attract a new generation of workers to an industry with a clouded past.[78]

With profits in the industry rising, it was no longer eligible for a recession cartel; so when the cartel expired in 1990, it was not renewed. (It should be noted that the MOT's informal "price guideline" system remained in effect.) And the 1987 shipbuilding law was also allowed to lapse in 1992. For the first time in sixteen years, the shipbuilding industry was no longer under formal government regulation.

IMPLICATIONS OF THE SHIPBUILDING CASE

The structure of the shipbuilding industry, like that of the industries in the first three case studies, gives us important clues to the economic and political strategies pursued by the firms. In the shipbuilding industry, as in synthetic fibers, the major firms were able to exit relatively easily. The fact that these firms were already well diversified, possessed an existing technological base, and also had access to the necessary financial resources, made further diversification a logical and rational business strategy. This case also shows the importance of "strategic groups" since this industry was not homogeneous. In contrast to the majors the smaller firms were completely dependent on shipbuilding. Lacking other sources of income, they were hit hardest by the downturn in shipbuilding. They also lacked access to other technologies and to financial resources and so had two choices: bankruptcy or pursuing economic stabilization. Many of the domestic regulatory efforts of the MOT were designed to deal with problems faced by the smaller firms. As for labor, the large size of the labor force made adjustment much more difficult than was the case with synthetic fibers and aluminum; on the other hand, the large size of the

---

[77] A second cause for optimism stemmed from the Exxon-Valdez oil spill of March 1989. As a result of that environmental disaster, the U.S. Congress began to work on a bill that required all tankers operating in U.S. waters to have double-hulled bottoms. This regulation signaled that future demand for new or refitted oil tankers would continue to rise (*Japan Economic Almanac*, 1990, pp. 140–141).

[78] *Journal of Japanese Trade and Industry*, May/June 1990, pp. 22–24. According to this journal, one of the industry's tasks was to "shed [its] dark image . . . and to transform shipbuilding into the type of industry that can fulfill the hopes, dreams and expectations of young people" (p. 24).

major firms, plus their strong *keiretsu* ties, eased this adjustment burden to some extent.

Throughout this case study MOT bureaucrats seem to have acted with somewhat more discretion than did the MITI bureaucrats. In part, this is merely an impression of autonomy, one that results from the MOT's opaque policy deliberations. In particular, the discussions held within its main advisory group, the SSRC, have been much more closed than was the case with MITI. As a result, journalistic accounts tended simply to report the SSRC's final pronouncements, rather than delve into the inner deliberations to look for industry or political influence.[79]

The MOT did enjoy some autonomy in the sense that it played a mediating role between conflicting industrial interests. At almost every juncture in the policy process the MOT was in the position of mediating conflicting interests, both domestic and international. It was constantly in the middle of a conflict between the interests of the majors and the smaller firms over how the burden of adjustment should be divided. Further, it also had jurisdiction over a key domestic consumer of ships—the shipping industry—whose interests at times were diametrically opposed to the interests of the shipbuilders. As one MITI official sympathetically remarked, the MOT was forced "to walk a fine line between these competing pressures."[80] Having to reconcile such disparate interests has been a difficult task, but it has also given the MOT some leeway in balancing the competing claims it has faced. Because the policy demands of one group were in part offset by the demands of others, the MOT was able to avoid being "captured" by any of them.

The MOT also had to balance domestic concerns with intense political pressures from abroad. Especially during the mid-1970s, the shipbuilding issue became an international one and went beyond the MOT-industry relationship. As a result, other industries in Japan, along with their political and bureaucratic representatives, became involved in the issue. With these conflicting interests complicating the policy process, the shipbuilders at times were only one of many competing voices. And again in the late 1980s, changes in the external environment had a direct influence on the

---

[79] As an example, nearly every account of shipbuilding policy during the 1985–1988 recession focuses on the SSRC's June 1986 report, in which the SSRC called for a 20-percent reduction in capacity, the restructuring of the industry into groups, and the creation of a new shipbuilding law. Very few accounts mention that the shipbuilders themselves had already requested these measures and that the shipbuilders wanted the government to go even further in helping to restructure the industry. Also, these analyses tend to portray the SSRC as a mere appendage of the MOT, when in fact all relevant private-sector interests, including the shipbuilders and their labor unions, were represented in this forum. Keyser (1990) is one of the few to stress that the SSRC has played a mediating role, helping the industry come to a consensus.

[80] *Ekonomisuto*, Dec. 7, 1976, pp. 29.

domestic policy process. Domestic policy-making occurred within the constant backdrop of external constraints.

Although the policy-making environment has clearly been important, eventual policy outcomes still reflected the basic interests of the actors with the highest stakes in those outcomes—the shipbuilders themselves. MOT policies consistently balanced the interests of the small and large shipbuilders. In particular, the MOT's ultimate use of its formal and informal policy tools was consistent with the shipbuilder's desire to manage competition in the industry. Like the industries in the other case studies, the shipbuilders sought some form of government support for their stabilization efforts, which included production curtailments, efforts to reduce the industry's redundant capacity, and efforts to restructure the industry. Unable to enforce collective stabilization schemes on its own, the shipbuilders turned to the government to provide a forum for negotiating and then enforcing its stabilization and restructuring efforts. That eventual policy decisions fundamentally reflected the interests of the industry actors reinforces my contention that industry-level dynamics should be at the core of analyses of industrial policy in Japan. Without an explicit analysis of the goals and interests of key industry actors and of the ways conflicting interests among them are mediated and resolved, we cannot fully understand eventual policy choices.

INTEGRATED STEEL

The Japanese integrated steel industry in 1995 is not yet considered to be a declining industry. Although analysts have periodically announced the impending demise of the industry, its situation has not been nearly as dire as the experience of, for instance, shipbuilding, aluminum, or textiles. The steel industry has had to cope with cyclical downturns and looming industrial maturity but has not yet been faced with strong pressures for drastic industrial adjustment.[81]

As shown in Chart 7-4, the industry's capacity and output have declined slowly, albeit steadily, over the past 20 years. The industry experienced two cycles of slumping demand and excess capacity during this period: in the late 1970s and again in the 1980s. The industry saw its first signs of impending maturity during the domestic recession following the Oil Shocks. However, it remained a world-class competitor, and exports continued to increase through the mid-1980s. In the last half of the 1980s, it was forced

---

[81] The integrated steel industry involves the gigantic firms that produce molten steel from iron ore (using both blast furnaces and basic oxygen furnaces), which they then roll into plates, sheets, and other products. These firms are thus fully integrated from the raw material stage to the final product stage. The integrated steel industry's JSIC number is 3111.

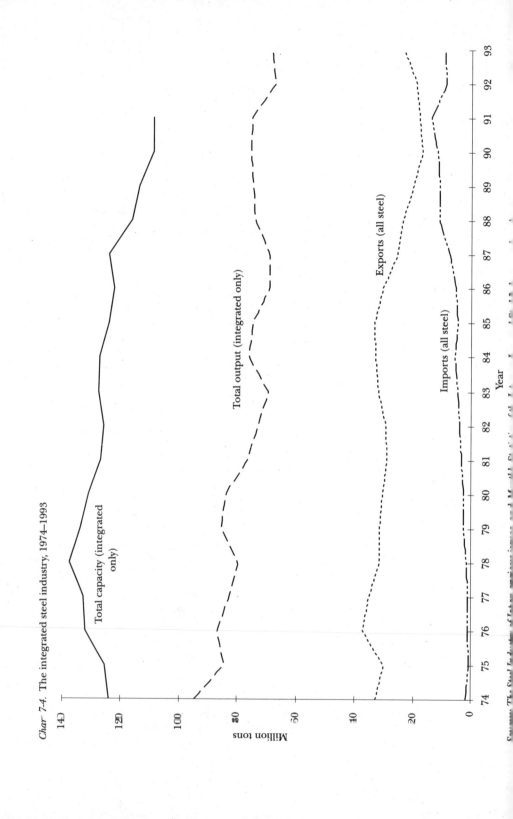

Chart 7-4. The integrated steel industry, 1974–1993

Total capacity (integrated only)

Total output (integrated only)

Exports (all steel)

Imports (all steel)

Million tons

Year

74 75 76 77 78 79 80 81 82 83 84 85 86 87 88 89 90 91 92 93

0   20   40   60   80   100   120   140

to deal with stiff international competition in Asia (especially Korea), in part spurred on by the rapid appreciation of the yen. The second slump was quite serious; between 1985 and 1990 Japanese steel exports were nearly cut in half while imports increased more than three-fold.[82] The industry received a temporary respite from these adverse trends during the so-called bubble economy of the late 1980s, but domestic demand again fell after the collapse of the bubble.

As a Type II industry, Japanese steel has faced conflicting incentives stemming from its industrial structure. Firms have had both the resources and interests to pursue economic adjustment in order to remain competitive. At the same time the high costs of adjustment for the industry's large labor force has also made political solutions such as stabilization or preservation seem attractive. Judging from structural factors alone it is not clear which direction a Type II industry will choose.

Japan's integrated steel makers have refrained from pursuing overtly political measures to stabilize the industry or preserve its status quo. Although the industry has received some compensation for its adjustment efforts it has not demanded political measures, such as industry-specific legislation, that would have slowed or stopped the adjustment process. The steel industry has also not asked for official recession cartels, at least since the mid-1970s.[83]

In addition, although the industry has tried to stabilize selling prices through informal means, these efforts have been largely ineffectual. There is considerable evidence that the industry has attempted to stabilize prices, either tacitly through collusion or under the auspices of MITI guidance. For instance, critics note that steel firms in Japan have been allowed to exchange information on production and pricing. In fact, since 1958 MITI and industry representatives have met every month to discuss industry conditions. Despite denials from the industry and from MITI that prices were not fixed during these meetings, suspicions remain that "under that system, administrative guidance played the de facto role of a car-

---

[82] Indeed, for a brief period in early 1990, Japan became a net importer of steel. Atsuhiko Takeuchi (1992) considers the 1986 Plaza Accord as the key turning point for the steel industry; as a result of this accord, the major steel firms "were forced to change their strategy management and initiated a 10-year restructuring survival program" (p. 189).

[83] This is surprising given the industry's past history and reputation as one of the most highly cartelized industries in Japan. Indeed, one of the industry's most powerful leaders, Inayama Yoshihiro, a former head of Nippon Steel, the Tekkō Renmei, and Keidanren, earned the nickname of "Mr. Cartel" for his activities in the 1960s (*Japan Economic Journal,* June 25, 1985). For one example of the FTC's suspicions, see *Business Japan,* Feb. 1976, pp. 18–19. The steel industry has been a constant target of FTC investigations of price fixing, especially because the oligopolistic nature of the industry makes tacit collusion easier to achieve than in other industries. FTC scrutiny has been high ever since the creation of Nippon Steel in 1970, because this giant firm has enjoyed a dominant market position that has raised concerns over its price leadership (*Japan Economic Journal,* Apr. 26, 1986; *Tokyo Business Today,* Nov. 1986, pp. 48–50).

tel in determining production levels for some steel products."[84] And through the early 1980s MITI "suggested" and "advised" the industry to curtail production in the face of declining demand.

By the late 1980s, however, whatever ability the industry ever had to regulate prices through formal or informal cartels had been largely eroded. This was due to increasingly fierce competition with other steel producers and also because of growing international criticisms and scrutiny. Steel-consuming industries had become unwilling to purchase higher-priced Japanese steel, especially in an era in which they themselves faced strong competition. The Japanese automobile industry was the main opponent of political solutions to preserve the steel industry. By the late 1980s, Japanese auto firms had strong incentives to switch to Korean suppliers of steel, especially as the Korean firms, led by the giant POSCO, had by and large closed the quality gap with the Japanese industry. The incentive to buy Korean steel was further increased by the need to cut costs in the face of severe international competition.[85] The auto firms now became the harshest critics of Japanese steel, arguing that the industry had become lax and "carefree" and thus had failed to keep pace with its Asian rivals. Now, the auto firms threatened to switch to foreign-made steel if Japanese steel did not improve its quality and lower prices to more competitive levels. This threat gave the auto firms strong leverage over the steel industry: as one analyst put it, "if Toyota decides it wants to use imported steel, there's nothing Nippon Steel can do to stop them."[86] The auto firms have acted on this threat twice in the 1990s. In 1991, shortly after Nippon Steel raised its steel sheet prices by 4 percent, imports of steel sheet began to rise. These imports counteracted the attempt to raise prices: faced with lower demand and falling prices, Nippon Steel was forced to cut back its output of steel sheet by 20 percent. And in April 1994 Mitsubishi Motors shocked the steel industry by becoming the first Japanese auto firm to contract with Korea's POSCO for the import of cold-rolled steel sheet. The steel indus-

---

[84] *Nihon Keizai Shimbun,* July 22, 1991. See Howell et al. 1988, pp. 202–249, for an involved discussion of business-government collusion in the Japanese steel industry. Keyser calls these practices "tacit inter-firm collusion sanctioned by the government" (1990, pp. 249–257). This system was finally abolished in July 1991. One steel industry executive offered an analogy to try to explain the apparent contradiction between the legal restrictions of the Anti-Monopoly Law and the tolerance of collusion in practice: "our constitution forbids a military, but we have the Self-Defense Forces!" (*Nikkei Weekly,* Aug. 3, 1991; *Industrial Review of Japan,* 1977, p. 71; and *Business Japan,* Apr. 1981, p. 23).

[85] From the early 1980s on, the auto industry has bargained hard with the domestic steel firms. See *Industrial Review of Japan,* 1981, p. 64, *Japan Economic Almanac,* 1987, p. 184, and *Japan Economic Almanac,* 1992, p. 142. Japanese auto firms were especially worried about the price of surface-treated steel sheet, which accounted for 6 percent of total auto manufacturing costs (*Nihon Keizai Shimbun,* Apr. 20, 1994; *Tokyo Business Today,* Nov. 1989, p. 41).

[86] *Japan Economic Journal,* Mar. 16, 1991. At one point auto executives hinted that it is "possible to produce vehicles by using 50 percent to 60 percent of [sic] imported steel, if not 100 percent" (*Daily Yomiuri,* June 25, 1994).

try initially decided to take a hard line against price concessions, but after Nissan and Honda also signed long-term contracts with POSCO, Nippon Steel agreed to cut its prices and offer rebates to the Japanese auto firms.[87]

Competition for two other large-scale consumers of steel has also prevented the steel firms from managing competition at home. As discussed in Chapter 5, the integrated steel firms were battling the domestic minimills for control of the largest consumer of steel, the construction industry. In particular, the minimills had clear advantages in terms of low costs and flexibility and were making concerted efforts to improve quality. As a result, they made strong inroads into some of the most lucrative construction markets. Similarly, the shipbuilding industry, once the second largest consumer of Japanese steel, pressured the steel industry for low-cost steel. In the 1980s many of the smaller shipbuilding firms had already switched to Korean suppliers of heavy plate, which was cheaper than the Japanese product and of similar quality. In the 1990s the larger shipbuilders were also moving in this direction.[88]

In short, the steel industry was in danger of losing all three of its largest customers to new competitors. These highly organized and politically powerful steel-consuming industries effectively deterred the steel makers from artificially raising prices, even temporarily. As was the case in the aluminum industry, these consumer industries who demanded low-cost steel had access to competitive alternative sources and could simply switch suppliers whenever the Japanese steel firms tried to manage competition in the domestic market. These consumers would also have opposed stronger attempts to preserve the industry or avoid adjustment, since a part of steel's adjustment costs would have been passed on to them.

Even if the steel industry could have overcome the opposition of these key industries, efforts at stabilization through the use of cartels would have been strongly opposed by Japan's trading partners. As discussed in earlier chapters, foreign (specifically, U.S.) criticisms of cartels have increased over time, and by the 1990s any efforts at cartelization would have caused

[87] Steel firms claimed that they had been encouraged by the auto firms to increase their capacity in surface-treating facilities in the late 1980s; now, for the auto firms to switch to Korean suppliers was likened to "a stab in the back" (*Nikkei Weekly*, Dec. 12, 1994; *Nihon Keizai Shimbun*, Apr. 21, 1994; *Daily Yomiuri*, June 25, 1994). Talking to the auto industry during negotiations, one steel executive remarked, "We made a huge investment in facilities to make high-quality steel sheets upon your request. [Our] poor business performance is partly your fault. Demanding a lower price without considering our long relationship cannot be called a mature attitude" (*Daily Yomuri*, Oct. 4, 1994). Other reports of auto-steel price negotiations include *Nihon Keizai Shimbun*, Apr. 5, 1991, Apr. 20, 1991, and Nov. 15, 1991, and *Nikkei Weekly*, Aug. 10, 1991.

[88] *Nikkei Weekly*, Dec. 12 1994. The Mitsubishi Group again led the revolt by entering into contracts for Brazilian steel plate; as a result, steel makers in 1993 and 1994 were forced to lower their plate steel prices (*Nihon Keizai Shimbun*, May 12, 1994 and Sept. 6, 1994).

a furious reaction abroad. Most recently, a new set of American guidelines was issued in December 1994 that allows U.S. antitrust officials to prosecute collusion that acts to restrain American exports even when it occurs in foreign countries. Thus, even if this collusion does not directly harm American consumers, foreign companies could be liable under American antitrust law. Significantly, the Japanese steel industry is frequently mentioned as a clear possibility for prosecution.[89] This latest development is yet another step in the evolution of international scrutiny, criticism, and involvement in the Japanese industrial policy process. As a result, international constraints on the use of formal or informal cartels have become increasingly difficult to ignore.

Instead of political solutions, the steel industry has taken the route of economic adjustment; in particular, the five major firms have each tried to restructure themselves through rationalization, overseas investment, and diversification. In the case of the steel industry this result was in part due to the domestic and international constraints discussed above. However, I agree with Keyser that the steel firms perceived—on their own—strong incentives to pursue a strategy of economic adjustment.[90] Like the shipbuilding firms, the steel firms have pursued adjustment in an effort to regain their competitiveness. In part, this result was due to certain structural advantages that have made the route of economic adjustment more feasible and thus more attractive. As a Type II industry, the steel industry has had ample access to capital and technology and has thus perceived some viable exit strategies. In addition, because the five majors are all core members of the various *keiretsu*, they have benefited from the support of affiliated firms. Other *keiretsu* members have been able to absorb a portion of the industry's excess labor and thus have helped to ease labor's adjustment burden.

As can be seen in Chart 7-4, the industry has responded to declining demand since the late 1970s by cutting back on capacity. First, between 1978 and 1982 firms shut down five of their 38 existing blast furnaces, totaling some 10.5 million tons, or 7.7 percent of the industry's overall capacity. The industry again cut capacity following the appreciation of the yen in 1987. Over the next three years the five firms closed another seven furnaces, leaving the industry with a total of 25 operating furnaces. In the process the industry's capacity fell by a further 15.3 million tons, a decrease of 12.3 percent. As a result of these capacity cuts the industry's operating rate improved every year since 1988, reaching the 70-

---

[89] See, for instance, *Nikkei Weekly*, Dec. 19, 1994. It is not clear whether the U.S. government will actually implement these new guidelines or what the results will be. Many European countries have joined Japan in criticizing this unilateral extension of U.S. domestic law and have vowed to resist any attempt at implementation.

[90] Keyser 1990, passim.

percent level in 1991 and 1992, the highest level since the First Oil Shock.[91]

The steel industry was one of the new industries designated for assistance under the so-called Adjustment Facilitation Law (Enkotsukahō) of 1988, MITI's follow-on legislation to the Tokuanhō and Sankōhō. One of the differences in this new law is that now MITI no longer designates industries, but rather specific classes of facilities; as Sekiguchi Sueo points out, however, this amounts to the same thing since these facilities are always specific to a particular industry and since the full range of integrated steel facilities was designated.[92]

Although government assistance has been welcomed by the industry, it has been the individual firms, not government policy makers, that have taken the initiative in cutting capacity.[93] Nippon Steel, for instance, decided in 1987 to close five of its oldest blast furnaces and to shut down completely its steel facilities in Kamaishi and Muroran. Although this was a difficult decision, Nippon Steel followed a hard-headed business rationale in closing these facilities: the firm wanted to concentrate production in its more modern facilities in Tokyo and Osaka. The other firms have similarly been guided by market realities to shut down their least competitive furnaces in favor of concentrating production in newer and more efficient plants.

These capacity cutbacks made necessary a drastic decrease in the size of the industry's labor force: between 1975 and 1990 the integrated steel firms cut their steel-related work forces exactly in half. The costs of labor adjustment, already high because of the sheer size of the work force, were made even higher because the industry was regionally concentrated. Some of Japan's oldest steel towns were located in rural areas that were already suffering from depression; closure of operations in communities such as Muroran or Kamaishi became potent symbols of the pains of industrial adjustment.[94]

In spite of these high costs, the process of labor adjustment has not raised a great deal of political controversy. Keyser, in her excellent description of labor adjustment in the steel industry, argues that this was because the firms did their utmost to minimize the adjustment burden for their workers and have made special efforts to avoid outright layoffs. As in our other case studies, firms have done their best to decrease their work

---

[91] The industry has long felt that it could be profitable even with operating rates below 70 percent (*Industrial Review Of Japan*, 1980, p. 62). Keyser (1990, pp. 196–206) gives a full description of firm-level capacity and employment reduction efforts. See also Park 1992, p. 69.

[92] Sekiguchi 1991, pp. 456–457; Tsūshō Sangyōshō 1984.

[93] For discussions of Nippon Steel's rationalization efforts, see Toriumi 1987, Takeuchi 1992, pp. 192–201, and Harvard Business School 1985, pp. 4–7. Nippon Steel's clear desire to close its aging facilities in Muroran and Kamaishi is also discussed in *Nihon Keizai Shimbun*, Mar. 6, 1984, *Japan Times*, Feb. 14, 1987, and *Japan Economic Journal*, Feb. 23, 1991.

[94] Keyser 1990, pp. 226–228; Park 1992; Takasugi 1987.

forces short of outright dismissals by cutting back on the hiring of new workers, relying on natural attrition of older workers, convincing workers to cut wages or restrain wage demands, and limiting working or overtime hours. Firms have also resorted to more drastic measures, including voluntary retirement.[95]

Finally, the steel firms have made strong efforts to retain their workers, either by transferring them to other divisions within the firm or to other related firms. In particular, all of the firms have tried to establish new companies outside the steel business and then have used these subsidiaries to absorb a portion of their redundant workers. Between 1985 and 1988 alone the five majors set up a total of 178 new companies and then transferred about 7,500 workers to them.[96] Keyser argues that approximately one-half of the workers who were released from the steel sector have ended up being re-employed by their firms. For instance, between 1987 and 1989 more than half of the 27,000 workers that were cut from the industry were transferred to related divisions and firms, while at least one-half of the 41,000 workers that were cut in the industry's next round of rationalizations were absorbed by more profitable divisions or transferred to affiliated firms.[97]

The steel workers union, the Tekkō Rōren (Federation of Iron and Steel Workers' Unions) has taken a stance similar to that taken by all unions in troubled industries in Japan: it has recognized that its interests depend on the health of the industry and that rationalization to cope with changing competitive conditions is inevitable.[98] Keyser argues that firms have been able to convince the unions that they are doing their utmost to minimize layoffs. According to Keyser, the labor unions have had a considerable voice in the labor adjustment process. Although initial adjustment proposals are put forward by the company, the unions are then consulted at every stage of the process, usually through the joint labor-management fo-

---

[95] Keyser (1990, pp. 212–214) reports that this method of labor reduction was the least popular with the unions, even though firms offered generous severance pay of up to 40 months. This is in contrast to the shipbuilding case, in which firms found themselves swamped with more volunteers for retirement than they could handle.

[96] For a list of steel subsidiaries and affiliates opened in 1986 and 1987, see *Japan Economic Almanac*, 1987, p. 187. See also Keyser 1990, pp. 220–223.

[97] Keyser reports that Nippon Steel planned to cut 19,000 workers between 1988 and 1990; of these, it planned to send 6,000 to its new business ventures. Nippon Kokan planned to transfer 60 percent of the 6,200 workers it cut to affiliated companies. Kawasaki planned to avoid layoffs altogether by shifting 50 percent of its 5,300 excess workers to related companies and transferring the rest within the company. And Sumitomo planned to transfer more than half of its 4,500 redundant workers within the firm. See Keyser 1990, pp. 196–206. These transfers were not without costs, however. In all cases the parent firms paid the difference between the worker's original wages and his wage with the new company, a difference that ranged on average from 33 to 40 percent. By the early 1990s these subsidy payments were becoming an increasingly heavy burden. *Nihon Keizai Shimbun*, Sept 10, 1993, and *Daily Yomiuri*, Nov. 23, 1993.

[98] Rōdōsha Chōsa Kenkyūkai 1990, pp. 298–303.

rums that have been established at both the enterprise and industry level. Also, the unions have had an effective veto over the rationalization plans put forward by the firms: Keyser contends that "if the enterprise unions had refused to endorse a company plan, the plan would not have been implemented."[99] During the 1987 retrenchment, for instance, the firms and unions held at least 12 rounds of talks, mostly centering on the firms' plan for relocating workers. In the end, "the union determined that workers would not be fired, but would instead be relocated to new business areas or absorbed by affiliated companies. Therefore, the union decided to accept the retrenchment proposals."[100]

The steel industry also pursued, and received, public policy support to help compensate workers and firms for the costs of adjusting labor. The steel industry first became eligible for industry-specific wage subsidies in 1983, when it was designated under the Employment Assistance Law. Under this legislation firms have received partial wage subsidies from the Ministry of Labor for retraining workers or assisting them in finding new jobs. These subsidies thus encouraged the "continued employment of surplus workers." The various labor-related subsidy programs have been quite generous, providing "up to as much as 70 percent in the case of retirement allowances, retraining fees, and transfer assistance."[101] These public assistance programs have been in the interests of both management and labor since they aim to facilitate and encourage the retraining and reemployment of excess workers.

Like the economic structure of the other concentrated industries, that of the steel industry has meant that firms have had the resources and capabilities to pursue a strategy of diversification. Especially after the Plaza Accord, individual firms have made strenuous efforts to diversify geographically through tie-ups with foreign firms or out of the industry altogether. All five majors have entered into joint ventures with steel firms in the United States. These investments helped the Japanese get around the various mechanisms that have protected the U.S. market since the late 1970s. In addition, the steel firms sought to follow the Japanese auto industry into the U.S. market: almost all of the industry's joint ventures focused on the production of auto-related sheet steel.[102]

---

[99] Keyser 1990, p. 242. Keyser also notes that the Tekkō Rōren and the Japan Iron and Steel Association have set up a joint Union-Management Discussion Group (1990, pp. 209–215, 243–244).

[100] *Japan Times*, Mar. 20, 1987.

[101] Keyser 1990, p. 44. These subsidies can last up to one year and cover from one-quarter to two-thirds of the employees original wages. Keyser 1990 also discusses labor issues in the steel industry (pp. 31–50, 228, 249).

[102] *Tokyo Business Today*, Nov. 1989, p. 44, provides a chart of the industry's joint ventures. Japanese steel had been active overseas since the mid-1970s in countries such as Qatar, Brazil, Mexico, and China (where it established the ill-fated Baoshan Works in Shanghai). See *Industrial Review of Japan*, 1979, p. 63, and *Industrial Review of Japan*, 1980, p. 63.

Second, the firms have tried to diversify out of the steel industry. Shortly after the Plaza Accord, all five steel firms announced ambitious plans to lower their dependence on the steel sector before the turn of the century. As shown in Table 7-4, each firm sought to diversify into four new fields.[103] First, the firms hoped that their experience with steel making would allow them to move into the production of "new materials," including products such as fine ceramics, carbon fibers, and amorphous metals. A second direction for diversification involved transforming large plots of land owned by steel firms into leisure-related projects. Nippon Steel, for example, built a new theme park—"Space World"—on the site of its old Yawata steel works. Third, most firms expressed a strong interest in the electronics and data communications industries. And finally, Nippon Steel, Nippon Kokan, and Kobe Steel planned to diversify into the promising field of biotechnology.[104]

As shown in the table, between 1985 and 1994 the industry has made some progress in reducing its dependence on the steel industry. Kawasaki Steel has made the most progress, reducing its steel sales by 13 percentage points. The industry's overall progress, however, has not been as dramatic as the industry had originally hoped, and none of the firms seems likely to reach its original diversification target. One problem has been that the steel industry was not a highly diversified industry to begin with. In contrast to the case of shipbuilding, the Japanese steel industry has remained concentrated largely on steel. For example, the industry's leader, Nippon Steel, in 1975 depended on steel for 96 percent of its sales, while steel sales for Kawasaki and Sumitomo Metals exceeded 80 percent. Also, steel industry executives are often criticized for being too traditional, arrogant, and unwilling to change. Most significantly, the steel firms have found that there are limitations or drawbacks to each of the sectors into which they have tried to diversify. Demand for new materials is limited; the future potential of the theme parks and leisure facilities is constrained by often unpopular locations and severely recessed economies; biotechnology demands technical know-how and market experience unfamiliar to the steel firms; and computers and electronics are already extremely competitive. Nippon Steel, for example, was quickly forced to withdraw from the

---

[103] Takeuchi 1992, pp. 195–203. See *Tokyo Business Today*, Nov. 1989, p. 45, for a summary of these diversification plans.

[104] In addition to these four main areas, the steel makers have also tried to diversify into a broad range of fields, including "language-teaching, production and marketing of hot-water heaters, restaurant operations, construction of homes for the elderly and even the raising of pigs" (*Japan Economic Journal*, Apr. 9, 1988). Keyser (1990, p. 223) reports that some steel firms are also involved in chicken feed and mushroom cultivation. For other discussions of the industry's diversification efforts, see *Japan Company Handbook*, various issues, *Japan Economic Journal*, Apr. 2, 1988, July 15, 1989, and Oct. 28, 1989, *The Japan Times*, May 9, 1988, *Mainichi Daily News*, Nov. 14, 1989, *Tokyo Business Today*, Nov. 1989, pp. 45–46, *Japan Economic Almanac*, 1989, p. 192, and *Japan Economic Almanac*, 1993, p. 131.

Table 7-4. Diversification efforts by the integrated steel firms, 1987–1994

Firm	Steel production goal (percent of total sales)	Diversification goals		Actual steel-related sales (percent of total sales)		
		Non-steel production goals (percent of total sales)	Target date	1975	1985	1994
Nippon Steel	60	Engineering (10); Electronics (20); Lifestyle development (10).	1995	96	90	82
Kawasaki Steel	58.5	Engineering (9); Chemicals (2.5); New businesses (30).	2000	88	83	70
Nippon Kokan	50	Engineering (25); Urban development (12.5); Electronics, New materials, Biotechnology (12.5).	2000	69	77	70
Sumitomo Metal	61.5	Engineering (12.3); Electronics (10.8); New materials (8.5); Service industries (6.9).	1995	84	81	72
Kobe Steel	32	New materials (24); Engineering (24); Electronics, Biotechnology, etc. (20).	1995	65	54	50

SOURCES: *Japan Company Handbook*, various issues; *Tokyo Business Today*, Nov. 1989, p. 45.

laptop computer industry when it found that the field was too fiercely competitive. Kawasaki Steel's efforts to enter the potentially lucrative semiconductor market also failed. Kawasaki reasoned that this market would continue to expand for the next decade so assumed that "there [would] be enough room for newcomers"; it further blithely assumed that its experience at mass production would be applicable to the production of semiconductors. However, it does not have strong ties to users of semiconductors, an advantage enjoyed by all current semiconductor producers. In addition, the semiconductor industry was already the subject of intense trade frictions and pressures from abroad, including demands for a guaranteed share of the domestic Japanese market. Given these obstacles, Kawasaki's future prospects in the semiconductor industry remain uncertain. An unidentified critic of Kawasaki's efforts may have been prophetic when he noted: "Should Toshiba, Hitachi or other electronics makers try to enter the steel industry, they will never be able to catch up with us. The converse is also true. We may well become a second-rate maker in the [semiconductor] sector."[105]

Overall, the steel industry has had no choice but to try to adjust to new economic realities. In part, this was due to the role of the major consumer industries, as well as by the U.S. government: most likely, these actors would have strongly opposed any concerted effort by the steel industry to use public policy to preserve or protect itself. But the steel industry should be given the credit for directing its own adjustment—it was the individual firms that tried to anticipate future market trends and that made great efforts to restructure themselves. This was made possible in part by the industry's structure, which has allowed firms to pursue certain options, such as diversification and overseas investment, that are not available to other industries. In addition, these diversification efforts have made labor adjustment somewhat less costly, since firms have been able to re-employ up to one-half of their excess workers. Whether these efforts will prove to be sufficient to deal with future periods of economic distress remains to be seen.

[105] *Japan Economic Journal*, July 15, 1989. In spite of these apparent difficulties, Nippon Kokan and Nippon Steel have followed Kawasaki Steel into the semiconductor field (*Japan Economic Almanac*, 1993, p. 130).

PART III

INDUSTRY ACTORS,
THE POLICY-MAKING ENVIRONMENT,
AND POLICY CHOICES

CHAPTER EIGHT

The Structural Determinants of Industry Behavior

In this chapter I assess the industrial organization hypotheses that I set out in Chapter 2. I contend that there is an identifiable link between the industrial organization of each industry type and the economic and political responses industry actors have chosen. The critical factor has been the extent to which industry actors have enjoyed viable and attractive economic alternatives. Industry actors in concentrated industries have had such economic alternatives open to them, and have had stronger incentives to pursue them than they have had to pursue the route of politics. Conversely, industry actors that have lacked such economic alternatives have had higher incentives to pursue political solutions. In other words, what industry actors have demanded from policy makers has depended in part on what they could or could not achieve in the economic arena.

These industrial organization variables help to explain the general tendencies and patterns of responses taken by industry actors. Although the exact nature of policy choices also depends on the policy-making process, these hypotheses do help to establish a baseline of expectations about actor preferences and behavior. It is important for any societal-based approach to specify actor preferences and interests in an a priori fashion; too often, actor preferences are discussed only in ex-post-facto terms.

INDUSTRIAL CONCENTRATION

The degree of concentration in an industry is the most important of the structural variables. All of the large and diversified firms in the concentrated industries followed some form of economic adjustment strategy. These firms enjoyed important advantages in terms of access to necessary resources: they had access to sufficient capital to finance their adjustment strategies, were able to use their technological resources and experience to diversify into other industries, and were able to pursue economic adjustment through overseas investments. Aluminum is the most striking example of economic adjustment—the industry had little trouble in reducing domestic capacity and was able to completely relocate itself overseas. Both synthetic fibers and the major shipbuilding firms, already highly diversified to begin with, made great progress in diversifying out of their respective businesses: the synthetic fiber firms used their background in chemicals to diversify into new materials, while the shipbuilders expanded their plant and engineering operations. In addition, the synthetic fiber firms were able to invest heavily abroad. Finally, the steel industry is now in the process of diversification out of the industry, although it has not yet made as much progress as originally planned.

As a result of their adjustment efforts, all of the firms in these industries were able to lower their dependence on their original core business and thus reduce their incentives to defend the existing market status quo. The political demands of these industries were therefore not as strong as those in the less concentrated industries: although firms and labor did try to stabilize the industries' conditions and sought compensation for their adjustment efforts, they did not try to stop the adjustment process entirely. And even when these industries did try to manage competition at home their efforts tended to be less intense and of shorter duration than was the case in the fragmented industries.

In stark contrast, firms in the fragmented industries did not have the luxury of pursuing adjustment strategies. These firms did not have access to adequate financial and technological resources and so for the most part found adjustment strategies to be beyond their capabilities. Lacking a diversified technological base to begin with, most of these firms were simply unable to diversify into other industries. Similarly the vast majority of small firms lacked the resources to shift their operations overseas through direct investment. In short, capital and labor proved to be less flexible than they were in the concentrated industries. As a result, the only adjustment option available to these firms was exit through bankruptcy.

With no attractive or viable adjustment options open to them, these firms instead had higher incentives to turn to political solutions to their problems. As we have seen all of the fragmented industries thus made strong efforts to manage competition at home through the cartelization of production and by controlling investment and capacity levels. These efforts were more intense and of longer duration than they were in the concentrated industries. Coal mining and cotton textiles were beneficiaries of industry-specific legislation that allowed them to legally regulate production, investment, and capacity. These laws gave the industry greater leeway to set up production cartels, capacity registration systems, investment controls, and other mechanisms to manage the supply side. For more than a decade the steel minimills tried to utilize public policy to manage competition in an industry that was inherently unmanageable.

This initial focus on the concentration of industries is a useful first approximation of the preferences of the different industry types. One major modification is in order, however: some of these industries were not completely homogeneous.[1] Both the shipbuilding and cotton spinning industries, for instance, exhibited dual structures, with large and small firms existing side by side. In other industries, differential access to the *keiretsu* was a factor in individual firms' response strategies. In most cases all firms were either members of the *keiretsu* (as in aluminum, synthetic fibers, and steel) or were not (as was the case with the minimills), but in some industries (shipbuilding, cotton spinning, coal mining, and paper), only the largest firms enjoyed ties to the *keiretsu*. Finally, some industries were divided in terms of competitiveness. This was especially clear in the minimill industry, which was composed of two strategic groups, the highly competitive outsiders and the less competitive insiders.

Industries were therefore not always monolithic entities with unified interests and preferences. For instance, the large shipbuilders were able to pursue diversification and adjustment, whereas the smaller firms were essentially locked into the shipbuilding industry; not surprisingly, it was the latter that pushed more strongly for political measures. This industry's dual structure also helps us to understand why the shipbuilding industry was the most aggressive of the concentrated industries in its efforts to manage domestic competition. Similarly, the larger cotton spinners tended to be more diversified and flexible and so were less ardent in their pursuit of political solutions than the smaller firms. Also, the less competitive insider minimills were the ones to push for political solutions, whereas the more competitive outsiders preferred to leave outcomes to the market.

Thus, although the initial hypotheses are indicative of the general direction of the reactions of these industries, we also must be sensitive to divisions among industry actors in order to understand the nuances of intra-industry bargaining and the resulting policy dynamics.

THE SIZE OF THE LABOR FORCE

The labor variable helps to explain the dynamics of the labor adjustment process. The costs of labor adjustment have varied depending on the industry's structure, and as a result, the mechanisms and process of ad-

---

[1] Porter 1980.

justment have also differed. One such difference concerns the ability of firms to maintain their commitment to "employment stability." Many analysts have pointed out that Japanese firms have made at least a tacit commitment to guarantee employment for their workers and that they tend to think of labor as a relatively fixed cost. In this arrangement, firms and labor have reached an agreement in which firms do their best to avoid laying off their redundant workers. I have found that management in all industries has indeed tried to preserve this practice but that their ability to do so has depended on the industry's structure.

Labor adjustment in the Type I industries was the least complicated and costly, since the industry's large firms had little difficulty in absorbing the relatively small labor force. In the case of synthetic fibers, all firms were able to pare their labor forces without having to resort to significant layoffs. In particular, their efforts to diversify into new lines of business allowed firms to retrain and re-employ a large portion of their workers. And because all firms enjoyed ties with the *keiretsu*, they could transfer at least a portion of their workers to related firms. Labor adjustment was especially smooth in the aluminum industry, in which large *keiretsu*-affiliated firms had to absorb only a minuscule labor force; it is thus not surprising that adjustment in this industry was the least politicized of all of Japan's troubled industries. The low costs of labor adjustment in Type I industries reinforced the tendency of this industry type to pursue economic adjustment rather than political solutions.

The labor adjustment process in Type II industries proved to be more difficult. Certainly, firms in this industry type did their best to avoid laying off their redundant workers. For instance, both shipbuilders and steel firms tried to trim their work forces by using creative measures such as freezing new hires and cutting work hours, and were also able to shift a number of their workers internally or to related firms. However, the sheer size of the work force strained the ability of firms to absorb their excess workers. The need to absorb large numbers of workers has given firms even greater incentives to pursue the economic adjustment strategy of diversification. By developing new businesses, either internally or externally, firms have been able to retain workers they otherwise would have fired. Although exact figures are difficult to find, it appears that most large firms were able to absorb between one-quarter and one-half of their redundant workers in this manner. The high costs of labor adjustment also gave firms incentives to seek compensation through public policies, such as wage and unemployment subsidies.

However, firms in the fragmented industries have faced higher labor adjustment costs. Like their larger counterparts, they did their best to maintain at least a tacit commitment to stable employment. The problem was that these firms were not able to utilize the same adjustment mechanisms available to the larger firms: they could not transfer workers internally or to affiliated firms, or create new jobs by diversifying into other fields. Thus, the severity of the industry's decline quickly overwhelmed their ability to honor their tacit commitment to employment security. When times became bad, firms had no alternative but to dismiss a large number of their workers. The guarantee of stable employment was a luxury available only to the more concentrated industries.

Management and labor in Japan have generally avoided large-scale confrontations and controversy.[2] In part this can be attributed to the organization of Japanese labor. Because the most important unions in Japan have been organized along enterprise lines, workers find that their interests are intimately tied to the fate of their individual firms. Thus, union leaders have tended to cooperate in their firm's efforts to restructure or to regain competitiveness. Union leaders have taken a highly pragmatic approach and have tended to sacrifice jobs in the short term in the hope of preserving jobs in the future. The case studies in this book illustrate this tendency: in each industry the labor force was cut by between 40 and 50 percent in the first decade after the onset of economic distress.

This is not to say that Japanese labor is a completely weak and subordinate partner to capital, however. Labor has secured from management at least the tacit commitment to employment security. Also, in practice, Japan's enterprise unions are usually fully consulted before any labor-related move is made; some analysts have even argued that labor enjoys de facto veto power over the decisions made by firms.[3]

The labor adjustment process was also relatively smooth because of the choices that were made by the firms. First, all firms went to great lengths to honor their commitment to preserve employment security. This was true especially of the largest firms, but even the smallest ones did not simply fire their workers at the first sign of hard times. The fact that firms have done their best to retain workers was appreciated by the labor unions and made the process of labor adjustment smoother and less confrontational. Further, firms in the concentrated industries have been able to ease the costs of labor adjustment by pursuing diversification, efforts that are almost always endorsed by the labor unions, since their workers are then retrained for jobs in the new business operations. Also, when adjustment strategies were unattainable or too costly, as was the case with the frag-

---

[2] The fact that these labor-intensive industries reached their decline phases during a period in which the Japanese economy was booming also helped to reduce the burden of labor adjustment. Although precise calculations are impossible, the costs of adjusting labor, either through internal or external labor markets, were surely lower while the economy was growing rapidly. Similarly, the fact that many industries in the 1980s and 1990s were more concerned about future labor *shortages* has also made massive unemployment less of a concern.

[3] Keyser 1990.

mented industries, labor and management found that they shared a mutual interest in protecting the industry, and often worked together to lobby the government for political solutions. This relationship was particularly striking in the coal mining industry where, after a period of intense labor-management strife in the 1950s, the miners and the mining firms jointly pressed their demands for subsidies and other measures to ease the costs of unemployment.[4]

INDUSTRY STRUCTURES AND INDUSTRY PREFERENCES: A WEST GERMAN PROBE

These industrial organization hypotheses do help us to understand the general behavior of the industry actors in Japan's troubled industries. However, if these hypotheses are to have more general explanatory power, they should be applicable to distressed industries in other countries as well. In this section I conduct a cursory examination of how some German industries have responded to economic distress. I look first at the coal mining industry in Germany as an example of a Type IV industry. Then I examine in turn iron foundries (Type III), aluminum (Type I), and integrated steel (Type II). In each case I am concerned with the relation between an industry's structure and its responses to economic distress. This is not a comprehensive test of my original hypotheses, as I am only relying on existing secondary materials to see if actors in different industry types have behaved in expected ways. Furthermore, I do not try to assess the broader policy environment in Germany. The policy environment in the Japanese case is highly situation-specific, having different effects both across and within industries, so surely, this policy context will differ in the German case. In particular, the external context will be very different. A comprehensive comparison of industrial policy making in Japan, Germany, and other countries is beyond the scope of this book.

Michael Trebilcock describes coal mining as "the only example of a West German industry in long-term decline which has received maintenance assistance from the federal government on a large scale."[5] Although the German government has often cited the need to secure a domestic source of energy, it has also been motivated by a more deeply rooted desire to avoid economic and social upheaval.[6] Throughout the 1970s the government assisted the industry with import quotas and tariffs, assistance

---

[4] Kume 1993, pp. 167–168. Kume further argues that the private-sector unions have been less confrontational than the public-sector unions because they have had to face market competition, especially internationally.

[5] Trebilcock, 1986a, pp. 289–290.

[6] Taylor 1992.

for rationalization, subsidies for transportation, and domestic purchasing arrangements with the German steel and electric power producers.[7] Public policy support has not been aimed at helping the industry to restructure. Instead, at least through the 1980s German policy "was directed at *preserving* the industry's existing shape."[8] This public policy support is likely to continue; according to one union leader, "this sector will need subsidies not just temporarily, but forever."[9]

Although I have not looked into the exact nature of the responses of industry actors, this policy outcome is at least consistent with my hypotheses. I suspect that both firms and labor, lacking attractive adjustment options, saw no choice but to pursue political channels. I would expect that the critical factor in this case was the lack of viable or attractive economic alternatives on the part of the coal mining firms. In addition, the large size of the labor force most likely made economic adjustment very costly and difficult and thus made political solutions more attractive.

However, as in the Japanese case, firms and unions have avoided long-term confrontation and have been able to cooperate in dealing with economic distress. In part this was because the German unions, like the Japanese unions, took a pragmatic approach. They recognized that decline was inevitable and that "their duty (as this was, they believed, their only realistic option) was to cooperate with management and government to cushion [the impact of adjustment] on those individuals and communities affected, and secure the best terms for those remaining in the industry."[10]

One of the few examples in the secondary literature of a Type III industry in Germany is the iron foundry sector. The lack of case studies is not surprising, since Type III industries have little political clout or organizational power and so tend to be ignored in most countries.

The iron foundry industry is highly fragmented: firms are very small and are mostly independent or family-owned.[11] This structure has made it difficult for firms to leave the industry (other than through bankruptcy). According to Colin Appleby and John Bessant, the "independent foundries often have little alternative expertise" and so have exhibited a high degree of endurance, finding themselves unable to diversify, a condition which makes economic adjustment enormously difficult.[12]

At the same time, the industry's lack of political power has limited its ability to achieve political options: the industry has realized that, "in em-

---

[7] Taylor 1992, p. 50; Trebilcock 1986a, p. 290.

[8] Taylor 1992, p. 52; emphasis in original.

[9] Trebilcock 1986a, p. 290.

[10] Taylor 1992, p. 57.

[11] The industry had over 1,000 establishments and around 70,000 workers; in addition, there were 30,000 workers in the nonferrous foundries (Appleby and Bessant 1987, p. 203).

[12] Appleby and Bessant 1987, p. 184.

ployment terms, it is relatively insignificant and cannot realistically hope for sector-specific support."[13] Although this sector is about the same size as the Japanese minimill industry, the German foundries have not received similar levels of public policy support. Rather, the German government has essentially let the industry cope with market forces on its own.

In contrast, the aluminum industry (Type I) has shown a much greater degree of economic flexibility: in the face of declining demand after the oil crisis, the domestic industry went though a period of drastic consolidation. Prior to the Oil Shocks six firms operated smelters in Germany, but by the 1980s, only one domestic firm, VAW, operated a domestic smelter (two foreign firms, Alusuisse and Alcan, also continued to operate in Germany). Firms in this industry were thus able to achieve more drastic economic adjustment, in a shorter period of time, than the fragmented German industries were able to achieve.[14]

Firms in the German integrated steel industry (Type II) have followed a mixture of economic adjustment and political strategies to cope with long-term economic distress. On the economic side, ever since the world-wide steel crisis of the 1970s German firms have made concerted efforts to rationalize, reduce capacity, and trim their labor forces. In part, this reflected their pragmatic realization that "it makes no sense to fight modernization."[15] The German industry has also made strong efforts to diversify, first up the value-added chain into higher-grade steel, and then out of steel and into unrelated sectors. For instance, the largest firm, Thyssen, has concentrated on mechanical engineering, transportation, and environmental technologies, while the second largest firm, Krupp, has focused on construction and plant engineering. By the mid-1980s, only one-quarter of Thyssen's total sales were accounted for by steel.[16]

At the same time, the German steel industry has benefited from political support as well. During the crises of the 1970s, for instance, regional firms were allowed to form "crisis cartels," in which the smaller firms formed into larger groupings in order to stabilize competition. These efforts evidently lasted only for the duration of the crisis and did not lead to a major restructuring of the industry.[17] The German industry was also the beneficiary of efforts to cartelize the European industry, even though it

[13] Appleby and Bessant 1987, p. 207.

[14] Compared to the Japanese case the German industry has enjoyed some advantages. In part, this was because the German industry used coal, rather than oil, for its energy needs. Although this made the industry less competitive before the Oil Shocks, it also insulated the industry once oil prices began to rise. In addition, the German government was evidently more willing to provide subsidies to its industry (Kirchner 1988, pp. 78–79).

[15] Esser and Fach 1989, p. 224.

[16] Bain 1992, p. 29; Esser and Fach 1989, p. 228.

[17] Esser and Fach 1989.

did not actively pursue these measures. In the late 1970s, for instance, the European Community created Eurofer, an E.C.-wide cartel designed to promote stability and rationalization. This cartel, along with the so-called Davignon Plan, gave the industry "a breathing space in which to restructure and modernize."[18] More important, the German industry has benefited from import protection, aimed mostly at Japan. The German industry in the late 1970s wanted to prevent Japan from diverting its exports from the American market, which was then becoming more closed. Thus, in 1978 the German industry adopted a "minimum-price system" similar to the U.S. trigger-price mechanism and later that year also reached a voluntary restraint agreement with the Japanese.[19] The German industry's attitude towards these political measures was not entirely clear, however. According to some analysts, the most competitive German steel makers were actively opposed to the European-wide cartel, since across-the-board reductions would have hurt them most. In addition, they have evidently not pushed strongly for import protection.[20]

In terms of the adjustment of labor, there were some striking similarities between the German and Japanese experiences. First, labor adjustment in the two industries proceeded at about the same pace.[21] Second, the process of labor adjustment, although costly, was handled peacefully and without a great deal of strife. In both cases, labor-management conflict was avoided largely because labor was given a full voice in the adjustment process and, as a result, firms were compelled to avoid the outright dismissal of redundant workers. German firms, like their Japanese counterparts, have therefore resorted to other methods of reducing employment short of dismissals: early or voluntary retirement, shortening hours, and transferring workers to other jobs. In practice, this system has slowed down the process of adjusting labor, but it has had the advantage of "contribut[ing] to *peaceful* and *orderly* industrial adjustment, and hence to maintaining industrial and social calm in a period of rapid economic change."[22]

Some have noted that German unions have an advantage over the Japanese unions because their access to the policy process is guaranteed by law. Through the system of "co-determination," in which the unions are guaranteed representation on the works councils and other labor-management negotiating bodies, the German unions enjoy "considerable powers of consultation and co-determination on redundancies, redeployment

---

[18] Trebilcock 1986a, pp. 282–283.
[19] Trebilcock 1986a, pp. 282–283.
[20] See Esser and Fach 1989, p. 240, and Trebilcock 1986a, p. 283.
[21] Between 1974 and 1987, the German industry's labor force was cut by almost forty percent (Esser and Fach 1989, p. 142). In Japan, the labor force was trimmed by 50 percent between 1975 and 1990.
[22] Thelen 1987, p. 141; emphasis in the original.

and retraining of personnel."[23] In contrast, in the Japanese case, labor's access to the adjustment process is based on tacit understandings that have developed between firms and labor.

However, despite this important difference in the institutional/legal relationship between management and labor, the process of labor adjustment seems remarkably similar and seems to have produced similar results. It is perhaps the case that what German labor has won through the legislative process Japanese labor has won through more tacit means.

I contend that the experiences of these German industries are at least *roughly* similar to the responses seen in the Japanese cases. I do not make strong claims as to the universality of these industrial structure hypotheses; I do not pretend to be able to explain all of the behavior of Germany's troubled industries using my original hypotheses. But it seems to me that these hypotheses are useful in providing an indication of how the different industry types will react to economic distress.

I leave it to those more familiar with the German case to assess the validity of my discussion and interpretations. Certainly the internal and external policy environment in the two countries differs, although at first glance these differences do not appear to be decisive. Unfortunately, a discussion of these differences goes beyond the scope of this chapter. But my main argument is that, in Germany as well as in Japan, an industry's structural characteristics will be a central determinant of the political and economic preferences of industry actors, and that these preferences will be a central part of the dynamics of the policy-making process.

[23] Marsden 1987, p. 192.

CHAPTER NINE

Rethinking Government-Industry Relations in Japan

Understanding the industrial policy-making process in Japan must begin with an understanding of the preferences and interests of firms and labor, the main industry actors affected by policy. In troubled industries, these actors, far from being "responsively dependent" on the bureaucrats, have been involved in all phases of the policy process and have had a visible impact on Japanese policy choices.

In each of the case studies, industry actors have sought to stabilize their economic environment and have tried to mobilize public policy to help alleviate the costs of adjustment. In particular, they have tried whenever possible to "manage competition" domestically, either in the short term through cartelization or over the long term through collective cutbacks in capacity. It may seem strange for distressed industries to desire cutbacks in production or capacity, but by coordinating output in the face of declining demand, they can achieve the long-term benefit of managing competition, propping up selling prices, and thus stabilizing profits. Without such stabilization measures, troubled industries run the risk of falling into damaging price wars, plunging profits, and the threat of spiraling bankruptcies. Cartelization helps to reduce these risks, especially for the least competitive firms in the industry.

The intensity of these pressures and demands has differed according to the type of industry. The fragmented industries have lacked viable economic alternatives and so have tended to pursue the whole range of political solutions, from measures that stabilize competition to policies that smooth out or delay the adjustment process. Political solutions were most evident in the Type IV industries, cotton spinning and coal mining, which lacked economic alternatives for both firms and labor. In contrast, the concentrated industries had an easier time adjusting economically and so have not pushed so strongly for political solutions to preserve themselves; their policy demands were often limited to maintaining a degree of stability and receiving adequate compensation for the costs of adjustment. Firms in Type I industries, such as synthetic fibers and aluminum, spent more of their energy pursuing economic adjustment rather than political solutions.

Japan's policy choices have consistently reflected the fundamental interests of these industries. In particular, all industry types have benefited from formal or informal cartels that have allowed them to enforce industry-wide efforts to manage competition, stabilize market conditions, and shield themselves from adjustment pressures. Government policy for the fragmented industries has gone a step further in helping the industry slow down and delay the adjustment process. In particular, industries like cotton spinning and coal mining have benefited from industry-specific legislation that has allowed them to regulate output and capacity levels. Finally, although Japan has avoided explicit import protectionism, it has, like many other industrialized nations, sought to shield its industries from pressures to adjust.[1] In other words, Japan has used different policy instruments to achieve the same political goal.

Final policy choices in each of the case studies have not merely coincided with industry preferences; rather, it was the industry actors themselves who were the driving force behind those policies. They have often been the source of policy initiatives and proposals, and they have always been active and involved in the policy process. Their influence was seen in case after case of specific policy decisions, across industries, and over time.

First, industry actors have often initiated the policy process. Of course, finding the *original* source of policy initiatives is a difficult task; far too often, however, analysts of Japanese industrial policy simply assert that policy initiatives have come from MITI bureaucrats. This simplistic assumption certainly makes the analysis easier—one need only investigate MITI's thinking and interests—but it leads us to ignore a crucial aspect of the policy process. In each of my case studies I have shown that it was the industry actors who were responsible for establishing their predicament as a policy issue in the first place. Firms and their labor forces carried on intense and detailed discussions of their economic problems well before the issue became public or became part of the public policy agenda. These actors were aware of their industry's problems and had clear preferences for specific solutions. At times they had to overcome internal divisions and conflicts of interest among firms or between labor and management, but once

---

[1] Although Japan has largely avoided import protectionism thus far, one should remember that only one industry, cotton textiles, has lobbied openly for it (and with some marginal success).

a consensus position evolved from this internal mediation process (usually accomplished through the industry associations), the position invariably dominated subsequent public discussions. Thus, it was the industry actors who determined the parameters of the industrial policy debate.[2]

Second, industry actors have always been actively involved in all aspects of the policy-making process. They have enjoyed both informal as well as formal access to the bureaucrats and to the politicians. Much of this input has occurred at the level of the industry association, although individual firms and unions have also lobbied on their own. In addition, industry actors are always represented on governmental advisory committees, the *shingikai*.[3] In every case, industry actors have had a great deal of impact on policy-related deliberations; I found no cases in which policy makers made any decisions without extensive discussion and consultation with the relevant industry actors.

Thus, industry actors have often had a visible impact on policy choices. These choices have at times reflected verbatim the requests and pressures of the industry. The industry-specific laws for the textile industry, for instance, were virtually identical to the proposals originally put forth by the industry association itself.

In the formation of cartels, the industries have actively pursued stabilization of supply-side conditions; without exception, they have gone to the bureaucrats for help in enforcing these efforts. Because cutbacks in production or capacity require short-term sacrifices, firms will only cooperate if they know that other producers are similarly bound. In all of these cases industry actors first tried to manage competition on their own but usually found that effective enforcement was beyond their capabilities. They thus sought government regulation as a necessary outside enforcement mechanism. Whenever the bureaucracy used its informal guidance powers or its formal regulatory powers, it was ratifying and supporting actions that the industry was already taking. Industry actors have lobbied MITI to enforce strict, and at times burdensome collective cutbacks, often asking for ever deeper cuts in production or capacity when existing efforts were not sufficient to stabilize the market or restore long-term profitabil-

---

[2] Conversely, I have found very few instances in which MITI has taken policy initiatives in the absence of strong cues, pressures, or requests from industry actors. And MITI has almost never initiated policies that industry actors have not favored. (The sole exception to this was the initiation of liberalization during the early 1960s, a policy which was opposed by most of the cotton spinning firms. It is important to recall, however, that MITI by the mid-1960s had retreated in the face of strong industry opposition.)

[3] As Samuels (1986) has argued about different industries, MITI is simply unable to exclude these actors from being formally represented in these bodies. Of course, mere representation is not a guarantee of influence—indeed, in many cases MITI has favored the interests of producers over the interests of labor, consumers, and taxpayers. But I have found little evidence that MITI has been able to "disenfranchise" any of these groups (Young 1984, 1986).

ity. Key examples of this behavior can be found in all four of my main case studies.[4]

In many cases, industry actors have had to apply heavy pressures to convince the bureaucrats to intervene on their behalf. For instance, in the 1950s and 1960s the cotton spinning industry had to lobby intensely to convince MITI to help enforce collective cutbacks in production and capacity. In other cases industries have had to overcome MITI's reluctance to use its informal administrative guidance powers to enforce implicit cartel arrangements; this was evident in the synthetic fiber industry in the 1970s and especially in the minimill industry in the 1970s and 1980s. There is very little evidence that MITI would have acted to create these cartels in the absence of industry pressures, and there is absolutely no evidence that MITI ever forced these industries to behave contrary to their self-defined interests.

Industry actors in troubled industries of course have not received everything they have demanded and may not have always demanded all that they desired (a subject to which I will return shortly). But no one—not even the most extreme proponent of a society-centered approach—expects any particular group to achieve all of its theoretically limitless policy demands. But in these case studies industry actors have played such an active and central role in the policy process, and have gotten their way so often, that their role simply cannot be ignored. It is absolutely necessary to analyze the interests of industry actors—or perhaps even to make these interests our central focus.[5]

I should emphasize that the analysis in this book has covered only one class of industry, those in distress. However, the central policy role that industry actors have played in this class suggests that they may have played a central role in all cases of industrial policy making.[6] Even in cases of industrial policy for growth industries, in which fewer controversies arise between the bureaucrats and industry actors, analysts must consider the extent to which policy choices reflect the interests of the industry actors

[4] Chalmers Johnson and E. B. Keehn have recently ridiculed Mark Ramseyer and Frances Rosenbluth for claiming that Chinese coolies once hired slave masters to help overcome collective action problems. In a typical rejoinder, Johnson and Keehn (1994, p. 14) state: "It evidently never crossed the minds of these savants of coolie motivation that their conclusion is so preposterous that it could be established (if at all) only empirically—by some on-the-spot discovery of a hitherto unknown guild of Chinese masochists." In the case of Japanese industry I find ample evidence that industry actors have turned to the MITI bureaucrats to help enforce collective action, and have asked for painful regulations in the short run, hoping for long-term benefits. I argue that industry actors have done so for rational, not masochistic, reasons.

[5] Richard Samuels (1986, p. 19) made a similar plea nearly a decade ago, yet since that time most analysts of industrial policy have continued to focus almost entirely on the state. The major exceptions are Friedman 1988 and Noble 1988. See also McKean 1993, pp. 82–85.

[6] McKean 1993, pp. 82–85.

involved. That is, we must always consider who or what groups we should expect to be involved in the policy process, and what sorts of policies they should logically favor. I think it is incumbent on those who portray MITI as dominant to go beyond their initial assertions and show how MITI has actually overruled or deflected industry interests. The notion that industry actors are "responsively dependent" on state policy makers should be demonstrated empirically rather than accepted as an unquestioned assumption.

THE DOMESTIC POLICY ENVIRONMENT: THE PERMEATED BUREAUCRACY

The initial focus on the interests of industry actors is an indispensable step in explaining policy choices, but it is only a first step. We must also analyze the broader policy environment and trace the process through which these actors attempt to achieve their interests. The broader policy-making environment can constrain the range of possible policy choices: an industry may find that preferred policy choices may only be attainable at high or prohibitive political costs and may thus be dissuaded from pursuing policy goals they otherwise would prefer. Conversely, at times the policy-making environment makes some goals more attainable than others: for instance, the existence of certain policy tools may motivate actors to pursue goals they would not otherwise consider.

The industrial policy-making environment in Japan is usually described as centering on the industrial-policy bureaucrats, and in particular the MITI bureaucrats.[7] Although I describe MITI as "permeated" and "responsive," it does not lack autonomy altogether. MITI bureaucrats have had their own ideas about how industries should react to economic distress and at times have been able to limit some of the more egregious demands of industries under their jurisdiction. Bureaucratic autonomy was highest when more than one interest was involved, particularly when consumer industries had a strong stake in the policy issue. In those cases MITI bureaucrats had to play a mediating role between conflicting interests.[8]

[7] The following discussion refers only to MITI, but a similar analysis applies to MOT bureaucrats as well.

[8] The role of consumer industries was most notable in coal mining, aluminum smelting, shipbuilding, and integrated steel. The consumer industries in these cases—steel and electric power in the case of coal mining, the aluminum rollers in the case of aluminum smelting, the domestic shipping industry in the case of the shipbuilders, and the auto makers in the case of integrated steel—were all relatively organized, relied on products of the troubled industry for a good portion of their inputs, and were themselves faced with either economic distress or severe competition at home or abroad. Consumer industries in the other case studies either faced difficult organizational barriers or had relatively low stakes in the troubled industry.

Most of the evidence in my case studies, however, suggests that currently popular, extreme versions of the "bureaucratic dominance" view of Japan's political economy are badly misleading. First, as I discussed earlier, industry actors have by no means been "responsively dependent" on bureaucratic direction or influence. Of all the assumptions of the capitalist developmental-state approach this is the most profoundly mistaken (as well as the most prevalent). Second, MITI has not been able to act as an autonomous and dominant bureaucracy, free from political and interest group pressures. Rather, it has been the bureaucrats who have been the responsive actors, reacting to pressures emanating from the distressed industries. MITI's autonomy has thus been permeated by the very actors that the bureaucratic-dominance approach would have us dismiss.

Third, MITI has not acted like a capitalist developmental state. I found absolutely no evidence that MITI has acted to "preempt the costs of economic adjustment," or to force industries to adjust against their will.[9] In fact, MITI has more often acted to *slow* the adjustment process than to speed it up. Rather than seeking to rationalize and downsize Japan's least competitive industries, MITI has been compelled to spend more of its time, energy, and resources on stabilizing and preserving them.

Finally, MITI regulation has consistently supported the *least* competitive firms in each industry. MITI policies to create a more stable economic environment, such as pro rata or across-the-board cuts in production or capacity, have tended to help the least competitive firms survive and to hold on to their market shares. These policies thus hurt the most competitive firms, whose market shares would have increased otherwise.[10] MITI's support for the least competitive firms in an industry was nowhere more stark than in the minimill case, in which MITI consistently tried to rein in the most dynamic firms, the competitive outsiders led by Tokyo Seitetsu. MITI's crackdown came at the behest of the less competitive firms, which were more intent on regaining stability than in regaining their competitiveness.

Thus, to the extent that MITI was able to favor the interests of some firms over others, it consistently favored those with the least competitiveness or growth potential. Far from promoting competitiveness, then, Japan's industry policies have helped the laggards survive and have

[9] Thus, I disagree with the assertions of Katzenstein (1985, pp. 23; 1988, pp. 281–284) and Trebilcock (1986b, pp. 223–242).

[10] And in some cases the largest (and more competitive) firms even undertook greater proportional cutbacks in capacity, thus alleviating adjustment pressures on the smaller firms; the shipbuilding and cotton spinning industries are clear examples of this. Analysts have noted that the Japanese Ministry of Finance adopted a similar approach, known as the "convoy system," to regulate domestic banks, in which regulation helped to keep the most and least competitive banks moving at a similar pace. This form of managed competition is seen in all cases of troubled industry policy as well.

tended to hurt the interests of the most competitive firms. Nothing could be farther from what we should expect of a capitalist developmental state.

Mark Tilton has recently presented an alternative explanation of MITI's objectives for troubled industries that focuses on supply security. He has suggested that MITI pushed for cartels in two troubled industries, cement and petrochemicals, because it was worried about maintaining a secure, domestic source of supply of basic materials.[11] While this interpretation may fit his two cases, however, it makes less sense when one looks at the totality of distressed industries in Japan. As I have shown, MITI provided the strongest support to industries that were the least "strategic," as was the case with the cotton spinners and the minimills, for which MITI implemented more numerous cartels and stronger stabilization measures than for any other industry.[12] In contrast, MITI did less to ensure domestic supplies of the more strategic materials, aluminum, synthetic fibers, and steel. If MITI was truly worried about stable domestic supply, why should it care more about cotton shirts and cement than about aluminum or steel?

MITI's policies toward the cement and petrochemical industries, I suggest, are consistent with the view that the industry actors themselves desired stability and protection through the formation of cartels. Since Tilton does not focus on the industries' desires or lobbying efforts, we cannot come to any final conclusions here. I suspect, however, that if one looks for the evidence, one will find that the behavior of the firms in these two industries was not unlike the cases I have analyzed—that is, that they favored the cartels not because MITI wanted them, but because they themselves did, and that these industries actually lobbied MITI to enforce their cartelization efforts. Furthermore, I suggest that the arguments about "supply security" may have originated with the industry actors themselves. The minimills, for instance, argued in the 1970s that Japan needed to retain the ability to recycle scrap—a nice argument, but one that few outside the minimill industry took very seriously.[13] Although MITI officials at times have justified policy decisions in terms of a concern for supply stability, I have not found compelling evidence that this has driven MITI's thinking or policy behavior.

---

[11] Tilton 1994.

[12] The coal mining industry was considered to be strategic in the immediate postwar period, given Japan's dependence on energy. In that period, however, MITI led the country away from coal toward petroleum, and it was only *after* the Oil Shocks, when Japan should have desired to maintain a domestic energy source, that MITI finally pulled the plug on the industry.

[13] I am reminded of the U.S. government's justification for giving the textile producers import protection on the grounds that if the United States had to fight a war, it would need a domestic supply of military uniforms. Arguments like these most likely reflect the self-serving interests of the industry rather than serious concerns on the part of the government.

That MITI has been so supportive of the least competitive industries and the least competitive firms is understandable if we view MITI as a political organization that is susceptible to pressures from particularistic interest groups and their political allies. MITI has had strong organizational incentives to intervene to stabilize industries in trouble: its interest in maintaining industries under its jurisdiction, dependence on the industry for information and policy cooperation, and above all, the desire to avoid politicization and controversy. In case after case, MITI's developmental goals have yielded to its political goals. That is, MITI has pursued overall development of the economy only when it did not raise the potential for politicization of a specific policy issue. But when faced with potential controversy MITI bureaucrats have had to walk a fine line between the desire for effective economic development and the desire to avoid politicization. This dilemma has led MITI to invariably compromise its developmental goals in favor of the particularistic concerns of the industry actors.

Industrial policy bureaucrats have also been susceptible to pressures from party politicians. Industry's threat to mobilize their political allies to apply pressure on the bureaucrats has constrained bureaucratic behavior. In a few cases industries have turned this latent threat into an active one, and when the party politicians have intervened heavily in the policy process their support has usually been decisive.

These findings are thus consistent with the recent assertions by Ramseyer and Rosenbluth.[14] Although I am basically sympathetic to the rational-choice approach which they espouse, I have major reservations with their recent formulation. First, Ramseyer and Rosenbluth so exaggerate the strength of political constraints on the bureaucrats that they open the rational-choice approach up to unwarranted ridicule and outright rejection.[15] Second, their arguments are more often asserted than convincingly demonstrated with empirical evidence. In my case studies the politicians were never as central to the policy process as Ramseyer and Rosenbluth would lead us to expect. Rather, for the most part, party politicians have remained uninvolved and on the periphery of the policy process; their influence thus remained limited to the murky world of "anticipated reactions." (Of course, Ramseyer and Rosenbluth can interpret this lack of involvement as the strongest evidence of the power of the politicians: that

[14] Ramseyer and Rosenbluth 1993.

[15] See, for instance, the often unfair criticisms offered by Johnson and Keehn 1994 and Clemons 1994 (the latter goes so far as to compare rational choice theory to the AIDS virus). Ramseyer and Rosenbluth would have done well to make some of their assertions into hypotheses, and to acknowledge the work of other scholars whose findings parallel their own, even those who do not utilize the language of rational choice. Such changes would have forestalled some of the more extreme reactions that their book engendered. See Green and Shapiro 1994.

is, they can assert that docile bureaucrats in these cases are perfectly anticipating the wishes of their political masters, thus making political intervention unnecessary. The problem here is one of falsifiability: exactly what evidence can disconfirm the notion of "anticipated reactions?" As currently formulated, *any* bureaucratic behavior can be twisted *post hoc* to be consistent with initial assertions. Even talking to the actors involved is not enough, for bureaucrats who express indifference to the threat of political interference may simply be misunderstanding structural constraints.)[16] Finally, the excessive focus on politicians obscures the importance of the industry actors themselves. In my case studies, I have found that the most salient feature of the policy process was that industry actors were often able to gain much of their demands on their own, through direct interactions and bargaining with the bureaucrats. In many cases, these industry actors prevailed even when they did not enjoy strong ties to the politicians or could not credibly threaten to mobilize political support. Clearly, some other policy dynamics—not simply the power of the politicians—were at work here.

INTERACTIONS WITH THE BROADER
POLICY-MAKING ENVIRONMENT

It is important that we specify the parameters of the policy-making environment correctly. Too often analysts of Japan's political economy have equated the policy-making environment with the Japanese bureaucracy; more recent analyses now focus primarily on the party politicians. As I have already noted neither of these sets of actors has been as central to the policy process as their advocates have argued: the bureaucrats have tended to be responsive to industry demands while the politicians have largely been peripheral to the entire process.

Furthermore, I argue that merely studying the "iron triangle" relationships between industries, bureaucrats, and politicians, will not give us the full story, because these actors are all constrained and influenced by the broader policy-making environment. This environment transcends the bureaucrat-politician nexus to include two other elements. On the domestic level, policy choices are influenced by the domestic antitrust environment; over time, antitrust constraints have grown, making it more difficult for industry actors to pursue cartelization. On the international level, external factors have exerted significant constraints on the domestic policy process,

---

[16] As Kernell (1991, p. 369) puts it, the method of "poking and soaking"—by which I take it he means process tracing, interviewing, and the like—will not refute his rational-choice assumptions. Again, one has to wonder: exactly what evidence can possibly be found to falsify this assertion of "anticipated reactions?"

and these have grown over time as Japan's position in the international economy has changed.

As I have described in detail in the case studies, Japan's antitrust environment has changed considerably over time. In the 1950s and 1960s the FTC was politically and organizationally weak and thus exerted few constraints on MITI's industrial policy. In this permissive antitrust environment, industry actors could appeal to a full range of policy tools, from formal recession cartels to informal administrative guidance, to help enforce their collective efforts to manage the supply side. Invariably, industry actors turned to these policy tools when they found that they were unable to enforce cartel behavior on their own.

In some cases the permissiveness of the antitrust environment encouraged industries to pursue options they might not otherwise have pursued. The minimill industry in the 1970s, for example, found the industry insiders facing such high obstacles to collective action (especially the existence of the competitive outsiders) that they could not hope to enforce cartel behavior on their own. Without strong outside enforcement mechanisms, combined with the perception that MITI could be persuaded to use these tools, it is doubtful they would have pursued cartelization as vigorously as they did. Similarly, other industries realized that through organization and political pressure they could convince policy makers to intervene on their behalf; this knowledge in some cases changed the calculations of industry actors. Thus, the prospects that policy support would be forthcoming has provided some disincentives to adjust and may have had the effect of slowing the adjustment process.[17] Key examples can be found in the cotton spinning, coal mining, and shipbuilding industries.

Over time, however, the FTC has become more assertive and aggressive in enforcing antitrust provisions. During the 1970s an increasingly vigilant FTC has chipped away at the use of informal administrative guidance, and especially MITI's traditional policy tool, production curtailments through *kankoku sōtan*. The key event was the prosecution in 1974 of the Petroleum Cartel, in which the industry (and by extension, MITI) was found guilty of collusive behavior. This court challenge had a visible impact on the policy process: throughout the 1970s and especially in the 1980s industry actors and MITI found it very difficult to resort to this traditional policy tool. FTC restraints on the use of *kankoku sōtan* were most visible in the minimill and shipbuilding cases, in which the FTC made it absolutely clear that the industries should pursue the more formal recession cartels. In addition, even these formal cartels have come under attack, with the FTC over time becoming less willing to approve them. During the 1960s

---

[17] See Tsuruta 1983 and Yamamura 1982.

industry actors considered FTC endorsement to be nearly automatic, but by the 1980s industry actors had to more clearly meet the criteria for a recession cartel before the FTC would give its approval.

Although the FTC is not yet as strong and assertive as its supporters would like it to be, it has been able to exert ever stronger restraints on cartel behavior. Furthermore, the FTC has been bolstered by pressures from Japan's trading partners. Since the mid-1980s American trade negotiators have focused more attention and scrutiny on the trade-stifling effects of domestic cartels. Most visibly in the Structural Impediments Initiative (SII) talks held between 1989 and 1991, the United States has pressured Japan to strengthen its antitrust enforcement capabilities and to refrain from excessive cartelization.[18]

By far the more important change in the broader policy environment concerns Japan's international context. Industrial policy for distressed industries tends to be seen as predominantly a domestic issue, but in every case study in this book the international environment has had a visible and growing impact, although its exact nature has varied across industries.

On the one hand, the international environment has been a source of opportunity for some industries. In particular, firms in the concentrated industries have benefited from an important economic adjustment option, namely the ability to shift some of their excess domestic capacity overseas through direct investment. The most notable example of this was the aluminum smelting industry, which essentially relocated its entire domestic base overseas. The synthetic fiber firms and the steel firms have also been active in overseas investments. In this sense, the mobility of capital in the concentrated industries has made economic adjustment less difficult. Among the fragmented industries only a handful of the largest cotton spinners and, more recently, the largest paper firms have had even limited success with this adjustment strategy.

Overall, however, the international environment has served as a growing constraint on the options open to industries. First, a number of industries have been forced by international pressures to "voluntarily" restrain their exports. Examples include the cotton spinners in the 1950s, the synthetic fiber firms in the late 1960s, and integrated steel in the 1970s. The most striking example of this "voluntary" restraint was the shipbuilding industry, in which the European shipbuilders effectively deterred the Japanese industry from increasing its share of the international market above 50 percent. In all of these cases international political pressures have ex-

---

[18] Merit Janow and Leonard Schoppa differ in their assessment of the effectiveness of these demands. Janow (1994, p. 70) argues that "Japanese antitrust enforcement activities have increased to a degree perhaps unimaginable before SII." Schoppa (1993, pp. 362–363) contends that Japan made only minimal concessions in strengthening antitrust enforcement.

acerbated the industry's domestic problems of excess capacity and also have prevented industries from using "export deluges" to rid themselves of excess production. As a result, industries have been forced to seek solutions to their problems at home, through domestic regulation.

Second, external constraints have eroded the ability of industries to manage competition in the domestic market. Indirectly, the growing openness and internationalization of the Japanese economy meant that industry actors could no longer hope to prevent imports from undermining domestic cartel arrangements. What may have been possible in the 1950s, when the Japanese economy was still relatively closed, was becoming more difficult by the 1980s. Foreign governments have become increasingly aware of the stifling effects of domestic cartels and administrative guidance on trade and have been much quicker to criticize and complain about such regulations. Foreign criticisms were especially important during the 1980s and 1990s in industries such as shipbuilding, paper, aluminum, synthetic fibers, and steel. Foreign governments have also become more critical of Japan's declining-industry legislation on the grounds that these laws have tended to prop up domestic industries rather than encourage them to adjust; these criticisms have been one reason the Japanese government weakened subsequent versions of the legislation.

Finally, the international environment has constrained Japan's ability to use policy measures to protect its troubled industries from import competition. In an era in which foreign governments have desperately tried to remove barriers to the Japanese market, new import barriers are not likely to be tolerated. In this environment, efforts by Japan to raise overt protective barriers are likely to be completely unacceptable to its trading partners. And as Japan's trading partners have become more aware that informal policy measures have been used to shield the domestic market, pressures on Japan to end these policies have also increased.[19] Japan's responsiveness to these foreign criticisms is likely to grow even stronger in the future. Japan today has an enormous interest in maintaining access to markets abroad and is extremely sensitive to threats to this access. As a result, policy makers are now more likely to take foreign complaints into account in formulating industrial policy. Thus, industries will find it increasingly difficult to resort to formal or informal measures to shield themselves from import pressures.[20]

---

[19] As one example of informal barriers to imports, the cotton spinners have tried to put pressure on domestic buyers and importers to refrain from dealing with foreign suppliers, pressures that were also bolstered by government bureaucrats.

[20] Constraints on import protection have domestic roots as well: efforts by troubled industries to protect themselves from imports encourages internationally minded industries to op pose these efforts. Industries that rely on exports, for instance, fear that attempts to protect

In sum, both elements of the broader policy-making environment have changed dramatically over the past five decades, leading to greater constraints on the choices and behavior of bureaucrats, politicians, and firms and labor. In the 1950s, industry actors were not strongly constrained by domestic antitrust considerations, and international pressures and scrutiny were still weak. In this policy-making environment the policy process for troubled industries was predominantly a domestic one in which industries and MITI had access to a full range of policy options. As a result, they were freer to manage competition in the domestic market. Since then, both antitrust considerations and the international dimension have changed. Although firms and labor are still the central actors in the policy process, the range of policy choices open to them has narrowed.

INTEGRATING INDUSTRY ACTORS AND THE POLICY ENVIRONMENT

The approach I have adopted in this book diverges from three tendencies apparent in the works of theorists of international political economy who stress either international or institutional explanations. These theorists have tended to limit their analyses to a single level, have focused on how structural features constrain the behavior of actors, and have stressed the static nature of these structural elements.[21]

First, my approach begins with the interests of industry actors as the core of the explanation, but also tries to integrate disparate elements of the policy-making environment, including Japan's international context. This integrative approach may be less parsimonious than approaches that stress only one level, but it has the advantage of allowing us to explore the interactions of actors with the different elements of their environment. This approach also provides us with a richer and more fruitful explanation. Put another way, telling the story from only one perspective will give us an extremely distorted view of the Japanese policy process. International-level approaches, for example, might lead us to expect that Japan will forgo import protection, but will be unable to capture the essence of

---

the domestic market will jeopardize their access to markets abroad, and thus become involved in the policy process for distressed industries. More influential are actors from industries that consume products produced by a troubled industry. These firms have had strong interests in maintaining access to cheaper inputs, including foreign supplies, and have thus been adamant opponents of allowing the troubled industry to protect itself from imports. Thus, industries desiring import protection must overcome the opposition of Japan's trading partners, other industries, the bureaucrats, and the politicians.

[21] Ikenberry et al. 1988.

the domestic policy process—the interplay between societal and institutional actors. Similarly, a focus on Japan's state institutions, or more specifically on the bureaucrats, would provide a different part of the story, but would miss the dynamics that are both internal and external to the state—that is, the role that societal actors play and the opportunities and constraints afforded by the international environment.

Second, international- and institution-centered approaches exaggerate the extent to which actors are constrained by their external environment. Those who focus on the international system, for instance, argue that the international distribution of power has enormous constraining effects on the behavior of states; at the domestic level, those focusing on institutions tend to stress how these arrangements constrain and determine the behavior of societal actors. I argue that while the policy-making environment may impose constraints on the range of choices open to actors, it does not *determine* what choices will be made. That is, actors will always have at least some degree of freedom of choice; in many cases these parameters are quite loose and wide. Structural constraints, whether domestic or international, cannot tell us when policy choices will be adopted, and often do not provide an adequate explanation of their content.

Third, structural theories tend to emphasize stability over change—that is, neither the international distribution of power nor the structure of domestic institutions is subject to rapid evolution. In contrast, I emphasize the dynamic nature of the environment: Japan's industrial policy-making environment has changed rapidly and constantly over time. It has also been subject to manipulation by industry actors. That is, environmental constraints are more elastic and flexible than portrayed by structure-based theories. Of course, industry actors often simply accept environmental constraints as being outside of their realm of influence. But if actors are able to manipulate their environment even to a limited extent, then our analysis must be able to deal with these dynamics.[22]

It turns out that industry actors in Japan have had some success in changing the policy parameters facing them, pushing these constraints in more desirable directions. Even politically weak industries have been able to change, reinterpret, or circumvent the structural constraints they face. To cite a mundane example, industry actors have successfully lobbied to convince reluctant bureaucrats to intervene on their behalf. Especially in cases of administrative guidance, these actors have had to overcome significant legal and international obstacles to achieve their policy goals. Furthermore, industry actors at times were able to make changes in the legislative environment itself. The cotton spinning indus-

---

[22] Frieden 1991, pp. 24–26.

try, for instance, through concerted political efforts was able to create industry-specific legislation that echoed the industry's basic interests. The creation of the Tokuanhō in 1977 is a second example of this influence. The Tokuanhō was a bill that the distressed industries themselves pushed very strongly. Finally, there are cases in which industry actors have been able to circumvent some very strong constraints on policy choices. The clearest example again comes from the cotton spinning case, in which industry pushed for some form of formal protection against imports. As discussed earlier, the industrial-policy environment throughout the postwar period has made it difficult, if not impossible, for industries to receive formal import protection. And yet the Japanese textile industry has been able to achieve a modicum of protection from imports through informal measures, such as pressures on buyers to refrain from "excessive" imports, as well as the imposition of informal voluntary restraints on its trading partners in Pakistan, Korea, and China. Further, the Japanese textile industry, in arguing that Japan should shift its status under the Multi-Fiber Arrangement from a supplier nation to an importer nation, has come close to overcoming these environmental constraints. Even the fact that the Japanese government has seriously considered this step cannot be explained without reference to the pressures emanating from the textile industry.

Analyses that integrate these different levels and elements will inevitably suffer in terms of parsimony. However, analyses that limit themselves to just one level—and especially those that consciously try to *exclude* other actors at other levels—often lead us to distorted explanations of the behavior that we observe. When sparse, parsimonious approaches do not provide us with adequate understandings, it is time to move toward more causally complex explanations. In other words, simplified theories and approaches are useful and usually preferable, but not when they lead us to overly simplistic analyses. Although we need to keep the different elements of the broader policy-making environment analytically distinct, I strongly endorse Gourevitch's plea for greater causal complexity in our analyses: "The historical reality of each case is too open, too uncertain, too plastic to sustain the reductionism involved in tracing outcomes back to one feature or even one combination of features of the system."[23]

The integrative approach I advocate here does have a clear explanatory focus—if forced to choose only one variable at only one level, I would stress the centrality of the preferences of industry actors. But we do not need to limit ourselves to just one level. Rather, an integrative approach allows us to trace the interactions and interrelationships between industry

[23] Gourevitch 1986, pp. 66–67.

actors and the broader policy environment they face. It is this dynamic process of *interaction* between choice and constraint that lies at the heart of my analysis and that, I believe, provides us with a better explanation of Japan's troubled industry policies.

References

Aggarwal, Vinod K. 1985. *Liberal Protectionism: The International Politics of Organized Textile Trade.* Berkeley: University of California Press.

Aggarwal, Vinod, Robert Keohane, and David Yoffie. 1987. "The Dynamics of Negotiated Protectionism." *American Political Science Review* 81, no. 2 (June): 345–366.

Alexander, Arthur J. 1994. "Japan's Policy toward Declining Industries: A Blueprint for Handling Economic Obsolescence?" *JEI Report* 4A (January 28): 1–21.

All Japan Cotton Spinners' Association et al. 1957. *The Story of the Japanese Cotton Textile Industry.* Osaka: All Japan Cotton Spinners' Association.

Anchordoguy, Marie. 1989. *Computers Inc.: Japan's Challenge to IBM.* Cambridge: Council on East Asian Studies, Harvard University.

——. 1990. "A Challenge to Free Trade? Japanese Industrial Targeting in the Computer and Semiconductor Industries." In Kozo Yamamura, ed., *Japan's Economic Structure: Should It Change?* Seattle: Society for Japanese Studies: 301–332.

Anderson, Douglas D. 1986. "Managing Retreat: Disinvestment Policy in the United States and Japan." In Thomas K. McCraw, ed., *America versus Japan.* Boston: Harvard Business School Press: 337–372.

Anderson, Kym, and Robert E. Baldwin. 1981. "The Political Market for Protection in Industrial Countries: Empirical Evidence." World Bank Staff Working Paper, no. 492. Washington, D.C.: The World Bank.

Appleby, Colin, and John Bessant. 1987. "Adapting to Decline: Organizational Structures and Government Policy in the UK and West German Foundry Sectors." In Stephen Wilks and Maurice Wright, eds. *Comparative Government-Industry Relations: Western Europe, the United States, and Japan.* Oxford: Clarendon Press: 181–209.

Bain, Trevor. 1992. *Banking the Furnace: Restructuring of the Steel Industry in Eight Countries.* Kalamazoo, Mich.: W. E. Upjohn Institute for Employment Research.

Barnett, Donald F., and Robert W. Crandall. 1986. *Up from the Ashes: The Rise of the Steel Minimill in the United States.* Washington, D.C.: The Brookings Institution.

Bethlehem Steel. 1983. "Japanese Government Promotion of the Steel Industry: Three Decades of Industrial Policy." Unpublished manuscript.

Blumenthal, Tuvia. 1976. "The Japanese Shipbuilding Industry." In Hugh Patrick, ed., *Japanese Industrialization and Its Social Consequences*. Berkeley: University of California Press: 129–160.

Boyd, Richard. 1989. "The Political Mechanics of Consensus in the Industrial Policy Process: The Shipbuilding Industry in the Face of Crisis, 1973–1978." *Japan Forum* 1, no. 1: 1–17.

Boyd, Richard, and Seiichi Nagamori. 1991. "Industrial Policy-Making in Practice: Electoral, Diplomatic, and Other Adjustments to Crisis in the Japanese Shipbuilding Industry." In Stephen Wilks and Maurice Wright, eds., *The Promotion and Regulation of Industry in Japan*. New York: St. Martin's Press: 167–204.

Boyer, Edward. 1983. "How Japan Manages Declining Industries." *Fortune*, January 10: 34–39.

Brown, Les. 1980. "Opening Remarks." In Raymond Cordero, ed., *The Market and the Mini: The Challenge of the Electric Furnace Steelworks*. London: Metal Bulletin: 3–11.

Calder, Kent E. 1988. *Crisis and Compensation: Public Policy and Political Stability in Japan, 1949–1986*. Princeton: Princeton University Press.

———. 1989. "Elites in an Equalizing Role: Ex-Bureaucrats as Coordinators and Intermediaries in the Japanese Government-Business Relationship." *Comparative Politics*, 21, no. 4 (July): 379–403.

Campbell, John Creighton. 1989. "Democracy and Bureaucracy in Japan." In Takeshi Ishida and Ellis S. Krauss, eds., *Democracy in Japan*. Pittsburgh: University of Pittsburgh Press: 113–137.

Chida, Tomohei, and Peter N. Davies. 1990. *The Japanese Shipping and Shipbuilding Industries: A History of Their Modern Growth*. London: Athlone Press.

Clemons, Steven C. 1994. "Japan Studies under Attack: How Rational Choice Theory Is Undermining America's Understanding of Other Nations." JPRI Working Paper, no. 1.

Curtis, Gerald L. 1988. *The Japanese Way of Politics*. New York: Columbia University Press.

Destler, I. M., Haruhiro Fukui, and Hideo Sato. 1979. *The Textile Wrangle: Conflict in Japanese-American Relations, 1969–1971*. Ithaca: Cornell University Press.

Dokusen Bunseki Kenkyūkai, ed. 1970. *Nihon no dokusen kigyō*. Tokyo: Shin-Nihon Shuppansha.

Dore, Ronald P. 1986. *Flexible Rigidities: Industrial Policy and Structural Adjustment in the Japanese Economy, 1970–1980*. Stanford: Stanford University Press.

Ekonomisuto Henshūbu, ed. 1978. *Asu no sangyō shinchizu*, vol. 2. Tokyo: Mainichi Shimbunsha.

Endo Kazuhisa. 1986. "Gōsen 4-hinshu ni okeru kōzō kaizen taisaku: Tokuanhō kara Sankōhō made." *Kasen Geppō* 459 (July): 12–20.

Esser, Josef, and Wolfgang Fach. 1989. "Crisis Management 'Made in Germany': The Steel Industry." In Peter J. Katzenstein, ed., *Industry and Politics in West Germany: Toward the Third Republic*. Ithaca: Cornell University Press: 221–248.

Export-Import Bank of Japan, Kaigai Tōshi Kenkyūjo. 1984. "*Kaigai chokusetsu tōshi ni kansuru ronbunshu*." Tokyo: Export-Import Bank of Japan.

Findlay, Christopher. 1988. "Steel Industry Development Strategies." Unpublished manuscript, Australian National University.

Frieden, Jeffry A. 1991. *Debt, Development, and Democracy: Modern Political Economy and Latin America, 1965–1985.* Princeton: Princeton University Press.

Friedman, David. 1988. *The Misunderstood Miracle: Industrial Development and Political Change in Japan.* Ithaca: Cornell University Press.

Friman, H. Richard. 1990. *Patchwork Protectionism: Textile Trade Policy in the United States, Japan, and West Germany.* Ithaca: Cornell University Press.

Fujii Mitsuo. 1971. *Nihon sen'i sangyō keiei-shi: sengo—menbō kara gōsen made.* Tokyo: Nihon Hyōronsha.

Garrett, Geoffrey, and Peter Lange. 1986. "Performance in a Hostile World: Economic Growth in Capitalist Democracies, 1974–1982." *World Politics* 38, no. 4: 517–545.

Gerlach, Michael. 1989. "*Keiretsu* Organization in the Japanese Economy: Analysis and Trade Implications." In Chalmers Johnson et al., eds., *Politics and Productivity: How Japan's Development Strategy Works.* Cambridge, Mass: Ballinger: 141–174.

Goto, Akira. 1988. "Japan: A Sunset Industry." In Merton J. Peck, ed., *The World Aluminum Industry in a Changing Energy Era.* Washington, D.C.: Resources for the Future: 90–120.

Gourevitch, Peter. 1978. "The Second Image Reversed." *International Organization* 32, no. 4: 881–911.

——. 1986. *Politics in Hard Times: Comparative Responses to International Economic Crises.* Ithaca: Cornell University Press.

Gowa, Joanne. 1988. "Public Goods and Political Institutions: Trade and Monetary Policy Processes in the United States." In G. John Ikenberry et al., eds., *The State and American Foreign Economic Policy.* Ithaca: Cornell University Press: 15–32.

Green, Donald P., and Ian Shapiro. 1994. *Pathologies of Rational Choice Theory: A Critique of Applications in Political Science.* New Haven: Yale University Press.

Hadley, Eleanor M. 1970. *Antitrust in Japan.* Princeton: Princeton University Press.

Haley, John O. 1987. "Government by Negotiation: A Reappraisal of Bureaucratic Power in Japan." In Kenneth B. Pyle, ed., *The Trade Crisis: How Will Japan Respond?* Seattle: Society for Japanese Studies: 177–191.

Hardin, Russell. 1982. *Collective Action.* Baltimore: Johns Hopkins University Press for Resources for the Future.

Harrigan, Kathryn Rudie. 1980. *Strategies for Declining Businesses.* Lexington, Mass.: D. C. Heath.

——. 1988. *Managing Maturing Businesses: Restructuring Declining Industries and Revitalizing Troubled Operations.* Lexington, Mass.: D. C. Heath.

Harvard Business School. 1985. "The Winter Age of the Japanese Steel Industry." HBS Case #685-050.

Heidenro Kihon Mondai Kenkyūkai. 1977. *Heidenro kihon mondai kenkyūkai hōkokusho.* Tokyo: Heidenro Kihon Mondai Kenyūkai.

Hirschman, Albert O. 1970. *Exit, Voice, and Loyalty: Responses to Decline in Firms, Organizations, and States.* Cambridge: Harvard University Press.

Hiwatari, Nobuhiro. 1989. "Organized Markets and the Restrained State: Institutions for Industrial Policy, Incomes Coordination, and Political Quiescence in Postwar Japan." Dissertation, University of California, Berkeley.

Horiuchi Toshihiro. 1985. "Gōsen sangyō ni okeru setsubi shōri to kyōdō kōi." *Nihon Keizai Kenkyū,* no. 14 (March): 22–46.

Howell, Thomas R., William A. Noellert, Jesse R. Kreier, and Alan Wm. Wolff. 1988. *Steel and the State: Government Intervention and Steel's Structural Crisis.* Boulder, Colo.: Westview Press.

Huntington, Samuel P. 1993. "Why International Primacy Matters." In Sean Lynn-Jones and Steven E. Miller, eds., *The Cold War and After: Prospects for Peace.* Expanded ed. Cambridge: The MIT Press: 307–322.

Iijima Banji. 1949. *Nihon bōseki-shi.* Osaka: Sōgensha.

Ikenberry, G. John. 1986. "The State and Strategies of International Adjustment." *World Politics* 39, no. 1: 53–77.

———. 1988. "Conclusion: An Institutional Approach to American Foreign Economic Policy." *International Organization* 42, no. 1: 219–243.

Ikenberry, G. John, David Lake, and Michael Mastanduno. 1988. "Introduction: Explaining American Foreign Economic Policy." *International Organization* 42, no. 1: 1–14.

Industrial Bank of Japan. 1988. "Nihon tekkōgyō no kin-miraizō." *Kōgin Chōsa* 5, no. 239: 2–115.

Inoguchi, Takashi. 1986. "Japan's Images and Options: Not a Challenger, But a Supporter." *The Journal of Japanese Studies* 12, no. 1 (Winter): 95–119.

Itoh, Motoshige, Kazuharu Kiyono, Masahiro Okuno, and Kotaro Suzumura. 1988. "Industrial Policy as a Corrective to Market Failures." In Ryutaro Komiya, Masahiro Okuno, and Kotaro Suzumura, eds., *Industrial Policy of Japan.* Tokyo: Academic Press: 233–255.

Iwasaki Tomoaki. 1977. "Heidenro kihon mondai kenkyūkai hōkokusho ni tsuite." *Tekkōkai* 127 (March): 58–69.

Iwata Katsuo. 1984. *Nihon sen'i sangyō to kokusai kankei.* Kyoto: Hōritsu Bunkasha.

Iyori, Hiroshi. 1986. "Antitrust and Industrial Policy in Japan: Competition and Cooperation." In Gary Saxonhouse and Kozo Yamamura, eds., *Law and Trade Issues of the Japanese Economy: American and Japanese Perspectives.* Seattle: University of Washington Press: 56–82.

Janow, Merit E. 1994. "Trading with an Ally: Progress and Discontent in U.S.-Japan Trade Relations." In Gerald L. Curtis, ed., *The United States, Japan, and Asia.* New York: W. W. Norton: 53–95.

Japan Development Bank. 1974. "Gōsei sen'i gyōkai jijō." Unpublished.

———. 1983. "Kami-parupu gyōkai." Unpublished paper. Tokyo: Japan Development Bank.

———. 1986. "Gōsei sen'i gyōkai jijō." Unpublished.

Japan Fair Trade Commission. 1976. *Shuyō sangyō ni okeru ruiseki seisan shūchūdo to hafindaru shisū no iten (1965–1974).* Tokyo: Japan Fair Trade Commission.

———. 1987. *Shuyō sangyō ni okeru ruiseki seisan shūchūdo to hafindaru shisū no iten (1975–1984).* Tokyo: Japan Fair Trade Commission.

Johnson, Chalmers. 1975. "Japan: Who Governs? An Essay on Official Bureaucracy." *Journal of Japanese Studies* 2 (Autumn): 1–28.

———. 1982. *MITI and the Japanese Miracle: The Growth of Industrial Policy, 1925–1975.* Stanford: Stanford University Press.

———. 1988. "The Japanese Political Economy: A Crisis in Theory." *Ethics and International Affairs* 2, no. 2: 79–97.

———. 1989. "MITI, MPT, and the Telecom Wars: How Japan Makes Policy for High Technology." In Chalmers Johnson et al., eds., *Politics and Productivity: How Japan's Development Strategy Works.* Cambridge, Mass: Ballinger: 177–240.

Johnson, Chalmers, and E. B. Keehn. 1994. "A Disaster in the Making: Rational Choice and Asian Studies." *The National Interest,* no. 36 (Summer): 14–22.

Kanebo. 1988. *Kanebo hyakunen-shi.* Osaka: Kanebo Kabushiki Kaisha.

Katzenstein, Peter. 1985. *Small States in World Markets: Industrial Policy in Europe.* Ithaca: Cornell University Press.

———. 1988. "Japan, the Switzerland of the Far East?" In Takashi Inoguchi and Daniel I. Okimoto, eds., *The Political Economy of Japan.* Vol. 2, *The Changing International Context.* Stanford: Stanford University Press: 275–304.

Katzenstein, Peter, ed. 1978. *Between Power and Plenty: Foreign Economic Policies of Advanced Industrial States.* Madison: University of Wisconsin Press.

Kernell, Samuel. 1991. "Conclusion: The Primacy of Politics in Economic Policy." In Samuel Kernell, ed., *Parallel Politics: Economic Policymaking in Japan and the United States.* Washington, D.C.: Brookings Institution: 325–378.

Keyser, Donna. 1990. "Japan's Response to the Crisis of Industrial Adjustment: An Alternative Approach to Understanding the Japanese Industrial Policymaking Process." Dissertation, Yale University.

Kindleberger, Charles P. 1973. *The World in Depression, 1929–1939.* Berkeley: University of California Press.

Kirchner, Christian. 1988. "Western Europe: Subsidized Survival." In Merton J. Peck, ed., *The World Aluminum Industry in a Changing Energy Era.* Washington, D.C.: Resources for the Future: 61–89.

Kitada Yoshiharu and Aida Toshio, eds. 1987. *Endaka fukyōka no Nihon sangyō: Kokusai sangyō chōsei no shinten to sangyō seisaku.* Tokyo: Ōtsuki Shoten.

Komiya, Ryutaro. 1988. "Introduction." In Ryutaro Komiya, Masahiro Okuno, and Kotaro Suzumura, eds., *Industrial Policy of Japan.* Tokyo: Academic Press: 1–22.

Kondo Hajime. 1976. "Heidenro sangyō no kōzō kaizen mondai." *Tekkōkai* 26 (June):26–29.

Krasner, Stephen D. 1987. *Asymmetries in Japanese-American Trade: The Case For Specific Reciprocity.* Berkeley: Institute of International Studies, University of California, Berkeley.

———, ed. 1983. *International Regimes.* Ithaca: Cornell University Press.

Kume, Ikuo. 1993. "A Tale of Twin Industries: Labor Accommodation in the Private Sector." In Gary D. Allinson and Yasunori Sone, eds., *Political Dynamics in Contemporary Japan.* Ithaca: Cornell University Press: 158–180.

Lake, David A. 1983. "International Economic Structures and American Foreign Economic Policy, 1887–1934." *World Politics* 35, no. 4: 517–543.

———. 1984. "Beneath the Commerce of Nations: A Theory of International Economic Structures." *International Studies Quarterly* 28: 143–70.

Lawrence, Robert. 1987. "A Depressed View of Policies for Depressed Industries." Paper presented at the Conference on U.S.-Canadian Trade and Investment Relations With Japan.

Lesbirel, S. Hayden. 1988. "The Political Economy of Industrial Adjustment in Japan: The Case of Coal." Unpublished manuscript, Australia-Japan Research Centre.

———. 1991. "Structural Adjustment in Japan: Terminating 'Old King Coal.' " *Asian Survey* 31, no. 11 (November): 1079–1094.

Little, Daniel. 1991. "Rational-Choice Models and Asian Studies." *Journal of Asian Studies* 50, no. 1: 35–52.

Lynch, John. 1968. *Toward an Orderly Market: An Intensive Study of Japan's Voluntary Quota in Cotton Textile Exports.* Tokyo: Charles E. Tuttle Company.

Lynn, Leonard H., and Timothy J. McKeown. 1988. *Organizing Business: Trade Associations in America and Japan*. Washington: American Enterprise Institute.

Macomber, John D. 1987. "East Asia's Lessons for Latin American Resurgence." In Jeffry A. Frieden and David A. Lake, eds., *International Political Economy: Perspectives on Global Power and Wealth*. 2d ed. New York: St. Martin's Press: 386–395.

Magaziner, Ira C., and Thomas M. Hout. 1980. *Japanese Industrial Policy*. Berkeley: Institute of International Studies, University of California.

Mainichi Shimbunsha, ed. 1978. *Naze? Sasebo jūkō kyūsai no 100 nichi*. Tokyo: Mainichi Shimbunsha.

Marsden, David. 1987. "Collective Bargaining and Industrial Adjustment in Britain, France, Italy, and West Germany." In François Duchêne and Geoffrey Shepherd, eds., *Managing Industrial Change in Western Europe*. London: Frances Pinter: 178–209.

Matsushita Masahito. 1972. "Gōsen sen'i Mēkā no karuteru ni tsuite." *Kōsei Torihiki*, March: 16–19.

McKean, Margaret A. 1993. "State Strength and the Public Interest." In Gary D. Allinson and Yasunori Sone, eds., *Political Dynamics in Contemporary Japan*. Ithaca: Cornell University Press: 72–104.

McKeown, Timothy. 1984. "Firms and Tariff Regime Change: Explaining the Demand for Protection." *World Politics* 36, no. 2: 215–233.

McMillan, John. 1994. "The Analytics of Industrial Restructuring." In Hong W. Tan and Haruo Shimada, eds., *Troubled Industries in the United States and Japan*. New York: St. Martin's Press: 29–45.

Millan, Les. 1980. "South East Asia: Mini Mills and Development." In Raymond Cordero, ed., *The Market and the Mini: The Challenge of the Electric Furnace Steelworks*. London: Metal Bulletin: 61–80.

Milner, Helen V. 1988. *Resisting Protectionism: Global Industries and the Politics of International Trade*. Princeton: Princeton University Press.

Misono Hitoshi. 1987. *Nihon no dokusen kinshi seisaku to sangyō sōshiki*. Tokyo: Kawade Shobō Shinsha.

Mitsubishi Ginkō. 1981. "Futsūkō denro gyōkai no genjō to henbō." *Mitsubishi Ginkō Chōsa*, no. 316 (August): 24–38.

Muramatsu, Michio, and Ellis S. Krauss. 1987. "The Conservative Policy Line and the Development of Patterned Pluralism." In Kozo Yamamura and Yasukichi Yasuba, eds., *The Political Economy of Japan*. Vol. 1, *The Domestic Transformation*. Stanford: Stanford University Press: 516–554.

Nihon Bōseki Kyōkai (JSA). 1962. *Sengo bōseki-shi*. Osaka: Nihon Bōseki Kyōkai.

———. 1969. *Bōshokugyō ni okeru kōzō kaizen taisaku no tenkai*. Osaka: Nihon Bōseki Kyōkai.

———. 1982. *Bōkyō hyakunen-shi—bōseki kyōkai sōritsu 100-nen kinen*. Osaka: Nihon Bōseki Kyōkai.

Nihon Kagaku Sen'i Kyōkai. 1974. *Nihon kagaku sen'i sangyōshi*. Tokyo: Nihon Kagaku Sen'i Kyōkai.

———. 1979. *Kasen bōseki shoshi*. Tokyo: Nihon Kagaku Sen'i Kyōkai.

Nihon Keizai Shimbun. 1979. *Sen'i sangyō: nokoru no wa dare ka*. Tokyo: Nihon Keizai Shimbunsha.

Nihon Rōdō Kyōkai. 1988. *Sangyō seisaku to rōdō kumiai*. Written by Hisamura Susumu. Tokyo: Nihon Rōdō Kyōkai.

Nihon Shakaito Seisaku Shingikai, Sen'i Taisaku Tokubetsu Iinkai, ed. 1968. *Nihon no sen'i sangyō.* Tokyo: Shakai Shimpō.

Nihon Zōsen Kōgyōkai 30-Nenshi Kankō Shōiinkai. 1980. *Nihon zōsen kōgyōkai 30-nenshi.* Tokyo: Nihon Zōsen Kōgyōkai.

Nihon Zōsen Shinkō Zaidan, ed. 1983. *Zōsen fukyō no kiroku: dai-ichiji sekiyu kiki ni taiōshite.* Tokyo: Nihon Zōsen Shinkō Zaidan.

Nimura Miyakuni. 1976. "Moeagaru tai-nichi hihan no jittai: Nihon shinshitsu o habamu kokusai karuteru," *Ekonomisuto,* December 7: 23–27.

Nisshin Bōseki. 1969. *Nisshin bōseki rokūjūnen-shi.* Osaka: Nisshin Bōseki Kabushiki Kaisha.

Noble, Gregory William. 1988. "Between Competition and Cooperation: Collective Action in the Industrial Policy of Japan and Taiwan." Dissertation, Harvard University.

——. 1989. "The Japanese Industrial Policy Debate." In Stephan Haggard and Chung-in Moon, eds., *Pacific Dynamics: The International Politics of Industrial Change.* Boulder, Colo.: Westview Press: 53–95.

OECD (Organisation for Economic Cooperation and Development). 1983a. *Positive Adjustment Policies: Managing Structural Change.* Paris: OECD.

——. 1983b. *Textile and Clothing Industries: Structural Problems and Policies in OECD Countries.* Paris: OECD.

Ogawa, Ichiro. 1984. "Administrative and Judicial Remedies Against Administrative Actions." In Kiyoaki Tsuji, ed., *Public Administration in Japan.* Tokyo: University of Tokyo Press: 217–227.

Ohashi Fujio. 1988. "Futsūkō denrogyō o megutte." *Tekkōkai* 38 (August): 2–8.

Okamoto Hirokimi. 1984. *Gendai tekkō kigyō no ruigata bunseki.* Kyoto: Minerva Shōbō.

Okimoto, Daniel I. 1989. *Between MITI and the Market: Japanese Industrial Policy for High Technology.* Stanford: Stanford University Press.

Olson, Mancur. 1965. *The Logic of Collective Action: Public Goods and the Theory of Groups.* Cambridge: Harvard University Press.

——. 1982. *The Rise and Decline of Nations: Economic Growth, Stagflation, and Social Rigidities.* New Haven, Conn.: Yale University Press.

Park, Ho Hwan. 1992. "Employment Adjustment in Steel Industry: The U.S. and Japan Compared." Dissertation, University of Illinois at Urbana-Champaign.

Patrick, Hugh. 1991. "Concepts, Issues, and Selected Findings." In Hugh Patrick, ed., *Pacific Basin Industries in Distress: Structural Adjustment and Trade Policy in the Nine Industrialized Economies.* New York: Columbia University Press: 1–32.

Peck, Merton J., ed. 1988. *The World Aluminum Industry in a Changing Energy Era.* Washington, D.C.: Resources for the Future.

Peck, Merton J., Richard C. Levin, and Akira Goto. 1987. "Picking Losers: Public Policy Toward Declining Industries in Japan." *Journal of Japanese Studies* 13, no. 1: 79–123.

Pempel, T. J. 1978. "Japanese Foreign Economic Policy: The Domestic Basis for International Behavior." In Peter Katzenstein, ed., *Between Power and Plenty: Foreign Economic Policies of Advanced Industrial States.* Madison: University of Wisconsin Press: 139–190.

——. 1987. "The Unbundling of 'Japan, Inc.': The Changing Dynamics of Japanese Policy Formation." In Kenneth B. Pyle, ed., *The Trade Crisis: How Will Japan Respond?* Seattle: Society for Japanese Studies: 117–152.

Pempel, T. J., and Keiichi Tsunekawa. 1979. "Corporatism without Labor? The Japanese Anomaly." In Philippe C. Schmitter and Gerhard Lembruch, eds., *Trends toward Corporatist Intermediation.* Beverly Hills: Sage Publications: 231–270.

Piore, Michael, and Charles Sable. 1984. *The Second Industrial Divide: Prospects for Prosperity.* New York: Basic Books.

Porter, Michael. 1980. *Competitive Strategy: Techniques for Analyzing Industries and Competitors.* New York: The Free Press.

Putnam, Robert. 1988. "Diplomacy and Domestic Politics: The Logic of Two-Level Games." *International Organization* 42, no. 3: 427–460.

Rajan, Mahesh, and Richard Brahm. 1994. "The Institutional Embeddedness of Corporate Strategies in Declining Industries: Findings from the Japanese Aluminum Smelting Industry." Paper presented to the Seventh Annual Meeting of the Association of Japanese Business Studies (AJBS), Vancouver, B.C., Canada.

Ramseyer, J. Mark. 1981. "Letting Obsolete Firms Die: Trade Adjustment Assistance in the United States and Japan." *Harvard International Law Journal* 22, no. 3: 273–320.

Ramseyer, J. Mark, and Frances McCall Rosenbluth. 1993. *Japan's Political Marketplace.* Cambridge: Harvard University Press.

Rōdōsha Chōsa Kenkyūkai, ed. 1984. *Zōsen. Kikai.* Tokyo: Shin-Nihon Shuppansha.

———, ed. 1990. *Tekkō.* Tokyo: Shin-Nihon Shuppansha.

Rosecrance, Richard, and Jennifer Taw. 1990. "Japan and the Theory of International Leadership." *World Politics* 42, no. 2: 184–209.

Rosenbluth, Frances. 1989. *Financial Politics in Contemporary Japan.* Ithaca: Cornell University Press.

Ruggie, John Gerard. 1983. "International Regimes, Transactions, and Change: Embedded Liberalism in the Postwar Economic Order." In Stephen D. Krasner, ed., *International Regimes.* Ithaca: Cornell University Press: 195–232.

Sabel, Charles F., Gary Herrigel, Richard Kazis, and Richard Deeg. 1987. "How to Keep Mature Industries Innovative." *Technology Review* 90, no. 3 (April): 27–35.

Saito Junko. 1987. "Zōsen fukyō no genjō to taisaku." *Chōsa to Jōhō,* no. 40: 1–16.

———. 1990. "Kōzō chōsei to zōsengyō." In Yaguchi Yoshio and Iwashiro Nariyuki, eds., *Sangyō kōzō chōsei to chiiki keizai.* Tokyo: Nōrin Tōkei Kyōkai: 23–39.

Sakota Masaaki. 1987. *Wagakuni gōsei sen'i kōgyō no hattatsu.* Tokyo: Sakota Masaaki.

Samuels, Richard. 1983. "The Industrial Destructuring of the Japanese Aluminum Industry." *Pacific Affairs* 56, no. 3: 495–509.

———. 1986. *The Business of the Japanese State: Energy Markets in Comparative and Historical Perspective.* Ithaca: Cornell University Press.

Sangyō Nenpō. 1987. "Gōsei sen'i: Kakō, ryūtsū dankai no saihen to saiteki kokusai bungyō taisei e." *Sangyō Nenpō*: 85–91.

Sangyō Seisaku Kenkyūjo. 1987. *Un'yushō: Sono yakuwari to seisaku.* Tokyo: Sangyō Seisaku Kenkyūjo.

Sangyō Seisaku Shi Kenkyūjo (History of Industrial Policy Research Institute). 1977. *Sengo sangyō gōrika to gijutsu dōnyū* (Postwar industrial rationalization and the import of technology). Tokyo: Tsūshō Sangyō Chōsakai Toranomon Bunshitsu.

Scherer, F. M. 1980. *Industrial Market Structure and Economic Performance.* 2d ed. Boston: Houghton Mifflin.

Schoppa, Leonard. 1993. "Two-Level Games and Bargaining Outcomes: Why Gaiatsu Succeeds in Japan in Some Cases But Not Others." *International Organization* 47, no. 3: 353–386.

Seiji Keizai Kenkyūjo, ed. 1958. *Nihon no sen'i sangyō*. Tokyo: Toyo Keizai Shimposha.

Seki, Keizō. 1956. *The Cotton Industry of Japan*. Tokyo: Japan Society for the Promotion of Science.

Sekiguchi, Sueo. 1991. "Japan: A Plethora of Programs." In Hugh Patrick, ed., *Pacific Basin Industries in Distress: Structural Adjustment and Trade Policy in the Nine Industrialized Economies*. New York: Columbia University Press: 418–468.

——. 1994. "Industrial Adjustment and Cartel Actions in Japan." In Hong W. Tan and Haruo Shimada, eds., *Troubled Industries in the United States and Japan*. New York: St. Martin's Press: 123–160.

Sheard, Paul. 1985. *Main Banks and Structural Adjustment in Japan*. Canberra: Australia-Japan Research Centre.

——. 1986. "Corporate Organisation and Structural Adjustment in Japan." Ph.D. Thesis, Australian National University.

——. 1987. "How Japanese Firms Manage Industrial Adjustment: A Case Study of Aluminium." Paper presented to the AJRC-JARC Joint Meeting, Australian National University.

——. 1992. "Corporate Organisation and Industrial Adjustment in the Japanese Aluminium Industry." In Paul Sheard, ed., *International Adjustment and the Japanese Firm*. New South Wales: Allen and Unwin: 125–139.

Shiono, Hiroshi. 1984. "Administrative Guidance." In Kiyoaki Tsuji, ed., *Public Administration in Japan*. Tokyo: University of Tokyo Press: 203–215.

Snyder, Jack. 1984. "Richness, Rigor, and Relevance in the Study of Soviet Foreign Policy." *International Security* 9, no. 3: 89–108.

Sone, Yasunori. 1993. "Structuring Political Bargains: Government, Gyōkai, and Markets." In Gary D. Allinson and Yasunori Sone, eds., *Political Dynamics in Contemporary Japan*. Ithaca: Cornell University Press: 295–306.

Stigler, George J. 1971. "The Theory of Economic Regulation." *Bell Journal of Economics and Management Science* 2, no. 1: 3–21.

Strange, Susan. 1979. "The Management of Surplus Capacity: Or How Does Theory Stand Up to Protectionism 1970s Style?" *International Organization* 33, no. 3: 303–334.

Suzuki Hiroaki. 1975. "Nagai tonneru ni hairu Nihon zōsengyō." *Ekonomisuto*, April 22: 59–63.

Suzuki, Takaaki. 1995. "The International and Domestic Politics of Japanese Government Spending in the 1970s and 1980s." Dissertation, Columbia University.

Suzuki, Takaaki, and Robert Uriu. 1994. "After the LDP: Political Actors and Structural Change." Paper presented to the 1994 Annual Meeting of the American Political Science Association, New York.

Takasugi, Shingo. 1987. "Collapse of a Steel Town." *Japan Echo* 14, no. 2: 22–27.

Takeuchi, Atsuhiko. 1992. "Strategic Management of Japanese Steel Manufacturing in the Changing International Environment." *International Review of Strategic Management* 3: 189–203.

Takeuchi Yuji. 1978. "Heidenro gyōkai ni tsunoru seisaku fushin." *Ekonomisuto*, February 28: 43–45.

Tan, Hong W., and Haruo Shimada, eds. 1994. *Troubled Industries in the United States and Japan*. New York: St. Martin's Press.

Tanaka Minoru. 1965. *Nihon no sen'i sangyō*. Tokyo: Shiseido.

Tanaka, Naoki. 1988. "Aluminum Refining Industry." In Ryutaro Komiya, Masahiro Okuno, and Kotaro Suzumura, eds., *Industrial Policy of Japan*. Tokyo: Academic Press: 451–471.

Tanaka Susumu. 1989. *Sen'i bijinesu no mirai*. Tokyo: Tōyō Keizai Shimpōsha.

Taylor, Andrew J. 1992. "Issue Networks and the Restructuring of the British and West German Coal Industries in the 1980s." *Public Administration* 70 (Spring): 47–65.

Tekkō gyōkai no keiei hikaku. 1980. Tokyo: Kyoikusha.

Thelen, Kathleen. 1987. "Codetermination and Industrial Adjustment in the German Steel Industry: A Comparative Interpretation." *California Management Review* 29, no. 3 (Spring): 134–153.

Thurow, Lester C. 1980. *The Zero-Sum Society: Distribution and the Possibilities for Economic Change*. New York: Basic Books.

Tilton, Mark. 1994. "Informal Market Governance in Japan's Basic Materials Industries." *International Organization* 48, no. 4 (Autumn): 663–685.

Tokutei Fukyō Sangyō Shinyō Kikin. 1982. *Kōzō fukyō sangyō no dōkō*. Tokyo: Tokutei Fukyō Sangyō Shinyō Kikin.

Toray. 1988. "Nihon no gōsen sangyō no kōzō kaizen ni tsuite." Unpublished.

Toriumi, Takashi. 1987. "Tough Times for Nippon Steel." *Japan Echo* 15, no. 2: 28–32.

Totten, George O., III. 1984. "The Reconstruction of the Japanese Shipbuilding Industry." In Robert L. Friedheim et al., *Japan and the New Ocean Regime*. Boulder: Westview Press: 130–172.

Toyobo Keizai Kenkyūjo. 1975. "Gōsen kōgyō no genryō mondai—sandai gōsen o chūshin ni." *Toyobo Keizai Kenkyūjo Kiho* 35 (May): 95–140.

———. 1977. "Kaigai chokusetsu tōshi ni kansuru oboegaki." *Toyobo Keizai Kenkyūjo Kiho* 38 (April): 50–88.

Tran Van Tho. 1985. "Nihon kigyō no tōnan ajia de no keiretsuka: Gōsen kōgyō no keesu (1960–1980)." *Nihon Keizai Kenkyū* 14 (March): 47–73.

Trebilcock, Michael. 1986a. *The Political Economy of Economic Adjustment: The Case of Declining Sectors*. Toronto: University of Toronto Press.

———. 1986b. "The Japanese Policy Approach to Declining Industrial Sectors." In Michael Trebilcock, *The Political Economy of Economic Adjustment: The Case of Declining Sectors*. Toronto: University of Toronto Press.

Tresize, Philip H., and Yukio Suzuki. 1976. "Politics, Government, and Economic Growth in Japan." In Hugh Patrick and Henry Rosovsky, eds., *Asia's New Giant: How the Japanese Economy Works*. Washington, D.C.: The Brookings Institution: 753–811.

Tsunabuchi Shōzō. 1980. *Toray: hanposaki o susumu keiei*. Tokyo: Nihon Keizai Tsūshinsha.

Tsuruta, Toshimasa. 1983. "A Criticism of Cartels in Ailing Industries." *Economic Eye* 4, no. 2: 7–9.

Tsūshō Sangyōshō, ed. 1972. *Shōkō seisaku-shi: Sen'i kōgyō*. Vol. 16. Tokyo: Tsūshō Sangyōshō.

———. 1978. *Tokutei fukyō sangyo antei ho no kaisetsu*. Tokyo: Tsūshō Sangyōshō Chōsakai.

——. 1984. *Sangyō kōzō kaizen hō no kaisetsu.* Tokyo: Tsūshō Sangyōshō Chōsakai.

——. 1988. "Sen'i sangyō no sangyō chōsei seisaku." Unpublished.

Tsūshō Sangyōshō, Kiso Sangyō Kyoku. 1973. *70 nendai no tekkōgyō.* Tokyo: Tsūshō Sangyōshō.

Tsūshō Sangyōshō, Sangyō Seisaku Kyoku. 1983. *Sankōhō no kaisetsu: Aratana sangyō chōsei e mukete.* Tokyo: Tsūshō Sangyōshō Sangyō Seisaku Kyoku.

——. 1988. *Kōzō tenkan enkotsukahō no kaisetsu.* Tokyo: Tsūshō Sangyōshō Chōsakai.

Tsūshō Sangyōshō, Seikatsu Sangyō Kyoku, and Sen'i Kōgyō Kōzō Kaizen Jigyō Kyōkai, eds. 1977. *Atarashii sen'i sangyō no arikata.* Tsūshō Sangyō Chōsakai.

Tsūshō Sangyōshō, Sen'i Kyoku. 1955. "Nihon mengyō no genjō to mondaiten." Unpublished document dated October 1.

Tyson, Laura D'Andrea. 1992. *Who's Bashing Whom?: Trade Conflict in High-Technology Industries.* Washington, D.C.: Institute for International Economics.

Uchino, Tatsurō. 1983. *Japan's Postwar Economy: An Insider's View of Its History and Its Future.* Trans. by Mark A. Harbison. Tokyo: Kodansha International, Ltd.

Un'yu 50-Nenshi Hensan Kyoku, ed. 1989. *Un'yu 50-nenshi.* Vol. 2. Tokyo: Kuresu Shuppan.

Un'yushō, ed. 1980. *Un'yushō 30-nenshi: Shiryō hen.* Tokyo: Un'yu Keizai Kenkyū Sentā.

Un'yushō Senpaku Kyoku Zōsenka. 1976. *Chūkogata kōzōsenjo kōji jōkyō.* Tokyo: Un'yushō, Senpaku Kyoku Zōsenka.

Upham, Frank K. 1986. "Legal and Institutional Dynamics in Japan's Cartel Policy." In Michele Schmiegelow, ed., *Japan's Response to Crisis and Change in the World Economy.* New York: M. E. Sharpe.

Uriu, Robert M. 1984. "The Declining Industries in Japan: Adjustment and Reallocation." *Journal of International Affairs* 38: 99–111.

——. 1988. "The Political Economy of Adjustment: The Case of Japan's Minimills, 1970–88." Pacific Economic Papers, no. 174. Australia-Japan Research Centre.

——. 1993. "Troubled Industries: The Political Economy of Industrial Adjustment in Japan." Dissertation, Columbia University.

U. S. General Accounting Office. 1982. *Industrial Policy: Case Studies in the Japanese Experience.* Washington, D.C.: General Accounting Office.

Uryu, Fujio. 1990. "Industrial Adjustment in Japan and the U.S.: The Case of the Textile Industry." The Program on U.S.-Japan Relations, Harvard University: Occasional Paper, no. 90-16.

Vogel, Ezra. 1985. *Comeback: Building the Resurgence of American Business.* New York: Simon and Schuster.

Weinstein, David, and Richard Beason. 1994. "Growth, Economies of Scale, and Targeting in Japan (1955–1990)." Harvard Institute of Economic Research Discussion Paper, no. 1644.

Wheeler, Jimmy W., Merit E. Janow, and Thomas Pepper. 1982. *Japanese Industrial Development Policies in the 1980's: Implications for U.S. Trade and Investment.* New York: Hudson Institute.

Yagi Hideo. 1989. *Ima tekkō sangyō kara me o otosuna.* Tokyo: Kanki Shuppansha.

Yamamura, Kozo. 1967. *Economic Policy in Postwar Japan: Growth versus Economic Democracy.* Berkeley: University of California Press.

——. 1982. "Success that Soured." In Kozo Yamamura, ed., *Policy and Trade Issues of the Japanese Economy.* Seattle: University of Washington Press: 77–112.

Yamawaki, Hideki. 1989. "International Competition and Domestic Adjustments: The Case of the Japanese Textile Industry." Pacific Economic Papers, no. 177. Australia-Japan Research Centre, Australian National University.

Yamazawa, Ippei. 1981. "Trade and Industrial Adjustment in the Asia-Pacific Region." In H. Kitamura, I. Yamazawa, and Y. Eguchi, *Prospects for Closer Economic Cooperation in the Asia-Pacific Area*. The Asian Club.

——. 1988. "The Textile Industry." In Ryutaro Komiya, Masahiro Okuno, and Kotaro Suzumura, eds. *Industrial Policy in Japan*. New York: Academic Press: 395–423.

Yasuki Hirohiko. 1989. *Wagakuni kyodai kigyō no koyō chōsei katei: Jigyōsho tan'i no koyō hendō* (1973–1983)." Osaka: Kansai Daigaku Keizai Seiji Kenkyūjo.

Yoffie, David B. 1983. *Power and Protection: Strategies of the Newly Industrializing Countries*. New York: Columbia University Press.

Yonekura Seiichi. 1994. "Fukyō karuteru to auto-saidā: Tokyo Seitetsu no jigyō tendai o chūshin ni." *Nenpō Kindai Nihon Kenkyū* 15: 195–221.

Yonezawa Yoshie. 1980. "Bōeki masatsu to sangyō chōsei." *Kikan Gendai Keizai* 39: 71–83.

——. 1988. "The Shipbuilding Industry." In Ryutaro Komiya, Masahiro Okuno, and Kotaro Suzumura, eds., *Industrial Policy of Japan*. New York: Academic Press: 425–449.

Young, Michael K. 1984. "Judicial Review of Administrative Guidance: Governmentally Encouraged Consensual Dispute Resolution in Japan." *Columbia Law Review* 84, no. 4: 923–983.

——. 1986. "Structurally Depressed and Declining Industries in Japan: A Case Study in Minimally Intrusive Industrial Policy." In Dick Nanto, ed., *Japan's Economy and Trade with the United States*. Washington, D.C.: Joint Economic Committee.

——. 1991. "Structural Adjustment of Mature Industries in Japan: Legal Institutions, Industry Associations and Bargaining." In Stephen Wilks and Maurice Wright, eds., *The Promotion and Regulation of Industry in Japan*. New York: St. Martin's Press: 135–166.

Zensen Dōmei. 1966. *Zensen Dōmei-shi (1951–1955)*. Vol. 3. Tokyo: Zenkoku Sen'i Sangyō Rōdō Kumiai Dōmei.

Zysman, John. 1983. *Governments, Markets, and Growth: Financial Systems and the Politics of Industrial Change*. Ithaca: Cornell University Press.

Index